THE GLOBAL CITY

THE GLOBAL CITY

NEW YORK, LONDON, TOKYO

Saskia Sassen

PRINCETON UNIVERSITY PRESS   PRINCETON, NEW JERSEY

Library of Congress Cataloging-in-Publication Data
Sassen, Saskia.
The global city : New York, London, Tokyo / Saskia Sassen.
p.   cm.
Includes bibliographical references and index.
ISBN 0-691-07866-1
ISBN 0-691-02567-3(pbk.)
1. Financial services industry— New York. 2. Financial services industry—
Japan—Tokyo. 3. Financial services industry—England—
London. 4. International finance. 5. International economic relations.
6. New York (N. Y.)—Economic conditions. 7. Tokyo (Japan)—
Economic conditions. 8. London (England)—Economic conditions.
I. Title.
HG184.N5S27 1991
332'.042—dc20   90-23017 CIP

This book has been composed in Linotron Caledonia

Princeton University Press books are printed
on acid-free paper and meet the guidelines
for permanence and durability of the Committee
on Production Guidelines for Book Longevity
of the Council on Library Resources

Printed in the United States of America

10 9   8 7   6   5   4

For Mara Van de Voort and Willem S. Van Elsloo

_____

Contents

Tables

Acknowledgments _____

THIS BOOK is part of a project that began many years ago. There are, then, many persons and institutions to thank, many more than I could list here.

Financial support for the research and travel came from several institutions: the United Nations Centre for Regional Development in Nagoya, Japan; the Revson and Ford Foundations, for a project on the employment of immigrant women in New York that was central to my research on low-wage workers and informal labor markets; the Chicago Institute for Architecture and Urbanism, for research on social class and space; the Department of Economics of the University of Tokyo, for generous support with research assistants during my stay in Tokyo; the School for International and Public Affairs of Columbia University, for support on research on labor markets as part of a larger project funded by the Andrew and Flora Hewlett Foundation.

There are other institutions that were central to my work. The Social Science Research Council through the Committee on New York provided assistance in the preparation of a major paper on New York City; the Economic Social Science Research Council of England supported an English-American team doing research on New York City and London; the Department of Urban Planning at MIT set up a team of U.S. and Japanese researchers working on deindustrialization and economic restructuring; the Development and Population Unit of City College of London provided various kinds of assistance, as did the Bartlett School of Planning. Many staff members of the Greater London Council and the various units after its abolition were particularly helpful. In Tokyo, many individuals and institutions were extremely helpful and often crucial to the research: the Tokyo Metropolitan Government and several of its staff members were unusually supportive and provided much important information. I also wish to thank staff at the Ministry of Labor, Ministry of Trade and Industry, and Office of Immigration of the Ministry of Justice. I am particularly indebted to Kalabao, an organization for immigrant workers set up by daily laborers in Japan, the poorest workers helping the most vulnerable newcomers.

Many colleagues and friends, as individuals and as members of research teams, need to be thanked: Susan Fainstein and Norman Fainstein, Manuel Castells, Janet Abu-Lughod, Bennett Harrison, Michael Storper, Ann Markusen, Michael Smith, Kiriro Morita, Peter Marcuse,

Ian Gordon, Michael Harloe, Nick Buck, Michael Edwards, Hidehiko Sazanami, Toshio Iyotani, Toshio Naito, Mika Iba, Tokue Shibata, Haruhi Tono, Naoko Iyori, Mako Yoshimura, Munesuke Yamamoto, and many others.

Research assistance was a major part of this study. Michelle Gittelman and Peter Marcotullio were key persons in the research on the financial markets and the trade in services. Sako Osaka helped with preparation of materials in Japanese. Wendy Grover used her detective instincts to get at much information on the informal economy. And then there was a group of students who worked little miracles with the entering of the text and preparation of tables, and all of it under the pressure of deadlines. Jesus Sanchez, Jerry Johnson, Brian Sahd, David Silodor, Karen Hemeleski, and Julie Burros were the most supportive assistants one could have wished for. I also need to thank Ted Reinert and Barbara Hemeleski for solving many a computer crisis when all seemed lost and Jinnah Mohamed for final preparation of tables. Gail Satler often took full responsibility for ensuring that the various parts of the project functioned smoothly and managed matters while I was away. I would also like to thank the many people at Princeton University Press for their support, particularly my editor, Gail Ullman, and her assistant, Cindy Hirschfeld, and Jane Low, in charge of editorial production. The copyeditor, Lyn Grossman, took on an unusually large burden of editing and proofing; I am immensely grateful for all her work.

It is my experience that in all major projects there are one or two individuals who play a critical role, one not necessarily related to time spent on the project, but more to the strategic character and the substance of their contribution. My single largest debt is to Zhen Wu from the Department of Urban Planning at Columbia University and to Professor Kiriro Morita from the Department of Economics at Tokyo University. Zhen Wu was an exceptional researcher, whose intelligence and determination made all the difference. She did a lot of the research on the producer services in London and in New York City for Chapters Five, Six, and Eight. Professor Kiriro Morita made the most important contribution to my research in Tokyo. He provided me with researchers and introduced me to several key people. His generosity and interest were exceptional.

And then there are those on the family front. My husband, Richard Sennett, and my son, Hilary Koob-Sassen, were a great source of support, love, and many a fine dinner. Without them there would have been so much less laughter and enjoyment.

THE GLOBAL CITY

One

Overview

FOR CENTURIES, the world economy has shaped the life of cities. This book is about that relationship today. Beginning in the 1960s, the organization of economic activity entered a period of pronounced transformation. The changes were expressed in the altered structure of the world economy, and also assumed forms specific to particular places. Certain of these changes are by now familiar: the dismantling of once-powerful industrial centers in the United States, the United Kingdom, and more recently in Japan; the accelerated industrialization of several Third World countries; the rapid internationalization of the financial industry into a worldwide network of transactions. Each of these changes altered the relation of cities to the international economy.

In the decades after World War II, there was an international regime based on United States dominance in the world economy and the rules for global trade contained in the 1945 Bretton Woods agreement. By the early 1970s, the conditions supporting that regime were disintegrating. The breakdown created a void into which stepped, perhaps in a last burst of national dominance, the large U.S. transnational industrial firms and banks. In this period of transition, the management of the international economic order was to an inordinate extent run from the headquarters of these firms. By the early 1980s, however, the large U.S. transnational banks faced the massive Third World debt crisis, and U.S. industrial firms experienced sharp market share losses from foreign competition. Yet the international economy did not simply break into fragments. The geography and composition of the global economy changed so as to produce a complex duality: a spatially dispersed, yet globally integrated organization of economic activity.

The point of departure for the present study is that the combination of spatial dispersal and global integration has created a new strategic role for major cities. Beyond their long history as centers for international trade and banking, these cities now function in four new ways: first, as highly concentrated command points in the organization of the world economy; second, as key locations for finance and for specialized service firms, which have replaced manufacturing as the leading economic sectors; third, as sites of production, including the production of innovations, in these leading industries; and fourth, as markets for the products and innovations produced. These changes in the functioning of cities have had a massive impact upon both international economic activity and urban form: Cities concentrate control over vast resources, while finance and specialized service industries have restructured the urban social and economic order. Thus a new type of city has appeared. It is the global city. Leading examples now are New York, London, and Tokyo. These three cities are the focus of this book.

As I shall show, these three cities have undergone massive and *parallel* changes in their economic base, spatial organization, and social structure. But this parallel development is a puzzle. How could cities with as diverse a history, culture, politics, and economy as New York, London, and Tokyo experience similar transformations concentrated in so brief a period of time? Not examined at length in my study, but important to its theoretical framework, is how transformations in cities ranging from Paris to Frankfurt to Hong Kong and São Paulo have responded to the same dynamic. To understand the puzzle of parallel change in diverse cities requires not simply a point-by-point comparison of New York, London, and Tokyo, but a situating of these cities in a set of global processes. In order to understand why major cities with different histories and cultures have undergone parallel economic and social changes, we need to examine transformations in the world economy. Yet the term *global city* may be reductive and misleading if it suggests that cities are mere outcomes of a global economic machine. They are specific places whose spaces, internal dynamics, and social structure matter; indeed, we may be able to understand the global order only by analyzing why key structures of the world economy are *necessarily* situated in cities.

How does the position of these cities in the world economy today differ from that which they have historically held as centers of banking and trade? When Max Weber analyzed the medieval cities woven together in the Hanseatic League, he conceived their trade as the exchange of surplus production; it was his view that a medieval city could withdraw from external trade and continue to support itself, albeit on a reduced scale. The modern molecule of global cities is nothing like the trade among self-sufficient places in the Hanseatic League, as Weber understood it. The first thesis advanced in this book is that the territorial dispersal of current economic activity creates a need for expanded central control and management. In other words, while in principle the territorial decentralization of economic activity in recent years could have been accompanied by a corresponding decentralization in ownership and hence in the appropriation of profits, there has been little movement in that direction. Though large firms have increased their subcontracting to smaller firms, and many national firms in the newly industrializing countries have grown rapidly, this form of growth is ultimately part of a chain. Even industrial homeworkers in remote rural areas are now part of that chain. The transnational corporations continue to control much of the end product and to reap the profits associated with selling in the world market. The internationalization and expansion of the financial industry has brought growth to a large number of smaller financial markets, a growth which has fed the expansion of the global industry. But top-level control and management of the industry has become concentrated in a few leading financial centers, notably New York, London, and Tokyo. These account for a disproportionate share of all financial transactions and one that has grown rapidly since the early 1980s. The fundamental dynamic posited here is that the more globalized the economy becomes, the higher the agglomeration of central functions in a relatively few sites, that is, the global cities.

The extremely high densities evident in the business districts of these cities are one spatial expression of this logic. The widely accepted notion that density and agglomeration will become obsolete because global telecommunications advances allow for maximum population and resource dispersal is poorly conceived. It is, I argue, precisely because of the territorial dispersal facilitated by telecommunication that agglomeration of certain centralizing activities has sharply increased. This is not a mere continuation of old patterns of agglomeration; there is a new logic for concentration. In Weberian terms, there is a new system of "coordination," one which focuses on the development of specific geographic control sites in the international economic order.

A second major theme of this book concerns the impact of this type of economic growth on the economic order within these cities. It is necessary to go beyond the Weberian notion of coordination and Bell's (1973) notion of the postindustrial society to understand this new urban order. Bell, like Weber, assumes that the further society evolves from nineteenth-century industrial capitalism, the more the apex of the social order is involved in pure managerial process, with the content of what is to be managed becoming of secondary importance. Global cities are, however, not only nodal points for the coordination of processes (Friedmann 1986); they are also particular sites of production. They are sites for (1) the production of specialized services needed by complex organizations for running a spatially dispersed network of factories, offices, and service outlets; and (2) the production of financial innovations and the making of markets, both central to the internationalization and expansion of the financial industry. To understand the structure of a global city, we have to understand it as a place where certain kinds of work can get done, which is to say that we have to get beyond the dichotomy between manufacturing and services. The "things" a global city makes are services and financial goods.

It is true that high-level business services, from accounting to economic consulting, are not usually analyzed as a production process. Such services are usually seen as a type of output derived from high-level technical knowledge. I shall challenge this view. Moreover, using new scholarship on producer services, I shall examine the extent to which a key trait of global cities is that they are the most *advanced* production sites for creating these services.

A second way this analysis goes beyond the existing literature on cities concerns the financial industry. I shall explore how the character of a global city is shaped by the emerging organization of the financial industry. The accelerated production of innovations and the new importance of a large number of relatively small financial institutions led to a renewed or expanded role for the marketplace in the financial industry in the decade of the 1980s. The marketplace has assumed new strategic and routine economic functions, in comparison to the prior phase, when the large transnational banks dominated the national and international financial market. Insofar as financial "products" can be used internationally, the market has reappeared in a new form in the global economy. New York, London, and Tokyo play roles as production sites for financial innovations and centralized marketplaces for these "products."

A key dynamic running through these various activities and organizing my analysis of the place of global cities in the world economy is their capability for producing global control. By focusing on the production of services and financial innovations, I am seeking to displace the focus of attention from the familiar issues of the power of large corporations over governments and economies, or supracorporate concentration of power through interlocking directorates or organizations, such as the IMF. I want to focus on an aspect that has received less attention, which could be referred to as the *practice* of global control: the work of producing and reproducing the organization and management of a global production system and a global marketplace for finance. My focus is not on power, but on production: the production of those inputs that constitute the capability for global control and the infrastructure of jobs involved in this production.

The power of large corporations is insufficient to explain the capability for global control. Obviously, governments also face an increasingly complex environment in which highly sophisticated machineries of centralized management and control are necessary. Moreover, the high level of specialization and the growing demand for these specialized inputs have created the conditions for a freestanding industry. Now small firms can buy components of global capability, such as management consulting or international legal advice. And so can firms and governments anywhere in the world. While the large corporation is undoubtedly a key agent inducing the development of this capability and is a prime beneficiary, it is not the sole user.

Equally misleading would be an exclusive focus on transnational banks. Up to the end of the 1982 Third World debt crisis, the large transnational banks dominated the financial markets in terms of both volume and the nature of firm transactions. After 1982, this dominance was increasingly challenged by other financial institutions and the innovations they produced. This led to a transformation in the leading components of the financial industry, a proliferation of financial institutions, and the rapid internationalization of financial markets rather than just a few banks. The incorporation of a multiplicity of markets all over the world into a global system fed the growth of the industry after the 1982 debt crisis, while also creating new forms of concentration in a few leading financial centers. Hence, in the case of the financial industry, a focus on the large transnational banks would exclude precisely those sectors of the industry where much of the new growth and production of innovations has occurred; it would leave out an examination of the wide range of activities, firms, and markets that constitute the financial industry in the 1980s.

Thus, there are a number of reasons to focus a study on marketplaces and production sites rather than on the large corporations and banks. Most scholarship on the internationalization of the economy has already focused on the large corporations and transnational banks. To continue to focus on the corporations and banks would mean to limit attention to their formal power, rather than examining the wide array of economic activities, many outside the corporation, needed to produce and reproduce that power. And, in the case of finance, a focus on the large transnational banks would leave out precisely that institutional sector of the industry where the key components of the new growth have been invented and put into circulation. Finally, exclusive focus on corporations and banks leaves out a number of issues about the social, economic, and spatial impact of these activities on the cities that contain them, a major concern in this book and one I return to below.

A third major theme explored in this book concerns the consequences of these developments for the national urban system in each of these countries and for the relationship of the global city to its nation-state. While a few major cities are the sites of production for the new global control capability, a large number of other major cities have lost their role as leading export centers for industrial manufacturing, as a result of the decentralization of this form of production. Cities such as Detroit, Liverpool, Manchester, and now increasingly Nagoya and Osaka have been affected by the decentralization of their key industries at the domestic and international levels. According to the first hypothesis presented above, this same process has contributed to the growth of service industries that produce the specialized inputs to run global production processes and global markets for inputs and outputs. These industries— international legal and accounting services, management consulting, fi- nancial services—are heavily concentrated in cities such as New York, London, and Tokyo. We need to know how this growth alters the rela- tions between the global cities and what were once the leading industrial centers in their nations. Does globalization bring about a triangulation so that New York, for example, now plays a role in the fortunes of Detroit that it did not play when that city was home to one of the leading indus- tries, auto manufacturing? Or, in the case of Japan, we need to ask, for example, if there is a connection between the increasing shift of produc- tion out of Toyota City (Nagoya) to offshore locations (Thailand, South Korea, and the United States) and the development for the first time of a new headquarters for Toyota in Tokyo.

Similarly, there is a question about the relation between such major cities as Chicago, Osaka, and Manchester, once leading industrial centers in the world, and global markets generally. Both Chicago and Osaka were and continue to be important financial centers on the basis of their man- ufacturing industries. We would want to know if they have lost ground, relatively, in these functions as a result of their decline in the global industrial market, or instead have undergone parallel transformation toward strengthening of service functions. Chicago, for example, was at the heart of a massive agroindustrial complex, a vast regional economy. How has the decline of that regional economic system affected Chicago?

In all these questions, it is a matter of understanding what growth em- bedded in the international system of producer services and finance has entailed for different levels in the national urban hierarchy. The broader trends—decentralization of plants, offices, and service outlets, along with the expansion of central functions as a consequence of the need to man- age such decentralized organization of firms—may well have created con- ditions contributing to the growth of regional subcenters, minor versions of what New York, London, and Tokyo do on a global and national scale. The extent to which the developments posited for New York, London, and Tokyo are also replicated, perhaps in less accentuated form, in smaller cities, at lower levels of the urban hierarchy, is an open, but important, question.

The new international forms of economic activity raise a problem about the relationship between nation-states and global cities. The relation be- tween city and nation is a theme that keeps returning throughout this book; it is the political dimension of the economic changes I explore. I posit the possibility of a systemic discontinuity between what used to be thought of as national growth and the forms of growth evident in global cities in the 1980s. These cities constitute a system rather than merely competing with each other. What contributes to growth in the network of global cities may well not contribute to growth in nations. For instance, is there a systemic relation between, on the one hand, the growth in global cities and, on the other hand, the deficits of national governments and the decline of major industrial centers in each of these countries?

The fourth and final theme in the book concerns the impact of these new forms of and conditions for growth on the social order of the global city. There is a vast body of literature on the impact of a dynamic, high-growth manufacturing sector in the highly developed countries, which shows that it raised wages, reduced inequality, and contributed to the formation of a middle class. Much less is known about the sociology of a service economy. Daniel Bell's (1973) *The Coming of Post-Industrial Society* posits that such an economy will result in growth in the number of highly educated workers and a more rational relation of workers to issues of social equity. One could argue that any city representing a post-industrial economy would surely be like the leading sectors of New York, London, and increasingly Tokyo.

I will examine to what extent the new structure of economic activity has brought about changes in the organization of work, reflected in a shift in the job supply and polarization in the income distribution and occupational distribution of workers. Major growth industries show a greater incidence of jobs at the high- and low-paying ends of the scale than do the older industries now in decline. Almost half the jobs in the producer services are lower-income jobs, and half are in the two highest earnings classes. In contrast, a large share of manufacturing workers were in the middle-earnings jobs during the postwar period of high growth in these industries in the United States and United Kingdom.

Two other developments in global cities have also contributed to economic polarization. One is the vast supply of low-wage jobs required by high-income gentrification in both its residential and commercial settings. The increase in the numbers of expensive restaurants, luxury housing, luxury hotels, gourmet shops, boutiques, French hand laundries, and special cleaners that ornament the new urban landscape illustrates this trend. Furthermore, there is a continuing need for low-wage industrial services, even in such sectors as finance and specialized services. A second development that has reached significant proportions is what I call the downgrading of the manufacturing sector, a process in which the share of unionized shops declines and wages deteriorate while sweatshops and industrial homework proliferate. This process includes the downgrading of jobs within existing industries and the job supply patterns of some of the new industries, notably electronics assembly. It is worth noting that the growth of a downgraded manufacturing sector has been strongest in cities such as New York and London.

The expansion of low-wage jobs as a function of *growth* trends implies a reorganization of the capital-labor relation. To see this, it is important to distinguish the characteristics of jobs from their sectoral location, since highly dynamic, technologically advanced growth sectors may well contain low-wage dead-end jobs. Furthermore, the distinction between sectoral characteristics and sectoral growth patterns is crucial: Backward sectors, such as downgraded manufacturing or low-wage service occupations, can be part of major growth trends in a highly developed economy. It is often assumed that backward sectors express decline trends. Similarly, there is a tendency to assume that advanced sectors, such as finance, have mostly good, white-collar jobs. In fact, they contain a good number of low-paying jobs, from cleaner to stock clerk.

These, then, are the major themes and implications of my study.

As a further word of introduction I must sketch the reasons why producer services and finance have grown so rapidly since the 1970s and why they are so highly concentrated in cities such as New York, London, and Tokyo. The familiar explanation is that the decade of the 1980s was but a part of a larger economic trend, the shift to services. And the simple explanation of their high concentration in major cities is that this is because of the need for face-to-face communication in the services community. While correct, these cliches are incomplete.

We need to understand first how modern technology has not ended nineteenth-century forms of work; rather, technology has shifted a number of activities that were once part of manufacturing into the domain of services. The transfer of skills from workers to machines once epitomized by the assembly line has a present-day version in the transfer of a variety of activities from the shop floor into computers, with their attendant technical and professional personnel. Also, functional specialization within early factories finds a contemporary counterpart in today's pronounced fragmentation of the work process spatially and organizationally. This has been called the "global assembly line," the production and assembly of goods from factories and depots throughout the world, wherever labor costs and economies of scale make an international division of labor cost-effective. It is, however, this very "global assembly line" that creates the need for increased centralization and complexity of management, control, and planning. The development of the modern corporation and its massive participation in world markets and foreign countries has made planning, internal administration, product development, and research increasingly important and complex. Diversification of product lines, mergers, and transnationalization of economic activities all require highly specialized skills in top-level management (Chandler 1977). These have also "increased the dependence of the corporation on producer services, which in turn has fostered growth and development of higher levels of expertise among producer service firms" (Stanback and Noyelle 1982: 15). What were once support resources for major corporations have become crucial inputs in corporate decisionmaking. A firm with a multiplicity of geographically dispersed manufacturing plants contributes to the development of new types of planning in production and distribution surrounding the firm.

The growth of international banks and the more recent diversification of the financial industry have also expanded the demand for highly specialized service inputs. In the 1960s and 1970s, there was considerable geographic dispersal in the banking industry, with many regional centers and offshore locations mostly involved in fairly traditional banking. The diversification and internationalization of finance over the last decade resulted in a strong trend toward concentrating the "management" of the global industry and the production of financial innovations in a more limited number of major locations. This dynamic is not unlike that of multisite manufacturing or service firms.

Major trends toward the development of multisite manufacturing, service, and banking have created an expanded demand for a wide range of specialized service activities to manage and control global networks of factories, service outlets, and branch offices. While to some extent these activities can be carried out in house, a large share of them cannot. High levels of specialization, the possibility of externalizing the production of some of these services, and the growing demand by large and small firms and by governments are all conditions that have both resulted from and made possible the development of a market for freestanding service firms that produce components for what I refer to as global control capability.

The growth of advanced services for firms, here referred to as producer services, along with their particular characteristics of production, helps to explain the centralization of management and servicing functions that has fueled the economic boom of the early and mid-1980s in New York, London, and Tokyo. The face-to-face explanation needs to be refined in several ways. Advanced services are mostly producer services; unlike other types of services, they are not dependent on proximity to the consumers served. Rather, such specialized firms benefit from and need to locate close to other firms who produce key inputs or whose proximity makes possible joint production of certain service offerings. The accounting firm can service its clients at a distance but the nature of its service depends on proximity to other specialists, from lawyers to programmers. Major corporate transactions today typically require simultaneous participation of several specialized firms providing legal, accounting, financial,

public relations, management consulting, and other such services. Moreover, concentration arises out of the needs and expectations of the high-
income workers employed in these firms. They are attracted to the amenities and lifestyles that large urban centers can offer and are likely to live
in central areas rather than in suburbs.

The importance of this concentration of economic activity in New York,
London, and Tokyo is heightened by the fact that advanced services and
finance were the fastest-growing sectors in the economies of their countries in the 1980s. It is a common mistake to attribute high growth to the
service sector as a whole. In fact, other major services, such as public
and consumer services, have leveled off since the middle or late 1960s in
the United States and since the 1970s in the United Kingdom and Japan.
In other words, the concentration of advanced services and finance in
major urban centers represents a disproportionate share of the nationwide growth in employment and GNP in all these countries.

The combination of high levels of speculation and a multiplicity of
small firms as core elements of the financial and producer services complex raises a question about the durability of this model of growth. At
what point do the larger banks assume once again a more central role in
the financial industry? And at what point do competition and the advantages of scale lead to mergers and acquisitions of small firms? Finally, and
perhaps most important, at what point do the sources of profits generated
by this form of economic growth become exhausted?

Over the last ten years, major economic growth trends have produced
spatial and social arrangements considerably divergent from the configuration that characterized the preceding decades. The economic sectors,
localities, and occupations that account for a large share of economic
growth today differ from those central to the immediate post-World War
II period. Most commonly, this process has been interpreted as the decline of old and the emergence of new industries, typically seen as two
somewhat unconnected events necessary for the renewal of all economy.
I shall challenge this disconnecting view, which means asserting that new
growth rests, to a significant extent, on deep structural processes of decline. The question of the long-term durability of the global city that I
have just posed turns on not seeing decline and growth as distinct. The
"high-flying" 1980s might emerge as a passing phenomenon, even as
manufacturing of the old sort continues to decline.

This systemic connection, I will argue, plays itself out in several economic arenas. I propose to examine this through several working hypotheses. They are the following: First, the geographic dispersal of manufacturing, which contributed to the decline of old industrial centers, created
a demand for expanded central management and planning and the necessary specialized services, key components of growth in global cities.

The move of large corporations into consumer services and the growing complexity of governmental activity further fed the demand for specialized services and expanded central management and planning, though they did not necessarily feed the decline of certain localities, as in the case of the dispersal of manufacturing. Second, the growth of the financial industry, and especially of key sectors of that industry, benefited from policies and conditions often harmful to other industrial sectors, notably manufacturing. The overall effect again was to feed growth of specialized services located in major cities and to undermine the economic base of other types of localities. Third, the conditions and patterns subsumed under the first two working hypotheses suggest a transformation in the economic relationships among global cities, the nation-states where they are located, and the world economy. Prior to the current phase, there was high correspondence between major growth sectors and overall national growth. Today we see increased asymmetry: The conditions promoting growth in global cities contain as significant components the decline of other areas of the United States, the United Kingdom, and Japan and the accumulation of government debt and corporate debt. Fourth, the new conditions of growth have contributed to elements of a new class alignment in global cities. The occupational structure of major growth industries characterized by the locational concentration of major growth sectors in global cities in combination with the polarized occupational structure of these sectors has created and contributed to growth of a high-income stratum and a low-income stratum of workers. It has done so directly through the organization of work and occupational structure of major growth sectors. And it has done so indirectly through the jobs needed to service the new high-income workers, both at work and at home, as well as the needs of the expanded low-wage work force.

This brief introductory chapter presents the main issues and arguments the book will develop. Part One discusses the major trends in the spatial dispersion of production and the reorganization of the financial industry. The focus here is on the geography, composition, and institutions that constitute the globalization of economic activity in the 1980s. This aims to be a straightforward empirical description of the composition and direction of international investment, service transactions, and financial flows. It entailed dealing with a vast amount of evidence, disaggregating in order to capture dimensions of interest to the analysis in this book and reaggregating in order to facilitate comprehension. The many tables in these chapters serve to summarize the details. The purpose is ultimately to understand how various forms of globalization in economic activity generated new forms of centralization, specifically, the rapidly growing agglomeration of specialized services and finance evident in major cities.

Part Two examines the industries that form the core in these cities and the national and transnational space economy of these industries. The purpose is to arrive at an understanding of the place of global cities in the organization of these industries, and to do so through an examination of the characteristics of the industries—rather than a detailed analysis of the economic base of the cities—in the context of national urban systems as well as an elemental global hierarchy of cities. Chapter Five examines the characteristics of the new components of centralization. They amount to a new basic industry: the production of management and control operations, of the highly specialized services needed to run the world economy, of new financial instruments. Chapters Six and Seven discuss the role of global cities in the new organization of the world economy, examining the development of these cities into sites of production for the new basic industry.

Part Three discusses some of the key aspects in the distribution of benefits and burdens of this particular form of growth. What is the range of jobs directly and indirectly sustaining the operation of this type of economic sector? And to what extent does the occupational and income distribution of these cities' resident work forces reflect the existence of a thriving profitmaking economic core? Chapter Eight examines how these transformations in economic activity generate a new labor demand and a new income structure in these cities. Chapter Nine examines the characteristics of the backward economic sectors that appear to thrive in these cities and seeks to understand what, if any, is the articulation between these two types of growth.

The concluding chapter discusses the political implications of these developments, addressing the following three questions. What are the political implications of concentration of the benefits of economic growth in global cities and in a stratum of high-income workers alongside the decline of what were once thriving localities and sectors of the work force? How does the consolidation of the world economy and of global centers for its control and management affect the relationship between nation and city, particularly between global cities and the nation-states they supposedly belong to? The final question concerns the durability of these arrangements: What are the conditions for the reproduction of this mode of growth?

The three central questions organizing this book can be simply put as follows. What is the role of major cities in the organization and management of the world economy? In what ways has the consolidation of a world economy affected the economic base and associated social and political order in major cities? What happens to the relationship between state and city under conditions of a strong articulation between a city and the world economy? These represent only a few of all the questions one could raise in a study about major contemporary cities. But these questions are strategic for understanding such cities from the perspective of the world economy—what moment in the global accumulation process is contained by or located in major cities? And they are strategic for understanding the interaction of local and global processes—how does the historical, political, economic, and social specificity of a particular city resist, facilitate, remain untouched by incorporation into the world economy? In this context, the contrasts among New York, London, and Tokyo should be illuminating, given their roles as leading world financial centers and their very different histories, economies, and cultures.

Part One ───────────────────────────

THE GEOGRAPHY AND COMPOSITION OF GLOBALIZATION

A LEADING ARGUMENT in this book is that the spatial dispersion of economic activities and the reorganization of the financial industry are two processes that have contributed to new forms of centralization insofar as they have occurred under conditions of continued concentration in ownership or control. The spatial dispersion of economic activity has brought about an expansion in central functions and in the growing stratum of specialized firms servicing such functions. Reorganization in the financial industry has been characterized by sharp growth, rapid production of innovations, and a proliferation of financial firms. These conditions, I argue, shifted the point of gravity in the industry away from the large, mostly United States, transnational banks that had once dominated the industry toward major *centers* of finance.

The fact that telecommunications and information technologies are essential to both processes has added yet another force for agglomeration. Finance and specialized services are major users of such technologies and need access to the most advanced facilities. These technologies, which make possible long distance management and servicing and instantaneous money transfers, require complex physical facilities, which are highly immobile. Such facilities demand major investments in fixed capital and continuous incorporation of innovations. There are, then, huge entry costs at this point for any locality seeking to develop advanced facilities. Established telecommunications centers have what amounts to an almost absolute advantage.

International transactions have expanded the scale and raised the complexity of these processes. However, the spatial and organizational logic at work is also evident at the national level. Whether internationalization is essential to the major outcomes, notably the acute pressures toward agglomeration in leading cities, is difficult to establish and is perhaps a question of theory. But the requirements that global production arrangements and markets bring about are a key factor in the organization of major industries and in the significance of specialized services for firms.

Furthermore, the fact of international transactions produces a specific regulatory question: What are the conditions that make international transactions cohere? This question becomes particularly compelling in the absence of a single dominant power, as was the United States after World War II, and of a treaty containing the rules for international transactions, a treaty made persuasive by the existence of such a power. The 1980s saw the proliferation of participants, acute competition, and an increasing internationalization in the ownership or control of capital. One of the questions guiding the deciphering of empirical details in Chapters Three and Four is whether the market as marketplace—more specifically, the leading marketplaces for finance and specialized services—provided the essential organizing element in the decade of the 1980s, a period of high competition, speculation, and profits. Was it precisely the centrality of the market in this brief period that explains its form?

Addressing these issues requires a detailed examination of the geography and composition of international transactions and the institutional arrangements through which such transactions take place. Much of the scholarship has focused on the geography and composition of the activities of large mutinational corporations. Has the growth of finance and services brought about significant differences in the composition of international transactions and in the corresponding institutional arrangements, as compared with the 1960s and 1970s? And does a change in composition entail a change in the types of locations and forms of articulation involved in international transactions? The international mobility of capital and its growing speed contribute specific forms of articulation among different geographic areas and transformations in the role played by these areas in the world economy. Have the properties of articulation been altered by the speed and growth of electronically integrated markets? In brief, is there a transformation in the spatial expression of the logic of accumulation and in the institutional arrangements through which it takes place?

The sharp growth in the monetary value of financial transactions and its highly speculative nature raise questions about the limits of this mode of growth. Is this a particular phase in the product cycle of these industries, which will be followed by greater standardization and concentration, less competition, and less innovation? How would such a development alter the pattern that emerged in the decade of the 1980s? The accelerated production of innovations and the rapid entry of new participants in highly profitable industries once dominated by a limited number of firms raise questions about the durability of this phase in a system with strong oligopolistic tendencies and a continuing dependence on mass markets.

The documentation of these issues focuses largely on its international components, these being the major ones. The decade of the 1970s was the crucial period when some of the new forms of geographic dispersal and internationalization, in the making since the mid-1960s, became fully evident. But the conditions for the exhaustion of certain of these patterns also developed in the 1970s, thereby facilitating the formation of new patterns of geography, composition, and institutional arrangements in the 1980s. The detailed documentation of international transactions in finance and services is intent on capturing the new patterns that emerged in the early and mid-1980s. These new patterns grew out of both the consolidation of some components of restructuring and the crisis of other components in the 1970s.

Chapter Two elaborates the concept of capital mobility so as to capture both dispersal and agglomeration. The ensuing two chapters document these processes. The question of economic concentration is central to this examination. Given the format in which many of the data are available, the simple form of this question, at this point, is: What countries account for the vast majority of the various flows under consideration? This should then set the stage for a more detailed analysis of concentration in the leading industries of the 1980s, specialized services for business and finance, the subject of Part Two of this book.

Two

Dispersal and New Forms of Centralization

DO CHANGES in the global flow of factors of production, commodities, and information amount to a new spatial expression of the logic of accumulation? Addressing this question entails a detailed examination of how that which we call the global economy is constituted. What are the geographic areas, industries, and institutional arrangements that are central to the current process of globalization, and how do they differ from those of earlier periods? Extracting theoretical insight from this empirical documentation requires elaborating the category of capital mobility to take it beyond the mere movement of capital across space. It must allow for the incorporation of not only the new forms of geographic dispersal, usually thought of as representing the mobility of capital, but also the new forms of centralization, which, I argue, are an integral part of the new forms of capital mobility. A theoretical elaboration of the concept of capital mobility that takes it beyond a locational dimension should also include the reorganization of sources of surplus value made possible by massive shifts of capital from one area of the world to another. Yet another aspect of the mobility of capital is the transnationalization in ownership, not only through foreign direct investment but also through mergers, acquisitions, and joint ventures, which raises anew the issue of the nationality of capital.

Key components of this process are the outflow of capital from old industrial centers (Bluestone and Harrison 1982; Massey 1982; AMPO 1987), the inflow of capital into newly industrializing countries (Fröbel, Heinrichs, and Kreye 1979), and the growth of transnational corporations (Vernon 1966; Herman 1982). These studies tend to posit the locational dimensions of capital mobility, or what Storper and Walker (1983) have termed the "locational capability" of capital. The most obvious and familiar image of the increased mobility of capital is the "runaway" shop, or the movement of manufacturing jobs from highly developed areas to less developed, low-wage areas. Perhaps as common an image is the instant transfer of money from one country to another.

But capital mobility, both as a process and as a theoretical category, incorporates a number of other components of importance to the analysis in this book. Capital mobility is constituted not only in locational terms but also in technical terms, both through the technologies that render capital mobile and through the capability for maintaining control over a vastly decentralized global production system (Sassen 1988).

Such an elaboration of the notion of capital mobility brings to the fore important questions about the broader organization and control of the economy in the current phase of the world economy. Increased capital mobility does not only bring about changes in the geographic organization of production and the network of financial markets. It also generates a demand for types of production needed to ensure the management, control, and servicing of this new organization of production and finance. These new types of production range from the development of telecommunications to that of specialized services that are key inputs for the management of a global network of factories, offices, and financial markets. And it includes the production of a broad array of innovations in these sectors. These types of production have their own locational patterns; they tend toward high degrees of agglomeration. In addition, the increased mobility of capital has reorganized the employment relationship. This subject has received attention in some aspects: the labor market dynamics leading up to and resulting from deindustrialization, and the low-wage labor enclaves of export processing zones. But other aspects of the employment relation have not been examined in the light of the increased mobility of capital: key trends in international labor migrations, notably the new illegal Asian immigration to Japan, and the formation of a broad stratum of medium-level workers with a global orientation in a context where school, family, and community are typically not so oriented. Here we introduce these concepts, which we return to in later sections of the book.

Mobility and Agglomeration

The implementation of global production processes by large corporations requires a certain type of international regime. The last clearly formulated such regime was the one associated with the Bretton Woods treaty, when the United States was the leading exporter of investment capital, consumer goods, and capital goods and the leading economic and military power. We can think of the 1970s as already containing the beginning of a new transnational logic in the form of multinational firms. But these were largely U.S. firms; they clearly were dominant, especially in banking; the dollar continued to function as the leading currency; and, notwithstanding severe economic and political decline of the United States in the world, the United States was still the dominant power. By the mid-1980s the dominant banks and the leading manufacturing firms were Japanese. The examination of the specific forms assumed by capital mobility in manufacturing, services, and finance in the 1970s and 1980s should allow us to *begin* addressing the question of how the world economy is organized.

The geographic dispersal of manufacturing is one of the more distinct traits in the current phase and one that has brought the issue of capital mobility to the fore.[1] There have been numerous plant closings in all major industrialized countries and transfers of production jobs to lower-wage domestic or foreign locations. There also have been overall declines in manufacturing employment in what were once established industrial centers, such as Detroit in the United States, or Manchester and Birmingham in the United Kingdom, and growing imports of components produced or assembled abroad and reimported for final product assembly.[2] Over the last few years there have been similar trends in Japan, including the shift of garment production to less developed domestic and foreign areas, as well as the shift of auto parts manufacturing to Thailand, South Korea, and Mexico. Evidence on direct foreign investment by the Unites States, the United Kingdom, and Japan describes shifts of manufacturing to foreign locations and the internationalization of manufacturing production in these three countries. More specifically, direct foreign investment in production for export is indicative of the existence of a global network of production sites set up by the firms of highly developed countries, insofar as this investment is geared toward production aimed not at the countries where the factories have been located but at the countries that provided the capital.[3]

[1] Plant closings in old industrial centers are probably the most dramatic instance. Disinvestment, shrinking, attrition, lack of maintenance—all these represent mechanisms for deindustrialization, which, while not as direct as plant closings, entail a severe erosion of the old industrial complex, both in the United States and in the United Kingdom (Bluestone and Harrison 1982; Massey 1984).

[2] Shutdowns are estimated to have eliminated 22 million jobs in the United States between 1969 and 1976 (Bluestone and Harrison 1982: 29). This trend continues. Plant shutdowns in 1982 alone resulted in 1.2 million jobs lost (Bureau of National Affairs 1982). In the United Kingdom, there was a 25% decline in manufacturing employment from 1978 to 1985. In Japan we are beginning to see a similar process. Mines, steel mills, and factories have been closed down over the last few years. In 1970 there were 250,000 miners; by 1985 there were 30,000. The steel industry will lose 100,000 jobs with the expected reduction of operations by the five leading companies. The auto and consumer electronics industries have shifted growing numbers of jobs to other Southeast Asian countries and now increasingly to the United States. During this same period direct foreign investment in low-wage countries rose strongly for all three countries, most of it for manufacturing and associated services.

[3] A growing share of this investment is for production or assembly of components imported from the highly developed countries and exported back after processing. A partial indicator of this is the value of goods brought into the United States under Tariff Items 806.30 and 807, which had a threefold increase from 1966 to 1978 (U.S. Department of Commerce, International Trade Administration 1980b, 1980c). The value of products com-

The decentralization of manufacturing is constituted in technical and social terms. Different kinds of processes have fed this decentralization. On the one hand, the dismantling of the old industrial centers in highly developed countries, with their strong organized labor component, was an attempt to dismantle the capital-labor relation around which production had been organized, often referred to as Fordism. On the other hand, the decentralization of production in high-tech industries was a result of the introduction of new technologies designed to separate low-wage, routine tasks from highly skilled tasks therewith maximizing locational options. Both, however, entail an organization of the capital-labor relation that tends to maximize the use of low-wage labor and to minimize the effectiveness of mechanisms that empower labor vis-à-vis capital. Thus, the term *dispersal*, while suggestive of a geographic aspect, clearly involves a complex political and technical reorganization of production as well. (For a full discussion see Sassen 1988.)

An important aspect of the mobility of capital not sufficiently developed in the literature is the transnationalization in the ownership and control of major corporations through foreign direct investment, mergers and acquisitions, and joint ventures. The United States has been one of the main objects of such investment and acquisitions. While the British and the Dutch have long been significant investors in the United States and continue to be so, the current phase has certain distinct traits. In the 1980s a range of investments and acquisitions took place that can be differentiated from traditional forms of investments and acquisitions, a subject I return to in Chapter Seven. One instance of this is the emergence of Southern California as the center for research and development, design, engineering, marketing, and management of the nine Japanese auto makers that now account for 30% of all cars sold in the United States. The actual manufacturing tends to be concentrated in the Midwest and in the South, and now also includes twin plants in northern Mexico. A second instance is extensive concentration of Japanese banks, securities houses, and other financial firms in New York City and, on a smaller scale, in Los Angeles. Japanese firms have created a large, complex, diversified base of operations in select locations of the United States. This is allowing increased and more direct participation in the economy, such as becoming lead managers in major real estate deals and producing cars here for export to Europe. There are many other examples. Japanese

---

ing from less developed countries represented only 6.3% of the total in 1966 but 44% by 1978. Most directly illustrative is the development of export processing zones, which began to be developed in the mid-1960s and represent an expansion of this strategy rather than its inception. How successful, or attractive, this strategy was is suggested by the fact that by the end of the 1970s there were about eighty such zones, mostly concentrated in Mexico, the Caribbean Basin, and Southeast Asia.

investors have bought up significant shares of major industrial firms, notably Firestone and the National Steel Corporation. The Tokyo-based NKK Corporation of Japan already owns half of the U.S. Steel Company and is expected to acquire another 40% of it, which would bring its ownership to 90% of what is the sixth-largest U.S. steel company. And major Arab investors are poised to acquire such legendary department stores as Harrod's in London and Saks Fifth Avenue in New York. These are huge acquisitions, with the Saks one estimated at $1.5 billion.

The Japanese case calls for a somewhat more detailed discussion, as it is less familiar and more unexpected, given a different organization of the economy. Restructuring in Japan has involved the shifting of a growing range of manufacturing to offshore locations, for example, textiles and auto parts; a shift from heavy and chemical industry to high-tech and knowledge-intensive industries; and the creation of Japanese international financial institutions. There has been a sharp increase in the number of workers employed abroad by the major Japanese manufacturers, an indication of the extent of internationalization and offshore production in such firms. From 1981 to 1987, Hitachi, a major producer of consumer goods, increased its number of employees abroad fivefold; Toshiba, threefold; Fujitsu, tenfold; and so on for a number of firms. For the three large auto manufacturers, this is a very recent process, and there are no figures available. But by 1987 Toyota had 7,516 workers abroad; Nissan, over 22,000; and Honda, 6,700. These numbers represented a not insignificant share of all workers directly employed by these companies, especially in the case of auto manufacturers; Toyota's core workforce in Japan was about 28,000; Nissan's, about 70,000; and Honda's, about 34,000.

In the last few years, Japanese firms have moved many of these operations to Mexico. As Japanese manufacturers have set up operations in the United States in order to avoid protectionist barriers, they have developed twin plant operations[4] with Mexico, especially to supply electronic and auto components (Echeverri-Carroll 1988).[5] Japanese twin

---

[4] The twin plant (or in-bond) program was designated through special provisions of both Mexican and U.S. law. Mexico allows duty-free imports of machinery and equipment for manufacturing as well as components for assembly under the provision that 80% of the plant's output be exported. Mexico allows complete foreign ownership of plants. The United States in turn charges import duties only on that portion of the value of a good that was added in the process of assembly or manufacturing in Mexico of U.S.-made components that are to be reimported into the United States.

[5] By 1988 the Japanese had thirty-nine *maquilas* (twin plant operations) on the Mexican side of the border, of which about 70% had set up operations after 1982 (Echeverri-Carroll 1988). While the vast majority of twin plants in Mexico are U.S. owned, Japan now accounts for 3.5% of the total, having surpassed all other countries as a group, except for the United States. In 1980 electronics plants accounted for 36% of total in-bond employment in Mex-

plants range from small operations employing between 25 and 50 people to very large ones employing 2,000 on several shifts. Auto-related plants have raised their share of employment in all Japanese twin plants in Mexico from 7% in 1979 to over 40% by 1988; this reduced the share of electronics plants from 71% to 49%. Many of these Japanese firms used to use assembly operations in Korea and Taiwan, from where the components were sent to Japanese firms in the United States or back to Japan.

Though on a much smaller scale, parallel patterns are evident in the organization of office work. There is a growing dispersal of routine office work. It is most evident in the United States and slowly emerging in the United Kingdom. It assumes a variety of forms, including the shipping or transmission of routine tasks to offices located abroad; shipping or transmission to suburban homes in the region where the head office is located; setting up offices, which are often whole divisions, in cheaper locations than that of the head office and frequently at great distance from the latter; subcontracting office work out to other firms; setting up back office operations at a short distance from the head office because the latter's location is too congested or expensive. The evidence suggests that these various forms are all increasing (Appelbaum 1984; Baran and Teegarden 1983; Nelson 1984). Probably one of the most rapidly growing forms of office work decentralization in the United States is the use of women working out of suburban homes. There is a considerable supply of well-educated women in suburbs, where the absence of adequate child care facilities and the paucity of job choices may lead them to prefer taking work at home. Firms with large amounts of data processing, such as insurance companies, have seized on this labor market.[6] The internationalization of this geographic dispersal of offices has been facilitated by the rather unrestricted flow and absence of tariffs on this type of data. Fur-

---

ico, and auto-related twin plants accounted for only 8.5% of such employment. By 1987 auto-related plants accounted for 21%. Of the thirty-nine plants in operation in 1988, eighteen were on the Texas border and were mostly auto-related manufacturing; seventeen were on the California border and were largely in electronics components; and four were in the interior of Mexico. The auto-related plants provided various parts to Honda and Mazda plants in the United States, as well as to plants jointly owned with U.S. companies. Electronics still dominates, accounting for twenty of the thirty-nine twin plants in operation as of mid-1988; but auto parts manufacturing is the fastest growing twin plant industry, having gone from three such plants in 1985 to eleven in 1988. This growth is directly tied to the expansion of Japanese manufacturing in the United States, especially auto manufacturing in Kentucky, Ohio, Tennessee, and Michigan.

[6] In their study on the insurance industry, Baran and Teegarden (1983) found that one company had relocated all its "personal lines" work to small towns in order to utilize the mostly white educated female labor force. The movement of semiskilled and skilled clerical work to small towns and suburbs appears to be increasingly common in the industry (Appelbaum 1984).

thermore, the international flow of such data fits into the expanding trade of services generally. The United States government has long sought to maximize the free trade of information and has put pressure on other countries to prevent the imposition of tariffs (U.S. Congress 1982).[7]

Transnational corporations are important in the international delivery of professional business services, in good part because they meet the need for continuous contact between the provider and the client (U.S. Congress, Office of Technology Assessment 1986). Business service firms serve foreign markets primarily through foreign affiliates. They do so in a range of ways—contractual arrangements, associated partnerships, equity participation. Statistics on large firms indicate that U.S. transnationals dominate the market for such professional services as accounting, advertising, management consulting, legal, and computer services. In some of these services, firms from France, Japan, and West Germany also have a significant share. Finally, a few less developed countries are gaining a place in the trade of certain professional services, notably computer software (UN Centre for Transnational Corporations 1989a).

A third area that has contributed to spatial dispersion under conditions of continued economic concentration is the entry of large corporations into the retailing of consumer services. It is the possibility of obtaining economies of scale on the delivery of such services and the expanding market for such services that have led large corporations to produce for the open market consumer services that used to be produced only by small, single-site firms. This has brought about what Levitt (1976) has called the "industrialization" of services. Elsewhere (Sassen 1988) I have discussed at greater length how standardization and economies of scale in service production and delivery are predicated upon the shifting of certain components away from the establishments where actual service delivery takes place and onto headquarters. These come to centralize planning, development, franchising, purchasing, and other such functions.[8] The result has been a growth of large new firms, or divisions

---

[7] There is great pressure from the United States to lift restrictions, long evident in Congressional debates about international trade in services (U.S. Congress 1982) and in GATT (1989) negotiations aimed at ensuring and maximizing the free flow of services. Furthermore, as happened with manufacturing plants, governments of various countries are trying to draw firms to locate offshore office facilities. These governments are providing subsidies to draw investors, including the training of workers for the facilities (Sassen 1988). The insurance industry, for example, has argued that in order to stimulate U.S. trade and investment overseas, constraints and restrictions on the insurance delivery systems in foreign countries need to be reduced in many less developed countries, where the risks to multinational corporations are high (UN Centre on Transnational Corporations 1989a).

[8] The globalization of markets and production together with product diversification demand the investment of greater resources in planning and marketing to reach the consumer. Advertising and consumer financing have become increasingly important compo-

within firms, engaged in service delivery via multiple retail outlets and centralization of specialized functions. This fragmentation of the work process, parallel to that in manufacturing, is evident in hotels, restaurants, various kinds of repair services, movie theaters, car rentals, photo development, retail outlets for a broad range of consumer goods, from food to flowers, and a vast array of other service activities, which used to be largely the domain of small, local, independent entrepreneurs.

The geographic dispersal of economic activity described by the three cases above can be conceived of as a redeployment of growth poles. Thus, the development of export processing zones represents a deployment of manufacturing capacity from highly developed to less developed countries and setting up back office operations or retail outlets outside the head office entails shifting jobs from central to more peripheral locations. Dispersal of growth sites could, in principle, pose obstacles to the incorporation of such dispersed growth into processes generating surplus for the sectors of capital that concentrate much of the ownership and control in the major economies. Conceivably, the geographic dispersion of manufacturing plants and of office work could have gone along with a decentralization in the structure of ownership and profit appropriation. The market would mediate to a much larger extent than it does today between production and accumulation; that is to say, the various institutional processes we call the market would replace many of the internal transfer mechanisms of large corporations.

But such a parallel decentralization of ownership has not taken place. The large size of firms has made it possible to internalize transaction and circulation costs, thereby reducing the barriers to capital circulation and raising capital's ability to equalize the profit rate. Continued centralization of ownership poses the task of operating a worldwide production system with plants, offices and service branches in a multiplicity of foreign and domestic locations. It has brought about new requirements for the control of the vast decentralized production system and labor force.

This entails implementation of a system for the provision of such inputs as planning, top-level management, and specialized business services. While such provision could conceivably be local, again, this has not happened. Firms with geographically dispersed plants, offices, and service outlets, as well as the firms that subsequently developed to service them, have tended to maintain considerable levels of centralized rather than localized provision of these types of inputs. As I will discuss at length in a later chapter, not only do the large industrial and trading corporations

---

nents in the final product or service. The rapidly growing franchising system puts a good share of the costs and risks on the delivery outlet (For a look from the bottom see pp. 371–400 in Light and Bonacich 1988). This is a form of vertical integration, I would argue, that is not in the Fordist mold.

have elaborate production and contracting networks, but the specialized producer services have also developed such networks. In both cases central headquarters management, planning, and control operations expand and require additional inputs. These may be produced in house or bought from other, specialized firms.

Several changes in the financial industry over the last decade are of significance to this discussion. Aggregate data on the industry mask the rather fundamental changes in its composition over the last two decades. In the 1970s there was a pattern of dispersal through the opening up of regional markets in many parts of the world as well as offshore banking to avoid the restrictive regulations in countries of origin. These developments were basically carried out under the aegis of the large transnational banks, the largest of which were from the United States. The form that capital mobility assumed in this industry at that time was similar to what had happened in manufacturing and services: a new, vastly expanded geography of economic activity that included a growing number of Third World locations along with the maintenance of economic control by large firms, mostly from the developed countries.

The onset of the so-called Third World debt crisis in 1982 continued to bring major changes to the industry, discussed at length later. For the purposes of this section what needs emphasizing is that its renewed concentration in and orientation toward major financial centers, beginning in the early 1980s, was not a mere geographic retrenchment but was in fact associated with new forms of capital mobility. These new forms were constituted basically through the development of a wide array of innovations, which had the effect of transforming more and more components of finance or financial assets into marketable instruments. We see an enormous increase in the liquidity of the industry and in the circulation of financial capital through the marketing of instruments rather than through lending. The central activity is now the buying and selling of instruments over and over again, thereby maximizing the circulation of financial capital. Deregulation and internationalization of major financial markets has raised the participation of investors and borrowers from all over the world. This poses the matter of control in the industry in a way parallel to that of the geographic dispersal of factories, though in a different form. Do deregulation and internationalization entail a decentralization in the ownership and control structure of the industry? I will argue that the fundamental axis for the circulation of this capital increasingly came to pass through New York, London, and Tokyo, rather than an expanding network of regional banking centers in the Third World, and that we see in this development of the financial industry yet another version of the new forms of agglomeration associated with the globalization of an industry.

Capital Mobility and Labor Market Formation

The increased mobility of capital has distinct effects on the formation of labor markets and the regulation of a global labor force. Increased capital mobility has brought about a homogenization of economic space, which conceivably could also have homogenized labor. On the one hand, there has been a worldwide standardization of consumer goods and decreasing differentiation among places in terms of the feasibility of producing a whole range of items for the world market, from apparel to electronic components. On the other hand, the dispersion of economic activity has contributed to the reproduction of structurally differentiated labor supplies and labor markets in this otherwise homogenized economic space.

The spatial and social reorganization of production associated with dispersion makes possible access to peripheralized labor markets, whether abroad or at home, without undermining that peripheral condition. Such labor markets remain peripheralized even when the jobs are in leading industries producing for the world market, for example, electronics production in Third World export processing zones. The historical tendency has been for workers employed in advanced sectors of the economy to acquire considerable economic power, that is, to become a "labor aristocracy." In different historical periods, this was the case in the auto, steel, and petrochemical industries. Under the organization of production prevalent today, even in a key industry such as electronics, labor needs can be met through a highly differentiated labor supply that corresponds to specific moments in the production process, that is—specific types of inputs. As a result, this high level of differentiation is not eroded by the incorporation of workers into an advanced sector of capital. Certain forms of the capital-labor relation can be maintained even in the most advanced and technically developed sectors of capital, such as sweatshops in the electronics industry. The geographic dispersal of economic activity can thus be seen as a tendency that ensures the reproduction of structurally differentiated labor supplies notwithstanding a context where global-sized firms have internalized the functions of the market and therewith homogenized their space of operation. Dispersion becomes a mechanism that operates against the tendency toward empowerment of workers in advanced sectors of capital and, at the limit, neutralizes the politico-economic consequences that Marx associated with the generalized increase in the capital intensity of production and that more recent analysts have associated with large, vertically integrated firms.[9] In this sense, the form

[9] At the same time, however, the greater spatial differentiation of labor can generate rigidities for capital. Storper and Walker (1983) note that neoclassic economists and location theorists have treated labor in the same terms as those for "true" commodity inputs and

of capital mobility entailed by the geographic dispersal of manufacturing is clearly yet another way in which the social compact represented by Fordism has been dismantled, even when assembly lines and mass production are retained at a transnational level.

There are also a number of economic activities that do not lend themselves to relocation. Notable among these are the large array of service jobs that need to be performed in situ: the staffing of hospitals and restaurants, the cleaning and maintenance of buildings, which cannot be moved—these need to be carried out where the offices, restaurants, and hospitals are located. Elsewhere (Sassen 1988) I have argued that the employment of immigrant workers, from highly trained personnel to unskilled laborers, may appear in this regard as a functional equivalent to the mobility of capital; but it is in fact a component of, rather than an alternative to, capital mobility insofar as (a) on the most general level, international capital mobility contributes to the formation of an international labor market and (b) more specifically, the economic restructuring associated with the current phase of capital mobility has generated a large supply of jobs and casual labor markets that facilitate the employment of disadvantaged foreign workers, and it has also generated a demand for specific high-level skills that can be met by workers from anywhere, as long as they have the required education.

The mobility of capital has contributed to new forms in the mobility of labor (Sassen 1988). The international circulation of capital has contributed to the formation of international labor markets. The major immigration flows to the United States, the United Kingdom, and now Japan are not haphazard in their origin. They are in good part rooted in the economic or political/military histories of their countries. The main countries sending immigrants to the United Kingdom were formerly part of the British Empire. The United Kingdom built "bridges" for the movement of capital, goods, and the military. But once the bridges are built, why would people not use them? Most immigrants to the United States come from countries where the United States has a strong economic or military presence. Finally, the recent formation of labor migration flows from several South Asian and Southeast Asian countries to Japan (discussed in Chapter Nine), would seem to confirm the model I developed in Sassen (1988). Through offshore production, foreign aid, investments and the spread of markets for Japanese consumer goods, Japan has built bridges with these countries. Furthermore, the internationalization of the economies of the United States, the United Kingdom, and now Japan, asso-

---

outputs and therefore have underestimated its importance in location decisions. Whether highly trained personnel or low-wage unskilled laborers, labor can become one of the key locational criteria.

ciated with the development of a strong economic or political/military presence in foreign countries, also contributes to the formation of the option to employ foreign workers—a subject discussed in Chapter Nine. Again, this is most evident in Japan today, a country that has never considered itself an immigration country and that has a strong ideology about the importance of racial homogeneity. It seems that the internationalization of the Japanese economy has brought with it the possibility of employing foreign workers in a country where this was inconceivable a few years ago. The formation of this kind of an international labor market can also be seen as contributing to the dismantling of the conditions that made Fordism possible.

Conclusion

In sum, central to my analysis of the mobility of capital is an elaboration that takes it beyond the notion of geographic locational capability. I seek to incorporate two additional elements. One is that the increased mobility of capital brings about new forms of locational concentration, which are as much a part of this mobility as is geographic dispersal. Furthermore, insofar as these new forms of agglomeration are associated with new forms of geographic dispersal, they do not simply represent a persistence of older forms of agglomeration, but respond to a new economic logic. This would mean that the question of why agglomeration persists in the face of global telecommunications capability is, in fact, the wrong question. This is not the persistence of old forms but the occurrence of new forms, precisely fed by the globalization and dispersal of economic activity that such telecommunications capability makes feasible. The question should rather be at what point the cost of this agglomeration will become so high that there will be strong inducements to develop forms of agglomeration of centralized functions that are not geographically determined.

The second element I seek to incorporate into the analysis of capital mobility has to do with the transformations in the capital/labor relation that such mobility entails. Hence, beyond a changed geography of economic activity there is a constitution of new relations among the various components of a particular location. Each type of location contains a specific form of these newly constituted relations. The locations of interest to this book are major cities, specifically New York, London and Tokyo, rather than for example, export-processing zones in Third World countries or back offices located in somewhat peripheral locations around major cities. In the case of major cities, I will argue in a later chapter that the casualization and informalization of a wide range of activities and the formation of a highly paid new professional class, are processes that can be shown to be strongly associated with the globalization of production and finance under conditions of continued economic concentration.

For the purposes of empirical analysis what needs to be extracted from the discussion here is that geographic dispersal is important to the understanding of growth in major cities today only insofar as this process has occurred under conditions of continued economic concentration. Given such conditions, the dispersal of economic activity brings about new requirements for centralized management and control. This leads to a subsequent task for empirical analysis: an examination of the actual work involved in running a highly dispersed (domestically and internationally) set of plants and offices and of the locational patterns of such work. If agglomeration economies are high, will these activities tend to be geographically concentrated, and if so, where? Major cities are obvious locations for activities geared toward the international market and transnational firms; yet there are elements in this chain of analysis that need further elucidation. Future chapters attempt this. But for now, the next two chapters examine the facts that describe the main trends discussed here.

Three

New Patterns in Direct Foreign Investment

DIRECT FOREIGN INVESTMENT (DFI) is one of several indicators of the processes of capital relocation discussed in the preceding chapter. It is a useful indicator because much of the geographic dispersion of production and of the reorganization in the financial industry are international rather than domestic. The intent here is not an exhaustive description of stocks and flows, but an identification of key patterns, magnitudes, and countries involved. The evidence discussed in this and the next chapter points to a realignment in basic trends. The massive increases in direct foreign investment by all developed countries in the 1960s and especially the 1970s have been overtaken by even more massive international financial investments in the 1980s. Furthermore, the already high domination of investment by a limited number of countries has continued to increase. Finally, in the 1980s the flow of direct foreign investment in services has grown more rapidly than in manufacturing and extractive industries.

There has been a pronounced transformation in the composition of direct foreign investment. During the 1950s, direct foreign investment, measured in terms of stocks and flows, was largely concentrated in raw materials, other primary products, and resource-based manufacturing. In the 1980s, it was primarily in technology-intensive manufacturing and in services. By the mid-1980s, about 40% of the world's total direct foreign investment stock of about $700 billion was in services, compared to about 25% in the early 1970s and less than 20% in the early 1950s. Moreover, direct foreign investment in services became the fastest-growing component of overall direct foreign investment flows. During the first half of the 1980s, more than half of all direct foreign investment flows (about $50 billion annually) were in services, with about two-thirds of this in finance and trade-related activities (UN Centre on Transnational Corporations 1989d). The most recent available data as of this writing point to a continuation of this trend in the second half of the 1980s.

Major Patterns

The most commonly used definition of direct foreign investment is that of the International Monetary Fund. It provides international guidelines for countries in compiling balance-of-payments accounts but does not specify a minimum ownership percentage to establish foreign ownership. In the most recent edition of the IMF *Balance of Payments Manual,* such investment is defined as "investment that is made to acquire a lasting interest in an enterprise operating in an economy other than that of the investor, the investor's purpose being to have an effective voice in the management of the enterprise" (IMF 1977). Most countries set ownership percentage levels, ranging from 5% all the way to 50% (IMF 1977: 4). The OECD has established a benchmark definition in order to make the data somewhat comparable. It recommends the inclusion of foreign affiliates in which a single investor controls less than 10% but has an effective voice in the management of the enterprise; it also recommends a variety of other indicators, such as participation in policymaking, exchange of managerial personnel, etc., to establish foreign ownership in marginal cases. The United States, through the Bureau of Economic Analysis of the Department of Commerce, has also adopted indicators that consider factors other than equity holding.

There has been a trend toward reducing the cutoff point that distinguishes direct foreign investment from other types of investments, in recognition of the fact that direct foreign investment can exist without ownership of voting shares. Large corporations may require only a small share in equity to have decisive influence in the management of an enterprise, and control may be obtained through nonequity, contractual arrangements. This is particularly important to an understanding of the place of foreign investment in services where nonequity arrangements are a common form for delivering services to a foreign location. This would be considered direct foreign investment as long as there is control over the foreign establishment. To consider zero-equity cases as direct foreign investment, does, however, create measurement problems (UN Centre for Transnational Corporations 1989c). The stock of direct foreign investments is a measure of equity and debt, and income from direct foreign investments is defined as a return on equity and debt investment, as distinguished from income from nonfinancial intangible assets associated with nonequity forms, which are categorized as "royalties and license fees."

The estimated world stock of direct foreign investment went from $66 billion in 1960 to $213 billion in 1972, reached over $549 billion by 1984, and reached $962.8 billion at the end of 1987. Five major patterns can be extracted from the vast amount of data on direct foreign investment over the last two decades. First, all developed countries increased their direct foreign investment in the less developed countries during the 1970s, reaching an average annual growth rate of 19.4% from 1973 to 1978 (excluding petroleum). In that decade, the strongest growth in investments was into less developed countries.[1] Investments in export-oriented production grew the fastest.

A second pattern emerged in the 1980s. Most countries reduced their levels of investment abroad and at the same time experienced declines in foreign investment inflows. Overall direct foreign investment declined in both the less developed and the highly developed countries. Between 1981 and 1983, such investment declined by one-third in the former and one-quarter in the latter. From 1980 to 1987, the average annual growth rate of direct foreign investment in developing countries was down to 1.9% (World Bank 1988). (See Table 3.1.) In the case of the United States, this rate went from 14% in the 1970s to 3.3% in the 1980–1987 period (*Survey of Current Business* 1988c: table 3).

Third, there was a sharp reversal in the position of the United States. Up to 1979, the United States had been the leading exporter of such investments. By 1981, it had become the leading recipient, and had fallen to second place as an exporter of capital, behind the United King-

TABLE 3.1

Average Annual Growth Rate of Direct Foreign Investment from Developed to Developing Countries, 1960-1987 (percent)

Period	Growth Rate
1960-1968	7.0
1968-1973	9.2
1973-1978	19.4
1980-1987	1.9

Sources: 1960-1978: OECD, *Recent International Direct Investment Trends* (1981). 1980-1987: World Bank, *World Development* (1988).

[1] In the 1970s, investments into less developed countries increased at an average annual rate of 18%, compared with 16% in the developed countries. However, a limited number of these account for most of the flow. The total direct foreign investment for all major industrial countries in developing countries went from $35 billion in 1967 to $76 billion in 1976 (ILO 1981: 2, 5). West Germany's direct foreign investment position went from $1.9 billion in 1970 to $5.9 billion in 1976; that of the Netherlands, from $2.2 billion to $3.5 billion; that of France, from $3.8 billion to $5.2 billion; and that of the United Kingdom, from $5.9 billion to $9.3 billion. In the case of the United States, it went from $8 billion in 1966 to $42 billion in 1980, accounting for half of all such investment in developing countries. The average annual growth rates of direct foreign investment for all major industrial countries grew significantly. They were 7% from 1960 to 1968; 9.2% from 1968 to 1973; and 19.4% from 1973 to 1978 (UN Centre on Transnational Corporations 1979: 5). In the case of the United States, the average annual growth rate from 1950 to 1966 was 11.7% for developed countries and 6.3% for developing countries. From 1966 to 1977 these rates were, respectively, 10.7% and 9.7%. From 1973 to 1980, they were 11.8% and 14.2%. (These figures exclude the petroleum industry.)

dom, where it stayed until 1984. Since then, the levels at which the United States absorbed direct foreign investment have reached historic highs; this trend is particularly noteworthy given the general contraction in foreign investment inflows experienced by most developed countries. (See Table 3.2.) Direct foreign investment in the United Kingdom declined from a high of U.S. $6 billion in 1980 to $1.9 billion in 1981 and in 1982; it rose again to U.S. $3.7 billion in 1983, a period when global foreign investment flows began to increase again. In the early 1970s, direct foreign investment in the United States represented less than 9% of all DFI by developed countries; by 1984, it was estimated at 60% of all DFI by developed countries, a share far higher than the 17% of the United Kingdom, the next largest recipient (U.S. Department of Commerce International Trade Administration 1984; UN Centre on Transnational Corporations 1985), and it constituted about 50% of global DFI in 1984 and in 1986 (IMF 1987b: table C14). Total DFI stock in the United States increased from U.S. $83 billion in 1980 to $328.9 billion in 1988. About 40% of this investment was accounted for by the United Kingdom and the Netherlands; Japan's share went from 6.5% in 1980 to 16.2% in 1988 (*Survey of Current Business* 1988a, 1989b). (See Table 3.3.)

A fourth pattern is Japan's rapidly growing role in global direct foreign investment. By 1982, Japan had become a leading exporter of direct foreign investment, with a gross outflow of $4.5 billion. That particular year, Japan surpassed the United Kingdom's $4.4 billion. This level was still far below the $7 billion and $10 billion gross outflows registered for the

TABLE 3.2

Inward Direct Investment Flows: SDRs and Percentage Distribution for Seven Countries, 1980-1986 (millions of SDRs and percent)

Country	Millions of SDRs [a]	% of Total
United States	122,962	60.5
United Kingdom	34,227	16.8
France	15,261	7.5
Australia	10,781	5.3
Netherlands	10,174	5.0
Italy	4,958	2.4
West Germany	4,909	2.4
Total	203,272	99.9

Source: IMF, *Balance of Payments Statistics Yearbook* [hereafter *Yearbook*] 38, pt. 1 (1987).
    Note: Percentages do not total 100 because of rounding.
    [a]   Standard Drawing Rights.

TABLE 3.3A

Direct Foreign Investment in the United States by Source, 1962-1988 (millions of U.S. dollars)

Source	1962	1966	1970	1974	1980	1987	1988
Canada	2,064	2,439	3,117	5,136	12,457	24,013	27,361
Europe*	5,247	6,274	9,554	16,756	55,226	186,076	216,418
United Kingdom	2,474	2,864	4,127	5,744	14,400	79,699	101,909
Netherlands	1,082	1,402	2,151	4,698	4,675	49,115	48,991
West Germany	152	247	680	1,535	6,716	20,315	23,845
Switzerland	836	949	1,545	1,949	4,675	14,686	15,896
France	183	245	286	1,139	3,392	10,119	11,364
Japan	112	103	229	345	5,398	35,151	53,354
OPEC	—	—	—	201	731	4,897	6,221
Other	189	238	370	2,706	9,320	21,651	25,496
Total	7,612	9,054	13,270	25,144	83,046	271,788	328,850

Sources: 1962-1974: *Survey of Current Business* [hereafter *Current Business*] 42–54 (1962-1974, various issues). 1980-1987; *ibid.* 68 (Aug. 1988). 1989; *ibid.* 69 (Aug. 1989).

* Total for countries listed below does not equal Europe total because not all European countries are listed.

TABLE 3.3B

Direct Foreign Investment in the United States by Source, 1962-1988 (percent)

	1962[a]	1966[a,b]	1970[a]	1974	1980	1987	1988
Canada	27.1	26.9	23.5	20.4	15.0	8.8	8.3
Europe	68.9	69.3	72.0	66.6	66.5	68.5	65.8
Japan	1.5	1.1	1.7	1.4	6.5	12.9	16.2
OPEC	--	--	--	0.8	0.8	1.8	1.9
Other	2.5	2.6	2.8	10.8	11.2	8.0	7.8

Sources: Same as Table 3.3A.
[a] Investment by OPEC excluded.
[b] Percentages do not total 100 because of rounding.

United Kingdom in 1980 and 1981. But it signaled Japan's major place among the capital exporting countries. It is worth noting that in 1983, when there was a general contraction in global foreign direct investment, Japan's decline was a relatively smaller one than the United Kingdom's if we consider the period beginning in the late 1970s, when the realignment of investment patterns was beginning to consolidate. This is further confirmed by the fact that in 1985 Japan's direct foreign investment rose to $12.2 billion and had almost tripled to $33 billion in 1987. For the first six months of 1988 it reached $22.8 billion, up 44.6% over the same period a year before (JETRO 1989: 7), with about half of this flow going to

the United States. Japan has surpassed most of the leading Western European capital exporters, such as West Germany, the Netherlands, and
France. But while these have typically also been leading recipients of
direct foreign investment, Japan has not until very recently. Gross annual
inflows of direct foreign investment had been between $250 million and
$400 million since the late 1970s, compared with $400 million to $1.6
billion in West Germany, $2 billion to $3 billion in France, $1 billion to
$2 billion in the Netherlands, and $2 billion to $6 billion in the United
Kingdom. From 1986 to 1987, direct foreign investment inflow into Japan
more than doubled, reaching a total of U.S. $2.3 billion in fiscal 1987
(though this is most probably an inflated figure, since it is based on the
required notifications of intent to the Ministry of Finance, some of which
may never take place) [JETRO 1989: 11].

In Standard Drawing Rights (SDRs), these figures are somewhat
changed because of the pronounced fluctuations in exchange values in
the mid-1980s, especially after 1985 in the case of the yen.[2] Japan's DFI
went from 1.8 billion SDRs in 1980 to 12.2 billion SDRs in 1986, clearly
a far more pronounced increase than the United Kingdom's increase from
8.7 billion SDRs in 1980 to 13.4 billion SDRs in 1986. (See Table 3.4.)
This put Japan in third place, behind the United States and the United
Kingdom. However, given the relatively low foreign investment in Japan, by the mid-1980s it had become the leading net exporter of direct
foreign investment.

A fifth pattern is the high degree of concentration in global direct foreign investment. Out of the global stock of $549 billion of direct foreign
investment in 1984, the United States accounted for 42.5%, the United
Kingdom accounted for 15.5%, and Japan accounted for 6.9%, or 65% of
the total. By the end of 1987, the United States's share was 31.5%, the
United Kingdom's was 18%, and Japan's was 10%, or 60% of the world
stock of direct foreign investment. In SDRs, total stock of these three
countries went from 347.5 billion in 1984 to 461.7 billion in 1988. (See
Table 3.5.) While the United States still accounts for much of direct foreign investment, its share of all flows has declined notwithstanding the
increased amount of such investment throughout the 1970s. This decline
is attributable to the rising levels of direct foreign investment by other
countries. Thus, from 1970 to 1974 the United States accounted for
51.8% of all direct foreign investment flows, and Japan accounted for 6%
of all such flows; in 1980–1984, the United States's share of flows had
declined to 17.3%, and Japan's share had more than doubled, to 12.5%

[2] In order to control for the pronounced fluctuations in the U.S. dollar and the yen,
especially in the 1980s, it is useful to use Standard Drawing Rights (SDRs) as the unit of
measure.

TABLE 3.4

Japan, United Kingdom, and United States: Direct Foreign Investment Flows, 1979-1986 (billions of SDRs)

	Japan			United Kingdom			United States		
	DFI Abroad	DFI in	Balance	DFI Abroad	DFI in	Balance	DFI Abroad	DFI in	Balance
1979	2.24	0.19	2.05	9.70	5.01	4.69	19.54	9.18	10.36
1980	1.84	0.22	1.62	8.74	7.78	0.96	14.80	12.99	1.81
1981	4.17	0.16	4.01	10.43	5.00	5.43	8.08	21.55	13.47
1982	4.10	0.40	3.70	6.51	4.85	1.66	2.22	12.57	14.79
1983	3.37	0.38	2.99	7.63	4.84	2.79	0.41	11.20	10.79
1984	5.80	0.01	5.79	7.88	0.28	7.60	2.82	24.73	21.91
1985	6.33	0.62	5.71	11.04	5.44	5.60	16.69	18.88	2.19
1986	12.22	0.20	12.02	13.37	6.60	6.77	24.24	21.04	3.20

Source: Same as Table 3.2.

(OECD, various years a; Bank of England, various years; U.S. Department of Commerce, International Trade Administration 1980c; *Survey of Current Business* 1981b, 1988c; MITI 1986; IMF 1987a, 1989; JETRO 1987a, b). Multinational corporations of the developed countries accounted for 97% of recorded flows of direct foreign investment in the early 1980s (UN Centre on Transnational Corporations, 1985: 15). A similar concentration is evident in the destination of global direct foreign investment in the early 1980s. By the mid-1980s, the United States was receiving over half and Southeast Asia was receiving another 35%.

A major, though distinct flow is the growing U.S. deficit. In 1981 the U.S. balance of trade registered a deficit of $27.9 billion; this figure rose to $112.5 billion in 1984, to $122.2 billion in 1985, and to $160.3 billion in 1987. The U.K balance of trade went from a surplus of $7.2 billion in 1981 to deficits of $1.3 billion in 1983, $5.9 billion in 1984, $2.5 billion in 1985, and $15.8 billion in 1987. Japan, on the other hand, had a steady increase in its surplus, which went from $20 billion in 1981 to $60 billion in 1985, and $96.4 billion in 1987 (OECD various years a; MITI 1986; IMF 1987, 1988c).

International Transactions in Services

Overall, the service sector is oriented to a domestic and local market. Only major firms in certain service industries, particularly producer services, have a significant degree of internationalization as measured, for

TABLE 3.5

Japan, United Kingdom, and United States: Direct Foreign Investment Stock, 1979-1988 (billions of SDRs)

	1979	1980	1981	1982	1983	1984	1985	1986	1987	1988
Japan										
Direct investment abroad	13.08	15.38	21.06	26.26	30.74	38.69	40.03	47.47	54.29	82.32
Direct investment in	2.60	2.56	3.37	3.63	4.16	4.55	4.32	5.32	6.36	7.74
Balance	10.48	12.82	17.69	22.63	26.58	34.14	35.71	42.15	47.93	74.58
¥/SDR	315.76	258.91	255.95	259.32	243.10	246.13	220.23	194.61	175.20	169.36
United Kingdom										
Direct investment abroad	53.02	62.10	73.76	76.51	80.87	93.14	98.41	109.48	119.22	136.43
Direct investment in	37.16	49.41	49.11	47.28	51.59	47.06	56.97	58.63	74.03	88.96
Balance	15.86	12.79	24.65	29.23	29.28	46.08	41.44	50.85	45.19	47.47
£/SDR	0.59	0.53	0.61	0.68	0.72	0.85	0.76	0.83	0.76	0.74
United States										
Direct investment abroad	142.61	168.87	196.18	188.33	197.91	215.75	209.62	212.40	217.09	242.92
Direct investment in	41.31	65.12	93.40	113.03	130.91	167.90	168.08	180.19	191.58	244.37
Balance	101.30	103.75	102.78	75.30	67.00	47.85	41.54	32.21	25.51	-1.45
$/SDR	1.32	1.28	1.16	1.10	1.05	0.98	1.10	1.22	1.42	1.35

Sources: IMF, Yearbook 38, pt. 1 (1987); ibid. 40, pt. 1 (1989).

example, by the weight of foreign sales in total revenues of a firm. For example, despite rapid growth of the service share in the U.S. economy, the international trade in services accounted for a small share in total services output (Candilis 1988). In 1985 service industries accounted for 70% of U.S. domestic product. Service exports other than investment income accounted for only 1.4% of U.S. domestic product. U.S. private service exports other than investment income (U.S. $44.2 billion) are small relative to merchandise exports (U.S. $214.4 billion).

The characteristics of non-tradable services tend to require production and delivery in one location, which explains why direct foreign investment is at this time the main mode of international service delivery. Measurement problems with international service transactions hinder a detailed analysis of investment and trade patterns in producer services. Several special studies launched to address these problems indicate an undercount in international service trade figures, particularly intrafirm trade, and in investment figures, particularly the exclusion of nonequity arrangements from direct foreign investment measures.[3] But the evidence strongly indicates that both the activities of transnational service firms and direct foreign investments in services have grown. The UN Centre on Transnational Corporations, which has accumulated one of the best data sets on these developments, has found that measurements based on sales and value-added are quite consistent with the measurements of direct foreign investment.[4] The United States is the country for which the most detailed data are available, which makes it possible to compare outcomes involving different types of measures (UN Centre on Transnational Corporations 1989d: 9). Because data on direct foreign investment stocks and flows are the only ones regularly compiled by a large group of countries, they are the most frequently used. While these data measure

[3] The data on the international trade balance are inadequate. There have been growing surpluses in "invisibles." But these cannot be fully attributed to the sales of services. On the other hand, some of the receipts of service industries are reported under the merchandise account. A full analysis on sources of information on service exports can be found in Economic Consulting Services (1981) and U.S. Department of Commerce, International Trade Administration (1980a). The data commonly used in descriptions of the service trade come from balance of payment data collected for the whole world by the Bank of International Settlement (BIS). In the United States, these data are then prepared by the Bureau of Economic Analysis of the Department of Commerce. According to these data, total service exports (excluding income on investments abroad) reached $35 billion in 1980 and $46 billion in 1985. These data have serious inadequacies. In response to criticism, the Office of Technology Assessment of the U.S. Congress has developed a more encompassing and precise measure.

[4] According to the UN Centre on Transnational Corporations, the best variable to measure the importance of transnational corporations would be the value-added of the affiliates controlled by these corporations, but no systematic data on this variable are available (UN Centre on Transnational Corporations, 1989c: 9).

foreign ownership of assets and capital flows, they omit various other aspects, for example, the share of joint venture partners and borrowing from local or international markets. These qualifications need to be borne in mind when reading the evidence presented here.

The distinction between trade, direct foreign investment, and other modes of delivery is important for conceptual and statistical purposes. In the case of direct foreign investment, transnational corporations are an important factor, and many of the questions raised in the case of industrial transnational corporations may also emerge for the case of services (GATT various years; UN Centre on Transnational Corporations 1989b). The Group of Negotiations on Services for the General Agreement on Tariffs and Trade (GATT) was given the task of drafting a framework for the case of services, particularly the definitional and statistical questions, on which to base principles and rules for trade in services. Coverage of the multilateral framework for trade in services, measures, practices, concepts, and rules on which agreement was reached was included in GATT's mid-term review ministerial declaration in April 1989 as the basis for further work. Studies of specific industries selected for study are under way: telecommunications, construction, transportation, tourism, and professional and financial services (including insurance) (UN Centre on Transnational Corporations 1989c). The mid-term review declaration also recognized that trade in services may involve cross-border movement of services, as well as cross-border movement of consumers and of factors of production (GATT various years).

International transactions in services can assume several forms. Services may be delivered to foreign markets directly, through the movement of people (either as providers or as consumers), through foreign affiliates in which the service provider has equity participation, licensing, or other nonequity mechanisms, and through commercial means, such as sales or representatives' offices (UN Centre on Transnational Corporations 1989c). In the case of nontradable services, direct foreign investment is the typical form of delivery. There is at this time no precise definition of trade in services. The two major forms of delivery are cross-border transactions and direct foreign investment.

The cross-border delivery of services is the only mode of delivery that has the characteristics of trade in goods, with the difference that only services embodied in goods (software or tapes, etc.) or those whose value-added can be put on paper (evaluations, drawings) can actually cross borders independently of producers.[5] Telecommunications technol-

[5] The case of services embodied in goods raises the question of their separability. Bhagwati (1984) argues that with specialization based on economies of scale, service activities will be "splintered off" and become part of interfirm transactions, which he views as technologically progressive, unlike the reverse case, when goods are splintered off from ser-

ogies make possible and can be expected to contribute to the growth of transborder data flows, especially for information-intensive services. This technology has raised the tradability of many of the professional services. But, surprisingly, this type of transborder flow still accounts for a very small share of international transactions in services (UN Centre on Transnational Corporations 1989c: 3–4). Telecommunications technology has raised intrafirm flows of services in transnational corporations and other corporate organizations.

The movement of persons is often a requirement for an international service transaction, either to buy or to provide the service. Travel is one of the four major services in terms of the balance of payments; it comprises various types of travel, including patients who go to a foreign country to buy medical services, tourists, and professional experts who go to a foreign country to provide a service, as is the case in many of the professional services. Providers may be unskilled construction workers, maintenance and repair workers, engineers, architects, lawyers, or managers. They may be working on their own account, on behalf of a firm in the country of origin, or for a foreign company in the country of destination.

Delivery through foreign affiliates is common given the characteristics of production of many services, such as hotel, retail banking, and car rental services, computer and office equipment maintenance, accounting, and advertising. Delivery can also occur through licensing and other nonequity mechanisms, for example, franchises. In the case of professional services, such as law or accounting, arrangements often resemble direct foreign investment arrangements. Transnational firms may do business and refer clients to a particular firm in a foreign country, that may or may not operate under the same name. In the case of the United States, it is clear that direct foreign investment is the most important mode of delivery of services by U.S. firms to foreign markets (UN Centre on Transnational Corporations 1989d: 8). Data from the *Survey of Current Business* (1987, 1988b) show that by far the biggest item is travel in cross-border transactions. While the total of cross-border transactions (of services) amounted to an estimated $70 billion in exports (or sales) in 1987, exports through affiliates abroad reached $209 billion, almost half of it through majority-owned nonbank affiliates and another 40% through banking affiliates.

Services delivered abroad by a provider are the most difficult to classify. Basically, such a transaction would be considered cross-border on the basis of four factors: (1) whether the producer's stay in the foreign

---

vices, which may leave behind a residue of relatively unprogressive, that is, technically static, services.

country is limited; (2) whether the producer's stay is not part of a broader movement of resources, as when a transnational corporation sets up a new branch and brings over managers and other employees; (3) the nature of the service rendered (for example, architectural work, as opposed to pure labor, as with immigrants); and (4) the conduit (is it a specific service rendered to a foreign client or part of the setting up of a foreign branch by a transnational corporation and thus internal to the firm rather than provided to a client?).

Trade in Services

Current balance of payments guidelines do not clearly define trade or cross-border transactions in services;[6] the definition is somewhat clearer for direct foreign investment, but it is not uniformly used by all countries. Gray areas in terms of definition are transactions related to the temporary presence abroad of a provider and delivery through nonequity arrangements, offices, and agencies.

For the case of services, there are two aspects of the definition that are important. One is the cutoff point in share ownership of foreign affiliates in order to distinguish trade in services from portfolio and other types of investment. The second is the duration of operations in a foreign country in the case of movement of personnel and machinery in order to distinguish such movement from cross-border transactions. In terms of equity participation, there has been a trend toward lowering the cutoff point distinguishing other types of investment.

The evidence suggests that an early factor inducing the internationalization of producer services firms was the internationalization of manufacturing and extractive industries (U.S. Department of Commerce, International Trade Administration 1980a; Economic Consulting Services 1981; UN Centre on Transnational Corporations 1985). Real growth in international trade in services was about 8% per annum from 1970 to 1980, similar to the growth in merchandise trade. After 1980, it declined to about 2.8% per annum, paralleling a decline in merchandise trade. However, by the mid-1980s the international trade in services was accelerating and surpassing the trade in merchandise, suggesting that it had

---

[6] Directly traded services are largely recorded in the balance of payments, while indirectly traded services are embodied in goods trade and are part of the trade account (Sapir and Lutz 1981). The latter is typically not counted in measures of service trade and hence most of the data are an undercount. Discussion of the problem in measuring service trade by use of balance of payments data can be found in Shelp (1981) and in Tucker, Sundberg, and Seow (1983). In 1984, the ten top trading countries accounted for almost 70% of world exports and 53% of world imports.

become less dependent on the latter and more connected to other conditions, such as the growth of investment income flows and finance.

The overall figures on the trade in services include as key components income from investment, including debt repayments, and travel and transportation. Investment income has grown faster than all other categories. Most of the growth of this component is in industrial and non-oil-exporting developing countries. Among the factors behind the increase in investment income flow is the rise in real interest rates in 1981, the increased debt of the less developed countries, and the growing debt service of the United States. Since 1980, real investment income flows have increased by 9% per annum. In 1984 exports and imports of investment income in industrial countries were about equal; by 1985, industrial countries had become net importers of capital. The trade in services for business, though small, was a growing share of overall service trade.

In the 1960s and 1970s, the international trade in services (transportation, tourism, investment income, and other services) accounted for one-fourth of total world trade; by 1984 it had increased to 29% of world trade and was worth U.S. $736.7 billion in imports. Table 3.6 shows service imports and exports in 1988 for major surplus and deficit nations. The world shows an overall deficit in service trade, which reached 63.8 billion SDRs in 1988. Half of it is composed of less developed countries' (LDC) deficits in investment income and transportation and a large deficit in transportation and other services among oil-exporting countries.

Table 3.7 compares developed, oil-exporting developing, and non-oil-exporting developing countries during 1975–1988. Developed countries presently dominate the trade, although their share is declining, with imports falling faster than exports. Non-oil-exporting developing countries, on the other hand, are increasing their share of trade, with growth in imports outpacing growth of exports. Only some highly industrialized countries are net service exporters. The largest volume of trade is among developed nations, while the net direction of trade is from developed to developing countries. In 1984 the developed countries accounted for 77% of world service exports and 66% of the imports. That same year the top ten trading countries (all OECD except Saudi Arabia) accounted for 68% of world exports and 54% of imports. However, the share of developing countries increased from 19% of the world trade in invisibles in 1973 to 29% in 1984. The non-oil-exporting developing countries have the largest deficits, mostly accounting for investment income flows, that is, debt repayments; this is especially true of Brazil and other Latin American countries.

The U.S. shares of world exports of services and merchandise both declined 3% between 1970 and 1985. But the United States still accounts for a large share of international service trade, with 18.1% of world ser-

TABLE 3.6

World Services Trade: Major Surplus and Deficit Countries, 1988 (billions of SDRs and percent)

	Total Credit (billions of SDRs)	Total Debit (billions of SDRs)	Net Services (billions of SDRs)	Imports as % of Total World Imports	Exports as % of Total World Receipts
United States	156.721	145.470	11.251	18.10	15.64
France	64.939	56.473	8.466	7.50	6.07
United Kingdom	109.975	97.793	12.182	12.70	10.52
West Germany	64.336	73.253	-8.917	7.43	7.88
Japan	83.349	91.787	-8.438	9.62	9.87
Italy	31.698	34.203	-2.505	3.66	3.78
Netherlands	28.308	29.432	-1.124	3.27	3.17
Switzerland	26.284	15.400	10.884	3.03	3.17
Spain	20.074	12.805	7.269	2.32	1.38
Canada	16.313	31.683	-15.370	1.88	3.41
Singapore	9.125	5.973	3.152	1.05	0.64
Mexico	8.315	12.248	-3.933	9.62	1.32
Australia	7.431	16.085	-8.654	0.86	1.73
Total world	866.072	929.889	-63.817	100.00	100.00

Source: IMF, *Yearbook*, 40, pt. 2 (1989).

Note: World services trade includes shipment; other transportation; travel; reinvested earnings on direct investment; other direct investment income; other investment income; other official goods, services, and income; and other private goods, services, and income.

vice exports in 1988. The main reason for the continuing surplus in services and growing deficit in merchandise trade is on the import side; while services were expanding globally, growth in the merchandise trade was aimed at exports to the United States. Between 1970 and 1984, U.S. purchases of merchandise imports rose from 15.4% to 19.1% of world merchandise imports, while U.S. purchases of service imports fell from 19.0% to 16.3% (see Table 3.8 for 1975–1988 data). Historically having been a large net investor overseas, the United States has had a large surplus in international investment income. Despite the pronounced decline in U.S. investments overseas, this category remains the strongest component in the U.S. service trade. By 1985, investment income accounted for over half of the total surplus in services. The decline in the surpluses since 1981 was due to the Third World debt crisis, increasing credit demands in the United States, high returns on investments in the United States, and the need to finance deficits in the merchandise trade.

Net U.S. service transactions declined in the period between 1977 and 1987, at a compound annual growth rate (CAGR) of −5.54% (*Survey of*

TABLE 3.7

Share in World Service Credits and Debits, 1975, 1980, 1985, and 1988 (percent)

	Credit				Debit			
	1975	1980	1985	1988	1975	1980	1985	1988
Transportation[a]								
Industrial countries	83.18	77.07	75.32	78.02	71.36	62.77	67.86	73.01
Nonoil developing countries	13.89	19.87	23.11	21.16	22.01	25.62	24.46	22.66
Oil-exporting countries	2.58	2.97	1.50	1.56	6.15	11.61	7.61	4.39
Travel								
Industrial countries	74.29	68.93	72.24	75.82	81.77	73.87	76.71	84.69
Nonoil developing countries	22.60	28.77	26.44	23.15	14.25	16.71	18.16	12.54
Oil-exporting countries	2.26	2.30	1.22	1.04	3.42	9.42	5.13	2.23
Investment Income[b]								
Industrial countries	87.76	79.70	81.47	85.59	70.93	69.17	70.45	78.42
Nonoil developing countries	5.24	9.43	6.65	4.70	20.24	20.42	21.35	14.71
Oil-exporting countries	6.46	8.92	7.19	4.62	8.13	6.81	4.58	3.45
Other[c]								
Industrial countries	83.45	79.00	78.34	82.91	75.27	62.02	60.80	71.76
Nonoil developing countries	15.71	17.28	17.62	14.92	15.55	16.97	17.35	14.90
Oil-exporting countries	0.51	2.05	3.76	1.89	8.66	18.19	18.85	8.73

Sources: IMF, *Yearbook* 33, pt. 2 (1982); *ibid.* 38, pt. 2 (1987); *ibid.* 40, pt. 2 (1989).

Note: Percentages do not total 100 because of certain nonreported transfers included by the IMF staff, unavailability of data for a specific category, and rounding discrepancies.

[a] Includes shipment and other transportation.

[b] Includes reinvested earnings on direct investment, other direct investment income, and other investment income.

[c] Includes other private goods, services, and income, and other public goods, services, and income.

Current Business 1988b). Receipts (exports) grew at a rate of 10.3% (CAGR), while payments (imports) grew even faster, at 14.05% (CAGR). Extrapolating from the above trends, by 1990 the deficit in total services could be U.S. $6.2 billion. In 1987, the major deficit items in order of size were government investment income, long a big deficit item, at U.S. $18.7 billion; travel and passenger fares, U.S. $8.8 billion; other transportation, U.S. $2.8 billion; military transactions, U.S. $2.1 billion, and other private investment income, U.S. $2.0 billion. Until 1987 there was a constant surplus, which peaked in 1982 at U.S. $24.6 billion and began declining rapidly in 1984. The major surplus item was direct net investment income, U.S. $35.3 billion, an item showing pronounced fluctua-

TABLE 3.8

United States: Share of World Trade, 1975, 1980, 1985, and 1988 (percent)

	1975	1980	1985	1988
		Credit		
Merchandise trade	14.82	12.20	11.33	11.40
Services trade	19.86	17.02	19.23	18.10
Transport	11.27	10.16	14.24	15.53
Travel	10.93	10.39	11.21	16.18
Investment income	36.53	25.76	25.73	20.47
Other	16.36	12.22	13.64	16.50
Private	12.64	7.67	9.70	13.67
Official	31.18	32.29	29.79	30.52
		Debit		
Merchandise trade	13.70	13.83	17.87	16.14
Services trade	13.48	16.69	14.83	15.64
Transport	10.57	8.90	15.10	13.23
Travel	15.08	10.04	16.87	17.48
Investment income	17.96	14.39	16.56	18.21
Other	11.08	0.85	10.26	10.86
Private	3.84	2.79	4.18	6.06
Official	34.66	23.79	29.43	30.18

Sources: Same as Table 3.7.

tions, due to changes in a broad range of conditions, such as interest rates and the value of the dollar. Another surplus item was royalties and license fees, U.S. $6.9 billion, probably a function of technology transfers.

In contrast to surpluses in merchandise trade, Japan's imports of services exceeded its exports, showing annual deficits of between 5 billion and 8 billion SDRs from 1980 to 1988 (see Table 3.9). Thus, in 1988, Japan had a deficit of 8.4 billion SDRs in its international service trade and a surplus of 71 billion SDRs in its merchandise trade. Among the largest items in its services trade deficit was the category "other private services." In 1988 Japan's exports of services totaled 83.3 billion SDRs, including investment income, and its service imports totaled 91.7 billion SDRs. These figures are significantly smaller than those for the United States. The most rapidly growing item was receipt of investment income, which rose from 8.5 billion SDRs in 1980 to 55.7 billion SDRs in 1988. The most significant changes in the composition of Japan's international trade in services were a decline in both exports and imports of transportation, mostly due to the decline in the demand for ocean shipping, and a substantial increase in other private services, including management

TABLE 3.9

Japan: Exports and Imports of Services, Investment Income, and Merchandise, 1975, 1980, 1985, and 1988 (billions of SDRs)

	1975			1980			1985			1988		
	Credit	Debit	Balance	Credit	Debit	Balance	Credit	Debit	Balance	Credit	Debit	Balance
Merchandise[a]	45.080	40.960	4.120	97.420	95.773	1.647	170.959	116.239	54.720	193.452	122.452	71.000
Total service	11.200	15.510	-4.310	24.202	32.921	-8.719	44.830	49.921	-5.091	83.349	91.787	-8.438
Transport[b]	5.300	7.020	-1.720	9.984	13.327	-3.343	12.264	14.883	-2.619	11.604	17.137	-5.533
Travel	0.210	1.130	-0.920	0.492	3.525	-3.033	1.120	4.729	-3.609	2.154	13.942	-11.788
Investment[c]	2.980	3.200	-0.220	8.539	7.884	0.655	21.777	15.046	6.731	55.775	40.106	15.669
Other[d]	2.710	4.160	-1.450	5.186	8.186	-3.000	9.670	15.262	-5.565	13.817	20.002	-6.785

Sources: IMF, *Yearbook*, 33, pts. 1 and 2 (1982); *ibid*. 38, pts. 1 and 2 (1987); *ibid*. 40, pts. 1 and 2 (1989).
a Includes international transactions in nonmonetary gold.
b Includes shipment and other transportation.
c Includes reinvested earnings on direct investment, other direct investment income, and other investment income.
d Includes other official goods, services, and income and other private goods, services, and income.

fees, advertising, licenses and royalties, and other such producer services.

Among the factors contributing to this change in composition were the internationalization of Japanese business and the rise in investment income. A comparison of trade and investment figures shows that major trends in this period were increased investments in finance and insurance, from U.S. $533 million in 1982 to U.S. $2.08 billion in 1984; in construction and real estate, from U.S. $619 million in 1981 to U.S. $1.21 billion in 1985; and in technology exports, from U.S. $578 million in 1978 to U. S. $1.02 billion in 1981. Another major trend was a decline in investments in primary industries, from U.S. $2.64 billion in 1981 to U.S. $747 million in 1983. The major partners are the United States and Japan. The most pronounced increase in Japanese direct investment in services in the United States was in real estate, which went from U.S. $396 million in 1982 to U.S. $10 billion in 1988, followed by that in finance, which rose from U.S. $570 million in 1982 to U.S. $2.8 billion in 1988. Investment in all services went from U.S. $9.6 billion in 1982 to U.S. $53.3 billion in 1988. (See Table 3.10.)

A comparison of the United States and Japan trade using SDRs to control for foreign exchange values shows considerable disparity in the absolute level of exports and similarity in the levels of imports. Service credits went from 19.2 billion SDRs in 1975 to 76.5 billion SDRs in 1988 for the United States and from 8.2 billion SDRs to 27.5 billion SDRs for Japan. The compound annual growth rate was 10% for the United States and 10.8% for Japan. Service debits from 1975 through 1988 increased from 18.1 billion SDRs to 66.8 billion SDRs for the United States and from 12.3 billion SDRs to 51.6 billion SDRs for Japan. This left an immense disparity in the net balance at +9.7 billion for the United States and −24.1 billion for Japan. The figures for the ratio of the services trade to the merchandise trade show growing dissimilarity—in the United States, from 0.22 in 1975 to 0.32 in 1988 on the credit side and stability on the debit side, at about 0.20; Japan's 1988 ratios were 0.14 on the credit side and 0.42 on the debit side. (See Table 3.11 for data for 1975–1988.)

Direct Foreign Investment in Services

The rapid increase of direct foreign investment in services is part of the more general internationalization of economic activity. The internationalization of industrial production through trade and direct foreign investment engendered a demand for support activities in trade, finance, ac-

TABLE 3.10A

U.S. Direct Investment in Japan: Selected Service Industries, 1982-1988 (millions of U.S. dollars and percent)

	Wholesale		Banking		Finance[a]		Services		Other		All Industries in Japan ($)
	$	% of Total FDI in Japan	$	% of Total FDI in Japan	$	% of Total FDI in Japan	$	% of Total FDI in Japan	$	% of Total FDI in Japan	
1982	1,093	17.18	166	2.56	312	4.80	42	0.65	85	1.30	6,407
1985	1,581	17.10	178	1.90	520	5.60	83	0.89	104	1.10	9,235
1988	3,473	20.60	262	1.60	1,258	7.50	206	1.20	325	1.90	16,868

Sources: Current Business 66, no. 8 (1986): tab. 12; *ibid.* 68, no. 8 (1988): tab. 11; *ibid.* 69, no.8 (1989): tab. 13.
[a] Excludes banking.

TABLE 3.10B

Japanese Direct Investment in the United States: Selected Service Industries, 1982-1988 (millions of U.S. dollars)

	Wholesale	Retail	Banking	Finance[a]	Insurance	Real Estate	Other	All Industries in the U.S.
1982	6,126	151	1,325	-570	169	396	339	9,677
1985	11,572	250	2,176	710	122	1,059	575	19,116
1988	18,390	346	3,895	2,863	-b	10,017	5,379	53,354

Sources: Current Business 65, no. 8 (1985): tab. 10; *ibid.* 66, no. 8 (1986): tab. 11; *ibid.* 69, no. 8 (1989): tab. 11.
[a] Excludes banking.
[b] Suppressed to avoid disclosure of individual companies.

TABLE 3.11

United States and Japan: International Service Credits and Debits and Service-Merchandise Ratio, 1975-1988

	Credits (millions of SDRs)		Debits (millions of SDRs)		Balance of Accounts (millions of SDRs)	
	U.S.	Japan	U.S.	Japan	U.S.	Japan
1975	19,236	8,220	18,111	12,310	1,125	-4,090
1980	35,119	15,663	31,621	25,037	3,498	-9,374
1985	55,056	23,053	58,792	34,875	-3,736	-11,822
1988	76,577	27,574	66,837	51,681	9,740	-24,107
	Ratio of Service Trade to Merchandise					
1975	0.22	0.18	0.22	0.30		
1980	0.20	0.16	0.16	0.26		
1985	0.26	0.13	0.18	0.30		
1988	0.32	0.14	0.20	0.42		

Sources: Same as Table 3.7.

Note: International service includes shipment; other transportation; travel; other official goods, services, and income; and other public goods, services, and income.

counting, law, etc. Thus, many service affiliates were, especially initially, established by industrial transnational corporations. The early 1970s saw the growth of the internationalization of service production by transnational corporations. And since then, the internationalization of service production has grown more rapidly than that of goods. Most of the services produced by transnationals are intermediate services, yet another indication that the internationalization of service production has followed industrial transnationalization. The growth of service transnationalization should not be seen as being at the cost of industrial transnationalization; they are deeply connected. We have a global economy in which a growing share of goods and services is being produced by transnationals.

The growing weight of services in the stock and flow of direct foreign investment has largely involved developed countries, where services account overall for about 40% of the stock in outward direct foreign investments, a share that is rising. Five countries, the United States, Japan, the United Kingdom, West Germany, and France account for a total of 70% of the world's total direct foreign investment stock, and the share of this stock accounted for by services ranges from 40% to 50% for each of these countries.

Flows have, clearly, increased even faster. During the first half of the 1980s, services accounted for over 60% of Japan's total investment outflows and for about 50% in the United States and the United Kingdom.

During the first half of the 1980s, the share of services in direct foreign investment inflows in other highly developed countries were 70% each for West Germany, Canada, and Australia, and 60% for France. In all of these and other highly developed countries, services attracted more direct foreign investment than did primary or manufacturing industries. The one important exception is Japan, where inward flows of direct foreign investment in services accounted for less than one-third.

In the United States, which has vast flows of direct foreign investment, services already accounted for a third of all stock abroad in the early 1950s. During the 1970s, a major new development was the strong shift toward the growth of the service share and a change in the composition of services. U.S. direct foreign investment in transportation, communications, and public utilities declined, and finance-related and trade-related services increased (Whichard 1981: 39–56). Between 1977 and 1986, the stock of direct foreign investment in services almost doubled, climbing from $60 billion to $119 billion, with the share rising to 43%; half of the increase in U.S. direct foreign investment abroad was accounted for by services (UN Centre on Transnational Corporations 1989d: 8–21). The United States is the largest recipient of direct foreign investment in services, with $110 billion of inward stock in services in 1986. Between 1980 and 1985, the stock of direct foreign investment in services increased more than in any other sector, by $55 billion compared with $45 billion for all other sectors combined. Six countries accounted for over 80% of this increase in the United States, with Japan and the United Kingdom each accounting for a quarter of that 80%-plus and Canada, West Germany, the Netherlands, and Switzerland accounting for the other half. Thus in both inward and outward direct foreign investment, services have increasingly gained share and now account for over half of global flows.

It is in Japan that services accounted for most of the rapid growth in outward stock of direct foreign investment over this period (UN Centre on Transnational Corporations 1989d: 11–14). Japan's direct foreign investment abroad increased by $61 billion from 1977 to 1985, of which 57% was in services; in the case of developed market economies, this increase was 63%. By the mid-1980s, the share of services in Japan's total stock of direct foreign investment had reached 50%. Of the total outflow of $22.3 billion in outward direct foreign investments from Japan in 1986, 77% was in services.

Flow data for the 1975–1980 and 1981–1985 periods show an increase in the share of services for most of the developed countries. In Japan the share of services was 41.8% in 1975–1980 and 62.2% in 1981–1985—an increase of 20% from one period to the other. In actual numbers, services were $4 billion and $9.4 billion, respectively. In the United States, the share of services was 34.3% in the first period and 53.2% in the second period—an increase of 19% from one period to the other. However, it should be noted that the overall decline in outward direct foreign investment in the United States did also affect the absolute volume of services, which actually declined from $15.6 billion to $9.1 billion, indicating that the decline in nonservice direct foreign investment was more severe. The share of producer services in the overall service sector in all the developed countries has also grown, going from 5% in 1970 to 7% in 1980 and 9% in 1985 of the share of services traded internationally. There is an uneven distribution of such exports among the developed countries and there are different service sector growth rates. The global share of services traded internationally rose from 7% in 1970 to 11% in 1980. This is low compared with the corresponding increases in agriculture, from 32% to 45%, and in manufacturing, from 30% to 55% (Clairmonte and Cavanagh 1984).

International Transactions in Producer Services

A particular concern here is international trade and investment in services for firms. To provide a general context for an examination of this trade, I used U.S. data and disaggregated the figures for service receipts in terms of a wide range of services (see Tables 3.12 and 3.13). The demand for business services has grown rapidly over the last decade. Initially the demand came from large corporations, which also explained the heavy incidence of international trade among service firms. Now there is an established world market for these services. The United States National Study on Trade in Services (U.S. Department of Commerce, Office of U.S. Trade Representative 1983) has estimated that 1980 worldwide service exports (excluding income on direct foreign investment, typically included in the service account) reached $370 billion, or 20% of world trade. This is a small figure compared with the $1,650 billion in global exports of goods and $600 billion in global direct foreign investment stock (UN Centre on Transnational Corporations 1985). But the trade in services is in part a function of these two other processes and should not be viewed as simply a numerically inferior quantity. The leading exporters of these services are all highly developed countries with high levels of internationalization in their economies (Table 3.14, while outdated, is one of the best estimates of this trade). Together, they accounted for 60% of the world's trade in services in 1980. These figures are, however, severe underestimates because they leave out sales by branches and affiliates in foreign countries. An examination of individual service industries (see Chapter Seven) makes it evident that these are also the foreign coun-

TABLE 3.12

United States: Direct Foreign Investment Abroad: Industry Detail for Selected Items (millions of U.S. dollars)

	1982	1985	1988
All industries	207,752	230,250	326,900
All services	66,483	77,856	133,423
Wholesale	20,317	22,790	34,401
Banking	10,317	14,461	16,120
Finance[a]	18,018	22,501	60,604
Finance	-9,397	-8,980	10,372
Insurance	7,268	8,322	12,677
Real estate	5,646	384	2,148
Holding company	19,597	22,775	35,407
Services	4,615	4,683	7,130
Hotels	493	548	799
Business services	2,191	1,882	3,069
Advertising	322	361	482
Management	593	683	686
Equipment rental	499	152	714
Computer and data	243	138	122
Other business services[b]	533	548	1,064
Motion pictures	685	664	971
Engineering	413	587	789
Health	58	398	647
Other services[c]	775	603	855
Transport	1,681	1,679	2,079
Communications	116	618	72
Retail	3,697	3,997	5,640
Other[d]	7,251	7,127	7,377

Sources: Current Business, 66 (Aug. 1986): tab. 37; *ibid.* 69 (Aug. 1989), tab. 30.

[a] Does not include banking.

[b] Includes research and development and testing labs, employment agencies, temporary help supply, and other business services.

[c] Includes automotive rental and leasing, accounting, auditing, and bookkeeping services, legal services, educational services, and other services provided on a commercial basis.

[d] Includes agriculture, forestry and fishing, mining, construction, and public utilities.

tries where leading firms with large numbers of foreign affiliates and branches are headquartered.

This points to an important distinction in a discussion about the international trade patterns of producer services, that between "transborder trade" and "investment trade" (U.S. Department of Commerce, Office of the U.S. Trade Representative 1983). Some producer service industries are more likely to centralize production in key locations and export their

TABLE 3.13

U.S. Sales to and Purchases from Unaffiliated Foreigners of Selected Services, 1986 (millions of U.S. dollars)

	U.S. Sales	U.S. Purchases	Balance
Advertising	94	77	17
Computer and data processing services	985	32	953
Database and other information services	102	15	87
Telecommunications	1,890	3,069	-1,179
Research, development, and testing services	305	76	229
Management, consulting, and public relations services	272	64	208
Legal services	93	41	52
Industrial engineering	95	75	20
Industrial maintenance, repair, installation, and training	448	143	305
Other[a]	135	99	36
Educational and training services	62	7	55
Sports and performing arts	32	21	11
Accounting, auditing, and bookkeeping services	21	29	-8
Total	4,419	3,691	728

Source: Current Business, 68, no. 10 (1988).

[a] The items listed for this heading do not sum to the total in the original source.

products. Management consulting, engineering services, and international legal services are examples. Other industries are more likely to export their services through direct foreign investment, that is, by setting up branches and affiliates abroad. Both forms of export have increased significantly over the last decade, and both are indications of the increased globalization in the economic activity of firms. Finally, and of equal importance to this analysis, there has been an increase in the incidence of foreign firms' exports in the overall service exports of the leading countries.

The most detailed data come from the United States, also the home of a very large number of transnational service corporations. Sales through affiliates of U.S. transnational corporations generally have exceeded direct exports and imports of private business services. Sales by majority-owned foreign affiliates (MOFAs) of U.S. corporations exceeded direct exports of private business services, which are recorded in the balance of payments. In 1984, sales by MOFAs totaled U.S. $67 billion, while exports by private businesses totaled U.S. $43 billion. Before 1980, sales by affiliates of foreign corporations were relatively small compared with direct imports in the first half of the 1980s.

TABLE 3.14

Top Eight Exporters of Services, 1980 (billions of U.S. dollars)

	Service Exports
United States	37.5
United Kingdom	37.1
West Germany	33.8
France	33.0
Italy	23.5
Japan	19.4
Netherlands	18.6
Belgium	14.9
Subtotal	217.8
World exports	370.0

Source: U.S. Office of Trade Representative 1983.

In 1986, the latest year for which data are available, the United States sold more services to unaffiliated foreigners (U.S. $4.4 billion) than it bought (U.S. $3.7 billion), producing an overall surplus (*Survey of Current Business* 1988b). Telecommunications services were the largest share of both sales and purchases and overall produced a deficit of over $1 billion. The other fifteen services considered registered a large surplus. Major surplus items were in sales of research and development, mostly to developing countries, followed closely by sales to developed countries. These are mostly government-sponsored research and consumer product testing, industrial maintenance, and repair services, which are mostly sales by U.S. aircraft manufacturers and hence tied to sales of military items, and rapidly growing exports such as management and consulting services and computer and data processing services.[7] The overall pattern in both sales and purchases is for service companies to buy services of their own industry. Thus, purchases by manufacturers are largest in industrial engineering, research and development, and management and consulting.

The Office of Technology Assessment (OTA) of the U.S. Congress has developed new measures in order to account for these variables. Under the concept of U.S. exports, OTA included not only direct exports by U.S. firms, but also direct exports by foreign firms located in the United States. Furthermore, OTA also considered the foreign revenues of U.S.

[7] Software services were two-thirds of the total; they consisted mostly of software and software rights, mostly for mainframes.

firms regardless of location. The first is a balance of payments criterion; the second, an ownership criterion (U.S. Congress, Office of Technology Assessment 1986: 38). Mid-range estimates of exports and imports are presented in Table 3.15. Exports amounted to $76 billion and imports to $59 billion. If we add to these figures those for U.S. revenues of foreign firms and foreign revenues of U.S. firms, we obtain a rather different level of activity. For example, in 1983 accounting had $350 million in direct exports; but if we include the sales of affiliates abroad, the total of U.S. services sold by U.S. firms in accounting reaches $4.2 billion. Advertising had $300 million in direct exports and $1.7 billion in affiliate sales. Construction and legal services, on the other hand, were among the few that registered much higher levels in direct exports than in affil-

TABLE 3.15
U.S. Service Balance of Payments, 1983 (OTA mid-range estimates, in billions of U.S. dollars)

	Exports (Receipts)	Imports (Payments)
Accounting	0.35	--a
Advertising	0.30	--a
Construction	4.80	0.85
Data processing	0.65	1.00
Education	1.95	0.20
Engineering	1.35	0.20
Franchising	0.65	--a
Health	1.75	--a
Information	1.45	0.50
Insurance	7.15	7.90
Investment banking/brokerage	4.80	4.55
Leasing	0.70	0.50
Legal	1.00	0.50
Licensing	5.20	0.80
Management/consulting	1.00	0.85
Motion pictures	1.90	0.90
Retailing	--a	--a
Software	2.55	1.10
Telecommunications	1.30	2.20
Transportation	17.10	19.10
Travel	14.10	15.80
Miscellaneous	5.30	1.90
OTA mid-range estimate	76.00	59.00

Source: U.S. Congress 1986: 38.
a Negligible.

iate sales. The combined figures for direct exports and affiliate sales range from $4.2 billion for accounting to almost $8 billion for construction, $3.75 billion for data processing, $16.75 billion for investment banking/brokerage, and $25 billion for retailing. Foreign revenues of U.S. service firms were estimated at $160.5 billion, with $92.4 billion in affiliate sales and $68.1 billion in direct exports. The comparative figures for U.S. revenues of foreign service firms total $122 billion, with $71.6 billion in affiliate sales and $50.3 billion in direct imports.[8]

The major trading partners of the United States are Canada, the United Kingdom, and Japan. Of the total sale of services, 55% were to developed countries, and 33% were to developing countries, with the remaining 12% sold to socialist economies. In both, telecommunications was the biggest item, with most sales to Canada, the United Kingdom, and Japan. In services other than telecommunications, most sales were to Japan, the United Kingdom, and Canada. A large share of sales to Japan was computer and data processing services (mostly mainframe software). The biggest developing country customer was Saudi Arabia, mostly for sales in research and development, testing, and industrial maintenance.

Regarding purchases, 50% were from developed countries, and 45% were from developing countries, with the remaining 5% from socialist economies. The trade was dominated by purchases of telecommunication services, with Canada, Germany, Japan, and the United Kingdom as major sellers. In nontelecommunications services, 75% were from developed countries, mostly from the United Kingdom, Canada, and Japan. Purchases from the United Kingdom were largest in management, consulting and public relations services, industrial maintenance, and industrial engineering. Purchases from both Canada and Japan were largest in industrial maintenance. It is worth noting that the United Kingdom and Bermuda account for over 80% of total insurance purchases; the latter is clearly a major offshore center of the global insurance industry. The Netherlands and Japan were the largest purchasers of construction, engineering and architecture services.

Information on firms in particular industries is useful here in order to establish whether these figures represent a very large number of affiliates. In accounting, for example, most of the ten largest firms in the world each had over 300 affiliates outside their home countries in 1982.

---

[8] This should also include *purchases* of services *in* the United States by foreign-owned firms located in the United States as well as local purchases by U.S. firms abroad. The data available do not allow a count of these transactions; they show purchases in the United States by nonbank U.S. affiliates of nonbank foreign firms. In 1982, these amounted to $440 billion, excluding other obligations and nonoperating expenses. A portion of this figure represents purchases of services.

The top eight accounting firms in the United States made over 40% of their income in 1978 from sales abroad, a figure that rises to over half of their income for the two largest (U.S. Department of Commerce International Trade Administration 1980a: 13–15). Accounting is probably the extreme case in terms of using affiliates to export services abroad. The top eighty-three advertising firms in the United States made 37% of their revenues abroad in 1980; for the top ten this share was 51.7% (Economic Consulting Services 1981: 85). While the incidence of foreign revenues is similar to that of accounting, the number of affiliates involved is smaller, and so is the share of exports accounted for by these. Legal services firms, on the other hand, do most of their business abroad through direct exports. Of the ten largest U.S. law firms in 1984, six had no foreign branch offices, three had fewer than six, and one had twenty-five such branch offices; however, among the one hundred largest firms, forty-six had foreign offices, mostly located in the major banking centers of the world. Examination of the available evidence on numbers of affiliates or branch offices abroad for major business service industries shows mostly sharp increases (For detailed industry studies see UN Centre on Transnational Corporations 1989b; Noyelle and Dutka 1988; Clairmonte and Cavanagh 1984). This is reflected in the fact that direct foreign investment in services has increased significantly, reaching 28.4% of all such investment in 1981 and over 50% by 1988.

Conclusion

There has been a fundamental transformation in the geography and composition of international economic transactions. Most remarkable is the emergence of the United States as the leading recipient of direct foreign investment and of Japan as the leading net exporter of such investment. Latin America is no longer the major recipient of direct foreign investment it once was, except perhaps for Brazil, and then largely São Paulo. Southeast Asia has replaced Latin America as the main location for direct foreign investment in manufacturing by highly developed countries. In terms of composition, the main developments were the rapidly growing weight of services in direct foreign investment and the immense volume reached by international financial transactions, discussed in the next chapter. Services now account for over half the global stock of direct foreign investment, a development of the 1980s that required even higher rates of increase in the flow of such investment during this period. Again, a handful of countries account for 70% of global activity in services. There is, then, a reconcentration of international transactions in the highly developed countries and a particularly high concentration of all activity accounted for by the United States, the United Kingdom, and Japan.

In terms of some of the questions organizing the inquiry in this book, several trends are of interest. First, transnational firms are central to the internationalization of services, with direct foreign investment one of the leading forms assumed by this activity. Telecommunications advances may increase the weight of transborder trade in services, but the properties of many services set limits to this mode of delivery. Second, in the case of professional services, foreign sales account for a very large share of all revenues among leading firms, reaching well over half in the case of accounting and advertising. This has reinforced the global market orientation in large cities that are key locations for such firms.

The 1980s were clearly a decade when the importance of services and finance rose sharply. The structures for international production and distribution of services and finance are in many ways quite different from those in extractive or manufacturing activities. The key production sites for the latter have often been in less developed countries; such countries are far less likely to play an important role in international transactions of professional services and finance, while such major cities as New York, London, and Tokyo are clearly central locations for these transactions.

These patterns point to a realignment in international investment. The large-scale increases in direct foreign investment in a multiplicity of locations during the 1970s, central to the internationalization of production, were followed by a subsequent phase of large increases in financial flows in the 1980s, on a scale that dwarfed the magnitudes of the earlier phase. The levels of concentration by country associated with this second finance-dominated phase would seem to be higher than those of the 1970s. But we also see here a realignment in the structure of concentration, a subject taken up in the next chapter.

Four

Internationalization and Expansion
of the Financial Industry

SINCE THE EARLY 1980s there has been a pronounced and rapid transformation in the volume of the financial industry, in its organization, and in the supply of and demand for financial products and services. Fundamental conditions for this transformation were the opening up of national markets through deregulation; a massive influx of funds into the markets through the growing participation of major financial institutions, notably insurance companies, pension funds, and trust banks; and the rapid production of innovations that transformed a large amount of financial assets into marketable instruments. Together, these developments had the effect in the early 1980s of raising the volume of the industry, accelerating the pace of transactions, and dramatically reducing the share of bank loans in industry volume. Bonds and equities as well as the marketing of hitherto illiquid instruments became the central components of the industry.

This transformation was both facilitated and partly induced by constraints on the earnings capacity of the large commercial banks that had dominated the industry since World War II. Regulations prohibiting banks from entering the securities market, massive Third World loan losses, and the more traditional type of business activity characterizing commercial banking reduced the participation of these banks in the highly innovative and speculative phase the financial markets entered in the 1980s. There was a rapid proliferation of smaller investment banks capable of seizing the opportunities of deregulation and internationalization of the financial industry through the development of new products and new markets.

Central concerns underlying the following examination of changes in the volume and composition of the industry are the durability of this phase of growth and the space economy it engenders. This chapter examines the empirical referents of the transformation in the industry, particularly the growing importance of securities and institutional investors, the formation of an international equities market, and the new role of Japanese investors. Deregulation and the production of innovations, two key aspects in the growth and internationalization of the industry, will be discussed in Chapter Five, as part of a broader examination of the producer services.

Conditions and Components of Growth

While aggregate measures of international financial activity show high growth rates from 1972 onward, there were radically different factors creating this growth in the 1970s compared with the 1980s. From 1972 to 1985, funds raised in the international financial markets grew by 23% per year on the average, compared with an average annual growth of 13% in world trade.[1] In the 1970s the major source of capital funds was massive oil revenues generated through the increase in the price of oil, and the key financial institutions were the large U.S. transnational banks in charge of selling much of this money. Thus, developing countries were a key element in the geography of financial activity, as both producers and consumers in international finance. In the 1980s, growth was linked to massive increases in international securities transactions, which became the main mode of cross-border borrowing and lending; the key institutions were securities firms and investment banks; and almost all these funds came from and went to developed countries.

In the immediate postwar period, there was no international financial market, and governments had close regulatory control over domestic financial activity and whatever foreign operations national firms engaged in. The first instance of a significant international financial market was the Eurocurrency market that developed in the 1960s. It came about and it grew in good part as a function of the effort by transnational corporations to avoid the regulations in their domestic markets and taxes on repatriated earnings. Up to the early 1970s, the international activity of banks mostly consisted of establishing foreign branches, subsidiaries and offices to service needs of nonbank corporations operating abroad: the financing of foreign trade, provision of credit in local currency to affiliates, and, at times, direct intermediation in local financial markets. This form of participation in international activity was linked to a direct presence abroad. The sharp increase in international banking activity in the

[1] An examination of overall capital inflows and outflows in the United States, the United Kingdom, and Japan can serve to illustrate the different magnitudes involved by comparing them with those of direct foreign investment. The global flow of direct foreign investment went from 42,254 million SDRs in 1980 to 79,205 million SDRs in 1986 (IMF 1987b: tab. C14). In contrast, the global flow of international portfolio investments reached 42,697 SDRs in assets in 1980 and increased to 153,982 SDRs in 1986 (IMF 1987b: tab. C15). Liabilities went from 2 trillion SDRs in 1980 to 2.6 trillion SDRs in 1986 (IMF 1987b: tab. B1).

1970s was largely organized by the large transnational banks located in the leading financial centers. This development, along with advances in telecommunications and information technology, made the use of local branches quite unnecessary. The decision by OPEC members to channel a major share of their earnings through the transnational banks produced an immense increase in these flows compared with the preceding decade. And OPEC price increases, along with other developments, made nations more dependent on banking funds. The assets of the major international banks grew by 95% from 1976 to 1980, with the U.S. banks by far the leading ones (Daly 1987). It was in this period that offshore banking centers and the Eurodollar market became important factors in international finance. These institutional arrangements sharply increased the mobility of banking capital through the avoidance of regulations and constraints typical of domestic markets. This development points to the growing power of the major transnational banks and the disintegration of the system for global trade contained in the Bretton Woods agreement.

The Third World debt crisis of 1982 undermined the leading position of U.S. transnational banks, and deregulation of domestic markets undermined offshore banking centers. What had once been essential elements of international financial activity—foreign banking branches in the 1950s and 1960s and offshore banking centers and transnational banks in the 1970s—had by the early 1980s become far less important. The leading financial centers in the world emerged as the key component in international finance. Banks' share of international financial activity fell sharply for much of the 1980s, and credit passed largely through securities markets and among developed countries.

Nonbank financial firms dominated the international financial markets in the 1980s. Among these, the most important ones were securities firms and financial services firms that covered a wide range of activities: stockbroking (investment portfolio management) and investment banking (underwriting, structuring of mergers and acquisitions). These institutions engaged both in traditional activity (in that interest spread is a source of earnings) and in risktaking (trading positions, underwriting new issues). There has been a sharp increase in cross-border acquisitions of financial firms and a sharp increase in the internationalization of mergers, acquisitions, and joint ventures among financial institutions.

This profound transformation could not escape its own consequences. The level of risk had grown to historic highs and had already begun to create concern among analysts before the October 1987 crash. The level of speculation built into this growth was extremely high; perhaps the only way this massive increase could have occurred was through speculation, epitomized by the futures market and corporate takeovers at exorbitant prices. This is a subject I return to in Chapter Five. The emergence of international markets and growing integration at the global scale meant that the October 1987 collapse in prices in New York became a world-wide collapse instantaneously. There follows a more detailed examination of some of these issues.

Formation of International Equity Markets

The current internationalization of the equity markets is quite different from the type of international transactions in equities before 1980. In the earlier period, Swiss banks, long the recipients of much foreign capital, acquired foreign equities to complement the limited investment opportunities within Switzerland. They were the leading investors in U.S. stocks during the 1960s and 1970s. Banks and investment companies in such countries as the Netherlands, Belgium, and Luxembourg, which have long functioned as recipients of foreign deposits, also engaged in this type of transaction, and Britain has had extensive overseas portfolio investments for a long time.

But there was no international market for equity transactions, and international capital investments were relatively small and limited to a few stock markets. Most of the financial markets were oriented to domestic investors and subject to foreign exchange controls. Access to equities listed in foreign stock markets was restricted, and there was no general, globalized distribution mechanism. Competitive pressures and the growing internationalization of other financial markets contributed to the rapid growth in international equity acquisitions. In Britain there was a strong increase in investments overseas, especially in the United States and Japan after foreign exchange controls were lifted. It was not until 1986 that the Japanese began to invest on a large scale in foreign equities. After the lifting of foreign exchange controls in Japan, most investment into overseas securities had gone into bonds, especially U.S. Treasury bonds.

Since the early 1980s, there has been an extremely pronounced growth in international transactions in equities and bonds. Deregulation and the vast amount of funds introduced by large institutional investors contributed to the rapid growth in cross-border investments in equities and the formation of an international market for equities. There is now an international equity market that is highly liquid and accessible, even though the integration of the various domestic markets involved is still quite limited. The production of innovations has also been of central importance in the expansion and operation of this market across national boundaries and in making more of these markets electronically integrated, as are those of New York, London, and Tokyo.

International transactions in equities may be of several types. Their purpose can be to use the equity opportunities present in stock markets in other countries considered to have better price/earnings ratios or, in the case of issuers, to gain access to abundant funds and new investment opportunities. The Japanese market had both of these conditions until recently; but a large number of smaller markets around the world also do. Alternatively, use of the international market for equities may be a response to limitations in the availability of funds in an issuer's domestic market.[2] For example, if an Italian corporation wants to raise a very large amount of capital by issuing stock, the use of foreign stock markets may be the only way of reaching that level. Finally, use of the international market may be a way of avoiding the limitations, restrictions, and costs of a domestic market.

The expansion of the market and the recency of this growth can be seen in various kinds of figures. Most stock markets around the world have experienced rapid increases in volumes and values, making them attractive to foreigners. Higher net returns than in the United States have occurred in many markets including those of Japan, the United Kingdom, West Germany, and France. Thus, from 1982 to 1987, capital returns in dollars were about 75 in the United States, compared with almost 500 in Japan, 150 in the United Kingdom, and 250 in France. Japanese acquisitions of U.S. equities went from $1 billion in 1980 to $22 billion by 1988. The holdings of foreign equities by U.S. pension funds had reached $22.5 billion in 1985 and almost doubled in 1987, rising to $42 billion. The participation of corporations in the equity markets has also increased strongly over the last few years.[3] In the United States, there has been an increase in the number of mergers and acquisitions and in large corporate repurchases of shares. This has meant raising vast amounts of funds to finance such acquisitions, and in the 1980s corporations chose to do much of this directly in the equity market rather than through banks.

Capitalization in stock markets grew rapidly in the 1980s. In December 1985, the United States accounted for 48.6% of global capital investment; Japan, 21.8%, a very large increase over earlier levels; the United Kingdom, 8.4%; West Germany, 4.9%; Canada, 3.3%; Switzerland, 2.3%; France, 1.9%; the Netherlands, 1.7%; and all other countries, 7.1%. The absolute levels were $1,178 billion in the United States, $528 billion in Japan, $204 billion in the United Kingdom, $118 billion in West

[2] In order to avoid the cumbersome procedure of becoming a reporting company in the United States, which is a requirement if a firm is to offer shares for sale, many foreign firms prefer to merely trade their shares here without the company's registering.

[3] In Japan the increased involvement of corporations has been through intercorporate investment in shares of customers and suppliers and by special investment trusts.

Germany, $81 billion in Canada, $56 billion in Switzerland, $45 billion in France, $40 billion in the Netherlands, and $173 billion in all other countries (Whittemore 1987: 142–43). The deregulation in the United Kingdom and the further deregulation in Japan since 1986 have raised the figures of overall international investment for these countries. By December 1989, capitalization had grown to $4 trillion in Japan, $3 trillion in the United States, and $823 billion in the United Kingdom (see Chapter Seven). These figures clearly show the strong growth of Japan.[4] The internationalization of investment can be seen in the increasing volume of purchases of foreign equity by individual and institutional investors. From very minimal amounts, they have increased steadily over the last decade, with the most pronounced increases beginning in the 1980s and growing rather rapidly.[5]

International equity issues reached $32 billion in 1986, a fivefold increase over 1983. Of these issues, a fifth of their value was represented by Euro-equity issues of European firms and almost half, or U.S. $15 billion worth, by issues of Japanese firms—a new development at that point.[6] It should be noted that many of the investors in new Japanese issues tend to be Japanese. They prefer doing this abroad in the Euromarket to avoid the regulations and the restrictions in their home markets. To put this in perspective, it is worth noting that the U.S. domestic market, long the world's largest market for new equity issues, offered U.S. $60 billion worth of new issues in 1986 and about U.S. $54 billion

[4] Another type of indication of the rapid and recent expansion of the international acquisition of equities is information on foreign stock purchases in individual countries. Foreign investment in Japanese stocks went from 1.1 billion yen in 1979 to 9.3 billion yen in 1985, 17 billion yen in 1986 (after the lifting of foreign exchange controls), and 23.3 billion yen in 1987 (Tokyo Stock Exchange 1988: 56). Foreign sales of Japanese equities went from 1.2 billion yen in 1979 to 10.1 billion yen in 1985, and then jumped to 20.6 billion yen in 1986 and 30.8 billion yen in 1987. On the other hand, Japanese investments in foreign equities in the Tokyo Stock Exchange in Japan went from 36 billion yen in 1979 to 1.3 trillion yen in 1985, 4.2 trillion yen in 1986, and 10.9 trillion yen in 1987. Japanese sales of foreign equities followed a parallel path, going from 44 billion yen in 1979 to 8.3 trillion yen in 1987 (Tokyo Stock Exchange 1988: 58).

[5] The international issues offered in the United States tend to be either issues sold by foreign companies or issues that are part of a larger offering in Europe, where the United States part is marketed as part of a global offering. Most of the foreign sales in the United States over the last few years have been the result of large corporations and shareholders wanting a larger market for their shares. This is the case with large companies, such as British Telecom and British Gas, when they became privatized and came out with huge new issues of stock.

[6] In the last few years the fastest growth has been by Japanese Trust Banks through special accounts called "Tokkin" in which corporate funds are managed for investment on a favorable tax basis. Given the recency of Japanese participation, the share of foreign equities in all holdings among Japanese investors is very small, though growing rapidly.

worth in 1987.[7] A recent development is the organization of simultaneous coordinated distributions of shares in several national markets when dealing with a very large issue. This was originally developed for the issue of 1 billion Texaco International shares. When the large public utilities in Britain were privatized, they also used this method. British Telecom used the United States, Canada, Europe, and Japan. U.S. corporations have also begun using this practice.[8]

The aggregate expansion of all equity markets points to a number of trends. First, a multiplicity of countries have had expansions in their equity markets. Second, the United States share of world capitalization, which stood at 57% in 1975, has declined to 34%, though increasing in absolute value.[9] Third, besides the expansion in total volume, there has been a continuation of high concentration in a few markets. Thus, the share represented by the United States, the United Kingdom, and Japan increased from slightly over 75% in 1975 to 85% in 1988 as a result of an immense rise in Japan's share of world capitalization, from 11.6% in 1975 to 41.1% in 1988.

Securitization of Finance

Direct raising of funds in the securities markets has affected the traditional role of banks as financial intermediaries. Securitization, the transformation of various types of financial assets and debts into marketable instruments, has been the vehicle for this disintermediation and for the massive expansion in the overall volume of the financial market. These

[7] Japanese investors showed a marked preference for high-yielding bonds, and purchased mostly dollar-denominated bonds. About three-quarters of all Japanese foreign bond purchases in the first nine months of 1985 are estimated to have been U.S. dollar-denominated bonds (bonds purchased in the United States and Eurodollar markets combined). Canadian dollars, Australian dollars, and British pounds accounted for most of the remainder. Early in 1986 there was uncertainty as to whether Japanese investors would continue to buy dollar-denominated instruments. This uncertainty was in good part due to the fact that the main buyers, such as life insurance companies, casualty companies, and trust banks, had begun to approach the limit of 10% of their assets that they are allowed to invest in foreign securities. A slowdown in acquisitions by these institutions was offset, however, by increased purchases by Japanese institutions not subject to this limit, such as commercial banks, Japanese corporations, and leasing companies.

[8] Japanese investors have more frequently hedged their purchases of foreign currencies by borrowing U.S. dollars short-term in the Euromarkets or by selling U.S. dollars forward as the dollar began to decline.

[9] In the United States the par value of outstanding publicly traded bonds and the market value of equity capital increased by five times from 1975 to 1986 (Salomon Brothers, Inc. various years). There has been a pronounced increase in the market value of securities relative to the value of gross domestic product.

are assets that were considered illiquid until recently. In the United States, where this process has been sharpest, the total value of securities increased from $22 billion in 1980 to $269 billion in 1986 (Salomon Brothers, Inc. various years). Securitization has required a vast production of financial innovations and raised the level of competition to new heights. It also required a vastly expanded market, achieved through deregulation of domestic financial markets and internationalization.

The total volume of financial assets and transactions in the international capital market in the 1980s increased significantly; yet the commercial banks experienced a considerable decline in their market shares, while other financial institutions, such as mutual funds, raised theirs. Central to the commercial banks' loss in market share in lending was the extensive issuing of commercial paper by the big corporations, a trend that is likely to continue and to spread to medium-sized corporations as well. Data on net borrowing by U.S. nonfinancial corporations show a doubling in securitized financing, from U.S. $45 billion in 1981 to U.S. $98.6 billion in 1986, almost all of it in the form of corporate bonds; in contrast, loans went from an almost similar level of U.S. $43.5 billion in 1981 to U.S. $27.1 billion in 1986 (Salomon Brothers, Inc. various years). Similarly, and especially in the United States, the banks' share of various kinds of consumer loans, such as auto loans, has shrunk as a result of a trend for manufacturers, notably in the auto industry, to acquire financial service firms.

Globally, as recently as 1982, international bank loans still accounted for a larger share of funds borrowed on international markets than did international bonds. By 1983 loans had fallen from U.S. $100 billion in 1982 to about U.S. $60 billion, a decline that continued down to U.S. $54 billion in 1985. Bonds grew from about U.S. $70 billion in 1982 to about U.S. $110 billion in 1984, U.S. $170 billion in 1985, and U.S. $229.8 billion in 1988. Thus loans suffered a decline in relative and absolute terms. In 1987 there was a resurgence in the use of loans, which grew to U.S. $80 billion in that year and to U.S. $116 billion in 1988. (See Table 4.1 for a breakdown of bonds and loans during 1985–1989. Inconsistencies among figures in Tables 4.1–4.4 are due to the use of different categories in original data.)

The recent resurgence of loans is in part attributable to the fact that during the last few years many large corporations have been undergoing financial restructuring and there has been a very large demand for funds in the capital markets and a need for immediate access when needed. Syndicated loans are a long-proven and reliable mechanism for raising money, and close working relations with a number of banks is an advantage in such a context.

TABLE 4.1

Funds Raised on International Markets by Type of Instrument, 1985-1989 (millions of U.S. dollars)

	1985	1986	1987	1988	1989ᵃ
International bonds	136,543.3	187,746.8	140,534.6	178,869.1	95,880.3
Foreign bonds	31,228.6	39,359.4	40,251.7	48,462.1	18,522.1
Special placements of bondsᵇ	1,300.0	1,000.0	—ᶜ	2,556.1	—ᶜ
Issues of bonds (total)	169,071.9	228,106.2	180,786.3	229,887.3	114,402.4
International bank loans	54,151.8	54,165.2	80,315.1	116,249.3	40,363.7
Loans by other international facilities	48,920.5	30,042.6	31,245.1	16,642.8	3,070.7
Foreign bank loans	6,988.8	9,061.1	11,342.8	9,357.7	1,854.4
Loans (total)	110,061.1	93,268.9	122,902.9	142,249.8	45,288.9
Total	279,133.0	321,375.1	303,689.2	372,137.1	159,691.3

Sources: OECD, Financial Statistics Monthly: International Markets (April 1988); ibid. (June 1989).
ᵃ Up to May 1989.
ᵇ Issues by development institutions placed directly with governments or central banks and, as from October 1984, issues specifically targeted to foreigners.
ᶜ Nil or no transaction over the period.

Overall levels of funds raised in the international capital markets have continued to grow. The major financing instruments in the international capital markets are straight bonds, syndicated loans, and Euro-commercial paper programs (see Table 4.2). In 1985 these three instruments accounted for over half of the total $280.9 billion in financing in the international capital markets, a share that climbed to 80% in the first quarter of 1988. The total for 1988 was $472.8 billion. The sharpest increase from 1985 to 1987 was the tripling in Euro-commercial paper, followed by the doubling of syndicated loans. Of the total $280.9 billion of such financings in 1985, 33.9% was in straight bonds, 12.8% in syndicated loans, 4.5% in Euro-commercial paper, 12.3% in note issuance facilities, including multiple component facilities, and 21% in FRNs[10] (including medium floating rate CDs). By 1988, of the total $472.8 billion in financing, 35.8% was in straight bonds, 26.7% in syndicated loans, and 12.6% in Euro-Commercial paper.

A breakdown by origin of borrowers (see Table 4.3) shows that the bulk of the financing went to OECD members, whose share rose from 75.8% in 1984 to 89.1% in 1987 and 94.3% in the first quarter of 1989. In the mid-1980s, borrowing by governments seems to have stabilized, espe-

---

[10] FRNs are floating rate note securities.

TABLE 4.2

International Capital Markets: Major Financing Instruments, 1984-1989 (percentage breakdown)

	1984	1985	1986	1987	1988	1989[a]
Straight bonds	29.6	33.9	36.5	30.9	35.8	39.3
Syndicated loans[b]	23.2	12.8	13.5	20.9	26.7	29.1
Of which: foreign loans	4.5	2.5	2.3	2.9	2.0	1.3
Euro-commercial paper programs[c]	-	4.5	15.2	14.2	12.6	7.1
Equity-related bonds	5.5	1.5	4.9	6.3	6.3	13.6
Note issuance facilities[d]	8.8	12.3	6.4	7.4	3.2	1.3
Shares	-	1.0	3.0	4.6	1.7	0.7
Nonunderwritten facilities[e]	-	3.8	2.2	3.9	4.3	3.6
FRNs[f]	19.4	21.0	13.2	3.3	4.9	2.2
"Managed" loans[g]	5.7	2.5	-	2.4	1.2	-
Convertible bonds	-	2.5	2.0	4.6	2.3	2.4
Other bonds[h]	2.0	1.2	2.0	1.0	0.5	0.5
Other backup facilities	5.8	3.0	1.1	0.5	0.5	0.2
Total	100.0	100.0	100.0	100.0	100.0	100.0
Total value in billions of U.S. dollars	$197.3	$280.9	$389.5	$383.8	$472.8	$480.0[i]

Sources: OECD, *Financial Market Trends*, no. 40 (May 1988); *ibid.*, no. 43 (May 1989).
Note: All data exclude merger-related standbys and renegotiations.
[a] First quarter.
[b] Excluding "managed" loans.
[c] Excluding programs for unlimited amounts.
[d] Including multiple-component facilities.
[e] Other than ECP programs.
[f] Including medium-term floating-rate CDs.
[g] Syndicated "new money" extended in connection with restructuring agreements.
[h] Zero bonds, deep discount bonds, special placements, and bond offerings not included elsewhere.
[i] At annual rate.

cially where creditworthiness was an issue in that there was resistance to lending to developing countries and Eastern European countries. OECD members are expected to increase their borrowing activity, especially through public sector organizations. In 1984, the four largest borrowers were the United States, which accounted for 17%; Japan, accounting for 10.8%; France, accounting for 6%; and the United Kingdom, accounting for 4.6%. Together, the United States, Japan, and the United Kingdom accounted for 32.3% of all borrowing. By 1987, their collective share had jumped to 43.7%; and by the first quarter of 1989, it had reached 50%, with increases in the shares of Japan and the United Kingdom. (See Table 4.4 for information on absolute borrowing levels.)

TABLE 4.3

Borrowing on International Capital Markets by Main Borrowers, 1984-1989 (percent and billions of U.S. dollars)

	1984	1985[a]	1986	1987	1988	1989[b]
	% of Total					
OECD area	75.8	83.3	90.9	89.1	91.1	94.3
Non-oil-exporting developing countries	14.5	7.5	4.0	5.9	3.7	2.0
OPEC	2.0	1.6	1.1	0.7	0.6	
Eastern Europe	1.7	1.9	1.0	0.9	1.0	0.9
Others	6.0	5.6	3.1	3.3	2.9	2.8
Total	100.0	100.0	100.0	100.0	99.3	100.0
In billions of U.S. dollars	$197.3	$279.6	$388.1	$392.9	$451.4	$120.0
U.S., U.K. and Japan	32.3	41.5	38.4	43.7	43.9	51.5
	Billions of U.S. Dollars					
United States	33.5	66.8	72.1	66.2	61.8	24.5
Japan	21.3	22.4	47.1	55.2	60.9	26.1
United Kingdom	9.0	26.8	30.0	50.4	75.4	11.2
France	12.1	15.6	25.8	18.8	28.3	6.4
Australia	9.8	18.2	24.5	18.9	19.8	3.8
Italy	6.3	10.3	15.9	16.1	14.7	4.8
Canada	8.8	11.6	25.8	13.9	21.2	10.4
West Germany	2.1	3.3	15.1	11.9	13.5	1.9
U.S., U.K. and Japan	63.8	116.0	149.2	171.8	198.1	61.8

Sources: Same as in Table 4.2.

[a] Figures for 1985 include international equities, Euro-commercial paper programs, and other nonunderwritten facilities.

[b] First quarter.

Some of the innovations already developed in the early 1970s assumed new dimensions and profitmaking properties in the unregulated and highly liquid markets of the 1980s. One such case is the market in futures, established in 1975 in the United States. Futures and options are risk management and funding vehicles. The aggregate open interest in financial futures and options grew from $0.2 billion in 1975 to $81 billion in 1980, and $391.9 billion in 1985 (Salomon Brothers, Inc. various years). By far the largest share was futures, at $253.7 billion in 1985. The most used trading instrument was futures and options written against contracts on interest-bearing securities.[11] The dimensions of this market

[11] In the mid-1980s, three-month Eurodollar futures contracts were the most actively

TABLE 4.4

Japan, United Kingdom, and United States: Funds Raised on International Markets, 1985-1989
(millions of U.S. dollars and percent)

	1985	1986	1987	1988	1989[a]
Total	$279,133.0	$321,375.1	$303,689.2	$372,137.1	$159,691.3
OECD area total	$229,959.1	$286,194.4	$263,000.5	$332,506.1	$148,033.8
Japan	$21,831.3	$35,283.3	$46,521.3	$54,130.3	$44,543.9
Share of total	7.8%	11.0%	15.3%	14.6%	27.9%
Share of OECD total	9.5%	12.3%	17.7%	16.3%	30.1%
United Kingdom	$20,940.3	$24,109.3	$33,026.2	$62,656.6	$13,693.0
Share of total	7.5%	7.5%	10.9%	16.8%	8.6%
Share of OECD total	9.1%	8.4%	12.6%	18.8%	9.3%
United States	$67,722.2	$55,702.7	$45,667.2	$47,485.3	$25,663.3
Share of total	24.3%	17.3%	15.0%	12.8%	16.1%
Share of OECD total	29.4%	19.5%	17.4%	14.3%	17.3%
Japan, United Kingdom, United States	$110,493.8	$115,095.3	$125,214.7	$164,272.2	$83,900.2
Share of total	39.6%	35.8%	41.2%	44.1%[b]	52.5%[b]
Share of OECD total	48.0%	40.2%	47.6%[b]	49.4%	56.7%

Source: Same as in Table 4.1.

[a] Up to May 1989.

[b] Discrepancies are due to rounding.

can be gathered from comparing the daily trading volume in treasury bond futures with trading in underlying cash bonds. As recently as 1978 the latter was three times as large as the former, but both were under a billion dollars. By 1980, trading in bond futures had overtaken trading in cash bonds, but barely so. By 1985, not only had there been a manifold increase in the volume of trading, but the futures market was three times the size of the cash bond market: $16 billion compared with under $5 billion for the cash bond market. There was a parallel dynamic in trading in stock index futures and trading in the underlying equity shares, pointing, again, to the sharp increase in speculative activity in these markets. Financial futures markets have now also been established in many cities outside the United States, facilitating offshore trading. The main futures

---

traded, accounting for 75% of trading activity, or an aggregate face value of $50 to $75 billion.

markets besides Chicago and New York are in London, Tokyo, Singapore, Hong Kong, São Paulo, and several other cities less important as financial centers, notably, Kuala Lumpur.

The Growth of Institutional Investment

Another important element in the massive expansion of the international financial markets is the growing participation of institutional investors—insurance companies, pension funds, investment managers, banks. Certain types of institutional investors have long been participants in the domestic market, and a few, notably the Swiss banks, have long been participants in international equity transactions. But others, particularly pension funds and the Japanese trust banks, are recent participants. Many of these institutions control vast amounts of assets. Pension funds in all the major developed countries have grown rapidly over the last years. Pension assets in Japan, which are managed by insurance companies and trust banks, have grown by 20% a year since 1980 (InterSec Research Corp. 1988). Corporations have also raised their participation in the equities market, particularly through mergers, acquisitions, and corporate repurchase of shares, in the case of the United States; and increase in intercorporate investment in shares of customers, suppliers, and special investment trusts, in the case of Japan.

The potential weight of institutional investors can be seen from the figures for pension funds (see Table 4.5). Foreign investment of such funds, a recent development, has grown strongly over the last few years (InterSec Research Corp. 1988). In the case of the United States, this investment grew from U.S. $3 billion in 1980 to U.S. $27 billion in 1985

TABLE 4.5
Pension Funds by Major Countries, 1985

	Total (billions of U.S. dollars)	Private Sector (%)	Public Sector (%)
United States	1,500	67.0	33.0
United Kingdom	225	74.5	25.2
Japan	210	47.6	52.4
Netherlands	110	50.0	50.0
Canada	100	50.0	50.0
Switzerland	70	64.3	35.7
West Germany	45	87.5	12.5

Source: "Global Investment Management," The Economist, Nov. 8, 1986.

and U.S. $42 billion in 1989, and is expected to reach U.S. $129.3 billion by 1990. In the case of Britain, these levels changed from U.S. $9.7 billion in 1980 to U.S. $34.4 billion in 1985 and are expected to reach U.S. $84.2 billion by 1990. In Japan the increase was the highest among all the industrialized countries, with the total going from U.S. $400 million in 1980 to U.S. $7.6 billion in 1985 and expected to reach U.S. $47.2 billion by 1990. Though rises in other major industrialized countries were less steep, it is important to emphasize that they all had rapid increases in their foreign investments of pension funds. The overall volume of such investment went from U.S. $19.3 billion in 1980 to U.S. $84.6 billion in 1985 and is expected to reach U.S. $309.4 billion by 1990. A large percentage of this investment has gone into equities.

By 1987 institutional investors in the United States represented 40% of all share ownership but 70% of all share trading. About half of the trading in New York City is done through specialized management firms. New York City is a leader in funds management, a highly competitive field with high levels of specialization. Investing abroad has expanded rapidly among portfolio managers, and many foreign offices of subsidiaries have opened, particularly in London, Tokyo, Geneva, and other major cities.[12]

In Europe, institutional investors account for a majority of all investors. They are mostly large banks, insurance companies, and investment trusts. They have not been as aggressive and involved in trades as their U.S. counterparts. Until recently equity markets in Europe were not very active. Deregulation in London, generally growing international investments in equities, and several large equity issues by European corporations have contributed to the activation of the equity markets in Europe. Institutional investors in Europe have been buying U.S. and Japanese equities.

In Japan, about 70% of share ownership is accounted for by institutional investors. It should be noted that most of the shares owned by large Japanese corporations are not traded but are part of long-term holdings based on intercorporate relationships. The participation of Japanese institutional and retail investors in the international equities market is very recent, particularly because of regulatory restrictions. High prices and low dividend yields in Japanese markets led investors to buy in the much cheaper U.S. and European markets.[13] The weight of Japanese in-

---

[12] Data on bank flows to many developing countries have become increasingly problematic because of banks' write-offs, debt swaps, and equity conversions as well as transfers of claims to nonreporting institutions.

[13] In 1989 Japanese investors bought large amounts of U.S. stocks and bonds, while non-Japanese, and especially Americans, have slowly been selling off their Japanese securities. In the first eight months of 1989, the Japanese made purchases of foreign shares, mostly

vestors in the international capital markets has become increasingly evident. There are several reasons for this. In the past few years, Japan's
huge current account surpluses have been exceeded by massive net long-
term private capital outflows. By 1985, such outflows were running at an
annual rate of over $60 billion, compared with a $40 billion current account surplus. Furthermore, 80% of these outflows were for purchases of
foreign bonds. The rate at which Japanese investors are expanding their
weight in the capital markets is suggested by the fact that net purchases
of U.S. non-Japanese equities and bonds doubled each year since 1982,
reaching $100 billion in 1986. The rate of growth in equities has been
even sharper, for example, from $1 billion in U.S. equities in 1980 to $22
billion right before the October 1987 crisis. There have been a number
of changes in the pattern of Japanese purchases of foreign securities.
There has been a very pronounced increase in turnover, reflected in
much higher purchases and sales of such securities. Furthermore, Japanese have acquired a more diverse array of financial instruments than was
typical in the past, when such purchases were largely in U.S. Government or Eurodollar bonds.

October 1987 and the Financial Markets

Several trends became evident in the international capital markets in
1987 and are continuing today. The most important development was the
increase of the syndicated loan market as a major source of international
financing. There was an increase both in volume and in the relative
standing of this market in the overall flow of international financing.[14] By
1988, syndicated loans accounted for one-quarter of total recorded borrowing facilities, and they accounted for 29% in 1989 (see Table 4.2). This
share was twice as much as in 1985 and in 1986. Total borrowing also
increased from $279.6 billion in 1985 to $480.0 billion (on an annualized
basis) in 1989 (OECD 1989b: 38).

The crisis in the stock market occurred at a time when large corporations all over the world were beginning major financial restructurings in-

---

U.S. shares, totaling $15 billion. During this same period, foreign investors made $14.5
billion of net sales of Japanese stock. This had the effect of lessening the influence of foreign
capital in the Tokyo market. In the early 1980s about 20% of the turnover in Tokyo was
attributed to foreigners, while now it is less than 10%. At the same time, Tokyo's influence
in the United States and elsewhere has grown steadily. Turnover on the Tokyo exchange
has risen above that in New York, and total value of Tokyo stocks has, since 1988, exceeded
the total value of shares listed on the New York Stock Exchange.

[14] Total borrowing includes international bonds and shares, syndicated credits, Euro-
commercial paper (ECP) and medium-term note (MTN) programs, underwritten note issuance facilities, and other committed and nonunderwritten facilities.

volving a large number of mergers, acquisitions, and takeovers. The October 1987 stock market crisis put constraints on the level of new equity capital that could be raised through the stock market and raised the attractiveness of alternative ways of raising capital. The attractiveness of the syndicated loan market for the provision of longer-term finance at favorable rates correspondingly increased after several years of decline.[15] That increase was also strongly related to other changes in the international financial markets, notably the loss of comparative advantage previously enjoyed by the Eurobond market for investors.[16] The syndicated loan market had in the past demonstrated its capability to raise large amounts of financing and to do so rapidly and through financing packages meeting the specific requirements of a firm. It is also worth noting in this context that one of the effects of the uncertainty and volatility in the securities markets was, according to some analysts, to bring back the attractiveness of "relationship banking" and close customer/bank relations. Under these conditions, the secure access to a large array of financing alternatives provided by banks became increasingly attractive.[17]

A more detailed examination of the absolute increase in borrowing in the international capital markets and its changed composition shows the following. Total borrowing in these markets stood at $388.1 billion in 1986, $381.7 billion in 1987 up to the October stock market crisis, and $441.4 billion from November 1987 to March 1988. This rather gradual increase masks pronounced shifts from securities to loans, the former declining from $240 billion in 1986 to $180.5 billion in the period Novem-

[15] It is interesting to note that despite the increase in the price of the associated services, contractual spreads and facility fees are very low compared with past standards (OECD 1989a). This raises the relative competitiveness of bank loans.

[16] External bond offerings experienced a severe contraction in 1987 after years of increases. Gross issues at current exchange rates increased by 51.7% from the first quarter in 1985 to the first quarter in 1986, and again by 35% for the next year-on period; in the subsequent 1987 year-on period, they declined by over 22%. In constant exchange rates, the contraction of 1987 was about 29%.

[17] By the end of 1987, total outstanding international bank claims (all claims on nonresidents plus foreign currency claims on domestic residents) of reporting banks exceeded $5.1 trillion, with a yearly growth rate of 24.5% from 1986 to 1987, compared with 6% in 1984, 10% in 1985, 18.6% in 1986. Much of this increase was not a function of actual lending but of the positioning of the banks, specifically, an increase in interbank claims. Total external assets, in fact, increased by a parallel amount over that period. However, net international lending, while increasing at significantly lower rates than the 24.5% rate of 1987 overall bank lending, did grow after a period of stagnation, from about 8% in 1984 and 1985 to 10% in 1986 and 13% in 1987. Bank cross-border claims grew by some $800 billion, to over $4.1 trillion by the end of 1987, representing a 55% increase in terms of flows and the largest annual increase ever recorded (OECD 1988b). International interbank claims are cross-border claims of reporting banks on one another in addition to foreign currency interbank assets within individual countries. From a 7% growth rate in 1984, these claims rose by almost 14% in 1985, 27% in 1986, and 28% in 1987.

ber to March 1987 while loans increased from $52.8 billion to $141.4 billion. The most pronounced trend over this period was the large increase in the share of syndicated loans and in that of Euro-commercial paper over the last quarter of 1987 and the first of 1988, an indication of the crisis in the securities market. While securities did recover from a low of about 35% of all international borrowing, rising to almost 50% of all such borrowing in the first quarter of 1988, this was still a reduction in that market's share, which had stood at well over 50% for much of 1986 and early 1987.[18]

The Eurobond market was the most severely hit by the October crisis in the stock market.[19] Nonetheless, issuing activity again increased, indicating the flexibility of that market.[20] In the first four months of 1988,

[18] The absolute figures for net lending in international markets also show pronounced increases. Net lending consists of net international bank lending and net external bonds, minus that part of external bonds that is double-counted because it is handled by banks. Net new bank and bond lending stood at $130 billion in 1983 and increased to $175 billion in 1985, to $245 billion in 1986, and to $315 billion in 1987 (Bank for International Settlements 1987).

[19] The Eurobond market, notwithstanding significant growth after the October 1987 crisis, still is viewed as one with disadvantages. The October crisis showed that large-scale shifts away from the Eurobond market can take place when a major currency, such as the dollar, experiences problems. Central to the post-October 1987 recovery of the Eurobond market was the perception of future interest rate levels. A strong point in this market is the high quality of borrowers, who are largely top-ranked governments and top-grade corporations. Better pricing and improved liquidity have also strengthened this market. Its high degree of flexibility has allowed both borrowers and investors to move rapidly across various segments of this market in response to changes in currency rates and interest differentials. Under these conditions, the Eurobond market may return to its basic role as a "reliable" source of long-term funding and a good outlet for international portfolio investment. The recovery of this market in 1988 after a 22% contraction in the volume of issues in 1986 was very pronounced. But this market is quite sensitive to unfavorable developments in international economic and financial conditions, notably fluctuations in exchange rates and the possibility of increases in long-term interest rates in several key financial centers. This has contributed to the increased differentiation in the market: the strong preference for the offerings by highly rated borrowers and the growing difficulty of access by second-tier corporations. There is also a strong preference for short-term maturities because of this market's sensitivity to actual and prospective shifts in interest rate differentials.

[20] Competitiveness with the domestic bond markets has been enhanced by two factors, which have been important in the current recovery of the Eurobond markets. One is the return to pricing new offerings in line with market expectations and beginning to pay more attention to credit quality aspects. Secondly, there was an improvement in the liquidity of the secondary market, and investors acted on it. Notwithstanding these improvements, there is still concern among investors that this market may have difficulty with rapid adjustments of Eurobond portfolios when great volatility may require it. In the short-term markets, the Eurobond market is an important channel of international intermediation. It has improved its organization and its competitiveness vis-à-vis domestic markets, conditions that have led to its strong growth over the last years. Corporations have placed a growing volume of funds in this market, which is seen as an alternative to more traditional forms of

issue volumes reached an annualized rate of about $250 billion, which would represent a 10% increase above the all-time record of 1986. But certain trends in the Eurobond market, already evident before the October crisis, such as the resistance by investors to long-dated issues, meant that in practice some market segments were functioning more as a short-term market than as longer-term sources of finance. Borrowers, in a situation of widespread financial restructuring, on the other hand, will tend to be interested in obtaining longer-term issues in order to secure low interest rates. The Eurocurrency market continued to grow, and appeared to become the primary source for international long-term finance for corporate borrowers, with a corresponding decline in the Eurobond market.

While conventional indicators, such as growth and inflation, suggested that world economic performance was satisfactory in the years after October 1987, the existence of growing balance of payments imbalances and the stock market crisis indicate the extent to which growth has been based on speculation. The syndicated credit market has, under current conditions, a number of attractive traits: broad availability of currency and maturity options, access to a wide range of national and international markets, cost-effectiveness, reliability. It can mobilize large amounts of money rapidly. These properties assume additional significance given the current requirements of a growing number of corporations for immediate access to a large amount of money due to financial restructuring, mergers, and acquisitions, both national and international. Credit lines are one such vehicle, essential when other markets, notably various segments in the securities markets, may be saturated. At this point, the syndicated market provides flexibility and cost-effectiveness, partly because of its attempt to become more competitive during the early and mid-1980s. As the demand on the syndicated credit market grows, that cost-effectiveness and flexibility of terms may be reduced somewhat.

But the new strength of the large banks in the international financial markets is not simply a return to the conditions of the 1970s. The old distinction between banks as institutions in charge of accepting deposits and creating loans, on the one hand, and fee-generating and underwriting activities of securities firms and investment banks, on the other, is increasingly weak as a result of deregulation. The large banks are strengthening their role in the new financial markets, not only as intermediary borrowers and lenders but also as agents facilitating direct lending and borrowing and other functions that resemble investment bank-

---

placement. Thus, nonbank investors have increased their participation significantly. The large number of investment-grade borrowers, the gradual extension of the market to other currencies beyond the dollar, and increasing linkages to domestic markets will all strengthen this market.

ing. Furthermore, among the hundred top transnational banks, twenty-six were Japanese by 1986; together, these twenty-six banks accounted for 40% of the total assets of the hundred top banks, an increase of 14% since 1978, mostly due to the expansion in the scale of their operations and only in minor part due to the rise of the yen (UN Centre on Transnational Corporations 1989b: 76–77). And seven of the top ten banks were Japanese, compared to only one in 1978. In 1986, U.S. banks accounted for 12% of the assets of the top hundred banks, down from 16% in 1978. Japanese banks have rapidly increased their business outside Japan, including intermediation between third parties for foreign clients; they have taken non-Japanese money, entered the domestic markets of several developed countries, and raised their share of underwriting and fee-generating income. By 1985 Japanese banks had 137 foreign offices in the United States, which accounted for 14% of all bank assets in the country (UN Centre on Transnational Corporations 1989b: 77), and 55 offices in the United Kingdom, which accounted for 22% of total assets in that country. Japanese banks have also acquired foreign banks and securities houses.

The large commercial banks in the United States, which until the turn of the decade had been by far the biggest in the world but had experienced constraints on their earnings due to the large number of problem loans to developing countries, eventually sought to strengthen their capital position in order to give better protection to depositors, other creditors, and the deposit insurance funds. In 1981, the three federal bank regulatory agencies—the Federal Reserve, the Federal Deposit Insurance Corporation (FDIC), and the Comptroller of the Currency—adopted minimum capital standards for banks and bank holding companies, a minimum primary capital requirement of 5.5% and a minimum total capital requirement of 6% of assets.[21] After those standards were implemented, the capital base of the banking industry became stronger; they issued common and preferred stock and long-term debt, and raised their loan loss reserves. The average primary capital ratio of the fifty largest bank holding companies in the United States rose from 4.7% in 1981 to 7.1% in 1986. There also were declines in levels of profitability, mostly among the small and medium-sized banks.[22] The poor quality of many real estate, energy, and agricultural loans contributed to the large num-

[21] The main components of primary capital are common stock, equity, perpetual preferred stock, loan loss reserves, and certain debt instruments that must convert to stock. Total capital consists of primary capital plus secondary capital instruments; among these are limited-life preferred stock and qualifying long-term debt securities.

[22] Return on assets, measured by net income as a percentage of average assets, declined from 70% in 1983 to 64% in 1986; return on equity, measured by net income as a percentage of average equity capital, dropped from 11.32% in 1985 to 10.23% in 1986.

ber of small-bank failures in 1986, mostly in oil and farm states and increasingly created problems for the large banks as well.

What we see, then, is a continuation of high levels of international financial activity after the crisis of October 1987, but with a rapid growth in the participation of large banks. By far the most important source of growth in the international capital markets from 1987 to 1989 was the market for syndicated credits, even though in absolute terms securities still accounted for half of all transactions in 1989. The late 1980s emerge as a period of massive demand for funds to finance huge takeovers and mergers, and the large Japanese banks emerge as the leading providers of funds.

Conclusion

There was a pronounced transformation in the financial industry in the decade of the 1980s. International financial activity in the 1970s was dominated by large transnational banks engaged in traditional banking activities. The vast surpluses of the oil-exporting countries in the 1970s were controlled by these banks, which loaned that money to Third World countries through traditional intermediation activities. The 1980s were dominated by the transformation of often hitherto unmarketable financial instruments into securities and by financial institutions other than the transnational banks, mostly investment banks and securities houses. While the geography of the 1970s was one that included less developed countries as crucial areas, both as providers of capital and as buyers of loans, the 1980s saw sharp increases in the weight of highly developed countries as exporters and buyers of capital. In addition, the regulatory framework in the 1970s had pushed the large banks toward the creation of offshore banking centers, but the 1980s, with rapid deregulation of many key markets in the highly developed countries, saw the growing importance of major cities as financial centers and a repatriation of much of the capital held in offshore banks.

Of significance to the analysis in this book is the increased importance of the marketplace and of leading financial centers in the reorganization of the financial industry. While financial markets continue to fulfill traditional supply and demand functions, a second type of activity has grown immensely in the major financial markets. It is the often highly speculative buying and selling of instruments and the experimentation with new ones. This activity goes beyond the servicing of investors and savers traditionally fulfilled by the banks. Utility originally was attached to the actual need for what was traded; that is, a loan satisfied the need for money. Today, tradability is utility. And the more rapid the buying and selling afforded by an instrument, the greater the utility. These markets have grown in size, complexity, and scope to the point that they support a large array of specialized firms, a massive volume of trading, and a highly advanced capability for the production of more and more instruments. The greater value added in the financial industry comes from the skill- and capital-intensive activities of financial institutions: market making, underwriting, product development, mergers and acquisitions, and risk management. In this sense, describing the current situation as disinter-mediation creates a distortion; it is rather that what were historically the main intermediaries lost immense ground in the 1980s. One could say that the financial markets, rather than banks, have become the key loca-tions for intermediation functions. While banks are a simple mechanism of intermediation, the financial markets are complex, competitive, inno-vative, and risky. They require a vast infrastructure of highly specialized services.

Part Two _____

THE ECONOMIC ORDER OF THE GLOBAL CITY

THE CENTRAL PATTERN emerging from the discussion in the preceding chapters is the vast growth in international financial activity and service transactions. A second major pattern is the increasing concentration of this activity in highly developed countries, and particularly in the United States, the United Kingdom, and Japan. This indicates a transformation in the composition and the geography of the global economy.

Several aspects are of interest to an inquiry about the place of cities in this transformation. Producer services, financial transactions, and the complex markets both entail are a layer of activity that has been central to the organization of major global processes in the 1980s. To what extent is thinking in terms of the broader category of cities as key locations for such activities—in addition to the more narrowly defined locations represented by headquarters of transnational corporations or offshore banking centers—useful to an understanding of major aspects of the organization and management of the world economy? The scholarly literature has made important contributions to the analysis of the geography and composition of the international activities of large corporations and banks. But a whole layer of activity that is part of the formation, implementation, and maintenance of global-level processes is only partly encompassed by the activities of transnational corporations and banks.

We posit that the transformation in the composition of the global economy accompanying the shift to services and finance brings about a renewed importance of major cities as sites for certain types of production, servicing, marketing, and innovation. In addition, the internationalization of mergers, acquisitions, and financial transactions makes cities "neutral" centers for management and coordination, for the raising and consolidation of investment capital, and for the formation of an international property market.

The existence of such locations with a pronounced orientation to the world market raises a question about their articulation with the nation-states to which they belong. There is some literature addressing this question for the case of free trade zones and offshore banking centers, particularly since their formation involves an explicit policy of considerable autonomy from various regulations in the host state. But there is very little on cities from this perspective. Cities are clearly a very different and a far more complex and multifaceted case. Yet it would seem important to examine cities with such a question in mind, especially cities where the dominant economic sectors are oriented to the global mar-

ket and have been the object of considerable foreign investment and acquisition. These developments also raise a question about the impact of
these developments on national urban systems. A new body of scholarship is beginning to address some of these questions. One distinction
between earlier analyses and this more recent recasting is the attempt to
theorize the discontinuity between a region or locality and the national
state to which it belongs.

The most fundamental and rapid shifts in the 1980s have taken place
in the financial industry. Central components of this transformation have
been the internationalization of the industry, the institutionalization of
investment, the production of innovations, and the central role assumed
by nonbank banks, all issues discussed in Chapter Four. There are economic and technical conditions that have affected financial markets ev-
erywhere. Among these are the high and erratic interest rates since the
1973 oil crisis and its aftermath; the implementation of a floating exchange rate system in 1973, which facilitated and promoted the internationalization of capital markets; and the rapid increase in government deficits, which led to large-scale issuing of government bonds. The last was
an important factor, which stimulated the development of open markets
in the financial system.

Against a background of major developments in computer and telecommunications technology and its commercial applications, these conditions promoted the production and the increasing demand for financial
innovations and specialized financial services. Furthermore, these inducements and possibilities for new markets entailed a high level of internationalization in the financial markets. Some form of the internationalization of the capital market has been in place for a long time. The
formation of the Europaper market, over two decades ago, represented
the existence of an unregulated market in a world where the other markets were regulated. But the recent changes represent a qualitatively different development.

The evidence on the composition and growth patterns of the economies of major cities clearly points to the weight of finance and producer
services, their above-average growth over the last decade, and their disproportionate concentration in such cities. It is important to this analysis
to gain a clear understanding of the nature of these industries, the conditions for their growth, the determinants of their concentration in major
cities given telecommunications advances that would conceivably allow
for spatial dispersal, the limits to such locational concentration, and the
limits to their growth. Risk and debt have emerged as essential elements
in the growth of finance. What does this tell us about the durability of
this model of growth? In addition, we need to examine the production of
innovations, a key factor in the development of these industries over the

last decade. One set of questions concerns the conditions under which such production of innovations can take place and to what extent the pronounced locational concentration of these industries in major cities is linked to a particular phase in the development of industries characterized by rapid production of innovations.

The focus of Chapter Five is on the development of producer services into a key input and on the development of finance not only into a key service industry but also into an industry with its own products and sphere of circulation—an industry to be distinguished from traditional banking and financial services. Chapter Six examines the space economy of producer services. The purpose here is to understand two distinct issues. One is whether the composition of producer services varies in different types of cities in the national urban system of each of these countries. For example, is New York City a different kind of location for producer services than Los Angeles or Chicago? Similar questions will be asked about the cities of the United Kingdom and Japan. The other issue of interest here is what the space economy of these leading industries reveals about the urban system in each of these countries. Chapter Seven carries these questions to the global scale, focusing in turn on two distinct issues. One is whether New York, London, and Tokyo, rather than merely competing with one another, actually constitute a sort of transnational urban system, each with somewhat distinct functions in the new leading economic sectors. The other concerns the relative position of these three leading financial and business centers compared to other major cities in the world and vis-à-vis one another.

Five

The Producer Services

ADVERTISING, ACCOUNTING, and business law are all producer services that were already in use in the late 1800s or early 1900s. And Taylor's time and motion studies are an early example of management consulting. How does the growth and role of these services in the current period differ from their growth and role in earlier decades? A similar question can be raised about finance, as it has long been an important industry in the major industrial economies. Does its growth over the last decade, especially in international and nonbank finance, represent a distinct phase? The evidence to be discussed strongly suggests that there has been a major transformation in the characteristics of the producer services and of finance, and that there has, furthermore, been a major transformation in the role these industries play in the economies of major industrialized countries and in the internationalization of these economies. A thorough discussion along these lines requires a detailed examination of the characteristics of production of these industries, their role in the economy, and their markets.

Producer services can be seen as part of the supply capacity of an economy. "They influence its adjustment in response to changing economic circumstances" (Marshall et al. 1986: 16) and represent a mechanism that "organizes and adjudicates economic exchange for a fee" (Thrift 1987). They are part of a broader intermediary economy. Conceivably these activities can be internalized by firms, and many firms do so, or they can be bought on the market. Producer services cover financial, legal, and general management matters, innovation, development, design, administration, personnel, production technology, maintenance, transport, communications, wholesale distribution, advertising, cleaning services for firms, security, and storage. Central components of the producer services category are a range of industries with mixed business and consumer markets. They are insurance, banking, financial services, real estate, legal services, accounting, and professional associations. These mixed markets create measurement problems only partly overcome by the fact that the consumer and business markets in these industries often involve very different sets of firms and different types of location patterns, a subject I return to later. Given the organization of the pertinent data, it is helpful to group these services under the category of "mostly producer services," that is, services produced for firms rather than individuals. I will refer to them, for convenience, as producer services.

In the initial analyses that resulted in the formulation of a distinct category of producer services (Greenfield 1966; Singelmann 1974; Singelmann and Browning 1980), the central notion was that these services supported production, whence the name *producer services*. It has now become evident that these services are also used in service organizations, both in the private and public sectors. The term *producer services* as used in this book, and increasingly by scholars on the subject, includes not only services to production firms narrowly defined but also those to all other types of organizations. The key distinguishing trait becomes the fact that they are services produced for organizations, whether private sector firms or governmental entities, rather than for final consumers; that is to say, producer services are intermediate outputs (Greenfield 1966). The relative simplicity of this definition should be placed in the context of the debates and the scholarship about services over the last twenty years, discussed later. The focus is on aspects that are critical to the analysis in this book.

Here we seek to examine the growth dynamic of these industries, their locational patterns, and the relations among agglomeration, specialization, and deregulation. There are several questions of interest. Do these services form territorial complexes with dense interfirm linkages as has been described for manufacturing plants that are small and specialized (Scott 1988; Piore and Sabel 1984)? And can we identify a distinct producer services complex in financial centers compared with industrial centers? How has the increased specialization in services intersected with advances in information and telecommunications technologies to facilitate standardization in production and expansion of the market to a global scale? And what does the potential for economies of scale and scope entail for the organization of the industry? Specifically does it strengthen tendencies toward concentration and/or vertical integration? (See Noyelle and Dutka 1988; Daniels 1985; Marshall et al. 1986.) How does the need for access to advanced telecommunications facilities shape the locational patterns of these services? Finally, what is the place of central functions in these territorial agglomerations?

The issue of deregulation plays a central role in many of the producer services, which differs in certain ways from its role in manufacturing. Several of the producer services have professional codes and governmental regulation covering the client-provider relation and the characteristics of products. This has created something akin to monopoly rights for legitimate professional practitioners, and it has affected the flow of these services, especially when more than one country is involved. In few of the major industries is the role of regulation as central as in the

financial industry. The existence of a highly developed regulatory framework requires a separate discussion. It is the subject of the second half of
this chapter. GATT negotiations on service flows and financial deregulation are two different versions of the pressure to internationalize these
industries. Major players are involved: extremely powerful firms in finance and in some of the major service industries, with growing market
shares and strong tendencies toward concentration.

Intimately linked with the question of deregulation in the financial industry are tendencies toward innovation and heightened risk. Innovation
has served the dual purpose of circumventing regulations and of expanding the market through the sale of new products and through mechanisms for raising capital. Deregulation has further facilitated expansion.
One outcome has been an immense increase in the total amount of debt,
a key feature of the growth in financial transactions in the 1980s. The
question is, How much risk can existing institutional arrangements absorb? The fact that risk and debt have been so central to financial growth
raises the broader question as to whether an urban economy can be based
on finance. In other words, can urban growth be driven by financial
growth the way it used to be driven by manufacturing growth and its
multiplier effects?

The first half of the chapter examines the matter of formal classification
of these industries and contains a detailed analysis of their evolution into
a key input for contemporary forms of economic organization, their characteristics of production, and their locational patterns. The empirical
elaboration of these various aspects focuses on the cases of the United
States, the United Kingdom, and Japan. The second section of Chapter
Five is a detailed discussion of deregulation in the financial industry and
the associated production of innovations. The details of regulatory frameworks in the three main countries are of central importance to understanding the extent of change in the industry and the new opportunity
structure for profitmaking. This section also attempts to examine the
broader organization of the industry in its current phase, the changing
weight of the large transnational banks and the rapid growth of other
types of financial institutions. A more speculative aspect of this discussion
is the extent to which we need to differentiate, on the one hand, between
banking and financial service activities that are services properly speaking and, on the other hand, financial activities that, I will argue, are no
longer usefully understood as services but are in fact more akin to commodity production, where the utility lies in the sale and resale of instruments rather than in the consumption of a service as is the case with
advertising or accounting.

The Category Services

Both neoclassical and Keynesian economics long ignored any distinction between the production of goods and that of services, let alone among service industries. Studies on the service sector basically conceived of it as a residual category that was neither the primary nor the secondary sector. As late as 1940 a book by Clark (1940: 34) contained the observation that the economics of tertiary industries remained to be written, and almost three decades later, Hill (1977: 336) could deplore its continued absence. This neglect was evident in many branches of economics and was partly an outcome of key assumptions about services. It is possible that the notion that services are not tradable led to their neglect in trade theory (Corden 1985). Hill (1977: 318–19) has posited that services cannot be analyzed in terms of conventional market exchange because they cannot be physically transferred from sellers to buyers and they cannot be stored. In urban economic analysis, the prevalent proposition about manufacturing as the export or base sector, the sector with multiplier effects, may have displaced the focus away from services. And the proposition about the unproductive characteristics of services and hence their retardant effect on economic development may have led to their neglect in international development theory (Kaldor 1966; Bacon and Eltis 1978). The more important theoretical elaboration of the services category came from such social scientists as Bell (1973) in the United States and Crozier (1963) and Touraine (1969) in France, who examined the implications of the growing weight of services in highly developed economies.

Much of the recent work on producer services represents an often-unwitting neoindustrial response to the notion of a postindustrial economy.[1] The economic crisis of the mid-1970s in major industrialized economies brought about a reexamination of the role of services in the overall process of accumulation and thus in the crisis. The low productivity typical of many service industries and hence the negative impact of the service sector on accumulation were seen as key factors in the crisis by many analysts. This crisis and its analysis also contributed to an increasingly critical and negative appraisal of the postindustrial thesis and its vision of a better society based on a service economy. In subsequent work there is a considerable distancing from broader sociological perspectives concerned with the larger impact of services on the social order and a nar-

---

[1] Understanding this group of industries as services for producers can be seen as entailing a neoindustrial logic and, at the limit, "an incapacity of conceiving of a development logic other than that of modern capitalist production" (Delaunay and Gadrey 1987: 124–25, my translation).

rowing of the focus to the characteristics of these industries in terms of output, location, and employment.

In some ways Galbraith (1969) and Fuchs (1968) are among the precursors of the current neoindustrial analysis of the notion of producer services and the technical bases of management. In *The New Industrial State*, Galbraith (1969) is fundamentally concerned with the importance and primacy of large industrial corporations but also focuses on advanced services produced inside such corporations. These are services necessary for the organization of large firms and their marketing strategies. Furthermore, while not examining the issues central to the postindustrial thesis, Galbraith does emphasize the importance of educators and scientists for the development of the technostructure he examines. Fuchs's (1968) analysis is, in this context, a landmark study. It is a nontheoretical, empirical analysis that emphasizes the distinctiveness of the service sector and simultaneously analyzes the differences among service industries. The book analyzes growth tendencies, productivity trends, cyclical behavior, specific forms assumed by wages and salaries, profits, and revenues in service industries. It includes a critique of conventional measures and shows their failure when it comes to measuring service industries. While not in the line of analysis of the postindustrial thesis as represented by Bell, Fuch's analysis does lead him to posit that service work is more personal and less alienating than industrial mass production. A further contribution to the specification of services can be found in Singelmann's (1974) characterization of service industries as having divergent economic behavior and social characteristics. He classifies the tertiary sector into distributive, producer, social, and personal services.[2]

In what is perhaps at this point one of the most sophisticated and thorough treatments of the scholarship on service industries, Delaunay and Gadrey (1987) organize the range of studies and types of analyses that have been produced over the last decade into three schools of thought, which they see as partly complementary. One is a conception that understands the growth of services as a move toward an information society (Machlup 1962; Porat 1976; Parker 1975). The second focuses on the changes in what we produce and how we produce it (Stanback 1979; Stanback et al. 1981); and the third analyzes how the industrialization of services results in a greater productivity and profitability of the sector, with a corresponding rearticulation with the process of accumulation (Aglietta 1979; Attali 1981). Some of these analyses seek to interpret recent trends in service growth from the perspective of one overarching category, such as

[2] Singelmann notes the very important point that Clark's law, establishing a positive correlation between growth in tertiary employment and per capita national income, holds for certain service industries but not, or only in a minor way, for others.

information or regulation. Others are more empirical and descriptive. What they share is a central concern with transformations in the formal structures through which work takes place.

For the purposes of the analysis in this book there are important elements in all three bodies of scholarship. Of central interest is the transformation in the formal structures of work and how this contributes to the expansion and demand for services. Important here is the notion that the growth in services over the last decade is associated with the increasing demand for services as intermediate or complementary inputs (Greenfield 1966), either directly for firms, for the distribution of goods, or for human capital formation. Of importance here, also, are theories of consumption explaining the expanded demand for consumer services that contributed to the growth of the service sector in an earlier period. Today, demand expansion in services is highly segmented and linked, to a far greater extent than in the past, to organizations.

Secondly, the scholarship focused on changes in the mode of production points to a number of trends important to my analysis. This type of conception makes evident a complementarity between changes in services and those in goods in the sense that the consumption by firms and individuals of increasingly diversified goods entails a growing demand for increasingly complex services (Williamson 1980). Similarly, the increasing size and diversification of firms has brought about a greater need for services, either produced internally or bought on the market (Stanback and Noyelle 1982; Marshall et al. 1986; Daniels 1985). The move of large corporations into the production and sale of consumer services has made possible economies of scale and mass production and distribution of services, which in turn generated additional needs for specialized services to run such a mass production and distribution system of consumer services.

The work of scholars such as Machlup (1962), Porat (1976), and Parker (1975) on the notion of an information society is of great importance to an understanding of fundamental characteristics of contemporary society. But for the purposes of the analysis in this book, it is a displacement of the central issues. The work by Attali (1981) on information as socially dependent and Stoffaes's (1981) distinction between information that is easily available and cheap and information that is difficult to obtain and expensive are of use in understanding certain aspects of the market for producer services. So is Delaunay and Gadrey's (1987) distinction between the information per se and the service through which it is provided. The latter aspect requires an examination of the actual activities involved and hence of jobs and places.

At the core of these analyses is an emphasis on an increasingly service-intensive mode of production and on the modernization and industrialization of service technologies. These analyses differ from the more

traditional conception, which sees services as nonstockable, nontrans-
portable, and not subject to mass production or scale economies (Stanback 1979).

In a major new book, *The Informational City*, Castells (1989) takes
these various analytical elements concerning the impact of information
technologies and develops a totally new conception about their impact on
urban and regional processes. Castells posits the emergence of a new
mode of sociotechnical organization, the "informational mode of development," which in the context of the restructuring of capitalism provides
the fundamental matrix of institutional and economic organization in the
current period. The effects of new information technologies on society
and space have been conditioned by the restructuring of capitalism. The
nature of space, place, and distance has been fundamentally modified.
This work represents one of the few that presents a broad, encompassing
theory connecting technological developments and transformations in the
organization of work to broader sociological questions.

Growth and Specialization

The elaboration of the services category and the consequent differentiation, especially between consumer and producer services, has led to a
reevaluation of the traditional characteristics attributed to services (that
services are not transportable, cannot be stocked or warehoused, and are
not subject to accumulation or export). The subsequent scholarship on
the producer services (Stanback et al. 1981; Singelmann and Browning
1980; Daniels, 1985; Wood 1987; Marshall et al. 1986) contains significant
evidence that producer services are much less likely to correspond to
these criteria than are typical consumer services.

Distinctions now abound. The work by Greenfield (1966) and Katouzian (1970) contributed to a differentiation among business-related services, consumer services which develop in the context of economic development, and personal services which tend to decline as economic
development proceeds. Other distinctions are between the public and
private provision of services and between blue-collar services and office-
based, or white-collar, services (Browning and Singelmann 1978; Noyelle
and Stanback 1985; Gershuny and Miles 1983). An important distinction
that has emerged in the literature is between the conventional view of
services as demand induced and "supply critical services" necessary for
economic development (Tucker and Sundberg 1988: 23–26).

In one of the most detailed and important studies on producer services, Marshall and his colleagues (1986) document how these types of
distinctions tend to neglect the extent to which services and other sectors
are essentially integrated and the fact that many occupations within man-

ufacturing are service occupations. Ultimately both services and goods are consumed together as part of final demand. The main distinction according to this study lies in the markets served. Producer services supply mainly business and government rather than individuals, but they do so in any sector, from agriculture through manufacturing to services. Such a conception goes beyond the notion of producer services as resulting from the demand for specialized services by manufacturing firms, the latter a long tradition that posits manufacturing as the base or export sector in an economy and hence views the growth of services as dependent on manufacturing and its growth. There is here a recognition of the fact that services are needed in production processes, hence going beyond consumer services, and that such processes are present in many spheres of the economy, not just in manufacturing (Galbraith 1969; Singelmann 1974; Marshall 1979; Greenfield 1966).[3]

There is now considerable evidence showing that beyond the demand by large manufacturing firms, there is the more general issue of the growing size, complexity, and diversification of firms in all sectors of the economy (Williamson 1978; Daniels 1985; Wood 1987; Marshall et al. 1986; Stanback et al. 1981). These conditions are now seen as central to the growth of the producer services. The merging of highly diverse firms has further added to the complexity of management and the need for highly specialized inputs. Growing size and diversity in the components of a firm entails increasing separation of functions, often resulting in geographic dispersal. The overall result is an increase in the level of complexity at central headquarters. These are not simply centers for administration and control, but also centers for decisions about product development and expansion and mergers and acquisitions in a multiplicity of industries. Finally, central headquarters have to function as a "center for orientation of the firm within the business environment" (Daniels 1985: 160; see also Stephens and Holly 1981). This environment has become increasingly dynamic and complex in terms of legal and financial regulations and the national and international aspects of both. Governments also encounter this growing diversity and are consumers of producer services.

Product differentiation and the resultant market differentiation emerge as yet another set of specialized conditions that must be brought together at the higher levels of a corporation. Greater product differentiation expands the marketing and selling functions of a firm. The increase in the research intensity of production also creates new demands on the central headquarters of a large, diversified firm. Rapid development of innova-

---

[3] This type of analysis is to be distinguished from the discussion on the export sector and the multiplier effect (Blumenfeld 1955).

tions requires support to incorporate such innovations into the production or organizational process of a firm. New technologies generate new organizational requirements if they are to be used.

An important factor in the development of producer services industries was the growth of the large transnational corporations, particularly U.S. corporations. The increasingly complex and sophisticated multinational U.S. corporations, operating at both a global and national level, generated a demand for advanced intermediate service inputs. This put U.S. producer services firms in the forefront in terms of innovations and service offerings and made them operate on an international level. Manhattan became the center for advertising, new models of management, and international law firms (Noyelle and Dutka 1988). There were innovations in accounting, in business law, in advertising. Similar patterns can be seen in the producer services industries in other developed countries, though mostly less innovative and less aggressive in the search for markets.

In the postwar decades and into the 1960s, U.S. corporate structure was among the most advanced forms of complex organizations, and U.S. corporations generally led in the use of sophisticated intermediate inputs. These corporations represented an organizational structure rather different from that of the large trading, banking, and insurance firms of the British Empire or of other earlier empires. Many of the advanced producer services, such as international law or management consulting, were largely seen as unimportant to the functioning of the broader economy in the postwar period, especially since the needed inputs for large corporations were often produced in house.

By the late 1970s, the transformation in the organization and composition of economic activity had resulted in a sharp increase in the demand for these types of services, as all kinds of organizations—whether large transnationals or small domestic firms, whether private or public sector—began to use such intermediate inputs. Increasing specialization and increasing demand combined to induce rapid growth in the freestanding market of business service firms.

In the 1940s, accounting in Britain, for example, was mostly organized in small, single-site partnerships. Most of the business was personal and oriented to the consumer market and small private company accounts. Changes in the organization of the economy and in the regulations covering accounting and financial practices have produced a large increase in the demand for accounting services and have transformed the organization of the industry, with a sharp increase in the number of large firms and mergers and acquisitions. In 1948, the largest twenty accounting firms controlled about a third of the audits listed in the Stock Exchange Year Book; by 1979, this share had jumped to almost 70% (Briston 1979).

Changes in the structure and in the scale of firms have resulted in a demand for inputs, which have become increasingly specialized and at the same time generalized, as more and more firms have these characteristics and hence this demand. Producer services can be traded in the market or within organizations, from the head office of a multisite firm to a branch or subsidiary. Whether the production of these services is internalized by a firm or bought on the market depends on a number of factors. Among these are the availability outside the firm of certain services, the degree of specialization, the strategic quality of service for a firm, the cost of alternative sources of supply of a service, and the difference in cost between producing the service in house and buying it on the market (Greenfield 1966; Williamson 1978).

In what has become a classic on the services industry, Stigler (1951) posited that the growing size of markets would increase both specialization and the realization of economies of scale in the production of such services. Stanback et al. (1981) have noted that Stigler failed to see that specialization preceded the possibility of realizing economies of scale. The increasing specialization of service functions that first arose within the large firm indicated to entrepreneurs that there was a market for these services, whence we see the development of a specialized producer-services industry. Producing certain highly specialized services inside the firm has become increasingly difficult because of the rising level of specialization and the costs of employing in-house specialists full time. Greenfield (1966) argues that specialization is the key factor pushing toward externalization. Specialized firms are in a position to sell their services to a diversity of firms and to continue developing their products and incorporating the latest innovations. Eventually, a large demand reduces the price of such producer services to small firms that otherwise would have been unable to buy such services. This in turn further expands the specialized services industry. The development of such a market entails a specialization of inputs in the production of such services and a standardization of outputs; that is, these services can be sold to a large number of firms. The specialization of inputs explains why there is a freestanding market of such services with a large number of small firms. The standardization of outputs with its corresponding expansion of the market points to the possibility that large corporations may also move into this market, as they are doing with consumer services. This would entail a shift of highly specialized functions to headquarters and the downgrading of what are now producer services firms to outlets for the sale of such services.

The available evidence suggests that U.S. firms in advertising, accounting, and management consulting were in the lead of this development. The growth of a service economy has entailed a fundamental transformation in the organization of work (Stanback et al. 1981). One aspect is the sharp growth in the use of intermediate service inputs across industries and markets. It could be argued that this transformation has been decisive in the shift to service-dominated employment in an increasing number of industries.

In terms of markets, Marshall and his colleagues (1986) posit that producer services can be classified as (1) services produced by firms for their own consumption; (2) services produced by firms whose purpose is to sell such a service (these are the specialized service firms that constitute a freestanding market of such firms); or (3) services produced for other firms by firms that meet demand from both firms and consumers (these are mixed consumer and business market firms).

The available evidence shows that the freestanding producer services industry is growing fast and accounts for rising shares of GNP, a subject I will return to in detail. Thus we know that a large share of these inputs are bought. Several studies have examined service employment inside firms (Miles 1985; Marshall 1979, 1982). They found some evidence that the subcontracting out of services is growing. This subcontracting can involve routine operations, such as cleaning and transportation services, or highly specialized services. The development of certain office technologies can both favor in-house production by facilitating the work and at the same time induce subcontracting given rapid changes in technologies and machines (Miles 1985).

One can identify yet another phase in the growth and specialization of producer services, especially the most advanced of these. This new phase corresponds to the transformation in the geography and composition of the global economy in the 1980s. The expansion of the financial markets, securitization, the growing complexity and scale of mergers, acquisitions, and joint ventures, and the increasingly international character of these operations, all raised the demand for specialized service inputs and innovations. Producer services firms entered a phase of accelerated development of new offerings. Competition and deregulation induced both growing specialization and diversification, as well as a strong orientation toward the global market. This brought about strong pressure to build international networks and consequently pressure toward market concentration. In the second half of the 1980s, there were a considerable number of mergers and acquisitions among accounting firms, advertising firms, securities brokers, and financial services firms. Among the top firms, a sharp tendency toward concentration and larger market share became evident.[4] In some industries, such as accounting, the growth of

---

[4] Noyelle and Dutka (1988: 12–13) have estimated that the world market of advertising, accounting, and management consulting (on the basis of market shares of the largest firms)

transnational corporations and banks had long been inducing large size and numbers of affiliates.[5] But the patterns of concentration evident by the late 1980s were on another order of magnitude.

Location and Agglomeration

A very different body of scholarship addresses the locational patterns of firms. From the perspective of classical location theory, access to transportation is one of the key variables determining a firm's locational choice; of less importance is labor availability. To these two factors Weber (1909) eventually added a third factor, agglomeration economies. From a traditional perspective, services are not subject to storage or transportation to their point of consumption, making these industrial location models inadequate for services.

At most, Christaller's (1966) central place theory can be seen as appropriate to explain consumer service location, since there is a strong correspondence between the size of the local market and the volume of service activity (Daniels 1985: 71–104). Indeed, much of the evidence we have on consumer services tends to suggest a strong correspondence between population distribution and consumer services. This is less so for cities where the diversity of the economic base affects locational choices. In Christaller's model the assumption is that suppliers of goods and services make their location decision on an isotropic plane over which a rural population with equal levels of purchasing power is uniformly distributed. This model makes it possible to establish the spatial organization of service activities in a region.[6]

There is not much literature on whether the growth of services has led

was, respectively, U.S. $20 billion, $40 billion, and $20 billion in 1984, on the assumption that the largest U.S. firms accounted for about half of the world market in these industries. Saatchi and Saatchi have estimated that in 1986 the eight largest advertising agencies controlled 20% of billings worldwide, compared to 12% in 1976 by the twelve largest (cited in Noyelle and Dutka 1988).

[5] A key factor in the expansion and transformation of the accounting industry has been the change in the organization of the large client firms. Increasing size and diversification, along with geographic dispersal, generate very specific accounting requirements. Accounting services are needed at a national and international level and for a broad range of activities that are not narrowly defined as accounting, such as setting up accounting models for complex organizations and factoring-in different regulatory systems when more than one country is involved. The capability to serve different regional markets for one client has been developed largely through acquisition of regional firms, facilitated by the prevalence of small and medium-sized accounting firms, especially once the emergence of large accounting firms eroded the marketplace of independent firms (Jones 1981).

[6] Daniels (1985: 75) discusses a number of empirical studies that have confirmed the validity of the model for consumer services, especially in rural areas.

to centralized or decentralized location patterns or on the comparative
locational economies of high-value and low-value service activities or of
highly innovative compared with routine services. Daniels (1985) tested
several of the hypotheses on locational patterns of services using data for
the European Economic Community, covering 1973–1979 (Keeble,
Owens, and Thompson 1982). The evidence supported the hypotheses
that consumer services are more evenly distributed than producer services and that they lack a strong contrast between central and peripheral
locations. Producer services were found to be highly concentrated in central places, with gradually reduced representation in the less central
places. The evidence points to a strong relationship between central
regions and relative specialization in producer services. Central places
are becoming increasingly specialized in producer services, while peripheral regions are increasingly specializing in consumer services. However,
the evidence also shows that some of the less central regions are growing
faster in terms of population and are showing higher growth rates in producer services, even though in relative terms they have underrepresentation of such services and increasing representation of consumer services. In the United States we can see similar patterns in cities, with a
higher specialization in producer services in major cities, but higher
growth rates, especially in the last few years, in a second tier of cities.
Again, these higher growth rates do not undermine the overrepresentation of producer services in the major cities. We return to this subject in
Chapter Six.

In the case of producer services, then, many of the assumptions underlying the distribution of consumer services are not valid or only mar-
ginally so. Precedents to the analysis of location patterns in producer services can be found in the studies of office location concerned with
understanding their concentration in urban places. Among these are
studies that inferred the existence of agglomeration economies from such
locational concentration (Haig 1972; Armstrong 1972); studies that analyzed communication linkages between offices (Gad 1975; Goddard
1975); more behavior-oriented studies focused on the influence of decisionmaking processes on locational outcomes (Edwards 1982); and the development of microeconomic models based on such evidence (Tauchen
and Witte 1983). Generally, the locational patterns of offices are understood in terms of the higher bidding power of offices for central locations,
with a resulting spatial hierarchy, in which higher-level offices tend to be
more centrally located than lower-order offices (Armstrong and Milder
1984).

The literature on the relation of firms to their spatial strategies has
largely focused on manufacturing. I would like to examine whether some

of the key propositions are applicable to the case of producer services and to what extent the differences in tradability and delivery modes between goods and services alter the propositions generated by the discussion on manufacturing.

Much of the recent debate on vertical integration and disintegration has focused on questions of economies and diseconomies of scope, the extent to which a firm integrates upstream or downstream. Scope economies are a major factor in the costs of organization: These are costs of coordination, which increase as a firm integrates up- and downstream, and transaction costs, which increase with reductions in vertical integration and the resulting growth of market exchanges. Many authors have posited that the system of high levels of vertical integration and centralization of capital is being superseded by a variety of developments: more disintegrated systems of industrial organization, entailing complex interfirm linkages; large firms using increasing numbers of subcontractors; niche markets offering both innovative and traditional small firms some protection from competition with large corporations; industrial districts consisting of integrated networks of small firms (Dunford 1989). Increases in the market for specialized inputs and growing advantages of buying such inputs or subcontracting out for them rather than producing them in house furthered the expansion of the market for small specialized firms. Various authors have pointed out that it is not certain that this represents a new model of development in that flexible specialization is often merely an adaptation to economic instabilities. And if the new types of demand that have fueled the growth of small, innovative, flexible firms, become more standardized and widespread, it is likely that the conditions for industrial organization now underlying those firms will be transformed and routinized or integrated into large firms. Furthermore, the immense costs of research and development can eventually force mergers and joint ventures. The propositions about a new model of development posit an increased extent and density in market relations. But vertical disintegration and the other trends described above may result in more interfirm planning and organization rather than in greater market density. There have been new forms of centralization in the specialized manufacturing districts of northern Italy, which served as one of the key cases for the model of flexible specialization and density of market linkages. Finally, much of the small, competitive, highly innovative character of industrial organization evident in "Silicon Valley" in the United States or in Cambridge in the United Kingdom may be related to the early stages of the life cycle of electronics products and the fact that entry costs were low (Dunford 1989: 14–15). Thus, the development of small firms is not simply a process of vertical disintegration; it will tend to be associated with fields of technological breakthrough and innovation.[7] Today, electronics production is determined largely by vertically integrated firms, and entry costs are enormously higher than they were in the 1960s. In the producer services, we find the three types of firm organization evident in electronics: vertically integrated firms, integrated networks of small firms, and independent small firms.

Producer services tend to require a diversified resource base and, in certain industries, considerable investment. Reaching the necessary concentration of suppliers and customers that makes this possible and feasible tends to contribute to location in urban areas of a certain size. Some studies (Daniels 1975; Pred 1977, 1976) emphasize the centrality of information and knowledge in the operation of many services, and especially producer services. If information is central, "then the location of these services can be interpreted within the context of the demand for information, the way it circulates and who exchanges it" (Daniels 1975: 113). Since a central attribute of information is that it is spatially based (Pred 1977), proximity emerges as a key to the activity of obtaining information; that is, information will circulate through specific places and not others. One could, then, in principle, establish the differential accessibility to information offered by different types of locations (Daniels 1975: 113).

The locational concentration of producer services is in part explained by the characteristics of production of these services. These characteristics, in conjunction with the ascendance of such services in economic activity generally, both domestically and worldwide, are helpful in explaining the centralization of the management and servicing functions that have fed the economic resurgence in major cities. Producer services, unlike other types of services, are mostly not as dependent on vicinity to the buyers as consumer services. Hence, concentration of production in suitable locations and export, both domestically and abroad, are feasible. Production of these services benefits from proximity to other services, particularly when there is a wide array of specialized firms. Such firms obtain agglomeration economies when they locate close to others that are sellers of key inputs or are necessary for joint production of certain service offerings (Stanback and Noyelle 1982: 17–18). This would help explain why while New York City continued to lose corporate headquarters throughout the decade, the number and employment of firms servicing such headquarters kept growing rapidly (Cohen 1981; Conservation of

[7] In the United Kingdom, small and innovative high-tech firms for very specialized products for particular high-profit niche-markets are the base of the Cambridge high-tech belt, but there are limitations to the growth and staying power of many of these firms (Dunford 1989: 18). Often, small size is a stage in the development of firms that is important in a period of basic technological change. Some high-tech firms are not production oriented and need constant interaction with research centers.

Human Resources Project 1977; Drennan 1983). Another kind of agglomeration economy consists of the amenities and lifestyles that large urban centers can offer the high-income personnel employed in the producer services. In brief, the fact that producer services are relatively independent of proximity to the buyers, combined with the existence of agglomeration economies, makes possible both the concentration of production in suitable locations and the export to other areas, domestically and abroad. As a result, we see the development of global centers—for example, New York and London—and of regional centers—for example, Denver and Birmingham—for the production of such services.

These general trends hold to different extents for the various branches in the producer services industries. The *U.S. National Study on Trade in Services* (U.S. Dep't of Commerce, Office of the U.S. Trade Representative 1983) notes that some industries lend themselves more readily to transborder trade and others to investment trade. (See also Chapter Three.) Advertising and accounting, for example, have tended to establish a multiplicity of branch offices because of the importance of dealing directly with clients.[8] Broad networks of branches and affiliates have contributed to the importance of central functions in headquarters of service firms; these branches are more than mere service outlets and carry out important production functions. Management consulting, engineering, and architectural firms, on the other hand, have not tended to set up branches and affiliates, but, rather, have kept all functions in centralized locations. Delivery of these services can often assume the form of a good—a drawing or a disk, for example. Or it may require the specialist to go to the site.[9] These locational patterns are also affected by the existence of regulatory restrictions, especially when foreign locations or international trade is involved.

An additional set of issues arises from the extent to which technical developments can increase the tradability of services. Noyelle and Dutka (1988), the *U.S. National Study* referred to above, and the UN Centre on Transnational Corporations (1989c) do not expect tradability to increase in any significant way; on the contrary, the expectation is that the current

[8] The most significant influences on the location of service activity by transnational corporations in recent years have been regulatory changes and technical advances in transborder data flows (Dunning and Norman 1987: 47; UN Centre on Transnational Corporations 1989c; Sauvant 1986). Advances in technology may reduce the need for direct foreign investment as a mode for international movement of services; such advances may also further promote such investment by reducing the transnational costs of cross-border activities.

[9] The new immigration law in Japan allows for an increase in the number of foreign lawyers who can be admitted. In a country with an extremely closed legal system, where international law firms are still not common, employing lawyers trained in countries with which Japanese firms do international business is one way of gaining access to that expertise.

trend of a growing gap between the level of direct exports and that of foreign investment in services will continue. Noyelle and Dutka (1988) further argue that attempts by countries to impose trade restrictions also can determine the extent to which technical developments may be fully utilized. These authors point out that advances in computerization and communications technologies are "making it increasingly feasible to design service production procedures in the form of software and to store inputs and outputs in electronic memories" (1988: 90). The effect of such developments is to separate production from consumption, in both time and space, and allow greater centralization of production, as is the case with goods; yet the authors stress that we should not underestimate the differences between goods and services (see also UN Centre on Transnational Corporations 1989d). Noyelle and Dutka (1988: 91) found a dual tendency toward centralization, resting on scale economies, and toward decentralization, resting on the computerization of routine procedures. But customization rather than mass production is the overarching organizing tendency. What this type of decentralization allows is the provision of a customized product to a client insofar as the computerization of the tasks allows for specific adaptations at a reduced cost. This trend contributes to the weight of headquarter functions but in a way that differs from the tendency toward the centralization of location.

Finally, in examining locational patterns and exports, it has become evident that exports that take place through direct foreign investment can contribute to direct exports from the home country or central headquarters. The Office of Technology Assessment (U.S. Congress 1986) estimated that of the $76 billion in service exports for 1983, $8 billion were exports to U.S. affiliates abroad. This figure is an underestimate since it includes only intrafirm exports of insurance and investment firms to affiliates. The ability to serve clients in the home country is more and more frequently associated with the ability to serve the firm in foreign locations as well. Given customization and specialized markets, profitability may be increasingly linked to the possibility of operating internationally. The geography of the corporate structure has increasingly become global for many of the top firms.

Marshall et al. (1986) found that the existence of a corporate hierarchy in the organization of firms also is one of the determinants of locational patterns for producer service firms. The high concentration of producer services in the greater London area and Southeast region "cannot be understood simply as a response of service activities to changes in the cost of sites or variations in communications costs" (p. 227). The fact that large manufacturing firms concentrate their national headquarters and many of their administrative research and technical functions in the London region while branch offices are distributed over a wider geographic territory to serve local markets may have contributed to a parallel corporate hierarchy in producer services, or in the case of single-site producer service firms, to such services being located where the headquarters and administrative functions are. The decline in central office employment in other regions of the United Kingdom during the 1970s may have been partly linked to the many takeovers in the early 1970s of the provincial firms headquartered outside the Southeast or London region (Howells and Green 1986). Insofar as these takeovers were by firms headquartered in the London region, they would have induced further locational concentration of producer services in this region, given that what were once headquarters in provincial areas had now become branch offices of firms headquartered in the London region.

But changes in corporate structure and markets for producer services are also linked to specific local conditions. Changes in the business and consumer markets for these services, the reorganization of suppliers' companies, and changes in the labor process are each "bound up with locational changes" (Marshall et al. 1986). In the United Kingdom, Wood (1984) found all of these conditions to have influenced the locational patterns of producer service firms and the reorganization of large firms in these sectors, especially from the mid-1970s onward. Notable patterns are the preferences for developing the resource base in existing sites rather than moving to other locations and for serving more peripheral markets from more central locations rather than setting up firms in the former.

These conditions and locational patterns all have the effect of further building up areas with already large concentrations of producer service firms. The need to serve clients who have decentralized their offices actually may reduce the feasibility of following clients to all their dispersed locations, and thus furthers centralization of the servicing firms. From the perspective of the decentralizing client it would seem that a central marketplace becomes important in that this is the way to find out what producer service firms are doing and with which firms to contract. Thus from both directions there is pressure on producer service firms to centralize, either following a corporate model or opting for a central location in order to obtain agglomeration economies.

At the same time, as lower-level divisional offices are increasingly concerned with routine operations that can indeed be separated physically from central headquarters given telecommunications advances, the need for face-to-face contact in the work done by central headquarters increases (Daniels 1985: 163). It is at the divisional level that telecommunications has made a lot of difference in reducing the need for face-to-face contact, while at the same time increasing the complexity of central headquarter functions, the importance of access to a wide variety of sources of information, and the capability for managing, processing, and utilizing all these diverse sources of information (Sassen-Koob, 1986).

The size thresholds to attain agglomeration economies can vary considerably for different types of firms and different types of scale economies (Isard 1956). Beyond a certain size, diseconomies may emerge, as congestion, costs of housing, and the length of the trip to work may all contribute to raising the costs of production and reducing the quality of overall services provided by the city (Alexander 1979; Daniels 1975; Goddard 1975; Goddard and Pye 1977). It is worth noting that research on office location patterns in the London area shows that savings in rents and salaries through office decentralization beyond eighty miles from the city are outweighed by the increase in communication costs.

A particular form of agglomeration evident in the case of producer services is that of the corporate service complex, pointing to a set of linkages internal to the complex (Conservation of Human Resources Project 1977; Drennan 1983; Stanback and Noyelle 1982; Goddard 1973; Gad 1979). A number of studies have examined the evidence on such complexes and the linkages among offices of different types. These studies have found that many linkages are a product of functional connections between firms and a range of specialized service firms that meet a specific demand. Furthermore, it also has become evident that corporate complexes do not need to be geographically proximate, as, for example, in a central business district (Browne 1983; Drennan 1983; Conservation of Human Resources Project 1977; Cohen 1981).[10] This can assume at least two forms. Regardless of where they are headquartered, firms can use the producer services available in such cities as New York or London. The key is that the producer services market is geared to corporate needs. Alternatively, a geographically dispersed multisite firm can make use of a particular producer services market for all its various divisions and branches.

Development of the telecommunications infrastructure requires massive investments and continuous incorporation of new technologies, dis-

---

[10] Browne studied the relationship between high-tech firms and business services in New England and found that they were not confined to locations in the same narrowly defined area. The initial premise in her study was that high-tech firms, management consulting firms, and computer service firms would tend to be located in the same location. But she found a high incidence of management and consulting firms in locations where high-tech firms are underrepresented. It is not evident to me how significant this finding is, as I would have expected management consulting to have a strong presence in a city like New York, which has no high-tech sector to speak of. Clearly it becomes important to disaggregate these industries, since they may contain a number of very different components. Thus, the initial premise—that somehow high-tech and these specialized services form a corporate complex—may be flawed. Furthermore, we cannot assume that an industry such as management consulting is limited to one type, in this case a high-tech, manufacturing-based, corporate complex.

coveries, and innovations. Telecommunication facilities have not been widely dispersed; while the technology has made possible the geographic dispersal of many activities, the distinct conditions under which such facilities are available have promoted centralization of the most advanced users in the most advanced telecommunications centers. Even though a few newer urban centers, notably in the U.S. South, have built advanced telecommunications facilities, entry costs are increasingly high, and there is a tendency for telecommunications to be developed in conjunction with major users, which are typically firms with large national and global markets. Indeed, Moss (1988) found a close relation among the growth of international markets for finance and trade, the tendency for major firms to concentrate in major cities, and the development of telecommunications infrastructures in such cities. Firms with global markets or global production processes require advanced telecommunications facilities. And the acceleration of the financial markets and their internationalization make access to advanced telecommunications facilities essential. The main demand for telecommunication services comes from information-intensive industries, which, in turn, tend to locate in major cities that have such facilities.[11] New York has at this point the largest concentration of telecommunications facilities in the United States. By 1984 it accounted for one-third of all optic fiber networks installed in the United States. Its Teleport is still among the most advanced, along with Tokyo's.[12] Intelligent buildings are another feature of the current office complex in any major city. These are buildings with built-in telecommunications facilities and wiring, to which all users of the building have access.

The space economy of technological innovation appears to follow the same pattern of dispersal and agglomeration (Moss 1986; Castells 1989). The most ecompassing analysis can be found in Castells (1989). He posits

[11] Moss points out that by law new communications lines in the United States have to follow already established rights of way; intercity lines generally follow the lines of the last century's railroad lines. What were once major transportation nodes are likely to be major telecommunications centers today. The new fiber-optic networks will tend to follow this pattern in addition to connecting new high-growth locations, particularly in the South. They primarily connect major metropolitan areas. The advantage of fiber-optic technology is its clarity and freedom from interferences, which are multiple in the major metropolitan areas. But satellites are more versatile. The new fiber-optic technology will tend to reinforce existing patterns of concentration of information-intensive industries that need access to advanced telecommunications facilities.

[12] There are about twenty teleports planned in the United States. The one in New York City will provide access to communications satellites, has seventeen earth stations located in Staten Island, and is connected to Manhattan by a fiber-optic line. Other intraregional systems are being developed in the New York area, which rely on coaxial cable; these include digital termination systems, among others (Moss 1988).

that restructuring processes under way in the electronics industry produce a locational logic characterized by the strengthening—notwithstanding urban crisis and economic downturns—of centers for high-level innovation, which will command and be at the heart of a globally dispersed production system. Secondary "milieux of innovation" will continue to develop but increasingly not as a function of innovation but rather as a function of decentralization of some aspects of the process of innovation. And offshore production will continue, but with strong upgrading by the automation of routine operations and the increased offshoring of advanced manufacturing processes. Thus, a spatial division of labor will remain as a distinct trait of information technology industries (Castells 1989: ch. 2).[13]

The tendency for firms to consist of many highly diverse branches or divisions, the growing size of firms, and the tendency to be multisite all have made the components of information to which central headquarters need access more diverse and raised the importance of precision in that information. Location thus has assumed a new importance, as some places will provide better access to information than will others. Travel as an alternative to locating in a central place loses comparative advantage in proportion to the level of spatial concentration of key resources. The marketplace, in the narrow sense of the word, assumes new importance as well—becoming a place where access to information is facilitated and where clients can gain access to a multiplicity of specialized firms. Certain urban centers emerge as servicing centers. Some are highly specialized—medical health centers, insurance centers—while others are more general, offering specialized services of all sorts, the agglomeration itself making more and more specialized firms economically feasible. This in turn contributes to increasing the importance of such cities as markets where client firms can buy any specialized service and hence an inducement to buying on the market rather than producing in house. Foreign firms and governments can also buy in such markets. Some cities emerge as specific marketplaces for a global clientele.

[13] On the issue of new tendencies toward concentration, Ernst (1986) foresees the emergence of strategic alliances between a few major electronics systems corporations. Castells (1989) predicts that insofar as innovation is central to the industry, large firms will tend to establish networks of subcontracting in order to maintain commercial control over the innovative smaller firms without creating obstacles for them. Small, innovative firms are increasingly dependent on large corporate firms that operate worldwide. But these large firms can keep the same spatial division of labor: milieux of high innovation along with decentralized manufacturing. The difference, Castells points out, is that the spatial logic of information technology producers is being "drawn inside the organizational structure of large corporations" (Castells 1989: 125).

Deregulation, Innovation, and Risk in the Financial Industry

A key argument in this book is that in the 1980s the place and characteristics of the financial industry underwent a sufficiently fundamental transformation to raise questions about the adequacy of grouping this industry
with the other producer services. This argument was partly documented
in Chapter Four and is further developed here. In Chapter Four, I
sought to show that the accelerated transformation of debt and assets into
highly marketable instruments has made many of the financial markets
akin to commodity markets, where the value of the instrument lies in its
resale potential; financial markets have become less and less like service
markets, where the value of the service lies in its utility to the buyer.
Parallel trends are evident in certain components of the real estate market, a subject I return to in Chapter Seven. But there is yet another way
in which the financial services industry is quite different from other producer services. This difference lies in the enormous weight of governmental regulation, much more so than in other highly regulated producer
services, such as accounting and law. In these latter industries, much of
the regulation is contained in professional standards. It is impossible to
discuss the financial industry without discussing regulation. This section
contains a detailed discussion of regulatory frameworks.

One of the main aspects that emerges from an examination of the regulatory frameworks in major developed countries is that central developments in the financial industry in the 1980s did not fit well into the
regulatory frameworks in place in the decade of the 1970s. At the same
time, the absence of constricting regulations, as in the case of West Germany, did not necessarily lead to the type of expansion and internationalization evident after deregulation in countries such as the United States
and Japan. There was clearly a more specific combination of conditions
at work in those countries where finance underwent sharp growth and
internationalization. This would also seem to be suggested by the fact
that countries with quite diverse regulatory frameworks—the United
States, the United Kingdom, and Japan—underwent regulatory changes
that left them with more similar types of financial markets and market
areas for different kinds of financial institutions.

The possibilities for new financial markets emerged in a context where
the regulatory framework in some of the leading financial centers contained various types and levels of restriction. The regulatory apparatus in
many of these countries typically led to closure in the domestic financial
markets. Regulations mainly concerned interest rates on financial instruments provided by financial intermediaries; statutory distinctions among

areas of business, notably between commercial banking and the securities markets, as well as a number of finer separations; and regulations, notably exchange controls, that separated domestic and international financial markets. Eventually developments in the financial markets and the characteristics of regulatory frameworks created a number of conflicts.

These conflicts led to the production of various financial innovations to resolve the problem or avoid the regulation. For example, technical developments made possible different types of cash management services and retail banking services that circumvented the statutory separation of business areas between commercial banks and securities firms or financial services. The growing levels of international circulation of capital in a context of considerable closure in domestic financial markets was central in the growth of the Euromarkets. Financial innovations "arise as a device for the private financial sector to solve or to circumvent conflicts between the newly developing economic and technical conditions and the old statutory framework and regulations which played an important role in the past but have become obsolete" (Suzuki, Y. 1987: 156). At the same time, deregulation, a recognition by governments of this situation, has further facilitated the development of financial innovations.

The internationalization of the financial markets and the production of innovations to circumvent restrictions put pressure on leading participants, such as the United States, Japan, and Western Europe to harmonize their financial regulations. At a time when the financial market consisted mostly of national markets, differences in the financial systems of various countries carried less weight than at a time of rapid internationalization.

To provide a context for the transformation of the last few years, the next section examines the main characteristics of the regulatory frameworks of the United States, United Kingdom, and Japan and the main components of the deregulation. The ensuing section will then discuss the impact of deregulation on the financial markets, including the production of innovations.

Deregulation in the United States, United Kingdom and Japan

Of importance in this brief description of several major financial systems in the world today, are (1) the extent and similarity of the transformations in systems that have functioned for a long period with their own distinct types of regulations and (2) what these transformations amount to and entail for the financial industry and the national economies of the main countries involved. The components of deregulation will vary according to the existing regulatory framework and the characteristics of the financial market in a country.

Among major financial centers, Japan and the United States have strong similarities in their regulatory frameworks. This is not surprising given the participation of the United States in the postwar organization of Japan's financial system. The Glass-Steagall Act of 1930 in the United States and the Securities Transaction Law in Japan, modeled after that Act, establish a strong separation between commercial banking and the securities industry. Several of the European countries have no such separation, permitting a financial institution to engage in both banking and securities transactions. The strongest difference between the European countries, on the one hand, and Japan and the United States, on the other, is the statutory separation of business areas. The Western European countries are more likely to have a universal bank model, which lacks the statutory separations of business areas and regulations on interest rates typical in the United States and Japan. The German universal bank is probably the quintessential European model. Compared with the United States, until recently the United Kingdom has had less regulation in certain aspects of the financial markets and more regulation in others, notably fixed commissions. The 1984 deregulation in the United Kingdom eliminated a number of these constraints and restrictions, making the United Kingdom more similar to its European counterparts. The United Kingdom, however, still has a higher degree of regulation than does West Germany.

West Germany's banking system is far more concentrated than that of the United States, with six large banks dominating commercial banking. However, the degree of concentration in German banks is less than that in the United Kingdom. There are more than 600 municipally owned banks, whose combined deposits are far larger than those of the six Grossbanken. Furthermore, the degree of competition and absence of regulatory constraints have been much higher than in the United States and United Kingdom. The German banking reform of 1967, which lifted controls on interest rates, was in many ways a precursor of what many of the Western European countries implemented a decade later (Mastropasqua 1978) and Japan and the United States are implementing today. One author (Hoffman 1971) described the German Grossbanken as "financial department stores" in that they offer a wide array of financial services, which commercial banks in the United States would not have been allowed to offer until recently.

What matters about the West German case is that notwithstanding the "universal banks," it did not become a leading financial center.[14] This is

[14] West Germany was never opened up to foreign law firms, and much of the legal work

an indication that the regulatory framework is only one element in the current situation. Indeed, it would suggest that the inducements for the transformation in the industry come not from deregulation but from broader economic developments and that deregulation is, rather, a response or adjustment to such developments. Both the United States and Japan had regulations on interest rates until more recently than Britain and West Germany. In 1978 the United States deregulated interest rates by lifting Regulation Q. Over the last few years, Japan has deregulated various interest rates, but the process is not yet complete. The United Kingdom had already deregulated interest rates in the early 1970s.

There were many attempts before 1980 to enact legislation that would deregulate the financial services industry. They were unsuccessful until regulatory changes were mandated by the Depository Institutions and Monetary Control Act of 1980 (DIDMCA) and the Garn-St. Germain Depository Institutions Act of 1982. One consequence of these changes is that depository financial institutions "today are more alike than they were at the end of World War II" (Cooper and Fraser 1984: 17). This legislation was not very different from much earlier proposals made by formal studies sponsored by the government, particularly the Hunt commission study in 1970 and the Financial Institutions and the Nation's Economy Discussion Principles prepared by the House Banking Committee in 1975. It is then worth noting that only when the changes in the financial markets made it evident that regulatory changes were also needed was the legislation passed.[15]

---

typically required by financial institutions was taken care of in house by the large German banks. This was probably facilitated by the fact that the German financial institutions did not move aggressively into the new financial markets and product lines. London and Paris emerged as the main centers for international law firms. Paris also concentrated much of the international arbitration work under the auspices of the International Chamber of Commerce, which was headquartered in Paris. The Eurodollar market was central to the expansion of London's international law firms. Hong Kong is a major center for international law firms covering the Pacific Rim; the industry is dominated by large U.S. and English firms. New York firms control New York and the U.S. market; London firms control the London market; Tokyo is a highly protected and closed market. There is considerable room for expansion and new markets among middle-level corporations in Europe, particularly where mandated audits are a fairly recent requirement. Public sector entities are seen as a new potential market. In addition, there is growing diversification in business service firms; for example, the top advertising firm Saatchi and Saatchi, Compton offers polling, marketing, and other services. Asset management for high-worth individuals is also seen as a new potential market for accountants and lawyers.

[15] The Hunt Commission recommended that nonbank depository institutions be allowed to offer transactions accounts and be given greater lending authority. Similarly, the Principles study prepared by the House Banking Committee recommended permission for all depository institutions to offer transactions accounts. The DIDMCA of 1980 explicitly allowed nonbank depository institutions to offer such accounts. And the Garn-St. Germain Act of 1982 allowed depository institutions to offer deposit accounts that were fully com-

While the framework for regulation is quite similar, the larger structure within which it functions and the objectives of regulation differ in Japan and the United States. The primary purpose of regulation in the United States has been to restrain competition in order to reduce risk, especially for banks since these are in charge of managing money owned by others. The constraints targeted intermediation finance. The regulatory framework and objectives were set by the Glass-Steagall Act as a response to the collapse of the banks during the Great Depression, a collapse that meant that not only the banks, but also all those who had entrusted their money to the banks, experienced losses. A second aspect incorporated regulation into policy to support the housing sector through savings and loans associations, backed up by the development of the mortgage market (Cargill and Garcia 1985).

In Japan, regulation was aimed at promoting and facilitating the industrialization of the country and, to that end, investment into export-led growth. An extensive regulatory framework was instituted to separate the domestic financial markets from the international ones. A key focus was the regulation of interest rates both on intermediation finance and on bonds and debentures in the primary market; this elaborate set of regulations was facilitated by a rather centralized regulatory structure. The Ministry of Finance and the Bank of Japan are the major regulatory agencies.[16] A third regulatory agency is the Ministry of Posts and Telecommunications, which oversees postal savings accounts.[17]

Commercial banking in the United Kingdom is far more concentrated than in the United States, probably an important factor facilitating regu-

---

petitive with money market funds. Technological developments and a proliferation of innovations in the financial services were major pressures to pass the 1982 legislation, which contained several parts addressing specific and mostly technical details of the operations and regulations of depository institutions. However, in many ways, both the 1980 and the 1982 legislation were principally concerned with rescuing thrift institutions; these were in crisis because of their fixed interest rates at a time when interest rates were extremely high, as was the case in the late 1970s. The disparity between the earnings from their fixed-rate accounts and the rates they had to pay to attract funds had led to numerous bankruptcies. Congress feared that this crisis could spread to other parts of the financial system and also feared the effects of a thrift industry crisis on the availability and cost of mortgage credit.

[16] The Ministry of Finance oversees commercial banks and other private financial institutions, and the Bank of Japan is in charge of monetary policy and foreign exchange market operations.

[17] In the United States on the other hand, the regulatory structure contains a multiplicity of regulatory agencies and levels of regulation. At both the federal and state levels, there is a variety of agencies. The most important of these at the federal level are the Federal Reserve Bank Board, Federal Savings and Loan Insurance Corporation, Federal Home Loan Bank Board, Federal Savings and Loan Insurance Corporation (part of the Federal Home Loan Bank Board), National Credit Union Administration, and Securities and Exchange Commission.

lation and cooperation without the highly formalized mechanisms found in the United States.[18] It is dominated by a few major "clearing banks," which until 1968 numbered eleven but were merged into six. In 1983, four of the London clearing banks accounted for 95% of all bank deposits and operated more than 12,000 branches. These banks were highly profitable (*Bankers Monthly* 1981; Cooper and Fraser 1984: 76–80). An important development for commercial banks in the United Kingdom was the enactment of the 1971 Competition and Credit Regulations Act of the Bank of England which had the effect of stimulating competition and can be seen as a precursor to the provisions of the United States International Banking Act of 1978 and DIDMCA. An additional effect of the Act was, as happened in the United States, to broaden the scope of commercial banks and blur the distinctions from the functions of other kinds of depository institutions. As in the United States, we see an increased diversification within the various types of depository institutions. It is important to note that, while the Bank of England exercises direct and indirect regulatory power over the financial system, many of the most recent changes toward greater competition and diversification have taken place as a consequence of economic trends rather than as a response, induced by regulation, to the Bank's interventions.

Up until the early 1980s, the United States had a system of controls and restrictions on international capital flows and international banking affecting both foreign financial institutions in the United States and the activities of U.S. institutions abroad. This contributed to the development of offshore banking and of the Euromarket in London. From 1971 to 1981, a period of capital abundance, foreign branch assets of U.S. banks had a sixfold increase, from \$55.1 billion to \$320 billion. A study by the UN Centre on Transnational Corporations (1981) found that six countries accounted for 76% of the assets of all transnational banks in 1978. The United States was the leading owner. Only a few years later, deregulation in the United States brought back much of the offshore capital, brought in new foreign capital, and contributed to changing the position of the large U.S. banks in the financial markets.

In Japan the government exercises strong control over the financial system (Pigott 1983). Much financing in Japan is actually provided by

[18] Compared with other major financial systems, the U.S. system is generally far less regulated and less concentrated. The two areas where the U.S. system is more regulated are in the separation between commercial banking and the securities industry and in the geographic restrictions placed on depository institutions. The second is central in explaining the larger number of institutions and lesser concentration. An indication of this is provided by the shares of total deposits accounted for by the largest five banks in these countries. In 1980 these ranged from almost 62% in West Germany to 34.5% in Japan and 19% in the United States (OECD 1981).

government financial institutions. Japan has seventy-six commercial banks, with thirteen of these, the large "city banks," in a dominant position. Central to the regulatory framework, implemented after World War II and under revision today, are separation between short-term and long-term financing and specialization along functions, notably the separation between commercial banks and securities firms. There were and still are some controls on interest rates and on sources of financing for financial institutions, as well as a variety of restrictions on activities and portfolio holdings. The lifting of restrictions in 1978–1979 gave commercial banks access to the money market, and changes in the basic banking law in 1982 further diversified the activities of banks. Most recently, restrictions on foreign banks have been reduced, and several interests rates have been lifted. Even though interest controls remain, there has been an opening in the financial system for both Japanese and foreign banks.

Deregulation in Japan has been facilitated by the weaker separation of areas of business and the fact of a unified regulatory system. There are fewer financial institutions, the distinctions among them are not as strongly delineated as in the United States, and the regulatory structure is simple. There is no dual state-federal regulatory system, there are fewer regulatory agencies, and they are extremely strong and thus can coordinate their actions. These characteristics need to be put in the context of a much more stable macroeconomic performance in postwar Japan than in the postwar United States. Perhaps the fact that the Japanese had the universal bank model of the Europeans before the post-World War II restructuring of the Japanese financial system under U.S. influence also helped in the deregulation of the separation of business areas.

Deregulation of the market was central in Tokyo's development into a leading international financial center. The implementation of the offshore market in Tokyo in December 1986, along the lines of New York's International Banking Facilities, and the further deregulation of the domestic financial market all have contributed to Tokyo's ascendance.[19] They fed the role of the yen as a financing and investment currency, a role that has increased immensely.

While in both countries the growing importance of disintermediation created pressures for easing restrictions on depository institutions, there were different forces at work. A key factor pushing deregulation in the United States was high and volatile interest rates. In Japan, on the other

[19] Overall, deregulation of the financial markets in Japan has tended to benefit capital outflows more than it has benefited the inflow of capital, particularly investments in short-term securities, such as Treasuries. This is partly because of structural problems and partly because of cyclical effects. Over the last few years, there have been efforts to facilitate capital inflows, particularly through the improvement of short-term domestic markets (Gyooten 1987: 123–24).

hand, it was the increase in public sector deficits, which in turn resulted in the development of a government bonds market. This put pressure on the government to deregulate interest rates, the main focus of deregulation thus far. The high interest rates of the 1970s in the United States in a context of high inflation created severe problems for institutions subject to Regulation Q, notably savings and loans associations which got money through short-term deposits and allocated it to long-term, fixed-rate mortgages. This threatened stability in the whole financial system, and led to the lifting of Regulation Q, which had been functioning as a housing promotion policy by facilitating loans to finance housing.

In Japan, where inflation and interest rates had been fairly stable since 1977, the pressure for deregulation was linked to the ending of the high growth period in 1973 and the emergence of the government as the primary borrower. Up till then, the main borrowers had been corporations undergoing high growth. To issue and sell a large quantity of government bonds, the government had to set interest rates at market value and deregulate the sale of government bonds by the issuers in the secondary market. One result was the development of a primary and secondary market for government bonds. This in turn caused disintermediation, since interest rates on intermediation instruments were still regulated, even though since 1975 the Japanese government had been rather more willing than the U.S. one to keep rates in line with market rates (Suzuki, Y. 1987).

In Japan, the statutory separation of short-term and long-term finance and between banking and trusts is not as strong as in the United States. Some of the barriers are now in practice minimal on the lending side, since all banks are engaged in both short-term and long-term lending. But on the liabilities side, this distinction remains in the late 1980s. Since it is problematic, numerous practices circumvented the existing regulatory framework. For example, deposit banks circumvent the separation of business areas by accepting long-term deposits denominated in foreign currencies or borrowing long-term funds in the Euroyen market. The statutory separation between banking and trusts is less strict in Japan than in the United States. Furthermore, the entry of foreign banks that are "universal banks" into the trust business, permitted since 1985, has further eased the separation. The separation between banks and securities firms is also less strict in Japan. By the mid-1980s, banks were allowed to collaborate with securities firms in the formation of syndicates for the purchase of government bonds and to become dealers with securities firms in the government bond market; finally, banks can hold corporate bonds and corporate equities in their investment portfolios, all types of transactions not allowed banks in the United States (Cargill 1986).

There are some less obvious and less attractive consequences of the deregulation legislation. The greater competition among financial institutions, while leading to higher deposit rates and lower loan rates, may still carry higher prices for consumers of certain financial services insofar as depository institutions can now charge for them. Also, since competition reduces profitability, the number of independent depository institutions will tend to shrink and concentration grow. Cooper and Fraser (1984) point out that already in the early 1980s one estimate put the potential decline in the number of U.S. commercial banks at between 30% and 50%. The last few years have certainly seen the collapse of a number of banks and mergers of others. Yet another estimate is that there will be a three-tier structure consisting of a few national-level firms offering a broad range of financial services, highly specialized firms offering low-priced services, and several firms specializing in less price-sensitive markets.

Innovation and Risk

Innovations have changed the nature of financial risk in several ways, both for traditional types of assets held by banks and for new types of instruments. Recent innovations have made it possible to assign market value to such assets as securitized loans and contracts—instead of, as was customary, basing their values on historical values and correcting these when an asset was acquired or sold, thus letting the market set the value.[20]

The increase in these types of instruments has raised the overall level of risk for banks. Such instruments go beyond the typical credit risk that banks have had, the default of a borrower or any party committed to a future exchange.[21] The new instruments (swaps, options, long forward

[20] In the United States, financial transactions are secured through a system of financial disclosure and rating, established as a response to the 1929 crisis, whereas in Japan they are secured through collateral. Now there is great pressure to replace the Japanese system with a disclosure and rating system akin to that of the United States. This pressure arises from the deregulation of interest rates and the development of the equities market as well as from the internationalization of financial transactions. Exceptions have already been put in place, notably the issuance of Euroyen bonds and domestic bonds without collateral by large firms since 1984, and, since 1985, transactions without collateral. The use of collateral is increasingly problematic with deregulation and internationalization and the associated increase of direct financing of nongovernmental borrowers. The rise of disintermediation and the decline of the banks' share in financing have created pressure to do away with the collateral requirement.

[21] Banks will have to factor in the risks of this new type of value assignment, notably market fluctuations. In addition, assets or contracts that do not involve an extension of credit, such as currency swaps, contain substantial credit risks.

dated exchanges, provision of letters of credit or purchases of revolving underwriting commitments) create "huge aggregate volumes of credit risk at all times" (Edwards 1987: 148).

Probably the best known of these innovations is the so-called junk bond, a high-risk, high-yield security that facilitates debt financing. Many small and less creditworthy companies did manage to expand by raising money through such high-risk, high-yield instruments. Several analysts have argued that junk bonds made financing available to smaller, less prestigious, and less powerful corporations in the United States and hence benefited the economy by strengthening the smaller companies and creating jobs. This is indeed, the data suggest, one of the outcomes of the development of this type of debt financing. But it is estimated that about half the funds raised through junk bonds in the decade of the 1980s have been used for corporate takeovers or for corporate reorganization to avoid unsolicited takeover bids.[22] The Securities Data Company, of Newark, New Jersey, found that $71 billion of the $153.7 billion issued between 1980 and 1989 in junk bonds went to acquisitions-related activities rather than to expansion of productive capacity and hence creation of new jobs. About 7% of the value of these issues was placed in the portfolios of savings and loans institutions.

The impact of innovations on the financial system is a complex issue on which there is no agreement. Some argue that the main effect has been to raise the efficiency of this market. Others argue that the main impact has been to raise the level of risk in the financial system. Edwards (1987) maintains that regulations that should have limited the risk exposure in the financial system have created the opposite effect. In the United States, financial innovations have used either regulatory loopholes or existing regulations that subsidize and thereby encourage institutional risk-taking.

Without the government guarantees and subsidies built into this system, such high risks would not be taken. They are made possible by the distinct nature of this market, characterized by strong links between the government and the financial industry. In the United States, the availability of last-resort lending from the Federal Reserve and a widespread

[22] See Congdon (1988) on the growth of debt. Financial deregulation produced a variety of innovations in venture capital and the financing of mergers and acquisitions. Congdon (1988: 186–87) points out that leveraged buy-outs are one of the best examples and "illustrate all that is best about American finance and entrepreneurship . . ." but that "it is difficult to be so enthusiastic about . . . the use of 'junk-bonds' to finance take-overs" (1988: 186). Congdon argues that leveraged buy-outs will, indeed, tend to produce better management, while this is not necessarily the case with the use of junk bonds, insofar as those involved are not necessarily better managers and assume such onerous debt that no matter how experienced management might be, it could not raise the rate of growth of a company to 14% or over, the interest rate on many junk bonds.

deposit insurance system in effect constitute a federal guarantee of the soundness of U.S. financial institutions and, indirectly, of the stability of the financial system. Firms can take on additional risks without paying the market price for such risk, and creditors and depositors similarly feel comfortable with a high level of risk because of government guarantees and hence further contribute to this skewed market operation.[23] In this sense the government gives the various participants in the market a subsidy equal to the differential between the true market price of risk and the price they pay for that risk given government guarantees (Edwards 1987: 149).

The extent to which growth in the financial industry has been based on debt and risktaking is well illustrated by two developments: the recent losses in major financial firms and those in the savings and loan industry. About a year after the October 1987 stock market crisis, but especially toward late 1989, several major firms on Wall Street and in London's City suffered large losses. The sharp decline in prices on the Tokyo stock market in January 1990 also created potentially major difficulties for several major Japanese financial institutions. On Wall Street, record-breaking losses were posted by such prominent firms as Shearson Lehman Hutton, Inc., while others, like Drexel Burnham Lambert, collapsed under the weight of debt. Major firms are also experiencing sharp reductions in activity and are laying off hundreds of employees. This has had a secondary effect on a broad range of businesses, from restaurants to clothing stores. Since stock market prices fell in October 1987, about 40,000 employees on Wall Street have lost their jobs. All major stock markets go through cyclical ups and downs and crisis periods. But the last few months of 1989 saw the beginning of what appears to be a far more severe drop in volume and activity than in the downturns of the 1960s and 1970s.

One of the major banks in London, Midland, experienced a severe fall

[23] According to Edwards (1987), this guarantee is increasing and reaching levels that are unsustainable. The aggregate value of deposit insurance guarantees is higher than the present system can handle or than was foreseen by the founders of the deposit insurance system in 1933 (Edwards 1987: 149). The insurance reserve on U.S. insurers is insufficient to meet the de facto guarantees, which are higher than the de jure guarantees. The gap between the de jure and de facto guarantees is bridged through a whole array of financial innovations. There is today de facto financial insolvency in the financial system. Edwards (1987) maintains it is necessary either to implement a system that shifts the burden of insolvency to the stockholders and creditors and away from federal regulatory agencies and taxpayers or to implement the regulatory constraints that correspond to the current federal system. It would seem that the current crisis in loans and savings institutions in the United States fully confirms the analysis by Edwards (1987). Every new risk taken on by firms represents an expansion of the federal government guarantee and obligation. Under these conditions, innovation and risktaking raise the profitability of financial operations.

in its profits in the early 1990s, to the point that it was considered unusual for recent banking history. The conditions that brought about Midland's decline are shared by many financial institutions, even though Midland is considered to be the weakest of the big four clearing banks of the City. And in Tokyo, two of the top five Japanese city banks, Daiichi Kangyo and Fuji, were experiencing difficulties due to interest rates and property losses. A major concern is the possibility of a massive unloading of securities owned by Japanese banks in that this could bring down international stock and bond prices. The fact that Japanese banks own largely Japanese stock would seem to counteract the effects on international markets but not necessarily on Japanese ones. One serious problem in Japan is that Japanese banks are allowed to count 45% of unrealized gains on securities investments toward their basic capital. Thus, capital ratios have been sharply reduced by the decline of the stock market. New international standards coming into effect in 1993 will pose additional burdens since Japan has not imposed the more demanding criteria guiding banks in the West. Finally, Japanese banks have put up only 20% as loan loss reserves against Third World loans. According to one firm, Yamaichi, when all these factors are put together, Japanese banks will require either $29 billion of new capital or a $216 billion reduction in outstanding loans—"the equivalent of wiping out Barclay's Bank" (*Independent*, April 25, 1990, 23) to raise capital ratios to the 1993 standards.

In the early 1990s, the General Accounting Office of the U.S. Congress estimated that the savings and loan bailout could reach as high as $500 billion, which was about twice the level of earlier estimates. Less than a year earlier, in July 1989, the government's estimate had been $257 billion. The actual level will depend on the performance of key sectors of the economy, notably the real estate industry, where many of these institutions made heavy investments. This makes it a far larger rescue for the government than several other recent such rescues combined, most notably the combined cost to taxpayers of the defaults in the 1970s of New York City, the Chrysler Corporation, and the Lockheed Corporation.

The increase in the cost estimate is due to the rapidly growing number of troubled institutions, the decline in real estate values, and the increase in interest rates on bonds to finance the rescue. According to some estimates, up to 600 institutions in the savings industry will eventually have to be bailed out. By early 1990, the number of institutions controlled by the government stood at over 350. This higher estimate will require new legislation because the level authorized by Congress only a year earlier was insufficient. In 1989 a special agency was set up to handle the rescue, the Resolution Trust Corporation. The need for an additional agency stemmed from the collapse of the Federal Savings and Loan Insurance Corporation, which guarantees deposits. This agency had accumulated losses of $87 billion at the time it had to be closed in mid-1989.

The deregulation of savings and loan institutions was a crucial element in the crisis of the industry because it allowed institutions to go beyond their traditional domain of collecting consumer deposits and making home mortgage loans. Some of these institutions invested relatively large sums, given their holdings, in highly speculative investments in real estate and in so-called junk bonds. Similar strains are also becoming evident in the large commercial banks.

Production of innovations on the international capital market has declined from late 1986 levels. While there has been continued use of already established innovations, such as swaps, futures, and options, there have not been many new capital instruments with novel interest and exchange rate characteristics brought to the market, and those that have been brought have not drawn much interest. There has been a mixed experience for investors with other innovative products introduced over the last few years, which have not produced the profits, liquidity, and/or risk limitation they were expected to produce. This holds for many floating-rate instruments as well as equity-linked ones. The retrenchment in the Eurosecurities market beginning in early 1987 and accelerating rapidly after the October crisis also contributed to a contraction in the range of marketmaking in highly specialized segments of this market.

One question that arises is whether a continuation of this slowdown in the production of innovations could induce a shift away from the international market and from securitization. According to OECD analysts, such a slowdown would not necessarily be a negative development in itself "to the extent that it would enable market participants to re-assess the pros and cons of existing instruments in a less favorable environment than the one in which they were created" (OECD 1988a). Finally, these analysts point out that both investors and borrowers seem to be more interested in the smooth functioning of the market, which could lead to greater use of "traditional" forms of financing.[24]

[24] The stock market crash of 1987 induced a change in thinking on Wall Street, leading to an attempt to reduce volatility. The New York Stock Exchange suddenly began to call for "circuit breakers," ways to halt the market and provide a brief cooling off when it rose or dropped sharply, rather than a massive chain reaction. The New York Stock Exchange took out a full-page advertisement in several newspapers in early December 1989 to declare that it would try to increase stability. "Excess volatility is a serious threat to our nation's capital markets and the American economy," asserted John J. Phelan, Jr., the Exchange's chairman. Tokyo has had such mechanisms for years. In Tokyo, a range of formal and informal mechanisms reduced price fluctuations after the October 1987 crisis. On Wall Street, the Big Board began to consider ways to stop program trading (a computer-driven strategy which could be a source of volatility, according to some experts). Japan's government, on

Technical developments in computer and telecommunication technology have been more rapidly applied in Japan and the United States than in Europe (Suzuki and Yomo 1986). Given the higher rate of financial innovations, the existing statutory separation between areas of business also has created more urgent conflicts or barriers than in the European countries. Partly as a result, there are greater similarities between Japan and the United States than between these two countries and Europe. They respond to a somewhat similar set of constraints.

Conclusion

Producer services have become central components in the work process of both goods-and service-producing firms. The development over the last two decades of a broad array of new producer services is both a response and a further inducement to this centrality. The expansion in the use of such services as intermediate inputs is linked with the broader technical and spatial reorganization of the economy. The introduction of computer technology and satellite transmission of data has altered the work process in both goods- and service-producing firms even when their products have not changed. Transferring what were once production jobs and blue-collar service jobs into computers and attendant technical jobs has brought about a greater need for specialized servicing, from engineering design to data processing. The supply of such a wide array of intermediate specialized services has itself contributed to the demand for them: It is now customary for firms and government agencies to use outside consultants of various sorts, even when these may replicate the work of internal staff. Finally, participation in a world market has created a need for a range of specialized services, and these have in turn facilitated the development of a world market. In brief what is characteristic in the contemporary phase is the ascendance of such services as intermediate inputs and the evolution of a market where they can be bought by foreign or domestic firms and governments.

The financial industry has functioned as one of the key producer services, with growing participation in all sectors of the economy. But it has also contributed to the development of a rapidly growing range of markets for the circulation of its products. Deregulation, internationalization, and innovation have been central in this development. And so have been risk-taking and speculation.

The deregulation and internationalization of the financial system in ma-

the other hand, was slow in introducing stock index futures, which are necessary for many forms of program trading, and has made it difficult to do program trading on a large scale.

jor developed countries have taken place notwithstanding differences among these systems in their regulatory frameworks, their histories, and the economies within which they function. The depth of these regulatory changes under highly varied conditions is an indication of the extent of the internationalization of the financial industry and of the weight of its transformation. And the enormous increase in the volume and value of financial transactions is an indication of the highly innovative and speculative character of the industry in the 1980s.

Six _____

Global Cities: Postindustrial Production Sites

How does the spatial and technical transformation of economic activity described in the preceding chapters play itself out in major cities? A central thesis of this chapter is that the industrial recomposition in the economic base of global cities is not simply a result of the general shift from a manufacturing to a service economy. Besides the vast set of activities that make up their economic base, many typical to all cities, these global cities have a particular component in their economic base—a component rooted in those spatial and technical changes—that gives them a specific role in the current phase of the world economy. Thus, while all cities contain a core of service industries and the leading cities of a country have long contained key banking functions, the argument here posits a more novel and specific process.

This thesis can be broken down into three parts. The first part posits that geographic dispersal of factories, offices, and service outlets and the reorganization of the financial industry over the last decade have contributed to the need for new forms of centralization for the management and regulation of the global network of production sites and financial markets. The work of management and regulation as well as the production of the needed inputs will tend to be concentrated in major cities. The second part of the thesis is that these new forms of centralization entail a shift in the locus of control and management: In addition to the large corporation and the large commercial bank, there is now also a marketplace with a multiplicity of advanced corporate service firms and nonbank financial institutions. Correspondingly, we see the increased importance of cities such as New York, London, and Tokyo as *centers* of finance and as centers for global servicing and management. In other words, this is not merely another instance of large firms' externalization of these functions. The third part of the thesis is that the production of a wide array of innovations in services and finance has been central to the transformation of economic activity. Cities have emerged as key locations for the production of such innovations.

There is a large body of scholarly literature on urban and metropolitan regions which addresses both the conditions necessary for the particular forms of growth that major cities make possible and the recurrent processes of dispersion of those same components of growth. Much of this literature emphasizes the continued seedbed function of major cities in the context of periodic cycles of overcrowding, congestion, and emergence of agglomeration diseconomies, followed by partial resolutions through spatial dispersal. There is also a vast literature on the relation of such major cities to other cities in an urban system, the latter typically conceived of as nation based. A balanced urban system is thought to promote the diffusion of growth across the national territory and thereby to secure spatial integration.

The question for us is whether the transformation in the economy has altered the propositions about cities, their regions, and national urban systems contained in that literature.[1] The decline of manufacturing and the shift to service-dominated employment, the rapid growth of producer services, and the further service-intensification of the economy, are trends evident in all three cities. Conceptualization about the nature of the urban system or urban hierarchy in developed countries is mostly derived from a particular historical phase—one where mass production largely for the domestic market was the dominant fact in these economies. What does the sharp growth in international financial and service transactions and the growth of New York, London, and Tokyo as leading international business centers mean for the urban hierarchy and spatial integration of the national economy in each of the three countries? What happens to the diffusion of growth from the top through the urban hierarchy when the top is oriented to the global market? There is an important critical literature that never has accepted the notion of mutually beneficial exchanges in the urban hierarchy and posits that cities function as surplus-extracting and concentrating mechanisms vis-à-vis their hinterlands. Is this proposition at all altered by the rise and internationalization of producer services and finance? Do New York, London, and Tokyo function as such a surplus-extracting mechanism vis-à-vis a "transnational hinterland"?

This chapter seeks to examine these issues through a detailed analysis of the space economy of the producer services in order to specify the type of location that New York City, London, and Tokyo constitute for these industries. The preceding chapters examined the conditions for and limits to the growth of finance and producer services (the major growth sec-

[1] Many scholars have argued that most developed economies are characterized by a rank rule city size distribution and that this represents a condition of equilibrium. Conversely, some have posited that it is the existence of an integrated space economy that produces a rank size distribution (Christaller 1966). Harvey (1973), on the other hand, argues that the appropriation and redistribution of surplus value is one of the key properties of city systems. The integration of the space economy organized along the urban hierarchy or contained in the urban system is an expression of the "process which circulates surplus value in order to concentrate more of it" (1973: 237–38).

tors in these three cities). This chapter provides a detailed analysis of the role of New York, London, and Tokyo as locations for the producer services and finance, and the limits to that role; the forms, if any, of integration of these new growth sectors into their larger metropolitan regions and into the general economy of the countries; and, finally, the differences, if any, between these cities and other major cities in the United States, the United Kingdom, and Japan.

The three countries under study represent considerable diversity in their urban systems. London, which accounts for 16% of the U.K. population is as close to a primate city as one could find in a highly developed country.[2] The United States has a multiplicity of large cities, none accounting for more than 4% of the total population. Japan has a major industrial center in Osaka, and while Tokyo is clearly the dominant city, there are several other major cities, particularly Osaka, once the leading industrial center in the country. The contrast between these three countries and the presence of major industrial centers in the Japanese urban system should allow us to detect differences in the composition of producer services in finance-oriented compared with manufacturing-oriented cities. Furthermore, comparing what were once major industrial cities in the United Kingdom with those in Japan should illuminate the relation between manufacturing and producer services—specifically, whether the growth of producer services is predicated on a strong manufacturing sector. Finally, in the case of the United States today, Chicago and New York present strong contrasts, with Chicago the center of the once-leading agroindustrial complex in the country and New York emerging as the major financial center in the 1980s. As a financial and business center Chicago was oriented toward its hinterland and represented a case of strong regional integration. What happens when such a regional industrial complex enters severe decline? Is this reflected in a decline and/or transformation of the producer services sector? And to what extent does the growth of the financial markets in Chicago present new conditions or seedbed functions for the growth of a different type of producer services? Los Angeles, a major recipient of foreign investment, with a strong orientation to the dynamic Pacific Rim, is considered to be the leading rival to New York's prominence as an international financial and business center. What is the position of Los Angeles vis-à-vis New York?

I will isolate the producer services to examine these questions. The

[2] The distribution of city sizes that is considered normal responds to a rank rule, where the second-largest city is one-half the size of the largest, the third is one-third the size of the largest, and so on. Mathematically, this is rendered through a log-normal distribution. The notion is that such a distribution will promote overall development, while urban systems with a primate city, where the largest city is inordinately larger than the rest, are not seen as conducive to development.

purpose here is not to describe the overall economic base in these cities. That will be part of the discussion of the broader socioeconomic order in Part Three of the book. The purpose here is to isolate the producer services and to carry out a comparative analysis of New York, London, and Tokyo and of their place in their national urban systems. Do New York, Tokyo, and London function as expected according to prevalent models of the urban system, diffusing growth along the hierarchy and contributing to the spatial integration of the economy?

The evidence shows clearly that in all three countries the growth rates of producer services were higher at the national level than in those cities. Moreover, the evidence shows that this higher national growth rate has not eroded the disproportionate concentration of producer services in major cities. This raises a question about the possibility of a new phase in the process of service-dominated urbanization that has been occurring for several decades now. This growth in overall services was particularly strong when manufacturing and wholesale trade were the key components in the economic base. Now that manufacturing has declined significantly as a share of employment in major cities and a new type of services, producer services, has grown rapidly and become a leading sector, there may be a different meaning to the notion of service-dominated urbanization.

The first section of this chapter is a discussion of general trends in the location of producer services, taking up where the preceding chapter left off. The second section examines producer services and finance in the context of what are often thought of as urban hierarchies. This discussion is intended to situate these cities in the space economy of the producer services in their respective countries. The next chapter will examine the place of London, New York, and Tokyo in global terms.

Location of Producer Services: Nation, Region, and City

A number of major trends are evident in the available data on the geographic distribution and composition of producer services industries in the United States, the United Kingdom, and Japan. There is no doubt that this is a significant growth sector in all three countries. The question is the specific role played by cities, especially New York, London, and Tokyo, in the organization of this sector. The main patterns described below begin with the level of the nation and conclude with that of the central business district in each of these three cities over the last decade. (For a brief comparison of classifications of producer services in these three countries, see Appendix A.)

A first trend evident in all three countries is that national employment growth in producer services was higher than total national employment and, furthermore, higher than in the leading cities (see Tables 6.1 through 6.3). This raises a question as to the composition of the producer services in different locations, specifically, the possibility that this sector is constituted quite differently in a leading city from what it is in the rest of a country.

TABLE 6.1A

United States: Growth in Total Employment and Producer Services Employment, 1977-1987

	1977	1981	1985	1987
Total employment (N)	(64,975,580)	(74,850,402)	(81,119,257)	(85,483,800)
Growth rate (%)	—	15.20%	8.38%	5.38%
Producer services (N)	(9,804,104)	(12,328,104)	(14,803,684)	(15,552,713)
Growth rate (%)	—	25.8%	20.1%	5.06%

Sources: County Business Patterns, issues for the United States, 1977, 1981, 1985, and 1987 (U.S. Department of Commerce, Bureau of the Census).

TABLE 6.1B

United States and New York: Employment Changes by Industry, 1977-1985

	% Change	
	New York	United States
All industries	11	25
Construction	-30	25
Manufacturing	-22	-1
Transportation	-20	-20
Wholesale	14	23
Retail	17	26
FIRE	21	31
Banking	23	36
Insurance	-2	21
Real estate	8	33
Services	42	53
Personal services	-2	85
Business services	42	85
Legal services	62	75
Other	44	48

Sources: County Business Patterns, issues for New York and the United States, 1977 and 1985.

Notes: Except where indicated otherwise, New York refers to New York City. County Business Patterns data cover only private sector jobs.

The period of rapid growth in producer services was from the late 1970s to the mid-1980s. In the United States, while total employment increased by 15% from 1977 to 1981 and by 8% from 1981 to 1985, total employment in producer services for those same periods increased by 26% and 20%, respectively. In Japan we see, similarly, considerable disparity between the level of overall national employment growth and growth in those producer services for which there are individual data. Total national employment in Japan grew by 5% from 1977 to 1981 and by 4% from 1981 to 1985. In services, growth was 17% from 1977 to 1981 and 15% from 1981 to 1985. If we consider only the FIRE sector the growth rate was 27% during 1975–1985. In the United Kingdom, total employment fell by 5% during 1978–1985, while services employment increased by 41% and FIRE employment increased by 44%.

A second trend is that the share of producer services jobs in New York, London, and Tokyo is at least a third higher and often twice as large as the share of these industries in total national employment (see Table 6.4). But the actual shares are quite small, ranging from 4.2% in 1985 for banking, finance, and insurance in Tokyo versus 3% in Japan, to 13.9% in New York City versus 5.7% in the United States. In the case of business services, this relation remains, but at a slightly higher level. Thus, business services accounted for 5% of all workers in Great Britain in 1984 but for 10.2% in London. In the case of Tokyo, there was no separate measure for business services. It should be noted that both London and New

TABLE 6.2

Great Britain and London: Employment Changes by Industry, 1978-1985

| | % Change | |
	London	Great Britain
All industries	-4	-5
Agriculture, forestry, and fishing	11	-11
Energy and water	-20	-14
Manufacturing	-25	-24
Construction	-18	-24
Transportation and communication	-18	-13
Banking, insurance, and finance	32	44
Public administration and defense	13	18
Education/health/other	-10	-3

Source: Inner London Education Authority, The London Labour Market -- Facts and Figures (May 1987).
   Note: Except where otherwise indicated, "London" refers to what is usually called Greater London.

TABLE 6.3

Japan and Tokyo: Employment Changes by Industry, 1975-
1985

	% Change	
	---------------	---------
	Tokyo	Japan
All industries	3	10
Agriculture, forestry, and fishing	-33	-26
Energy and water	-40	--
Manufacturing	-12	4
Construction	1	12
Transportation and communication	5	5
Wholesale and retail	6	18
Finance and insurance	-5	26
Real estate	2	30
Public services	-20	3
Services	27	36

Sources: Tokyo Metropolitan Gov't, *Plain Talk About
Tokyo,* 2nd ed. (1984.); *Japan Statistical Yearbook,* 1986.

York City have lost a considerable number of insurance jobs over this
period, while they have gained jobs in finance. Thus, the difference between the share of insurance jobs in the city and the nation is much
smaller and, in London, increasingly so. Additionally, more disaggregated data on the producer services would reveal much higher differences for some of these industries in major cities compared with the nation. I will return to both points later in this chapter. (For a brief
description of the areas covered by the data and of how Tokyo is specified, see Appendices B and C.)

A third observation is that a considerable number of producer services
industries have very small employment shares, but together make a significant difference in the employment distribution of these cities. Besides
the examples discussed above, there are management consulting, advertising, engineering, and other highly specialized services. The evidence
for New York City and London shows that together the producer services, which include the FIRE group, accounted for 35.1% of all private
sector workers in New York City in 1985, up from 29.8% in 1977, and for
about 33% in London in 1984, up from 28% in 1971 (see Table 6.5). In
contrast, producer services accounted for 18.3% of all private sector
workers in the United States in 1985 and 16.6% of all private sector workers in the United Kingdom in 1984—about half the share such services
represented in New York and London, respectively. There are no comparative data available for Tokyo.

TABLE 6.4

Great Britain and London, United States and New York, Japan and Tokyo: Employment Share of
Selected Producer Services, 1970s and 1980s (percent)

	Producer Services as % of Employment				City's Total Employment
	Banking and Finance[a]	Insurance[b]	Real Estate[c]	Business Services[d]	as % of Total National Employment
1970					
London (1971)	4.0	2.6	0.7	6.3	16.0
New York (1970)	7.3	3.2	3.0	6.3	5.9
Tokyo (1975)	4.5[e]		1.9	--	11.0
Great Britain (1971)	1.6	1.2	0.4	2.9	--
United States (1970)	2.9	2.2	1.2	2.9	--
Japan (1975)	2.6[e]		0.7	--	--
1980/1981					
London (1981)	4.5	1.9	0.6	8.1	15.7
New York (1981)	10.2	3.4	3.0	8.3	3.9
Tokyo (1980)	4.2[e]		1.8	--	10.2
Great Britain (1981)	2.1	1.1	0.3	4.3	--
United States (1981)	3.4	2.3	1.3	4.1	--
Japan (1980)	2.8[e]		0.7	--	--
1984/1985					
London (1984)	4.8	1.7	1.0	10.2	16.6
New York (1985)	10.7	3.2	3.1	9.4	3.7
Tokyo (1985)	4.2[e]		1.9	--	10.2
Great Britain (1984)	2.4	1.1	0.6	5.0	--
United States (1985)	3.5	2.2	1.4	5.3	--
Japan (1985)	3.0[e]		0.8	--	--

Sources: Census 1971, England and Wales; Census 1981, England and Wales; Census of
Employment, 1984, (U.K.); Employment Gazette, (U.K.) 95, no. 10 historical supp. no. 2, (Jan. 1987);
County Business Patterns, issues for United States and New York, 1970, 1981, 1985, 1987; Japan
Statistical Yearbook, 1986.

[a] Covers SIC 60, 61, 62, 67 in the United States; SIC 814 and 815 in the United Kingdom; SIC J
and 67 (insurance) in Japan (see Appendix A).

[b] Covers SIC 63 and 64 in the United States; SIC 82 in the United Kingdom; SIC 67 in Japan.

[c] Covers SIC 65 and 66 in the United States; SIC 834 in the United Kingdom; SIC K in Japan.

[d] Covers SIC 73 in the United States; SIC 84 and 85 in the United Kingdom; SIC 839 in Japan.

[e] Combined category for Tokyo and Japan is finance and insurance.

Similarly, while the actual share of national employment is small, the
locational patterns of producer services employment give considerable
weight to these cities in the space economy of such services. Thus, in
1985 New York City accounted for 7.2% of national employment in producer services, compared with 3.7% of all U.S. employment. London has
an extremely high degree of concentration. These differences become

TABLE 6.5

New York and London: Share of Producer Services in
Employment, 1970s and 1980s

	% of Total City Employment	% of National Employment in Producer Services	% of Total National Employment
New York			
1977	29.8	8.3	4.2
1981	32.9	7.8	3.9
1985	35.1	7.2	3.7
1987	37.7	7.6	3.7
London			
1971	28.0	40.3	16.0
1981	31.0	34.1	15.7
1984	32.8	32.6	16.6

Sources: County Business Patterns, issues for United
States and New York, 1977, 1981, 1985, and 1987; Census of
Employment, (U.K.), issues for 1971 and 1981; Employment
Gazette, (U.K.) 95, no. 10, historical supp. no. 2 (Jan.1987).

even more evident if location quotients are used. Employment-based
quotients, with the overall share of producer services in national employment as the base, show a quotient of 1.9 for producer services in New
York City from 1977 to 1985, rising to 2.07 in 1987, and of 2.04 for London in 1971, down to 1.96 in 1984 (see Table 6.6). Comparing a particular
industry such as real estate, for which there is separate information on
Tokyo, there is a similarly high quotient (see Table 6.7). It was 2.42 in
New York City in 1977 and 2.2 in 1985; London's quotient was 2 in 1971
and declined to 1.75 in 1984; and Tokyo's declined from 2.44 to 2.28.
Slight declines in quotients are also evident in other individual producer
services, but these declines have not made a major dent in the overrepresentation of many of these industries in New York, London, and Tokyo, given the absolute growth of such services in these cities.

A fourth observation concerns the possibility of differences in the kinds
of producer service industries that are growing in the more central locations of a metropolitan area compared with the overall region. An important question concerning the location of producer services is their relation to and place in local labor markets. Again, when we examine
national-level data for all three countries, we see pronounced concentration and overrepresentation in key locations. What is the actual distribution within these key locations? The locational concentration of producer services in certain regions can conceivably assume more than one
pattern. It can be geographically concentrated or dispersed within such
a region. Furthermore, there may or may not be firm decentralization

TABLE 6.6

New York and London: Producer Services Location
Quotients, 1970s and 1980s

	Location Quotient
New York	
1977	1.98
1981	1.99
1985	1.92
London	
1971	2.04
1981	1.85
1984	1.96

Sources: County Business Patterns, issues for New York,
1977, 1981, and 1985; J. Howells and A. E. Green, "Location,
Technology, and Industrial Organisation in U.K. Services,"
Progress in Planning 26 (1986): pt. 2; *Census of Employment, 1984* (U.K.); *Employment Gazette,* (U.K.) 95, no. 2,
historical supp. no. 2; (Jan. 1987).
Note: Computed with national quotient as unity.

TABLE 6.7

New York, London, and Tokyo: Location Quotients for Real
Estate, 1970s and 1980s

	1970s	*1981*	*1984/1985*
New York	2.42 (1977)	2.22	2.20 (1985)
Tokyo	2.44 (1977)	2.33	2.28 (1985)
London	2.00 (1971)	1.59	1.75 (1984)

Sources: County Business Patterns, issues for New York,
1977, 1981, and 1985; *Japan Statistical Yearbook, 1977,*
1981, and 1985; *Census of Employment, 1984* (U.K.); *Employment Gazette,* (U.K.) 95, no. 2, historical supp. no. 2;
(Jan. 1987). *Census 1971, England and Wales; Census 1981,
England and Wales.*

along with territorial dispersal within regions of high concentration. Finally, in regions of high concentration with geographically dispersed producer services, there may or may not be considerable divergence among
the various locations within such a region in terms of the composition of
its producer services sector.

The English case is probably the most extreme instance of high concentration of national producer services employment in one region, significant territorial dispersal within that region, and indications of different industry composition in the central and peripheral locations of that

region. The Southeast accounts for 40% of national employment in producer services. But over the last two decades the highest growth rates have occurred in the more peripheral areas of the Southeast.[3] An examination of the different areas within the Southeast region and between the Southeast and its immediately adjacent regions reveals differences over time. When we disaggregate the growth of this whole southern area by year, it is evident that much of the growth in the immediately adjacent regions had its highest rates throughout the 1970s and that after 1978 the Southeast had relative growth compared with relative decline in adjacent areas. One possibility is that growth in the adjacent region is high-tech based, while growth in the Southeast is mostly related to the new financial and producer services complex that took off in the late 1970s. In that case we would be dealing with different economic complexes, each with a distinct space economy.

In the case of New York City, use of a broader regional and time frame shows that Manhattan already had a disproportionate concentration of FIRE jobs thirty years ago (see Table 6.8). Using the industrial distribution of the New York Metropolitan Region as the base (100), Hoover and Vernon (1962) calculated Manhattan's "specialization index" (location quotient) for FIRE in the New York Metropolitan Region at 169 in 1956 (100 being the regional norm). Harris (1988) shows that by 1980 it had increased to 195, an uncommonly high quotient. The rest of the core, consisting largely of the rest of New York City and one New Jersey county, suffered declines in the finance quotient. A second pronounced trend that emerges from such a broader perspective is the decline in manufacturing in the rest of the core, with the specialization index reduced from 121 in 1956 to 86 in 1980. If we juxtapose those figures with those on population and employment (see Table 6.9) it becomes evident that the rest of the core suffered severe losses in both over the last 30 years. In 1956 this area had 41.8% of the region's population and 23.6% of its jobs; by 1985 these shares had fallen to 32.4% and 16.2% (Harris 1988). The figures on population and employment show that, as in London, Manhattan's overall share of the region's jobs declined significantly, from 40.6% in 1956 to 27.2% in 1985. This decline further underlines the disproportionate concentration of FIRE and business services in Manhattan, a subject I return to in later sections. Clearly, the highest increases in the share of population and employment were in the outer ring. As in the case of London and the Southeast, an important question concerns regional integration: Are the components of that growth articulated with

---

[3] In contrast there were declines in the northwestern regions and below-average growth rates in the rest of the North. Furthermore, most of the employment growth in producer services in the adjacent regions (East Anglia, Southwest, and East Midlands) was in full-time jobs, which accounted for 71 to 82%. The declines in the northern regions in producer services jobs are associated with the decline of the manufacturing base in those regions.

TABLE 6.8

New York: Industrial Specialization in the New York Metropolitan Region (NYMR), 1956 and 1980

	% of Total NYMR Employment	Specialization Index Distribution (NYMR=100)			
		Manhattan	Rest of N.Y.C. Core	Inner Ring	Outer Ring
1956					
Manufacturing	28.2	69	121	117	128
Wholesale	6.8	145	83	68	45
Finance	4.8	169	46	68	35
1980					
Manufacturing	21.5	78	86	111	122
Transport	9.1	102	158	81	71
Wholesale	5.1	110	94	112	78
Retail	14.1	70	101	114	113
Finance	9.5	195	57	75	62
Business services	5.9	144	66	95	85
Personal services	2.6	108	104	200	85
Professional services	22.1	87	118	97	102
Public administration	4.8	104	117	88	91

Sources: Harris 1988, calculated from Hoover and Vernon 1962: 248; U.S. Census, Place of Work (1984).

other economic sectors in the region and, more specifically, with the major growth sectors in Manhattan over the last decade?

A fifth observation is that the central business and finance districts in each of these cities contains an extremely high concentration of these industries (see Table 6.10). Identification of a central business and finance district in each of these three cities poses problems in terms of definition and geographic breakdowns of the available evidence. A reasonable approximation is to use Manhattan for New York City, the City for London, and the three central business district wards (Chiyoda, Chuo, Minato) in addition to Shinjuku, a new major business center, for Tokyo. London's City is a far smaller geographic area than the other two. Manhattan shows the highest concentration for finance, insurance, and real estate employment, as well as for business services, accounting for about 90% of all FIRE employment and for 85% of business services in New York City in 1985 and 1987. This represents an increase in concentration of FIRE, from about 86% in 1970 and 1977. Business services, on the other hand, reduced their concentration in Manhattan slightly, from 88% in 1970. But both increased their share of Manhattan employment from 17.8% in 1970 and 23.5% in 1985 to 25.6% in 1987 in the case of FIRE, and from 8.4% to 12.7% in the case of business services.

There was a decline in the concentration of total London FIRE em-

TABLE 6.9

Population and Employment Distribution in the New York Metropolitan Region, 1956-1985

	% of Total NYMR Population			% of Total NYMR Employment		
	1956	1975	1985	1956	1975	1985
Manhattan	11.8	8.0	8.1	40.6	29.1	27.2
Rest of N.Y.C. core	41.8	32.1	32.4	23.6	19.0	16.2
Inner ring	29.7	28.8	29.5	23.5	27.9	27.9
Outer ring	16.7	31.1	31.0	12.3	24.0	28.7
Total NYMR ('000s)	(15,375)	(18,394)	(18,304)	(6,700)	(7,216)	(8,392)

Sources: Harris 1988, calculated from New York Metropolitan Transportation Council, Metromonitor (1986); Hoover and Vernon 1962: 6.

Note: The NYMR data for 1975 and 1985 are for a Tri-County Region that includes Fairfield County and other parts of Connecticut.

ployment in the City of London, from about 49% in 1971 to 45% in 1981. There was also a decline in the share of the City's work force employed in this sector, from 41% to 38%. This may be linked to the relatively greater expansion of related sectors as well as the spread of FIRE activities into the newly developed Docklands and other adjacent areas. The relative decline in the share of FIRE in the City is also partly attributable to the relocation of much insurance activity, a trend also evident in New York City. Business services have increased their concentration in the City from 11% in 1971 to 20% in 1981 and in the City's work force from 3.4% to 20%.

In the case of Tokyo, the available evidence is less complete at this time. While the central business district is officially defined by three wards, Chiyoda, Chuo, and Minato, the fourth added here, Shinjuku, is widely recognized as a new major business district (see Appendix B). In 1980, these four wards accounted for over 49% of all FIRE employment in Tokyo. But FIRE accounted for only 10% of total employment in these four wards, an indication of the degree to which most tertiary activities in the whole of Tokyo are concentrated in this area. The evidence does not allow for a separate analysis of business services at the ward level. If we exclude wholesale and retail services, 33% of all Tokyo's services are concentrated in the area, and these account for 22% of all employment in these four wards.

It is evident that the producer services as a whole have grown rapidly over the last decade and that they have grown more rapidly in the countries as a whole than in these cities. But these three cities continue to account for a disproportionate share of national and regional producer

TABLE 6.10

Manhattan, the City of London, and Tokyo's Central Business District (CBD): Share of Selected Industries, 1970s and 1980s (percent)

Manhattan	FIRE		Business Services	
	% of Total FIRE Jobs in New York City	% of Total Jobs in Manhattan	% of Total Business Service Jobs in New York City	% of Total Jobs in Manhattan
1970	86.0	17.8	88.1	8.4
1977	86.7	21.2	86.8	9.5
1981	88.7	22.2	86.5	10.7
1985	89.8	23.5	85.3	12.7
1987	90.4	25.6	85.2	12.7

The City of London	FIRE		Business Services	
	% of Total FIRE Jobs in London	% of Total Jobs in City of London	% of Total Business Service Jobs in London	% of Total Jobs in City of London
1971	48.7	41.2	11.2	3.4
1981	44.8	37.6	20.2	19.6

Tokyo CBD	FIRE		Business Services	
	% of Total FIRE Jobs in Tokyo	% of Total Jobs in Tokyo CBD	% of Total Business Service Jobs in Tokyo	% of Total Jobs in Tokyo CBD
1980	49.4	9.9	33.0	21.8

Sources: County Business Patterns, issues for New York, 1970, 1977, 1981, 1985, and 1987; Census 1971, England and Wales; Census 1981, England and Wales; Tokyo Metropolitan Gov't, Survey of Tokyo Day-time Population, (1983).

Note: Tokyo's CBD includes Chiyoda-ku, Chuo-ku, Minato-ku, and Shinjuku-ku.

services employment; their central business districts have especially high concentrations of these industries; and a growing share of the labor force in these cities is employed in such industries, particularly in business services. Two important questions emerging from these trends concern the place of other major cities in the space economy of the producer services, and the specific composition of these services in different types of cities. This is the subject we turn to next.

New Elements in the Urban Hierarchy

There are significant differences in the urban systems of these three countries. London has the highest degree of concentration, with 16% of national employment (see Table 6.11). Tokyo follows with 10% of national employment (see Table 6.12). In the United States, there are several large cities, and they account for a far smaller proportion of national employment: 3.7% in New York City, 4% in Los Angeles (county), and 2.6% in Chicago (see Table 6.13). Furthermore the level of discontinuity between the largest and subsequent cities also varies considerably in the United Kingdom and Japan (see Tables 6.11 and 6.12). In the United Kingdom, the next largest cities are far behind London in national employment share: Birmingham with 2.3%, Glasgow with 1.8%, Manchester with 1.3%, Edinburgh with 1.1%, and Liverpool with 1%. In Japan, the next largest cities have about half Tokyo's share of national employment: 5.6% in Nagoya and its prefecture and 6.9% in Osaka and its prefecture.

One question that arises is to what extent the devastation of manufacturing in the United Kingdom may have affected the urban system by

TABLE 6.11

United Kingdom: National Employment Share of Major Cities, 1971-1984 (percent)

	1971	*1981*	*1984*
London	16.01	15.71	16.61
City of London	1.39	1.40	1.50
Birmingham	2.14	2.21	2.27
Manchester	1.34	1.30	1.30
Liverpool	1.31	1.11	1.05
Glasgow	--	1.65	1.67
Edinburgh	--	1.04	1.11
Total U.K. employment (N)	(23,732,610)	(22,619,190)	(20,845,900)

Sources: Census 1971, England and Wales; Census 1981, England and Wales; Employment Census, 1984 (U.K.).

TABLE 6.12

Japan: National Employment Share of Major Cities, 1975-1985 (percent)

	1975	*1980*	*1985*
Tokyo	10.98	10.24	10.17
CBD	--	4.54	--
Nagoya (Aichi Prefecture)	5.06	5.47	5.58
Osaka (Osaka Prefecture)	7.47	6.84	6.86
Total Japan employment (N)	(52,973,000)	(55,749,000)	(58,113,000)

Sources: Japan Statistical Yearbook, 1977, 1982, and 1986.

TABLE 6.13

United States: National Employment Share of Major Cities, 1977-1987 (percent)

	1977	1981	1985	1987
New York	4.2	3.9	3.7	3.7
Manhattan	2.7	2.6	2.6	2.4
Los Angeles (L.A. County)	4.1	4.2	4.1	4.1
Chicago (Cook County)	3.4	3.0	2.7	2.6
Houston (Harris County)	1.4	1.7	1.5	1.4
Detroit (Wayne County)	1.2	1.0	0.9	0.9
Boston (Suffolk County)	0.6	0.6	0.6	0.6
Total U.S. employment (N)	(64,975,580)	(74,850,402)	(81,119,257)	(85,483,804)

Sources: County Business Patterns, issues for United States, New York, Illinois, Massachusetts, Michigan, Texas, and California, 1977, 1981, 1985, and 1987.
Note: Only private sector employment is included.

reducing the weight of cities such as Birmingham and Manchester. On the other hand, the weight of Osaka and Nagoya in Japan still reflects the phase of high industrial output, even though key sectors in basic industry are shrinking and there is a growing trend toward locating assembly plants offshore.[4] The dismantling of what were once basic industrial sectors is just beginning in Japan, whereas in the United Kingdom and the United States it reached a peak in the 1970s. The discontinuity in the United Kingdom between London and the next largest cities is further accentuated by the acute locational concentration in London of the leading growth sectors in the current period, a far higher level of concentration than is the case with New York City and Tokyo.

A third issue that arises is that of nonproduction employment in manufacturing. To what extent are many of the producer services jobs in industrial areas, such as Manchester, Nagoya, or Detroit, primarily linked to manufacturing, and quite distinct from the producer services jobs concentrated in cities such as New York, London, and Tokyo? Furthermore,

[4] By 1960, Tokyo, Osaka, and Nagoya were major international cities. At the end of the nineteenth century, these three cities had become key locations for capital, labor, and economic growth (Ishizuka 1980) and from then on were the location for large-scale development. The development of heavy industry and the chemical industry has been concentrated in Tokyo Bay, Osaka Bay, and Ise Bay. These three cities also concentrated machinery, computers, and office equipment production. Any of the benefits of export-led development were also concentrated in this area, since they contained the dominant export sectors (steel, autos, consumer electronics production). Hattori et al. (1980) saw the megalopolis constituted by these three cities as the key for centralization and operation on an international scale.

are manufacturing-linked producer services in the latter three cities different from those in industrial cities?

In order to address some of these issues and to understand the place of New York, London, and Tokyo in their national economies, there follows a detailed examination of the locational patterns of producer services across major cities.

In the United Kingdom, the location quotients for producer services generally, and business services in particular, indicate considerable unevenness. The most comprehensive study is by Marshall et al. (1986) on which much of the following discussion is based. The London area quotient for all services is 1.19; it rises to 1.61 for producer services and to 1.85 for office-based producer services. The next-largest quotient is for business services in smaller cities in the London metropolitan area, at 1.21. There are a few location quotients around 1, but most others for cities and metropolitan areas are considerably under 1, pointing to the extreme concentration in London. Using the classification developed by Peter Wood in Marshall et al. (1986) and 1981 census data yields a total of 4.1 million jobs in producer services in Great Britain, of which 1.219 million were in London and another 329,000 were in the greater metropolitan area. The London region accounted for a third of all producer services jobs. The disaggregated data indicate that London accounted for 34% of nonproduction employment in manufacturing, and almost 43% of producer services industry employment. The next largest concentration of producer services jobs was 10% in the Northwest.

The distinctiveness of the London metropolitan region can be seen in the fact that the other metropolitan areas in Great Britain experienced relative and absolute declines in producer services jobs, with an absolute loss of 38,000 jobs (Marshall et al. 1986: 85). On the basis of location quotients, the whole Southeast had 461,700 more producer services jobs than expected given its share of national employment. On the other hand, all other regions in Great Britain had fewer producer services jobs than expected. The most pronounced underrepresentation was in the East and the West Midlands. All nonmetropolitan areas had location quotients below 1. Furthermore, cities and towns in greater metropolitan areas other than London continued to be underrepresented in producer services employment. This indicates that the rapid growth of producer services for the nation as a whole has not overcome the significant overrepresentation in London, a pattern also evident in the United States and Japan.

Most of the divergence between the Southeast and the rest of the country is attributable to the producer services industries rather than nonproduction employment in manufacturing. While 97% of the excess of producer services jobs in the Southeast is accounted for by the pro-

ducer services industries, regions with higher concentrations of manufacturing also have relatively higher concentrations of nonproduction
employment in manufacturing. These regions also have an underrepresentation of producer services industry employment. However, at the same time, it is also worth noting that Marshall et al. (1986)
found that the Southeast, a major area for producer services industries,
had a higher concentration of nonproduction manufacturing workers per
1,000 workers in manufacturing than did any other region of the country.
Part of this is attributable to the heavy incidence of small, research and
development oriented firms in the area (Hall et al. 1987).[5] On the other
hand, areas with major concentrations of manufacturing have a lower incidence than would be expected given their manufacturing employment
(Marshall et al. 1986). Thus 41% of nonproduction employment is concentrated in the greater metropolitan London area, as well as 47% of
producer services industries employment. But the share that nonproduction employment in manufacturing represents of all producer services
employment in this area is 18%, the lowest in the country.[6] One question
raised by this difference is whether the devastating losses in manufacturing employment in Britain, which caused severe declines for Britain's
largely manufacturing-based cities other than London, are associated
with this pronounced underrepresentation. And to what extent is it a result of spatial reorganization in manufacturing, with the relocation of routine office work to small, low-cost urban areas, and of central functions to
London?

London has significantly higher values for its location quotients than
does the Southeast as a whole. This is partly because of the urbanization
effect: population size resulting in greater agglomeration and the influence of centrality on all services industries, especially those with considerable intermediate inputs (insurance, banking, finance).[7] London's location quotient in insurance, banking, finance, and business services was
over 2.00 both in 1971 and in 1981, the highest single value for any industry group, for all years and regions.[8] All regions, except for the South-

[5] Other evidence suggests that a good number of business services firms are small, low-
cost operations, such as cleaning services, and hence will prefer to locate in lower-cost areas
of the city.

[6] This would suggest that, given difficulties in obtaining measures of nonproduction employment in manufacturing, considering only the producer services industry may be adequate for an examination of producer service jobs in major cities.

[7] Greater London, similarly, has lower employment-based quotients than population-
based quotients, and here commuting is clearly a significant factor. Daniels (1985) argues
that the commuting effect should not be exaggerated since it is likely that differences in
levels of unemployment, activity rates for men and women, and the match between skills
available and those in demand also have some effect.

[8] In the population-based quotients, the levels of concentration in this industry group are

east, had quotients significantly below 1.00, hovering around 0.70 in this industry group. London parallels the case of large cities in the United States, which have extremely high location quotients for these industries.

Daniels (1985) calculated the population-based location quotients for six producer services industries in the nine economic planning regions in England and Wales, of which the Southeast is one. The majority of the quotients for 1971 and 1981 were below 1 (Daniels 1985: 85ff.). This indicates that underrepresentation was the typical pattern. The exception was the Southeast, where he found overrepresentation in both 1971 and 1981. He also found differences among the various industries in their degree of overrepresentation in the region. Thus, in 1981, insurance, banking, finance, and business services ranged from a quotient of 1.69 in the Southeast to 0.49 in Wales;[9] the professional services quotient ranged from 1.41 in the Southeast to 0.80 in the West Midlands, and the transport and communications quotient ranged from 1.39 in the Southeast to 0.68 in the West Midlands.[10] Other industries, such as the distributive trades, not unexpectedly, displayed far less variation among regions. They also reflected a stronger relationship with the distribution of the population.

These facts bring to the fore the question about London's role in promoting growth in the more peripheral areas of the metropolitan region and the Southeast in general. While 31% of jobs in 1981 in London were in producer services, an increase over the 1971 level of 28%, the highest growth rates were in the manufacturing towns in the Southeast and the East, with increases of over 50% from 1971 to 1981. Furthermore, in the cities and towns of the London metropolitan area, there were increases of about 40%, representing an increase of 96,000 producer services jobs from 1971 to 1981. But the magnitude of London's concentration of producer services jobs is indicated by the fact that the 40% increase in cities

---

even more pronounced, reaching 2.68 in 1971 and 2.86 in 1981. The values of the other regions rise only a little, if at all, when population-based quotients are used for this industry group.

[9] The second single highest value is that of transport and communication, with Greater London showing a population-based quotient of 2.12 in 1981, the same as in 1971, and an employment-based quotient of 1.58. The Southeast region had a quotient of 1.24 in 1971 and of 1.39 in 1981. For both the finance group and the transport and communication one, there is not much growth from 1971 to 1981 in Greater London's population- or employment-based quotient. The same can be seen for the Southeast region. Furthermore, employment-based quotients for the remaining industry groups show declines in Greater London, along with increases in population-based quotients.

[10] Employment-based location quotients show a narrower range for interregional differences. The Southeast still has values exceeding 1.00 for all service industries, but they are systematically lower than the population-based quotients. This difference may be partly attributable to commuting from other regions.

and towns outside London made for a total increase of only 6.8% for the region when we include London. To what extent are we dealing with a territorial complex, a geographically dispersed array of sites in the Southeast held together by the presence of London and its dynamic growth in these industries? It is also important to understand the composition of the small manufacturing towns of the South and the Southeast, which, at 50%, had one of the highest growth rates in producer services for this period.[11] Are these towns linked to the development of a high-tech manufacturing base, which in fact consists largely of various types of specialized service activities (Hall et al. 1987), but represents a very different economic sector from others in the Southeast in terms of market orientation and articulation with the London economy?

Case studies on the advertising, accounting, marketing, market research, computer service, and management consulting industries in Great Britain show them to be much smaller and more locationally concentrated than banking (see Wood 1984). This is particularly due to the high consumer market share in banking and hence locational patterns that follow population distribution. The degree of concentration varies among these industries. They are all overrepresented in the Southeast. Market-oriented services, such as marketing and market research, are most concentrated, with 84% of national offices in the Southeast, and more than 50% of their total offices in Greater London. Practically all provincial regions have underrepresentation of all these service industries except for accounting, also an industry with a strong consumer market, and, to a lesser extent, management consulting. Within these regions, there is a clear pattern of concentration in the major urban centers. Thus Birmingham accounts for 66% of advertising agents and 75% of management consulting firms in the West Midlands region; Manchester and Liverpool account for almost 87% of advertising agents and 54% of management consulting firms in the Northwest; and Glasgow and Ed-

[11] These patterns have been confirmed in a study using more disaggregated data both at the industry level and for smaller regions. Marquand (1979) examined the proportion of service employment in 126 metropolitan economic labor areas in Britain from 1971 to 1975 to identify differences in the distribution of producer, consumer, private, and public services. Within the producer services, the largest differential between Greater London and the rest of the country was in advertising and market research, with quotients of 4.44 and 4.35 for central offices. The Southeast while higher than the rest of Britain is significantly lower than Greater London, with quotients of 2.27 and 2.24, respectively. Other regions, such as the Southwest, had quotients as low as 0.31. The values for banking and insurance were lower; since these industries also contain consumer sectors, one would expect a relatively more even distribution. These data confirm and strengthen the overall pattern described earlier, where Greater London emerges with a disproportionate concentration in producer services. The overall picture is one of imbalance in the distribution of service industries.

inburgh account for 85.5% of advertising and 64% of management consulting in Scotland.

The evidence also suggests that the composition of the industries in the Southeast differs from that in the rest of the country. Thus, in computer services, the Southeast has a greater concentration of software and consulting, while the less central regions have a greater concentration of data processing. Furthermore, marketing services in the less central regions are more likely to consist of selling, distribution, and conference organization, while in the southeast there is a heavier incidence of research and consulting.

The assumption that business service industries are typically characterized by small, independent, single-site firms was examined by Marshall et al. (1986) through a comparison of the corporate status of offices in different regions of Great Britain.[12] The offices were classified as single-site firms, main offices of multisite firms, or subordinate offices of multisite firms. The evidence, limited and inadequate as it is, suggests that there are differences between the Southeast and other regions of Great Britain in the organizational form of firms. Single-site firms dominate in both the Southeast and the other regions, but they do so much more in the former—79% of management consultants and 88% of advertising offices are single-site firms in the Southeast, compared with 49% and 68%, respectively, in the provinces. Furthermore, provincial areas have a larger percentage of subordinate offices of multisite firms in all services, while the Southeast has more main offices. This is especially the case in management consulting, with 13% of offices in the Southeast being main offices, while in the other regions, 3% are main offices and 48% are subordinate offices. In the provincial areas, there is a strong tendency for single-site firms to be located outside main urban centers and for branch offices to be located inside such centers. This would suggest, perhaps, that small, independent firms will find a market in the more peripheral areas where large, multisite firms would not find it sufficiently profitable to operate. In the main provincial centers, on the other hand, large, multisite firms would have competitive superiority over small, independent firms.

We can see a corporate structure with multiple offices involving many different regions and with top headquarters likely to be in London. A study of business services in Birmingham, Leeds, and Manchester found that 33.4% of offices and over half of employment were in firms that were directly or indirectly linked with headquarter offices outside the local

[12] Information on these various industries comes from case studies, service employment statistics (which do not cover all service industries separately), and information provided by professional associations (see Marshall et al. 1986: 85, app. 2). Thus the results are not exhaustive.

economic planning region, mostly in Greater London (Marshall 1982). The same study also found that national service firms had expanded more rapidly during the decade of the 1970s than had local firms (Marshall 1982). What we are seeing is an expansion of the corporate service sector in provincial areas of Great Britain.

Using the Census of Employment data set of the Manpower Services Commission's National On-Line Manpower Information System (NOMIS), Marshall et al. (1986) constructed a hierarchy of urban-centered functional regions. The areas used were the 280 CURDS Local Labor Market Areas (LLMAs), which were defined through extensive analysis of the 1971 population, employment, and commuting data (Coombes et al. 1982). The London LLMA is at the top followed by urban areas in the London Metropolitan region and the rest of the country. This analysis produced two interesting findings. One is the greater disparity among these labor market areas in the distribution of producer services than in the distribution of services in general, which tend to have a location quotient of 1. The other is the absence of a hierarchy in the levels of concentration of producer services.

In sum, London's overrepresentation continued, within both the country and its metropolitan area. The representation of producer services in towns and cities of London's greater metropolitan area was brought above the national level in most cases. This indicates that this broader region accounts for some of the rapid national growth in producer services. However, while the growth rate in these was markedly higher than in London for the 1971–1981 period, in absolute numbers London's dominance is overwhelming. It is worth noting again that the relative dispersal within the London metropolitan area was much more pronounced in the early 1970s, and that from 1978 onward there was a relative decline in the growth rates outside London's metropolitan area and a relative increase in London's growth rate. There is a suggestion in this evidence that the Southeast region, which experienced significant growth rates in producer services in its various territorial components—surrounding towns and cities, nonmetropolitan areas, and South and Southeast manufacturing towns—owes its growth to the presence of a larger economic complex dominated by London. If this is the case, it is in the form of a complex economic subsystem, one with distinct components: high-tech and local producer services in the region and internationally marketed producer services in London. This would explain why the other regions and intraregional nodes have not experienced growth but, on the contrary, have tended to experience declines in producer services. Those regions have a very different economic base and have central nodes, the once-powerful manufacturing centers, in severe decline.

There is, then, a fundamental discontinuity between London and the

rest of the country, with pronounced overrepresentation in the former
and pronounced underrepresentation at other levels of the urban hierarchy, except for some smaller cities in the London metropolitan area. A
narrower definition of the producer services restricted to office-based
services, such as insurance, financial services, banking, and so on, yields
an even stronger concentration at the top and underrepresentation in the
subsequent levels.

The degree of concentration represented by London is significantly
higher than what we find in the United States or even Japan. In the
United States there is considerable dispersion in the distribution of producer services among a number of major urban centers, especially New
York, Los Angeles, and Chicago (see Table 6.14). There is clearly overrepresentation of these industries in all major cities. While there may
have been slight declines over the last decade in some of these industries, overall the sharpest concentration is still in New York City. Chicago
and Los Angeles also have considerable overrepresentation, but they are
a far second behind New York City. In 1977 New York City had 4.2% of
national employment, but 8.3% of all employment in producer services,
a share that declined to 7.2% in 1985 and was 7.6% in 1987. Chicago's
share similarly declined, from 4.2% in 1977 to 3.5% in 1985 and in 1987.
Detroit, Boston, and Houston, on the other hand, kept their shares of,
respectively, 1%, 1.2%, and around 1.8% virtually constant over the period from 1977 to 1987. And so did Los Angeles, with its share of 4.9%.
However, the total U.S. employment share of New York City has fallen
considerably, from 6% in 1970 to 3.7% in 1985 and in 1987.

When we disaggregate the information on growth rates and employment shares for various producer services industries, the overall patterns
tend to remain, with a few major exceptions, but the levels of overrepre-

TABLE 6.14
United States: National Employment Share of Major Cities in Producer Services, 1977-1987 (percent)

	1977	1981	1985	1987
New York	8.3	7.8	7.2	7.6
Los Angeles (L.A. County)	4.6	4.9	4.6	4.9
Chicago (Cook County)	4.2	3.8	3.5	3.5
Houston (Harris County)	1.7	2.0	1.8	1.8
Detroit (Wayne County)	1.0	0.9	0.8	0.9
Boston (Suffolk County)	1.2	1.2	1.2	1.2
Total U.S. producer services employment (N)	(9,804,104)	(12,328,104)	(14,803,684)	(15,552,713)

Sources: Same as in Table 6.13

sentation and growth tend to vary considerably among industries (see Table 6.15). Thus New York City's concentration in 1985 remained basically undiminished, but it was significantly higher in banking, at over 11%, and in legal services, at 8.6%, than in insurance, at 5.4%, or in business services, at 6.6%. On the other hand, Boston and Chicago generally had a greater share of insurance and legal services than of the other major producer services listed in Table 6.15 or of national employment in producer services. Similarly, Houston's highest shares were for the real estate industry and business services, clearly a function of the real estate boom of the late 1970s and early 1980s, even though it was already declining and creating a series of highly publicized bankruptcies. On the other hand, Houston's share of banking was lower even in 1981 than its share of all producer services, pointing in yet another way to the fact that major business components of such industries as banking and insurance have not followed the people and jobs that migrated to the South in the late 1970s and continue to service these regions from the old centers of the North, where they remain concentrated (Cohen 1981).

Organizing this information in terms of location quotients underlines the extent to which major cities have overrepresentation of most of these producer services, but with considerable variation in the degree of overrepresentation and type of industry (see Table 6.16). New York City is the premier banking center in the country, with a location quotient of 2.8 in 1977, 3.0 in 1985, and 3.2 in 1987. Boston is a major insurance center, with location quotients of 3.2 in 1977, 2.7 in 1985, and 2.6 in 1987. It is also, with San Francisco, the city with the second-highest location quotient in banking, going from 1.9 in 1977 up to 2 in 1985 and 2.2 in 1987; San Francisco's quotient stood at 2.5 in 1987, down from 2.8 in 1977. These quotients have magnitudes that clearly are describing a market that extends significantly beyond an average overrepresentation and reveals a highly specialized spatial organization of an industry. The figures for Los Angeles are underestimates of the extent of concentration because they cover the whole county, which corresponds far less closely to its main city than do other counties (such as Chicago's Cook County), while leaving out key business districts. The massive industrial complex and active harbor are central to the growth of producer services in the area, but will tend to create a demand for different types of services than those engendered by Los Angeles's expanding financial activities (Cohen and Zysman 1987).

One question we need to ask is whether there are significant differences among these cities in the composition of their industries. We need to know whether Boston is as specialized in international banking and finance as New York and Los Angeles and, if so, whether it is the same type of international finance. Secondly, the absolute size of the banking

TABLE 6.15

United States: National Employment Share of Major Cities in Selected Producer Services, 1977-1987

	Banking and Finance[a]	Insurance[b]	Real Estate[c]	Business Services[d]	Legal Services[e]
	City's Share (%)				
New York					
1977	11.7	6.5	10.1	8.4	9.4
1981	11.7	5.9	8.7	7.9	8.6
1985	11.3	5.4	8.2	6.6	8.6
1987	11.8	4.8	7.5	6.2	8.2
Los Angeles (L.A. County)					
1977	4.5	4.0	4.5	6.0	5.1
1981	4.9	3.9	5.6	6.0	5.5
1985	4.5	3.6	4.9	5.3	5.5
1987	4.3	3.5	4.9	5.1	5.6
Chicago (Cook County)					
1977	4.1	5.2	4.2	4.7	4.0
1981	4.2	4.5	3.8	4.0	4.0
1985	3.8	4.1	3.3	3.8	3.8
1987	3.6	3.9	3.3	3.1	3.8
San Francisco (S.F. County)					
1977	1.9	2.0	1.0	1.3	1.8
1981	1.6	1.2	0.9	1.3	1.9
1985	1.7	1.1	1.2	1.1	2.0
1987	1.5	1.0	1.0	1.0	2.1
Houston (Harris County)					
1977	1.3	1.2	2.1	2.6	1.4
1981	1.6	1.6	2.7	2.9	1.7
1985	1.7	1.2	2.4	2.1	1.7
1987	1.4	1.2	2.4	1.9	1.7
Detroit (Wayne County)					
1977	1.5	0.8	0.6	1.1	1.1
1981	1.0	0.7	0.5	0.8	1.1
1985	0.8	0.8	0.4	0.9	0.9
1987	0.8	0.7	0.3	0.8	0.8
Boston (Suffolk County)					
1977	1.1	1.9	0.7	1.1	4.5
1981	1.1	1.9	0.8	1.1	1.6
1985	1.2	1.6	1.1	0.9	1.7
1987	1.3	1.5	1.1	0.9	1.7
Atlanta (Fulton County)					
1977	0.6	0.9	0.9	1.1	0.9
1981	0.6	1.0	0.9	0.9	0.9
1985	0.6	1.1	0.9	1.0	1.0
1987	0.7	1.0	0.8	0.9	1.0
	National Employment ('000s)				
1977	2,096	1,498	862	2,307	392
1981	2,547	1,703	999	3,093	545
1985	2,862	1,806	1,145	4,272	685
1987	3,216	1,997	1,298	4,494	818

Sources: County Business Patterns, issues for United States, New York, California, Michigan, Illinois, Massachusetts, Georgia and Texas, 1977, 1981, 1985, and 1987.

[a] SIC 60, 61, 62, and 67.
[b] SIC 63 and 64.
[c] Real estate does not include SIC 66 (combined real estate and insurance).
[d] SIC 73.
[e] SIC 81.

TABLE 6.16

United States: Location Quotients of Selected Producer Services Industries, 1977-1987

	Total Employment (N)	Location Quotient				
		Banking and Finance[a]	Insurance[b]	Real Estate[c]	Business Services[d]	Legal Services[e]
New York						
1977	2,714,385	2.81	1.56	2.42	2.01	2.25
1981	2,941,325	2.98	1.43	2.22	2.02	2.19
1985	3,018,000	3.04	1.45	2.20	1.77	2.31
1987	3,122,583	3.23	1.32	2.05	1.70	2.25
Los Angeles (L.A. County)						
1977	2,647,263	1.12	1.00	1.12	1.48	1.26
1981	3,173,460	1.16	0.93	1.33	1.41	1.29
1985	3,345,520	1.09	0.87	1.18	1.28	1.34
1987	3,546,343	1.04	0.84	1.18	1.23	1.35
Chicago (Cook County)						
1977	2,189,598	1.22	1.54	1.25	1.39	1.18
1981	2,247,119	1.40	1.51	1.29	1.33	1.34
1985	2,187,992	1.41	1.51	1.22	1.41	1.42
1987	2,213,434	1.39	1.50	1.27	1.20	1.47
San Francisco (S.F. County)						
1977	490,748	2.79	2.94	1.47	1.91	2.64
1981	508,861	2.35	1.76	1.32	1.91	2.80
1985	520,167	2.66	1.72	1.88	1.72	3.13
1987	503,859	2.54	1.69	1.69	1.69	3.56
Houston (Harris County)						
1977	925,257	0.92	0.84	1.43	1.83	1.01
1981	1,256,765	0.63	0.93	1.20	1.65	0.95
1985	1,215,870	1.13	0.79	1.60	1.38	1.14
1987	1,156,357	1.04	0.89	1.78	1.41	1.26
Detroit (Wayne County)						
1977	797,342	1.22	0.65	0.41	0.89	0.89
1981	738,866	1.02	0.71	0.51	0.82	1.12
1985	698,986	0.93	0.93	0.47	1.05	1.05
1987	730,372	0.14	0.82	0.35	0.94	0.94
Boston (Suffolk County)						
1977	382,546	1.84	3.20	1.25	1.85	2.52
1981	452,189	1.81	3.12	1.25	1.74	2.62
1985	486,045	2.08	2.68	1.75	1.55	2.86
1987	498,241	2.24	2.59	1.90	1.55	2.93
Atlanta (Fulton County)						
1977	348,168	1.11	1.67	1.67	2.04	1.67
1981	394,565	1.13	1.89	1.70	1.70	1.70
1985	459,524	1.05	1.93	1.58	1.75	1.75
1987	487,170	1.23	1.75	1.40	1.58	1.75

Sources: Same as Table 6.15.

[a] SIC 60, 61, 62, and 67.

[b] SIC 63 and 64.

[c] Real estate does not include SIC 66 (combined real estate and insurance).

[d] SIC 73.

[e] SIC 81.

sector is likely to diverge dramatically from that in New York City given
the much smaller employment base of Boston, under half a million, compared with 3 million in New York, 3 million in Los Angeles, and 2.1
million in Chicago. Detroit, once the premier manufacturing city of the
country, has unexpectedly low representation in real estate, an indication
of its acute manufacturing losses. Given that Detroit is still the home of
major car manufacturers, it is worth noting its underrepresentation in
business services, legal services, real estate, and insurance. This situation
is reminiscent of the one in Britain, where what were once the major
manufacturing centers have underrepresentation of producer services.
One question that needs examining is the extent to which Detroit, like
those English cities, has primarily a manufacturing-oriented producer services sector. Finally, San Francisco, Boston, and New York have extremely high concentrations of legal services. To what extent is this associated with the fact that these three cities have the highest quotients
in banking and finance as well? This association is discussed in Chapter
Five.

A 1986 rating of the twenty largest U.S. banking centers classified by
cumulative assets of the nation's top hundred bank holding companies,
valued at U.S. $1,812.7 trillion, has shown that the top five account for
almost 60% of that value. New York alone accounts for almost 34% of the
total, with U.S. $611,701 billion. The top five in 1986 were New York,
San Francisco, Los Angeles, Chicago, and Boston. Dallas and Houston
were among the top ten. The top twenty banking centers accounted for
almost 90% of the total. Compared with 1979, the total had almost doubled, and New York City's share remained basically the same. On the
other hand, Chicago was ranked third in 1979 and Los Angeles fourth,
an order that was reversed in 1986. In terms of the value of cumulated
assets, Los Angeles almost doubled its value from U.S. $54.610 billion to
U.S. $112.134 billion in 1986. Chicago increased slightly, from U.S.
$78.435 billion to U.S. $85.912 billion. San Francisco, ranked second at
both time periods, is clearly an important banking center; though its
share has declined, from 14.3% in 1979 to 9.2% in 1986, the value of its
assets increased slightly, from U.S. $145,120 billion to U.S. $166,279 billion in 1986 (American Banker 1986; Moody's Investors Service 1984).
San Francisco and Chicago are clearly major banking centers, but this
appears to be partly a function of the past importance of these cities
rather than of highly dynamic growth over the last decade as is the case
with Los Angeles. A key question here is, again, the possibility of significant differences in the types of assets and transactions characterizing
these banking centers.

One question is whether New York City firms differ from those of other
major cities, notably Los Angeles and Chicago, in their type and level of

specialization. For example, research by Mollenkopf (1984) has shown that corporate legal firms in New York City have a high level of specialization and comparative advantage in international expertise. Large firms in Los Angeles and Chicago are expanding their markets and have opened branches in New York City and in regional growth centers. The large New York City firms, on the other hand, have set up branches in other major foreign international financial centers as well as in Washington, D.C., this city being a step in the international chain of transactions. The source of growth of these services in New York City has been the rise of investment banking. New York accounts for a third of U.S. corporate legal services employment and up to 50% of its profits. Using the Martindale-Hubbell Law Directory, I calculated the share of law firms in Manhattan, Los Angeles, and Chicago that have foreign branches. Manhattan had 78 such firms, Los Angeles had 39, and Chicago had 11 (see Table 6.17).

The level of specialization in many of the advanced services has increased. For example, large firms now tend to use several corporate specialized legal firms. Similarly, central to the growth of management consulting has been a high level of specialization oriented to institutional investment. Thus, while cities like Boston and Los Angeles used to have management consulting sectors that competed with New York's, the changes in the financial industry have created a specific role for New York City, and one that has carried much of the industry's growth (Mollenkopf 1984). This high level of specialization has brought about a need for and a dependence on a combination of other services and resources. There is a high level of contact among firms at the point of production. These firms can serve widely dispersed regional, national, and international markets, but at the point of production, agglomeration economies are high (Sassen 1988). New York City clearly, then, emerges as a desirable

TABLE 6.17
Law Firms with Foreign Branches: Manhattan, Los Angeles, and Chicago, 1988

	Total Number of Law Firms	Firms with Foreign Branches	
		Number	% of Total
Manhattan	1,147	78	6.8
Los Angeles	765	39	5.1
Chicago	567	11	1.9
Total	2,479	128	

Source: Martindale-Hubbell Law Directory, 1988 ed.

location, notwithstanding higher costs of operation than in alternative cities.

Chicago, the financial, marketing, and insurance center for the once powerful agroindustrial complex in the Midwest, raises interesting questions. To what extent is the composition of Chicago's producer services quite different from that in New York or Los Angeles because it is directly related to servicing of the agroindustrial base of the region, and to what extent has the decline of this complex and the growth of the futures market reoriented Chicago to the world market through finance? New York's producer services sector caters to a world market and is heavily internationalized, servicing or making transactions at the axis between a firm and the international market. Chicago's would seem to be much less so. Chicago's large export-oriented firms typically had high levels of vertical integration and extensive internal production of the necessary services. Now we may be seeing the beginnings of a freestanding producer services industry, fed by the growth of foreign investment in the region and of the futures market.

It is evident that these services have grown in Chicago. The proportion of producer services in Chicago probably follows a more expected pattern, somewhere between the acute overrepresentation of some producer services in New York, Los Angeles, and Boston and the marked underrepresentation in Houston and Detroit. From 1977 to 1988, average annual growth rates in several specialized services compared favorably with those of New York City (see Table 6.18). The difference lies in the prevalence of certain industry groups. Table 6.19 shows that Chicago's employment share in FIRE was 6.1% in 1981 compared with 11.5% in New York City; these figures increased to respectively 7.4% and 12.4% by 1985. One question here is whether part of the difference is explained by Chicago's sharp orientation to the agroindustrial complex now in decline and the differential impact of the global reorganization of the financial industry on each of these cities. One indication is the large concentration of foreign banks and financial firms in New York, which has increasingly outdistanced Chicago.

To ground the comparison of the three major cities in a broader complex of industries, I added the communications group (SIC 48) to FIRE, business, and legal services (see Table 6.20). The incidence in New York, at 31%, is significantly higher than in Los Angeles (18%) or Chicago (20.3%). But these levels are all above the 15% in the United States as a whole. By 1987, this share had risen to 32.7% in New York and 18.2% in Los Angeles and remained constant in Chicago. A sharp differential also emerges from a comparison of the location quotients of FIRE for New York City, Los Angeles, and Chicago, the three leading financial centers.

TABLE 6.18

New York and Chicago: Employment Growth Rates in Producer Services, 1977-1987

		Growth Rate			
		New York		Chicago	
SIC No.	Industry	1977-1985	1985-1987	1977-1985	1985-1987
60	Banking	15.4	5.6	11.9	-0.2
61	Credit agencies	49.3	9.4	25.4	15.1
62	Securities	73.0	33.1	74.0	12.8
63	Insurance carriers	-9.0	-1.6	-11.5	3.9
64	Insurance agents	33.5	0.1	15.0	15.8
65	Real estate	7.6	3.7	3.7	14.4
67	Holding and other investment	-8.6	4.0	77.0	7.0
73	Business services	47.0	8.3	51.3	-5.6
81	Legal services	58.7	14.6	67.5	17.9
86	Membership organizations	4.7	8.6	4.3	3.2
89	Miscellaneous services	38.6	14.4	32.9	10.4

Sources: *County Business Patterns,* issues for Illinois and New York, 1977, 1985, and 1987.

TABLE 6.19

New York and Chicago: Percentage Employed in Selected Industries, 1981-1985

	Total Employment (N)	% of Total Employment			
		Manufacturing	TCU[a]	FIRE	Services
1981					
Chicago	1,189,000	28.4	5.4	6.1	21.2
New York	2,760,000	16.0	6.5	11.5	23.3
1984					
Chicago	1,133,000	22.3	6.5	8.02	24.6
New York	2,719,000	14.2	6.2	12.62	25.2
1985					
Chicago	1,172,000	20.9	5.8	7.4	24.6
New York	2,930,000	14.0	6.5	12.4	26.5

Sources: *County Business Patterns,* issues for Illinois and New York, 1981, 1984, and 1985.
[a] Transportation, communications, and utilities.

The differences are much smaller for the quotients of services as a whole (see Table 6.21).

One particular instance of this uneven distribution of financial activity is the distribution of foreign deposits at the 200 largest banks in the United States. Table 6.22 shows that in 1986 New York City accounted for 68.8% of all foreign deposits in the 200 largest banks in the United

TABLE 6.20

United States, New York, Los Angeles, and Chicago: Employment in Information Industries, 1985

SIC No.	Industry	New York		L.A. County		Chicago (Cook County)		United States	
		%	N	%	N	%	N	%	N
48	Communication[a]	2.4	71,340	1.9	61,928	1.5	31,697	1.6	1,282,616
60-69	FIRE	17.3	521,402	8.0	268,379	10.2	223,501	7.4	6,004,136
73	Business services	9.4	283,906	6.8	226,346	7.4	162,264	15.2	4,272,20
81	Legal services	1.9	58,729	1.1	37,542	1.2	26,092	0.9	685,456
	Total employment	100.0	3,017,996	100.0	3,345,520	100.0	2,187,992	100.0	81,119,257
	Information industries as share of total employment	31.0		17.8		20.3		15.1	

Sources: *County Business Patterns*, issues for the United States, New York, California, and Illinois, 1985.
[a] Includes telephone communication, telegraph communication, radio and television broadcasting, and communication services.

TABLE 6.21

United States: Location Quotients of FIRE and Services in
Selected Locations, 1985

	FIRE	Services
New York to United States	2.334	1.310
Manhattan to New York	1.363	1.018
Manhattan to United States	3.181	1.334
Los Angeles (County) to United States	1.084	1.091
Chicago (Cook County) to United States	1.380	1.069

Sources: Same as Table 6.20.

States, a share that rose to 85.6% for the 10 largest banks. The respective shares for Los Angeles were 2.9% and 4.1%, while Chicago had 8.5% for the top 200 banks and none for the top 10. However, Chicago had a larger concentration of deposits in the top 200 banks than did Los Angeles. While both Chicago and Los Angeles had absolute increases in foreign deposits compared with 1976, they have not raised their share of all deposits, as has New York City, whose share increased by almost 12% and whose absolute value more than doubled, from $92 billion in 1976 to $194 billion in 1986.

In a classification of the 140 largest SMSAs for 1976 in the United States, Stanback and Noyelle (1982: 20–26) found a distinct relation between size and functional specialization. Of the sixteen largest SMSAs (population over 2 million), twelve were centers for the production and export of producer and distributive services, and the other four were governmental and educational centers. Of these twelve, four were global centers, and the remaining eight, regional centers. Furthermore, controlling for type of service export, the authors found a direct relation between size and type of service export. The larger the SMSA, the greater the weight of producer services compared with distributive services. It should be noted that the larger SMSAs, were once predominantly centers for the production and export of manufacturing.

On the other hand, the group of smaller SMSAs (population under 1 million) had the highest single concentration of "production centers," mostly in manufacturing. Indeed, a comparison of the location quotient of manufacturing in the smaller SMSAs for 1976 with that for 1959 indicated that the importance of manufacturing had increased. This increase was sharpest in SMSAs with populations under 0.25 million, where the manufacturing quotient went from 0.9 in 1959 to 1.13 in 1976. In contrast, in the largest SMSAs this quotient went from 0.99 in 1959 to 0.90 in 1976. In terms of shares of employment, the share of manufacturing rose as the size of the SMSA declined. On the other hand, the share of

TABLE 6.22
United States, New York, Los Angeles, and Chicago: Foreign Deposits at the 200 Largest U.S. Banks, 1976 and 1986 (billions of dollars and percent)

	United States		New York[a]			Los Angeles[a]			Chicago[a]		
	Number of Banks in Tier	Deposits (billions of dollars)	Number of Banks in Tier	Deposits (billions of dollars)	% of Deposits in Tier	Number of Banks in Tier	Deposits (billions of dollars)	% of Deposits in Tier	Number of Banks in Tier	Deposits (billions of dollars)	% of Deposits in Tier
1976											
Top 10	10	126	6	86	68.3	1	2	1.6	2	13	10.3
Remaining 190	190	35	8	6	17.1	3	3	8.6	5	2	5.7
Top 200	200	161	14	92	57.1	4	5	3.1	7	15	9.3
1986											
Top 10	10	195	6	167	85.6	2	8	4.1	0	0	0.0
Remaining 190	190	87	12	27	31.0	2	0.3	0.3	6	24	27.6
Top 200	200	282	18	194	68.8	4	8.3	2.9	6	24	8.5

Sources: "Annual Survey of Bank Performance," Business Week, Apr. 18, 1977; ibid. Apr. 6, 1986.
[a] "Percent of Deposits in Tier" means city's share of all U.S. deposits in tier.

the "corporate headquarters" complex declined with size, ranging from 20% in the largest SMSAs to 8.7% in the smallest. While this 1976 information is somewhat dated, the more recent information discussed here points to a strengthening of these patterns.

In sum, there is an enormous difference in national employment shares between major cities in the United States and those in the United Kingdom. Where London accounted for 33% of national employment in producer services, New York accounted for 7.6%. Compared to total employment shares, London's 16% is also significantly higher than New York's 3.7%. Yet in relative terms the two cities are parallel in that their share of national producer services employment is twice their share of all employment. But in the United States there is a group of cities, rather than a single one, in which a significant share of all employment in various producer services is concentrated. U.S. cities also have a tendency toward specialization, not evident in the United Kingdom or Japan. For example, Hartford is a small city well known for its large concentration of national insurance firms.

A detailed breakdown by producer services industries points to considerable variation among major cities in the United States. New York City has maintained its 11.8% employment share in banking, three times its share of national employment. In other major producer services, New York City is still strongly overrepresented, but declines in its employment share are evident, notably in insurance. New York City's shares of national employment in producer services are markedly higher than those of other major cities, such as Chicago and Los Angeles. There is a significant difference between New York's 11.8% employment share of banking in 1987 and Chicago's 3.6% or Los Angeles's 4.3%, and this disparity tends to hold for all of the other major industries, though at a less pronounced level. Furthermore, New York City has maintained this overrepresentation notwithstanding high growth in many of these industries throughout the United States as a whole.

The share of national employment accounted for by major cities in Japan (see Table 6.23) follows a pattern somewhere between that of the United States and that of the United Kingdom. There is a combination of medium-high shares of employment in the producer services along with a tendency toward declines in these shares. Thus Tokyo's share of finance and insurance declined from 17% in 1977 to 15% in 1981 and 14% in 1985. In real estate, this share declined from 26% in 1977 to 23% in 1985. The overrepresentation of these industries in Tokyo notwithstanding this city's declines in national employment shares is evident from the fact that Tokyo accounts for about 10% of all employment in Japan.[13] Nagoya's

---

[13] The centrality of Tokyo as an economic center is also suggested by its larger daytime

TABLE 6.23

Japan: National Employment Share of Major Cities in
Selected Producer Services, 1977-1985

	Finance and Insurance	Real Estate	Services
	City's Share (%)		
Tokyo			
1977	16.6	25.8	13.0
1981	15.2	23.9	12.5
1985	14.2	23.0	12.5
Nagoya (Aichi Prefecture)			
1977	5.0	4.3	4.7
1981	4.8	4.7	4.8
1985	4.7	4.3	4.8
Osaka (Osaka Prefecture)			
1977	8.5	12.1	6.6
1981	8.2	11.0	6.5
1985	8.2	11.3	6.6
	National Employment ('000s)		
1977	1,383	372	8,741
1981	1,577	427	10,288
1985	1,742	485	11,924

Source: *Japan Statistical Yearbook*, 1978, 1982, and 1986.

share of national employment in these producer services industries parallels its share of all services employment, which is between 4% and 5%
with a few fluctuations among the three periods under consideration.
Osaka, on the other hand, shows overrepresentation in its 8% share of
national employment in finance and insurance and its 12% share in real
estate compared with its 6.5% share of all service employment. These
levels remained practically the same during the three periods under observation, though there were changes in the absolute numbers. Finance

than nighttime population, with the latter decreasing over the last few years and the former
continuing to increase. Daytime population in the twenty-three central wards increased
from 1975 to 1980. The population flowing into Tokyo from other prefectures totaled 2.1
million in 1980, 95% of whom were commuters to places of work and schools from the three
adjacent prefectures (Saitama, Kanagawa, and Chiba). The flow of workers into the three
central wards (Chiyoda, Chuo, and Minato), which constitute the central business district,
is 2.3 million people—6.8 times the size of the 34,000 nighttime population of these three
wards. For all twenty-three wards, the daytime population is 10.61 million, while the nighttime population is 8.35 million. For Tokyo as a whole, the daytime population is 13.49
million and the nighttime population is 11.6 million.

and insurance and real estate have been central components of the rapid urbanization of the Japanese population outside of Tokyo, as well as of the rise in exports of industrial goods. It is not possible to separate the consumer market from the business one. It is quite possible that over the next few years there will be a shift in composition and in location as the urbanization of the Japanese population subsides and a larger share of direct exports is replaced with offshore production.

Table 6.24 shows location quotients for Japan's major cities. Tokyo's location quotient for finance and insurance is as high as London's at 1.82 in 1985 compared with London's 1.89; Tokyo also has an extremely high 1985 quotient of 2.28 for real estate, compared with New York City's 2.18. Again, as in these other cities, Tokyo has a far smaller overrepresentation of services as a whole, with a 1985 location quotient of 1.23, compared with London's 1.18 and New York City's 1.31. The other major cities in Japan, Nagoya and Osaka, have underrepresentation of all services. Among these cities, several conditions are evident. Both Osaka and Nagoya had underrepresentation in all services from 1977 to 1985. While Osaka had overrepresentation of both finance and insurance and real estate over this period, Nagoya had significant underrepresentation.

The second trend that emerges is that since 1977 the degree of overrepresentation of finance and insurance in these three cities has tended to increase, indicating locational concentration in major centers. The distribution of both finance and insurance and real estate follows the model

TABLE 6.24
Japan: Location Quotients of Financial and Service Industries in Major Cities, 1977-1985

		Location Quotients		
	Total Employment (N)	Finance and Insurance	Real Estate	All Services
Tokyo				
1977	5,620,000	1.57	2.44	1.23
1981	5,672,000	1.49	2.33	1.23
1985	5,910,000	1.82	2.28	1.23
Nagoya (Aichi Prefecture)				
1977	2,881,000	0.93	0.79	0.88
1981	3,049,000	0.88	0.85	0.86
1985	3,240,000	1.10	0.78	0.87
Osaka (Osaka Prefecture)				
1977	3,708,000	1.22	1.73	0.94
1981	3,811,000	1.20	1.60	0.86
1985	3,989,000	1.56	1.66	0.96

Sources: Same as Table 6.23.

of an urban hierarchy in a way that it does not in Great Britain; there is less discontinuity in Japan between Tokyo and the next major cities, even though this discontinuity has risen. A crucial question here is, again, How significant is the presence of a strong manufacturing sector in explaining the strong representation of producer services industries in several major cities rather than in just one? Secondly, is there in fact a discontinuity between Tokyo and the other two cities in terms of the composition of the overrepresented sector? To what extent is the overrepresentation in Osaka rooted in the existence of a very strong manufacturing base and in that sense quite different from one of the key sources of growth in the FIRE sector in Tokyo? In that case, the structure in Japan would, indeed, be similar to that in Great Britain, with the latter appearing diverse only because the devastation of manufacturing has severely affected the growth of producer services in manufacturing-dominated cities. This would lend support to my hypothesis that key components of the financial industry today are no longer oriented toward serving production.

More detailed data show that an increasing share of Japan's national economic activity is becoming concentrated in Tokyo.[14] Firm relocations away from other major urban centers in Japan have accelerated in the 1980s. From 1985 to 1989, 30,000 Japanese firms moved their head offices to Tokyo according to the National Tax Administration. A survey of 1,050 large foreign firms conducted in 1986 by a private consulting firm found that 78% had located their Japanese branches or affiliates in Tokyo. More suggestive than absolute size is the disproportionate concentration of certain types of workers and economic activities: Tokyo has 47% of Japan's certified public accountants, 35% of its artists and craftspeople, 52% of its computer software specialists, and 45% of its writers. A 1982 governmental study found that 84.7% of all Japanese television broadcasts, newspaper articles, pieces of mail, telephone calls, and other information transmissions originated in Tokyo. In 1980, Tokyo accounted for 30% of all sales nationwide, a percentage higher than the city's population share, indicating the region's role as a commercial center.

Terasaka et al. (1988: 166) point out that while the development of tele-

[14] A central component in the Japanese economy are the bank-centered business groupings (kinyu keiretsu) comprising a trading group (sogo shoshu); at the center is one of the large banks (the Big Six) and the entire industrial spectrum. The Big Six banks are Mitsui, Mitsubishi, and Sumitomo, descendants of the prewar saibatsu, and Fuji, Sanwa, and Dai-ichu Kangyo. All six are located in Tokyo. Sumitomo and Sanwa have joint headquarters in Osaka. As with some of the large industrial corporations, some of these dual joint headquarters may have more to do with the past and a firm's original location than with the present, and Tokyo is most likely the "real" headquarters (Rimmer 1986: 134–35). (See Fukuhara [1981] for changes in banking locations inside Japan.)

communications capability was expected to reduce the density of central offices in Tokyo, in fact during the last few years the number of headquarters in Tokyo's central wards has accelerated rapidly. In 1969, 56.5% of the headquarters listed in the main stock exchange listings were located in Tokyo and 20.3% in Osaka. In contrast, the 1981 Census of Business Establishments in Japan found that only 23.1% of all offices in the country were concentrated in Tokyo. This suggests that the overrepresentation is among certain types of firms. Almost 57% of firms with 5 billion yen or more in capital were located in Tokyo, compared with 38% of firms with capital between 100 million and 1 billion yen and almost 53% of those with 100 million to 5 billion yen.

A survey by the National Land Agency cited in Terasaka et al. (1988) found that of the companies surveyed with headquarters in Tokyo, 56.3% responded that the main reason for having headquarters in Tokyo was raising investment capital and financial investments; 45% said it was the necessity of a central location to oversee the branch offices and factories, often over a wide geographic area; 41.7% said it was access to goods and marketing; 36.4% mentioned obtaining information from business organizations; and 31.8% mentioned obtaining information from administrative agencies. Thus, one could say that besides the financial aspects of raising capital and investing it, matters that an information economy might supposedly have solved continue to be rather important reasons for locating headquarters in Tokyo notwithstanding high prices of land, higher wages and salaries, and other costs.

The number of foreign firms has also increased in Tokyo, both in absolute numbers and as a share of all foreign firms with offices in Japan. The Ministry of Finance found that in 1974, 279 foreign firms opened offices in Tokyo, of which 150 were nonmanufacturing firms. In 1982, the number of new offices opened was 412, of which 292 were nonmanufacturing firms; in 1983, there were 548 openings, and another 490 in 1984. By 1984, the total number of foreign companies in Japan numbered 2,256; almost 63% of these had offices located in the central wards in Tokyo, and another 22% had offices located in other parts of Tokyo within the twenty-three ward area. Only 15.6% were located in areas other than Tokyo. The degree of concentration in Tokyo was extremely high among financial firms and banks.

Rimmer (1986) compared Tokyo, Osaka, and Nagoya along five groups of activities and measures: industrial output, wholesale output, retail sales, bank deposits, and bank advances. Osaka's share (measured at the level of the prefecture, not the city) of national industrial output fell by over a third, from 23.4% in 1960 to 16.4% in 1980, and though Tokyo's share also fell, from 28.3% to 26.5%, it was clearly still the leading concentration. Nagoya increased its industrial output but failed to raise its share of bank deposits and bank advances, while its share of wholesaling decreased. In many ways Nagoya is an industrial city that has something of a "company town" rather than an international character. Osaka, on the other hand, is the major economic center outside Tokyo, and according to many geographers, Tokyo and Osaka are the key points in the urban system of Japan. Tokyo's share of wholesale output rose from 30.9% in 1960 to 42.3% in 1980, while both Nagoya and, especially, Osaka suffered severe declines in their shares, with Nagoya's share dropping from 11.8% to 9.4%, and Osaka's share dropping from 32.9% to 19.5%. In terms of their shares of retail sales, they were more or less constant, probably an indication of a stabilized population size. In bank deposits and advances, the two strong trends were growth in Tokyo's share and declines in the shares of Nagoya, from 8.8% to 6.7% and from 8.3% to 5.9%, and of Osaka, from 22% to 19% and from 24.5% to 19.6%. Tokyo's share grew from 38.7% of all bank deposits to 43.4% and from 43.2% of all bank advances in 1960 to 49.6% in 1980. Of the twelve major banks, ten had their headquarters in Tokyo.

Conclusion

The space economy of producer services in the United States, the United Kingdom, and Japan contains locations of acute concentration, along with rapid growth dispersed throughout these countries. Overrepresentation in major cities continues notwithstanding growth rates that are generally higher for the nation overall. This pattern raises a number of questions. One concerns the composition of producer services in different types of locations. The evidence suggests there is a pronounced difference between New York, London, and Tokyo, which have extremely high concentrations of producer services and a strong orientation to the global market, and other cities. Other major cities in the United Kingdom tend to have underrepresentation of such services and to be somewhat marginal to the international financial industry. In Japan, Osaka has strong overrepresentation of producer services, but a more detailed analysis shows that Tokyo's concentration in all major sectors with a global market orientation—from headquarters to stock transactions and foreign firms— has grown during the 1980s. In the United States, several major cities have sharp overrepresentation in producer services and are significant locations for international finance. But, again, a more detailed examination of the composition of producer services indicates that during the 1980s New York City consolidated its role as the leading international financial and business center in the United States and outdistanced Los Angeles on several counts, notwithstanding the latter's rapid growth.

The locational distribution of producer services follows, up to a point, the accepted urban hierarchy in each of these countries. The largest concentrations are in the top cities, London and Tokyo; and, in the case of the United States, where there are several leading cities, New York City is clearly the leading center for producer services. While there is, then, a pattern resembling an urban hierarchy, one can also detect severe discontinuities. The most extreme case is London: It concentrates 31% of all producer services jobs in the United Kingdom, while many of the old industrial centers have underrepresentation of producer services; and it accounts for 16% of employment in the United Kingdom, while the other major cities account for about 2% each. It would seem that rather than a diffusion of growth along the urban hierarchy, there is a clear divergence in growth paths. London's disproportionate concentration of producer services and strong global market orientation has functioned as the growth engine not just for London but for the Southeast; manufacturing decline has decimated key sectors of producer services in the old industrial centers. The disproportionate concentration of the most dynamic sectors in London and its region may have altered the nature of the urban system in the United Kingdom. Similarly, in Japan, Tokyo's increasing concentration of leading sectors, headquarters, the large trading houses and banks, and the most advanced manufacturing sectors is creating a greater differential between Tokyo and the next largest city, Osaka, once the most powerful industrial center in Japan. In the United States, Chicago, once the leading city in the massive industrial complex of the Midwest, has lost considerable ground to New York and Los Angeles.

Does the orientation of leading sectors to the global market contribute to altering the nature of the urban system as it has been understood for developed economies? That understanding presumes a high degree of national integration, enough to absorb considerable unevenness in development and Schumpeter's inevitable creative destruction. The evidence discussed in this chapter indicates that growth predicated on a global market orientation induces discontinuity in the urban hierarchy. It is perhaps becoming increasingly evident that the centrality of mass production and mass consumption was a crucial factor in creating a balanced urban system and national integration in these countries. To what extent is the lesser discontinuity in Japan due to the continuing manufacturing strength of other major cities, and to what extent are tendencies now evident in the United Kingdom, and in a different way in the United States, slowly emerging in Japan? Indications of this could be the growing concentration of all major headquarters, trading houses, foreign banks, firms, and financial markets in Tokyo and the gradual decline of Osaka as the major industrial center. Osaka has also lost share in the financial markets. The growing centrality of telecommunications for the organization of work may further reinforce these tendencies toward concentration.

Major cities tend to have overrepresentation of the main producer services industries: advertising, banking and finance, legal services. However, cities that were once major industrial centers and are now in severe decline, notably in the United Kingdom and the United States, often have underrepresentation of these services. This would indicate that there are different producer services complexes in industrial compared with financial centers. On the other hand, much of the growth of the latter is a function of exports to the global market, as the more detailed analysis of particular producer services in Chapter Five showed. What this may be indicating is the extent to which the question of overrepresentation is bound up with major cities being appropriate production sites and marketplaces for these services, rather than with the need to service the city's economic base. To what extent is the latter form of service, central to many models of the urban economy, the mode in manufacturing-dominated urban economies?

The overall growth of producer services since the 1970s can be seen as an indication of a major transformation in the organization of work. And it is this transformation that is perhaps the essence of a service economy. The service economy has usually been identified with the massive increase in consumer services. But the growth in consumer services was strongly associated with the phase of expanded mass production and the urbanization and suburbanization of the population. Perhaps it is more appropriate to think of the growth of consumer services not as a shift to a service economy but rather as a phase of economic development based on the centrality of mass production and mass consumption.

The complexity of the economy and of regulatory frameworks has raised the need for various intermediate service inputs in many organizations of both the private and public sectors. And computerization, the development of information technologies, and telecommunication have altered the organization of work. These are developments that have occurred across industries and localities, as is made evident by the overall growth of service inputs in all types of organizations and localities. This general development constitutes the real shift to a service economy.

In this chapter we saw that New York, London, and Tokyo had outdistanced other cities in their national urban systems. What about major cities in other countries? Is there any evidence of a pattern where the growth of international financial and service flows has had parallel effects on major cities oriented to the world market? Specifically, does global market orientation create more discontinuity with national urban systems and contribute to new forms of transnational interdependence among cities? Do we see the elements of a global urban system or transnational hanseatic league? We cannot answer all these questions here. Establishing the interdependence of cities beyond New York, London, and Tokyo is not easy, though it appears as an increasingly compelling question at a time when the nation-state is becoming a less central actor in the world (Sassen 1990). The next chapter begins to examine these issues.

Seven

Elements in a Global Hierarchy

NEW YORK CITY, London, and Tokyo have long been centers for business and finance. What has changed since the late 1970s is the structure of the business and financial sectors, the magnitude of these sectors, and their weight in the economies of these cities. In an earlier period, a limited number of large corporate headquarters and a few large commercial banks dominated a market characterized by high levels of regulation, low inflation, and moderate but predicable growth rates. High inflation in the 1970s, growing use by corporate borrowers of the Euromarkets, and the Third World debt crisis changed these conditions. Today, a large number of firms constitute the core of the business and financial sectors. These firms account for much of the office growth in the private sector and a large volume of economic transactions. The reorganization of the financial industry over the last few years has brought about fundamental changes, characterized by less regulation, more diversification, more competition, the loss of market share by the large commercial banks, and a massive increase in the volume of transactions. This chapter seeks to map the information about the financial markets presented in Chapters Four and Five onto major cities in order to situate New York, London, and Tokyo in a broader framework. The centrality of finance in the international transactions of these cities and the immense money value of the financial industry, which dwarfs that of all other industries, invite an examination of the interactions among these and other major cities.

With rare exceptions (Walters 1985; Chase-Dunn 1985), studies of city systems assume that the nation-state is the unit of analysis and that urban systems are coterminous with nation-states. But there are cases where one nation-state may encompass several urban systems and, conversely, cases where an urban system may encompass more than one nation-state. Nor does the case described by Hall (1966) in his landmark study, *The World Cities*, quite account for the transactions binding New York, London, and Tokyo today. In addition to the central place functions performed by these cities at the global level, as posited by Hall (1966) and Friedmann and Wolff (1982), these cities relate to one another in distinct systemic ways. The interactions among New York, London, and Tokyo, particularly in terms of finance and investment, suggest the possibility that they constitute a system. These cities do not simply compete with each other for the same business. There is an economic system that rests on the three distinct types of locations these cities represent.

The international mobility of capital contributes specific forms of articulation among different geographic areas and transformations in the role played by these areas in the world economy. This brings to the fore the existence of several types of location for international transactions. The most familiar are export-processing zones and offshore banking centers; others may yet have to be specified or recognized. Our question here is the extent to which major cities are one such location, though clearly one at a very high level of complexity.

These cities contain a multiplicity of international markets, major concentrations of foreign firms and of producer services selling to the world market, and they are the key locations for the international property market. The sharp concentrations of such activities constitute internationalized spaces at the heart of these large, basically domestic urban areas. In the preceding chapter, we examined the characteristics of these concentrations in New York, London, and Tokyo and their relation to the national urban system in each country. The first question here is, How do these three cities relate to one another and to the global market? The typical view has been that New York, London, and Tokyo compete among themselves and sharpen that competition by providing joint twenty-four-hour coverage of the markets. What is emerging out of the analysis of the multiplicity of financial and services markets concentrated in these cities is the possibility of a systemic connection other than competition—an urban system with global underpinnings. A second question concerns the place of New York, London, and Tokyo vis-à-vis other major cities, notably the important financial centers in Western Europe, such as Paris and Frankfurt, and other major centers in Asia, such as Hong Kong. These are all financial centers with a strong global orientation. Does a ranking emerge? Is there a global urban hierarchy?

Leading Financial Centers

It has become increasingly evident that mere population size is not sufficient to explain the level of a city's economic power in the world economy. Some of the largest cities in the world have no headquarters of major firms or banks. New York, London, and Tokyo, on the other hand, have disproportionate concentrations of top-level headquarters in the financial, industrial, commercial, and producer services sectors, even though they are far from being the most populous cities. Many of the large industrial transnational corporations that account for 70% to 80% of world trade in market economies are headquartered in these cities. Feagin and Smith (1987) examined all cities in the world with over 1 million population in 1982 and found that over 75% had no headquarters of the top 500 multinationals at all. Of the seventeen largest metropolitan areas, nine had only one headquarters or none at all, and the other eight ranged from fourteen headquarters in Los Angeles to fifty-nine in New York (see Table 7.1). In 1982, New York, London, and Tokyo accounted for 120 headquarters of the top 500 transnational corporations in the world. By 1987 this number had risen to 154. Most of the other headquarters were in large European cities and in major industrial centers in Japan (Feagin and Smith 1987: 6–7).

But headquarters are a less adequate measure of economic power than they were in the 1960s and 1970s. Firms are locating their headquarters outside major cities even if they continue to be dependent on the specialized services and financial firms concentrated in major cities.[1] Many

TABLE 7.1
Number of Headquarters of the Top 500 Transnational Firms
in the World's Seventeen Largest Metropolitan Areas, 1984

	Population ('000s)	Number of Top 500 Headquarters
Tokyo	26,200	34
New York	17,082	59
Mexico City	14,600	1
Osaka	15,900	15
São Paulo	12,700	0
Seoul	11,200	4
London	11,100	37
Calcutta	11,100	0
Buenos Aires	10,700	1
Los Angeles	10,519	14
Bombay	9,950	1
Paris	9,650	26
Peking	9,340	0
Rio de Janeiro	9,200	1
Cairo	8,500	0
Shanghai	8,500	0
Chicago	7,865	18

Source: Feagin and Smith 1987.

[1] In addition, very different types of firm organization by industry and country alter the meaning of size. The Fortune 500 list is not as appropriate for describing Japanese firms, especially the large trading houses, as it is for Western firms. The large Japanese manufacturing firms (Nippon Steel, Toyota, Hitachi, Kobe Steel, Nissan Matsushita) resemble Western firms, except for the prevalence of capital subcontractors (Sheard 1982). The large Japanese trading houses are huge, diversified firms, which together with General Motors,

of the headquarters now located in the center of New York, London, and Tokyo have international markets; national market firms which may carry considerable power and be major users of the specialized services and financial services in those cities, are increasingly located outside the center, either in the larger metropolitan areas of these cities or in other cities and towns. By 1989 New York City had only fifty-nine headquarters of the top 500 U.S. firms even though its weight as a financial center had grown immensely over the decade. Insofar as headquarters with international markets locate their firms in New York City this 10% of the top 500 represents considerable specialization. Tokyo, on the other hand, has been increasing its number of headquarters as the economy becomes increasingly international and Osaka and Nagoya are losing ground to Tokyo even in manufacturing headquarters. It is not clear whether this is an early phase of a process which eventually will lead to decentralization of headquarters as it did in New York City.

The massive expansion of the financial industry over the last few years can be illustrated by the figures on worldwide capitalization (see Table 7.2), which stood at U.S. $892 billion in 1974 and grew to $2.8 trillion (in constant dollars) as of September 1987, to $7.9 trillion as of September 1988, and to $10.1 trillion as of December 1989. The level of concentration of these transactions can be seen in the fact that about 80% of world capitalization from 1986 through 1989 was accounted for by New York, London, and Tokyo. The impact of the growth of the financial markets in these cities can be gathered from the appreciation of the equity market in their countries. According to data from Morgan Stanley (1988a, 1988b, 1990), during 1985 alone, the equity market appreciated by 27.2% in the United States, by 13.4% in Japan, and by 17.6% in the United Kingdom.

The market value of equities of domestic firms also confirms the leading position of New York, London, and Tokyo (see Table 7.2). In September 1987, before the stock market crisis, this value stood at U.S. $2.87 trillion in the United States, representing the equivalent of 64% of GNP, and it stood at U.S. $2.9 trillion in Japan, representing the equivalent of 119% of GNP. Third ranked was the United Kingdom, with U.S. $728 billion, representing 118% of GNP. The extent to which these values represent a disproportionate concentration of worldwide capitalization is indicated by the fact that the next largest value is for West Germany, which has a strong, thriving economy, but where domestic equities represented 23% of GNP and U.S. $255 billion in value. By December 1989, these values stood, in order of size, at $4.1 trillion in Japan, $3.0 trillion in the United States, $823 billion in the United Kingdom, and $362 billion in West Germany. At the time, the Tokyo exchange accounted for 90% of

---

Ford Motors, Shell, and Exxon were in the top hundred industrial groupings in the world in the 1989 *Times 1,000* listing (*The Times 1,000* 1989).

TABLE 7.2

Capitalization in Leading Stock Markets, 1987 and 1989 (billions of U.S. dollars)

	Sept. 30, 1987	Dec. 31, 1987	Sept. 30, 1988	Dec. 31, 1989
United States	2,871	2,216	2,348	3,027
Japan	2,896	2,978	3,335	4,102
United Kingdom	728	664	676	823
West Germany	255	207	215	362
France	185	154	183	339
Italy	128	109	115	166
Canada	244	201	231	290
Switzerland	165	133	133	190
Australia	132	83	129	138
Hong Kong	84	50	66	77
Total World	8,114	7,139	7,919	10,141

Sources: Morgan Stanley Capital International Perspectives, Oct. 1987, Jan. 1988, Oct. 1988, and Jan. 1990.

Note: Capitalization figures refer to the market value of equities of domestic firms, excluding unit trusts. Market values are converted into U.S. dollars at current exchange rates.

equities trading in Japan; New York accounted for 73% of trading in the United States; and London accounted for all trading in the United Kingdom.

The sharpest transformation occurred in Tokyo's stock market. At the beginning of the decade, it was small compared to New York and basically followed New York. In the second half of the 1980s, Tokyo became the largest stock market in the world and responded less sharply to fluctuations elsewhere.[2] This shift in financial power rests in good part on the huge amount of national wealth concentrated in Japan. In 1985 Japan had national assets worth $19.4 trillion; by the end of 1989, these had grown to $43.75 trillion. Beginning in 1984, the Nikkei 225 index of the Tokyo market outdistanced the Dow-Jones average. In 1988 the difference sharpened rapidly, and the Tokyo market came to be seen as a leader. It was also a rather stable market, with a much smaller decline after the 1987 crisis and a quicker return to the prior growth rate. It succeeded in supplying a steady pool of low-cost capital to the Japanese economy.

The number of companies listing stock on the Tokyo exchange in 1987 was 1,499, compared with 1,516 for the New York exchange and 2,101

---

[2] From 1987 onward, Tokyo's stock market was increasingly considered as a model to follow, one where the emphasis on stability differed from the model represented by New York. The Tokyo market had far less of a decline in 1987 and again in 1989 (New York: 7% decline; Tokyo: 2%). It closed in 1989 with a 31% increase over the prior year and largely without the sharp fluctuations evident in New York City. However, by January 1990, the plunge in prices that took place in New York toward the end of 1989 hit the Tokyo market.

for the London one. The number of foreign stocks listed on each was 52 in Tokyo, 59 in New York, and—a significant difference—584 in London. The total market value of stocks was U.S. $1.8 trillion in Tokyo, U.S. $2.1 trillion in New York, and U.S. $471 billion in London. The trading value of stocks was U.S. $955 billion in Tokyo, U.S. $1.3 trillion in New York, and U.S. $133 billion in London. The total number of member firms, however, diverged greatly: 93 in Tokyo, 611 in New York, and 357 in London. None of the other major stock exchanges in the world comes even close to the order of magnitude represented by London, New York or Tokyo.[3]

Finally, as the earlier discussion of producer services indicated, New York and London are leading producers and exporters in accounting, advertising, management consulting, international legal services, engineering services, information products and services, and other business services. They are the most important international markets for these services, with New York the world's largest source of service exports. Tokyo is emerging as an important center for the international trade in services, going beyond its initial role, which was restricted to exporting the services required by its large international trading houses.

The leading firms in advanced producer services have developed vast multinational networks containing special geographic and institutional linkages that make it advantageous for clients to use a growing array of service offerings from the same supplier. Global integration of affiliates and markets requires making use of advanced information and telecommunications technology which can come to account for a significant share of costs—not just operational costs but also, and perhaps most important, research and development costs for new products or advances on existing products. The need for scale economies explains the recent increase in mergers and acquisitions, which has consolidated the position of a few very large firms in many of these industries. These have emerged as firms that can control a significant share of the national and world markets. This has been particularly evident in accounting and advertising.[4] The top

---

[3] While the other stock exchanges in Japan are, in principle, significant markets given the large, powerful industrial corporations in their regions, they are on another order from that of the Tokyo Stock Exchange, which accounted for about 84% of all volume and value in 1987. This figure represents an increase in Tokyo's share of trading volume, which, while always high, had stood at about 56% in the early 1950s, the period of rapid industrial growth, increased to about 65% in the early 1960s, further rose to about 74% in the early 1970s, and reached around 83–85% in the late 1970s. Most of the share gained by Tokyo came from Osaka, which had 28% in the early 1950s and then systematically lost share over the ensuing years. Over this period, there was an overall increase in the volume of trading for all exchanges, from 425 million shares in 1949 to 118,931 million in 1980, 238,354 million in 1986, and 315,441 million in 1987, clearly showing that much of the increase in the absolute volume of trading is relatively recent.

[4] By 1983, the nine largest accounting firms in the world controlled over one-third of the

eight accounting firms have an immense advantage that rests on reputation: An audit by one of these accounting firms raises the status of the audited firm, inspires confidence in potential investors, and reassures government regulators.[5] The multinational advertising firm can offer global advertising to a specific segment of potential customers worldwide (Noyelle and Dutka 1988). These are important advantages for firms functioning in a world market. U.S. and U.K. law firms in New York and London have strong linkages to financial institutions in those cities, and this gives them a competitive edge over other firms (Noyelle and Dutka 1988; Thrift 1987; Leyson, Daniels, and Thrift 1987).[6] They may wind up doing business for firms from a variety of foreign countries because they have a comparative advantage within those leading financial centers. There has been growing concentration in law firms.

The Japanese are more likely to gain a significant share of the world market in some producer services than in others (Rimmer 1988). Construction and engineering services are examples of the former; advertising and international law, of the latter. It is illustrative to see the development over time of Japan's international contracts. Rimmer (1987) found that as recently as 1978, the United States accounted for sixty of the top two hundred international construction contractors, and Japan, for ten. By 1985, each accounted for thirty-four of such firms. In Japan, as in South Korea, the large-scale construction programs in the oil-exporting Middle Eastern countries during the 1970s were of central importance in the internationalization of the construction industry. Together, Japan and South Korea account for fifty of the sixty-one firms listed for Asia as a whole. Also of interest here is the locational distribution of Japanese international contracting. In 1978, 87% of all contracts were in the Middle East and other Asian countries; no contracts were registered for the United States. By 1985, the total Asian share was down to 47%, and the

---

world's accounting business (Bavishi and Wyman 1983). Most of these firms were Anglo-American partnerships. By the early 1980s, about thirty advertising firms dominated half of the world market. In the early 1980s, this group of transnational advertising firms was dominated by U.S. firms; this U.S. domination continued except for the British firm of Saatchi and Saatchi's becoming the single largest advertising firm in the world through a series of mergers and diversification.

[5] Several of the U.S. savings and loan associations now in bankruptcy were audited by major accounting firms, a factor that may have deterred more critical evaluation by third parties and government regulators.

[6] The geography of international law firms is quite different from that of advertising and accounting. International law firms are not closely connected to the geography of multinational corporations, but rather concentrated in major financial centers. Banks and financial firms are major users of international legal services. International legal services are also a highly regulated profession, which poses problems for international activity. Since major financial centers are international, they will tend to have a far greater need for and openness to such international legal firms.

North American share had reached 24%, most of it in the United States (Rimmer 1988). The trends in this particular industry follow the global pattern of direct foreign investment, with a growing concentration in the highly developed world, particularly the United States (see Chapter Three). In 1984, the United States emerged as the main area for locating Japanese factories, offices, and banks. The growth in Japanese construction contracting in the United States is directly linked with this development. The United States is today the leading market for Japanese international construction companies.

Globally, a ranking of the world's twelve largest banking centers based on cumulated assets and income of the world's top fifty commercial banks and top twenty-five securities firms in 1985 and 1986 shows once again the prominence of New York, Tokyo, and London (see Table 7.3). By 1985 Tokyo had become the leading banking center in the world in terms of cumulated assets. It is well known that Japanese banks have operated by asset growth criteria rather than profit growth criteria. The growth in assets can be seen, partly, in their growth from 1 trillion in 1985 to 1.8 trillion in 1986. But this immense increase is partly a function of the revaluation of the yen after the 1985 foreign exchange agreement. New York, ranked second, had an increase from U.S. $846 billion in 1985 to U.S. $904.8 billion in 1986. Paris was third, with $659 billion in assets in 1986. In France, especially since the nationalization of several major banks, there has been a very great concentration of banking assets among a few banks at the top, in contrast, for example, to the United States, where there is relatively less concentration than in most major industrialized countries. Osaka ranked fourth, with U.S. $366.7 billion in assets in 1985 and U.S. $557.6 billion in 1986. Osaka is the major industrial city in Japan and its second-largest stock exchange. But it is clearly a very far second behind Tokyo in terms of both cumulated assets and the size of its equity market. London, which in 1985 had been ranked above Osaka, by 1986 had fallen behind, though experiencing an absolute increase in the value of assets, from U.S. $376.3 billion in 1985 to U.S. $390.3 billion in 1986. (Osaka's increase was, as in the case of Tokyo, in part a function of the sudden increase in the value of the yen while London has a vast number of banks not included in this count.) Several European banking centers, such as Frankfurt, Amsterdam, and Munich followed. Perhaps surprising is the fact that Hong Kong ranked eleventh in 1985, with U.S. $68.8 billion, and twelfth in 1986, with U.S. $90.8 billion. This loss of place was attributable to the increase in the value of another Japanese banking center, Kobe, which went from fifteenth to eleventh place, again partly because of the changing value of the yen.

If these banking centers are ranked by income, there are some changes in the ranking. Tokyo remains first in 1986, with $6.4 billion accounting

TABLE 7.3

Top Twelve Banking Centers Ranked by Income and Assets of Top Fifty Commercial Banks and Top Twenty-Five Securities Firms, 1985 and 1986

Ranking by 1986 Income	1985 Income (millions of U.S. dollars)	1985 Number of Firms	1986 Income (millions of U.S. dollars)	1986 Number of Firms
Tokyo	2,922	20	6,424	22
New York	5,372	14	5,673	16
London	2,282	10	2,934	5
Paris	983	6	1,712	6
Osaka	617	4	1,261	4
Frankfurt	763	3	1,003	3
Zurich	337	1	826	2
Amsterdam	172	1	739	3
Basel	291	1	415	1
Hong Kong	348	1	392	1
Los Angeles	636	2	386	1
Montreal	605	2	354	1

Ranking by 1986 Assets	Assets (billions of U.S. dollars)	
	1985	1986
Tokyo	1,086.3	1,801.4
New York	846.0	904.8
Paris	543.7	659.3
Osaka	366.7	557.6
London	376.3	390.3
Frankfurt	228.8	306.8
Amsterdam	51.4	193.4
Munich	53.7	133.4
Nagoya	77.7	123.9
San Francisco	118.5	109.2
Kobe	61.2	107.1
Hong Kong	68.8	90.8

Ranking by 1986 Income-Asset Ratio	Income to Asset Ratio	
	1985	1986
London	0.606	0.752
New York	0.636	0.627
Los Angeles	0.621	0.617
Toronto	0.527	0.591
Zurich	0.502	0.524
Montreal	0.502	0.520
Basel	0.475	0.489
Hong Kong	0.506	0.432
Amsterdam	0.333	0.382
Tokyo	0.269	0.357
Frankfurt	0.330	0.327
Paris	0.170	0.260

Source: "Global Finance and Investment" (annual special report), *Wall Street Journal,* Sept. 29, 1986; *ibid.* Sept. 18, 1987.

Note: Cities are ranked by cumulated net income, cumulated assets, and average net income to asset ratio of the top fifty commercial banks and the top twenty-five securities firms in 1986.

for twenty-two of the world's top firms, up from twenty in 1985. This represents more than a doubling of the 1985 value, again partly a function of the value of the yen. New York, which until recently had been ranked first, with $5.4 billion in 1985, fell to second place in 1986, with $5.7 billion. It accounted for sixteen of the world's top firms in 1986 and for fourteen in 1985. London was ranked third, with $2.3 billion in income in 1985 accounted for by ten firms and $2.9 billion in 1986 accounted for by only five firms. Paris was fourth, with $983 million in 1985, $1.7 billion in 1986, and six of the top firms in both years. Osaka followed, again showing a doubling on its income, from $617 million to $1.3 billion and accounting for four of the top firms. Two interesting changes occurred with regard to Zurich, Amsterdam, and Los Angeles. Zurich increased its income from $337 million to $826 million, accounting for one of the top firms in 1985 and two in 1986. Amsterdam more than tripled its income and number of firms, with income going from $172 million to $739 million and the number of firms going from one to three; its rank rose from fourteenth in 1985 to eighth in 1986. Los Angeles, on the other hand, lost rank, going from seventh place in 1985 to eleventh place in 1986 and from a 1985 income of $636 million to $386 million in 1986. These changes in rank according to income for these three cities are in good part a function of the criterion for classification, which is an arbitrary cut at the top fifty commercial banks and top twenty-five securities firms. Minor shifts among these firms can produce significant changes in the rank according to income for the three cities. The huge growth of several Japanese banks by itself would push many large banks out of the top fifty. This type of classification is most helpful in understanding the location of these top fifty commercial banks and twenty-five securities houses, the latter far more concentrated.

Perhaps the most pronounced difference in the ranking emerges when top firms are classified in terms of the net income to asset ratio. London and New York are leading centers, while Tokyo falls to tenth. London's ratio was 0.75 in 1986 and 0.60 in 1985. New York's was slightly over 0.60 in both years, as was that of Los Angeles, which ranked third. On this criterion, Hong Kong, at 0.43, did better than did Tokyo, at 0.36, in 1986. This value for Tokyo represents an improvement over the 0.27 registered in 1985, reflecting the new emphasis on profit growth, rather than merely on asset growth, that is emerging in Japan. Paris ranked twelfth, with a 0.17 ratio in 1985, which rose to 0.26 in 1986, indicating the extent to which its high ranking in terms of income is a function of huge assets.

These rankings confirm the central position of New York, London, and Tokyo as banking centers. Moreover, by 1988, Tokyo, London, and New York accounted for forty-seven of the top hundred banks in the world and 60% of their capital (see Table 7.4); and they accounted for twenty-four

of the world's top twenty-five securities firms and 97.7% of their capital
(see Table 7.5). The ratios for net income to assets confirm the existence
of highly developed financial markets in London and New York. Finally,
the data point to the rapid rise of Tokyo and its potential for growth once
securitization is as developed as it is in New York and the associated
profit-expansion orientation gains ground over the asset-expansion orientation still prevalent in Japan and typical of more traditional types of
financial activity. Commercial banks in Japan are now under pressure to
raise their capital base in order to meet the new capital requirements
agreed on by the Group of 12 under the umbrella of the Bank for International Settlements in 1987.

When we compare the figures for deposits from and loans to foreigners
through deposit banks, it becomes evident that by far the most pronounced change has occurred in Japan on both counts and in the United
States regarding liabilities (see Table 7.6). Japan's borrowing from foreigners increased from U.S. $100 billion in 1982 to U.S. $845 billion in
1989, and its lending to foreigners increased from U.S. $90.9 billion in
1982 to $830 billion in 1989. In the United States, such borrowing dou-
bled over a five-year period, from U.S. $254.5 billion in 1982 to $572.95
billion in 1987, and rose to almost $700 billion in 1989, while lending
increased from U.S. $401.5 billion in 1982 to U.S. $660 billion in 1989.
The massive size of the United Kingdom as a banking center can be gath-

TABLE 7.4

New York, London, and Tokyo: Share of World's 100 Largest Banks, 1988

	Number of Banks	Assets		Capital		Net Income	
		Millions of U.S. Dollars	% of Total	Millions of U.S. Dollars	% of Total	Millions of U.S. Dollars	% of Total
Tokyo	30	484,759	36.51	4,862,509	45.64	12,420	28.94
New York	12	113,744	8.57	933,037	8.76	8,942	20.83
London	5	55,531	4.18	605,019	5.68	5,655	13.18
Tokyo, New York, and London	47	654,034	49.26	6,400,565	60.08	27,017	62.95
World	100	1,327,891[a]		10,653,417[b]		42,919[c]	

Source: "World Business" Wall Street Journal, Sept. 22, 1989.

[a] Banks are ranked by assets as determined by Worldscope. Figures are based on each bank's
1987 fiscal year results.

[b] Capital figures were available for 98 out of the 100 banks. They were available for all Tokyo, New
York, and London banks.

[c] Net income figures were available for 97 out of the 100 banks. They were available for all Tokyo,
New York, and London banks.

TABLE 7.5

New York, London, and Tokyo: Share of World's Twenty-Five Largest Securities Firms, 1988

	Number of Firms	Assets		Capital		Net Income	
		Millions of U.S. Dollars	% of Total	Millions of U.S. Dollars	% of Total	Millions of U.S. Dollars	% of Total
Tokyo	8	153,587	29.65	40,825	42.91	4,637	72.55
New York	12	303,479	58.58	47,543	49.98	1,419[a]	22.20
London	4	57,321	11.07	4,622	4.86	176[a]	2.75
Tokyo, New York, and London	24	514,387	99.30	92,990	97.75	6,232	97.50
World	25	518,017		95,130		6,392[a]	

Source: Same as Table 7.4

Note: Firms are ranked by assets as determined by Worldscope. Figures are based on each bank's 1987 fiscal year results.

[a] Net income figures were available for 18 out of the 25 firms. They were not available for 6 New York firms and 1 London firm.

ered from the U.S. $1 trillion in borrowing reached in 1989, up from U.S. $489.6 billion in 1982; lending to foreigners increased from U.S. $462.8 billion in 1982 to U.S. $894 billion in 1989. These three countries account for three-fifths of the total of such flows, the vast majority of which are processed in New York, London, and Tokyo.

One classification (Euromoney 1987) shows that in 1986 institutional investors controlled about 60% of the 130 largest investment funds worldwide. In 1986, these funds, all firms with over $13 billion in cumulated assets under management, accounted for U.S. $4.3 trillion in assets (included are pension funds, mutual funds, and funds managed by banks and insurance companies). New York had by far the largest concentration of institutional investment funds: In 1986, the United States accounted for 60% of the value held by the 130 largest funds, and half of this was concentrated in New York. Second ranked were Japanese institutional investors, with accumulated assets of U.S. $640 billion in 1986, accounting for 14.8% of the total for the top 130 institutions. Closely behind was Switzerland, with U.S. $540 billion and a share of 12.5%. The United Kingdom followed, but with a value that was half that of Switzerland, at U.S. $252.7 billion and a 5.8% share of the total.

Together with other cities in the region, the greater New York area accounted for almost 45% of the U.S. total. New York City alone accounted for $911 billion. The next largest concentration in the United States was in Boston, with $342 billion. It is worth noting that Chicago

TABLE 7.6

United States, United Kingdom, and Japan: Foreign Liabilities and Assets of Deposit Banks, 1982-1989 (billions of U.S. dollars)

	1982	1983	1984	1985	1986	1987	1988	1989
United States								
Liabilities	254.55	305.78	338.12	381.26	477.22	572.95	641.11	699.35
Assets	401.53	433.13	443.37	446.78	506.70	549.56	603.84	659.64
United Kingdom								
Liabilities	489.64	519.63	538.22	625.74	758.94	927.54	961.84	1,000.14
Assets	462.82	485.21	489.71	590.07	715.56	875.71	883.65	893.81
Japan								
Liabilities	100.00	106.65	127.05	179.31	345.99	592.03	772.42	845.78
Assets	90.90	109.06	126.92	194.62	345.33	576.83	733.69	830.04

Sources: IMF, *International Financial Statistics* 41, no. 8 (Aug. 1988); *ibid.* 43, no. 2 (Feb. 1990).
Note: Foreign liabilities are defined as borrowing (deposits) from foreigners; foreign assets are defined as loans to foreigners.

and Los Angeles accounted for significantly smaller amounts than did Boston: $133.2 billion and $90.1 billion, respectively. Hartford ranked above Chicago, with $186.2 billion, largely explained by the pronounced concentration of insurance firms in this city. (See also Tables 7.7 through 7.9 for additional data on insurance firm assets and transnational pension fund investment.)

The rapid increase in direct foreign investment in services is strongly linked with the high level of concentration in many of these industries and a strong tendency during the 1970s toward increasing market share among the larger firms. This is particularly the case for firms servicing large corporations. In accounting, the top nine firms increased their market share for large corporate audits (Bavishi and Wyman 1983). The market share for small and nonaffiliated firms declined from 28% in 1971 to 14% in 1981 in the United Kingdom, from 58% to 1% in Canada, and from 64% to 29% in Australia. In the London area, four firms controlled almost two-thirds of the fees generated by the world's top nine accounting firms. Yet, at the same time, small, independent firms are also finding specialized markets and thriving in large cities such as New York and London. In international legal services, there has been a growth of very large firms in New York, through both internal expansion and mergers. A similar situation prevails in London. The link between international law firms and financial firms has contributed to a centralization of law firms in major financial centers. For example, among the top ten foreign law firms in Hong Kong, half are from the United Kingdom and the other

TABLE 7.7

Cities Ranked by Cumulated Assets of the Twenty Five
Largest Insurance Firms, 1985

	Assets	City Rank
United States	544,548	
New York	198,175	1
Hartford	99,936	2
Newark	91,706	3
Philadelphia	44,736	6
Boston	26,594	8
Houston	20,688	10
Milwaukee	18,807	12
Springfield	15,597	14
Des Moines	14,927	15
Chicago	14,140	16
Japan	122,628	
Osaka	65,621	4
Tokyo	57,007	5
United Kingdom	58,339	
London	43,764	7
Edinburgh	14,572	13

Source: New York in the Global Economy: Studying the
Facts and Issues (New York: Regional Plan Association,
1987).

Note: Cities ranked 9th and 11th are the only ones in the
top 25 outside the U.S., U.K., and Japan.

half from the United States; in advertising, the world's five largest firms
control 38% of the Western European market, and about 56% each of the
Latin American and Pacific Area market (Noyelle and Dutka 1988: 103).

There are several distinct phases in the geography and composition of
Tokyo's area of transnational control. Tokyo's main area of control in the
1970s and early 1980s was over goods and commercial transactions in
South and East Asia (Rimmer and Black 1982), where it was and remains
the central power. However, in the 1980s, its links became strongest with
the United States, in terms of volume of transactions, joint ventures, and
acquisitions and, secondarily, with Western Europe. By the end of the
1980s, Tokyo had begun to strengthen its financial ties and investments
in Southeast Asia through its securities houses, and Japan proposed massive investments in Eastern Europe with Tokyo's banks the key players.
The opening up of the European market in 1992 may create a third major
power center there.

Linkages between Tokyo-based offices and major cities abroad indicate

TABLE 7.8
Foreign Investment Share in Private Sector Pension Assets
by Country, 1980-1990 (percent)

	1980	1985	1990
United States	1	3	8
Japan	1	8	20
United Kingdom	9	18	25
West Germany	2	3	6
France	1	2	4
Canada	7	8	10
Netherlands	4	9	15
Switzerland	4	4	8
Belgium	25	30	35
Australia	0	5	12

Source: "Investment Management Survey," The
Economist,   Nov. 8, 1986.

the extent to which New York was and remains in a commanding position. In 1981 Tokyo-based companies had 107 branches of various types
in New York, ninety-three in São Paulo, and fifty-two in Seoul (Miyakawa
1983). An analysis of overseas companies of Japanese manufacturing firms
shows that in 1975 Korea, Hong Kong, Taiwan, and Singapore accounted
for almost a quarter of all such companies, while North America accounted for 6.4%; by 1987, the U.S. share had grown to almost 21%, and
the actual number of companies had increased from 20 to 181, of which
160 were in the United States. Europe's total started at a higher level, accounting for 12% of all such companies in 1975 but went just to 13.7% in
1987, with England and West Germany accounting for the largest single
concentrations. A parallel trend has emerged with Japanese subsidiaries
in finance and insurance. By 1987 the United States had the single largest
concentration of such companies, followed by England and Hong Kong.

Leading Currencies in International Transactions

There are advantages in being the key international currency. First, the
country does not need to earn foreign exchange to pay for imports.
Hence the balance of trade matters less and domestic economic policy
can more easily accommodate a negative balance of trade. Secondly, the
country is less sensitive to exchange fluctuations because trade and capital transactions are largely denominated in the country's currency. Finally, the country's role as a leading financial international center is facilitated, although this role also varies according to whether there is a high

TABLE 7.9

Private Sector Pension Assets Invested Abroad by Country,
1980-1990 (millions of U.S. dollars)

	1980	1985	1990 (forecast)
United States	3,300	27,000	129,300
United Kingdom	9,700	34,400	84,200
Japan	400	7,600	47,200
Netherlands	1,500	5,400	15,900
Canada	2,000	4,100	9,000
Switzerland	1,300	1,700	6,900
West Germany	500	1,000	3,500
Ireland	300	700	1,400
Australia	0	500	3,700
Belgium	275	500	1,100
France	75	200	600
Rest of world	--	1,500	6,400
Total	19,350	84,600	309,200

Source: InterSec Research Corporation, *Foreign Investment of Private Sector Pension Funds 1980-1990,* Stamford, Conn. 1988.

or low level of internationalization in the capital markets. But there are also costs associated with this status of primary currency. Providing the rest of the world with liquidity often entails running a deficit on the current account or long-term capital account. Yet this deficit cannot exceed certain thresholds because this would undermine the role of key currency, a threat not only to the country itself but also to the global economic system. The need to maintain stability and balance in the exchange rate system also means that monetary policy is not free from the constraints associated with trying to keep such stability. Finally, being the key currency in a period of high internationalization in the financial markets means that large holdings can be amassed by foreign entities and hence make domestic monetary control somewhat less effective.

The costs associated with being the key currency require a country to have a strong economy and a strong place in world trade as well as world finance at a time of internationalization of the capital markets. The dollar today is still the key currency, even though other currencies, notably the yen, the German mark, and the Swiss franc, are gaining share. But the U.S. economy is increasingly incapable of maintaining a strong economy given the high budget and trade deficits. The rapid devaluation of the dollar since 1985 is testimony to that. The United States is thus also less capable in the current period of gaining the benefits associated with having the key currency.

As a currency, the U.S. dollar still plays the major role in the international financial system. But this role has declined. By 1984, the dollar's share was down to 65%, the German mark's share was up to 12%, and the yen's share was up to 5%. In 1985, 61% of the total issues of international bonds were still denominated in U.S. dollars. Even though the dismantling of the Bretton Woods agreement made possible the implementation of a multireserve currency system to replace the dollar standard system, the dollar is still the key international currency. The expectation that other currencies, such as the German mark, would be used more widely in world trade and finance has only partly been met. Now it is expected that the yen will play a much larger role.

There is, clearly, a growing imbalance between the role of the dollar in the international financial markets and the place of the U.S. economy in world trade. Against this imbalance, Japan, with its increasingly strong position in world trade and growing participation in the international financial market, emerges as a key second currency. However, Japan's economy, while very strong and growing, is highly sensitive to global forces, such as a decline in foreign demand for its products or an increase in the price of oil. Japan's economy is also highly sensitive to changes in the foreign demand for its products, foreign exchange rates, and financial markets. Its leading trading partner, the United States, has also become its leading investment recipient. From 1975 to 1986, the U.S. share of Japanese exports increased from 20% to 36%, and the U.S. share of Japan's foreign investment increased from 28% to 45%. Most Japanese portfolio investments are in dollar-denominated instruments.

The use of the yen in the international marketplace has increased as a result of deregulation in Japan and the implementation of the Euroyen market. Japan's large current account surplus, the magnitude of available funds in Japan through domestic savings and private sector earnings, and the low value of the yen until recently are all factors that have helped increase the use of the yen in the international capital market. In 1985, about $7 billion worth of issues in yen were made by non-Japanese corporations in Japan; Japanese banks extended $14 billion of credit in yen to foreign borrowers; and there were $8 billion worth of Euroyen bond issues. In only five years, the yen has gone from a very minor role to being the second or third key currency in the world capital market.

In the area of current transactions, the yen's role is still very minor compared with that of the U.S. dollar and the German mark. In 1985, only 36% of Japanese exports and 7% of imports were invoiced in yen. The distribution and use of yen are quite uneven. They are much higher in trading with China or Southeast Asia and in trade of machinery, where

Japan has a very strong competitive situation, and rather low in trading with Europeans. One factor that has contributed to this low proportion of yen invoicing in Japan's international trade is that the European Community accounts for a significant share of Japan's international trade. Finally, many of Japan's imports are primary commodities, such as oil, foodstuffs, and industrial materials, which have traditionally been traded in dollars.

These conditions suggest a distinction between the internationalization of the yen in world trade and in world financial markets. In world trade, the yen has encountered a number of structural problems that are quite different from those of the international financial market. The deregulation of financial markets and the greater internationalization of this market have facilitated the growing use of yen in the international financial market. On the other hand, the heavy share of commodities in Japan's international trade and the prevalance of the dollar in the commodities trade have not allowed for an equally pronounced internationalization of the yen.

The internationalization of the yen can be furthered by the provision of additional financial instruments that allow non-Japanese to invest in yen assets. Today, the degree of nonresident participation in Japanese short-term financial markets is significantly lower than in the United States. The 1986 opening of the Japanese market for a new type of short-term government note, the continuing deregulation of interest rates in certificates of deposit, and the opening of the Tokyo offshore market are all developments that should raise the participation of nonresident foreigners in the Japanese capital market by facilitating their access to liquid yen assets.

It is clear that a stable economic situation in Japan, economic policies that further certain forms of growth, a highly valued yen, and large surpluses in the current accounts are all necessary conditions. But by themselves they would not have resulted in the internationalization of the yen. There were explicit measures that needed to be implemented, and the Japanese government has been doing so. Deregulation in this sense is crucial to the internationalization of the yen and its greater participation in the international financial market.

The International Property Market

The rapid growth in the number of financial firms, services firms, and high-income workers concentrated in major cities has contributed to rapid growth of a high-price real estate market. The concentration of major firms and markets in New York, London, and Tokyo in particular has raised the importance of locating in these cities and has been a key factor in the development of massive construction projects. The active participation of foreign firms as investors and as buyers and users of real estate in these three cities has contributed to the formation of an international property market.

One distinct aspect of this process has been that the price of land in the 1980s in central New York and London appeared to be increasingly unrelated to the conditions of the overall national economy. Furthermore, the bidding for space was confined to specific locations, and did not necessarily spread to all available space in these cities. High, often foreign, bidders were clearly willing to pay an extremely high premium for a central location and had no interest whatsoever in a less central location. This led to a process of "rehabilitation" of what had been considered marginal areas and their reconstruction into "central" areas: the western side of midtown Manhattan and the old docks in London were made into prime office land. Only a few years earlier, these areas had been defined as undesirable, derelict, unworkable parts of these cities. The proposals for massive reconstruction of Times Square and its environs were central to this rehabilitation for corporate office uses. And so was using a stunning array of internationally known architects to make once "derelict" areas into glittering offices. The concentration of high-income workers, including employees of foreign firms, also brought about an expansion in the demand for space and a parallel rehabilitation of developed urban land for new residential uses. This was a process with a multiplicity of minor locations throughout these cities and several radical transformations of whole neighborhoods: the old warehouse district in Manhattan, which became fashionable as Soho, is probably the most accomplished of these transformations, with its concentration of famous and/or wealthy residents, luxury shops, and art galleries, with enough not-so-famous and even poor artists to ensure its "bohemian" aura.

While there were strong spread effects throughout the office and housing markets in these cities, there also were, perhaps less noted, discontinuities. The prices commanded by central locations and by the "right address" for offices or residences were extremely high. And while there was an overall increase throughout the metropolitan regions of these cities, there was considerable disparity between central locations and the rest. The notion of a gradual decline with distance from the center is inadequate to describe the land price gradient. The highest disparity was between central locations and the rest. There were and remain locations at the heart of each city close to the center that have been devalued, a long-term process that began with suburbanization in the interwar period in London and in the postwar period in Tokyo and New York. We return to this in greater detail in Chapter Nine. There was, then, considerable discontinuity in the functioning of the land market. This would also help explain the coexistence of abandoned empty spaces with extreme density, particularly in New York.

The central areas of these cities have become part of an international property market; and conversely, these central areas account for much of the international property market that has developed since the late 1970s. The entry of institutional investors into the financial markets has been a significant fact in the expansion of this market. Institutional investors have sought to internationalize their holdings generally. Corporations that operate internationally have reconcentrated and expanded their holdings in leading centers, part of a broader pattern of reconcentration.

But it would seem that other conditions had to come together for an international property market to come about. It is the existence of a multiplicity of other markets, and particularly leading markets, that raises the value of land in the leading financial centers. It is the highly international character of these markets and of the bidders that differentiates this property market and differentiates these cities from other major cities with desirable building stock. They become the arena for major architectural projects, with architects from various countries building in all three cities, further enhancing the value and difference of these cities. Seen from this perspective, the acquisition of a major share of Rockefeller Center by Japanese investors is less surprising. The emergence of Japanese firms as the major investors in New York City real estate at the end of the 1980s is a continuation of this trend and one that confirms the fact that Japan is now the largest net exporter of investment capital in the international market, as the United States was in the postwar era.

The highest returns are to be found in the leading international centers. While much attention has gone into the acquisition of New York real estate by Japanese investors, firms from many countries have bought up property in all three cities. They have emerged as transnational places where major architects from the world over will be found building one or more major buildings. New types of transactions have further strengthened and developed this market, notably new types of institutional investment, such as property unit trusts, new forms of finance, such as property leasing, and the emergence of a growing secondary mortgage market handled by investment banks and brokers that trade mortgages (Daly 1987; Feagin 1988). Buildings become commodities, which can be bought, sold, and resold as commodities, in a market that is autonomous from broader conditions in a national economy. The case of Tokyo is somewhat different and remains so notwithstanding new legislation, because of acute concentration in ownership, state regulation, and the common practice of intracorporate property deals.

The traditional strong cyclical trends in the real estate industry were sharply accentuated by the financial speculation in the 1980s, especially in major cities. The English firm Richard Ellis reported that in the mid-1980s, when these financial centers were experiencing sharp expansion, net rents in centrally located offices of prime quality reached £33 per square meter in London's City, £38.75 in midtown Manhattan, £27.17 in downtown Manhattan, and £37.10 in central Tokyo (Ellis 1985). After 1985 prices rose further, with Tokyo's prices jumping to unheard-of heights, notably U.S. $210,000 a square yard in late 1989 for top commercial space (see Appendix D for detailed information on 1985, when the steep rise began, to 1987). In New York and London, on the other hand, real estate prices and activity declined and something akin to a crisis was declared by industry analysts in 1989.

The major construction projects of the 1980s in these three cities are vast, represent massive investments, and involve a multiplicity of top-level financial, engineering, architectural, and other professional firms. New York's Battery Park City, built on a 92-acre landfill in lower Manhattan, should provide 6 million square feet of commercial space and 14,000 residential units. Part of the complex is the World Financial Center, designed by Cesar Pelli. The Times Square redevelopment project, estimated at $2.5 billion, covers a 13-acre area and will include the construction of four massive office towers, with construction scheduled to begin in 1990, after a decade of litigation because of strong opposition by community groups. Like Battery Park City, the Times Square development will implant a luxury complex in an area of the city that was until recently regarded as fairly unattractive.

In London, two of the largest urban redevelopment projects are under way. Canary Wharf is a 71-acre site on the historic Isle of Dogs, within the London docklands. The project, proposed by one of the leading architectural firms in the world, the U.S.-based Skidmore, Owings and Merrill, in collaboration with I. M. Pei, is a vast luxury complex of offices and residences with highly designed public spaces and parks, and about 10 million square feet of commercial space, primarily to meet the needs of London's financial sector. The second major project in London is the redevelopment of the old railroad yards at King's Cross. This is at this point the largest inner city redevelopment project in the whole of England and Europe. It involves a 125-acre site and will cost over £2.5 billion. Another leading architect, Norman Foster, is the main designer. The site is located on unused railway land on the northern fringes of London's West End.

In Tokyo there are about forty major projects either under way or being designed. Perhaps the best known is the Tokyo Teleport City, expected to provide residences for 60,000 people and offices for 110,000.

Another project, the Makuhari Messe, to be built on 438 hectares of land reclaimed from Tokyo Bay, is expected to provide housing for 26,000 people. The largest project is the New Tokyo Plan 2025, covering an area of 30,000 hectares and involving a massive land reclamation scheme. As proposed by Kisho Kurakawa, a leading Japanese architect, it would accommodate an estimated 6 million residents. The latest developments propose using underground spaces to create vast complexes of offices and residences. Among other projects are the Sumida River Okawabata Renaissance redevelopment of an old warehouse district along Tokyo's main river. It is being transformed into luxury offices and apartment complexes; the massive nearby dockyard will similarly be redeveloped. (For a more detailed description of these projects and their implications see Shibata 1988.)[7]

Conclusion

There is a growing concentration of foreign service and financial firms in New York, London, and Tokyo handling business on behalf of both host country firms and co-national firms operating in the host country. In this sense we can think of New York, London, and increasingly Tokyo as transnational centers for financial and service activity. While the governments involved are important participants in the approval and legitimacy of these arrangements, it is also the case that the lifting of restrictions on

[7] There has been a savage struggle within central Tokyo to accumulate enough small parcels to make possible the building of tall towers and large complexes. Companies have resorted to using the yakusa (or Japanese organized crime). A new character has emerged, the "jiageya" (land price raising specialist), who puts pressure on small-parcel owners to sell their lots and has been found to use criminal tactics if all else fails. According to Forbes magazine (December 14, 1987), large real estate companies were estimated to have spent about 10 billion yen in 1987 for the services of such gangsters. From 1974 to 1983, the supply of office space did not increase much. But building of many office towers had begun, so in 1984, in a single year, almost 100 hectares of office space were added in the central wards. By 1986, office space in these three wards together with Shinjuku, Bunkyo, and Taito had increased sharply. From 1981 to 1986, the floor space of office buildings increased by 321 hectares in the three central wards. There were particularly strong concentrations in Marunouchi, long the business district and the main location of banks, in Kasumigaseki, the main location for government offices, and in Shinjuku, the secondary urban center and the location for the new offices of the metropolitan government. Terasaka et al. (1988: 169) have pointed out that the growing use of advanced office machines has raised the space requirements per worker. In 1975 the per capita effective floor space in an office was 11.3 square meters; by 1985 it was up to 13.5 square meters. This, together with the rapid increase in demand due to business expansion, reduced the room availability in office buildings from 2.1% in 1975 to 0.4% in 1984, with continuing declines since then. Office rental prices have risen immensely.

direct foreign investment in the United States and increasingly in Japan
and the deregulation of the financial markets have created a whole arena
of economic activity where governments participate only minimally, and
in this sense we can think of these cities as containing transnational economic spaces for the operation of both domestic and foreign firms.

New York, London, and Tokyo have become the key locations for a
variety of other transnational activities. Illustrative of these are the formation of an international property market and the growing transnationalization of corporate ownership and control. In the 1980s these have
assumed characteristics that point to a distinct form of the internationalization of economic activity, one beyond customary types of direct foreign investment and acquisition. This is partly because of the
scale of acquisitions and investments and partly because of their concentration in central locations and in leading corporations. The acquisition of
a large share of Rockefeller Center and of the American Express Company by Japanese investors are outcomes that represent a discontinuity
with the nature and magnitude of earlier acquisitions.

One might raise the question as to whether these acquisitions are not
akin to U.S. investments and acquisitions in Latin America in the 1950s
and 1960s. But I would argue that the latter differ from what we are
examining here because they took place in a context of marked political
inequality, where the United States was clearly dominant and the U.S.
government was a central element in economic transactions. The transnationalization of ownership and acquisitions, which is particularly evident in the United States, is a rather different process, one where the
states involved are increasingly not participating and where the question
of the nationality of capital assumes new meanings—as for example, when
Japanese auto makers put twin plants in northern Mexico to make cheap
auto parts for their plants in the United States, where those exported
to Europe are also produced. In an earlier book (Sassen 1988) I posited
that the United States has emerged as a sort of international zone for
manufacturing and that New York in particular has become an international zone for the financial transactions and legal transactions that are
part of these arrangements.

The massive expansion of international financial transactions, the integration of stock markets into a global network, and the growth of international markets for producer services have become part of the economic
base of many major cities. But New York, London, and Tokyo concentrate a disproportionate share of these transactions and markets. They
contain the largest concentrations of leading producer services firms, the
top twenty-four securities houses in the world, sixty-three of the top one
hundred banks in the world, 84% of global capitalization, and the largest

concentrations of a variety of commodity and currency markets. The magnitude and composition of this concentration of transactions and markets in New York, London, and Tokyo is to a large extent an occurrence of the 1980s. And it is also, to some extent, built on debt and speculation, which raises a question about the durability of this form of growth.

Part Three

THE SOCIAL ORDER OF THE GLOBAL CITY

THE NEXT two chapters address the social order associated with this particular form of growth, which, according to standard economic criteria, is very successful, makes use of our most advanced technologies, and utilizes a large proportion of highly educated workers. Conceivably, this core of leading industries in the premier cities of the world economy could have the overall effect of raising the quality of life and the quality of jobs for large segments of both the work force and the rest of the population in these cities. And, conceivably, the profits and tax revenues these sectors have generated, even if we were to consider only tax revenues based on the prices of developed land, could have made it possible for the governments of these cities to help support those in the population who could not share in this new economic order. Such conditions should further the overall well-being of workers and other people in these global centers of finance and business services. Finally, the expansion of the stratum of highly educated professional and service workers could represent, in principle, the growth of an enlightened type of work force.

There is, clearly, no simple way of establishing this. There are only indications, such as income and occupational distribution, changes in the prevalence of poverty and incidence of impoverishment, the effects of this type of growth on other sectors of the economy, and the range of jobs sustaining the operation of the corporate and financial service economy, from high-salaried to low-wage occupations and from white-collar to blue-collar services.

The advanced sectors of the economies of these cities are indeed central and of great weight; but they do not account for all firms and jobs in these cities. One question concerns the relationship between advanced and less advanced sectors. Conceivably, growth in leading sectors of a city's economy could (1) be neutral regarding employment and wages in less advanced sectors of the economy; (2) promote growth in the other sectors under existing or enhanced wage and employment levels; (3) promote growth in other sectors but under conditions that represent a deterioration of employment and wage levels; or (4) constrain, block, or reduce growth in other sectors. Precise measures of these various outcomes either are impossible or would demand a whole treatise by themselves. Furthermore, there will tend to be multiple factors contributing to those outcomes; growth sectors may increase or reduce the weight of various factors, but it is unlikely that they would be the sole cause for a particular outcome. An analysis of forward and backward linkages or input-output tables would not overcome these problems or provide a satisfactory measure either. This, then, raises the matter of the validity of an inquiry about the effects of high-growth sectors on the rest of a city's economy and population.

The question, I would argue, can be addressed in a general way and still provide a meaningful answer. Does the success of the postindustrial core tend to reduce poverty and marginality for significant numbers of the population? Is there less poverty and marginality in today's major global centers for finance and services than there was two decades ago, a less "advanced" period of economic development, one where manufacturing still accounted for a third of all jobs and the telecommunications revolution had not quite taken hold in the economy?

Large cities have historically been places with significant concentrations of wealth and poverty, long-established households as well as transients, immigrants, and casual laborers. Have these conditions been affected by the transformation in the economic base of global cities? Did the presence of a thriving postindustrial economic core, which generated vast amounts of profit for a large number of firms and large revenues for the governments of these cities, manifest itself in a reduction of the poverty and transiency we expect to find in very large cities? What is the social dynamic whereby people become articulated with this growth? Does this growth circulate and incorporate large numbers of workers and firms, and under what conditions? We know that the growth of manufacturing after World War II had strong multiplier effects on other sectors, thereby promoting overall growth in manufacturing localities. Does today's postindustrial growth have the same effect? In brief, does a thriving postindustrial urban economy reduce the number of poor people, the unemployed, casual laborers, and the working poor? Does it represent social and economic development in the sense of incorporating a growing share of people into reasonably good working conditions?

Eight

Employment and Earnings

THE ADMITTEDLY PROVOCATIVE inquiry set out for Part Three of the book begins, in this chapter, with a straightforward description of the overall economic base of each of these cities. The focus is particularly on the employment and earnings distribution in each city and how they compare with that of the corresponding country. It completes the picture introduced in the preceding chapters, focused largely on the leading sectors of the economy—finance and producer services—with some detail on the place of manufacturing and services in these cities. This chapter seeks to establish whether the occupational and income distribution of the city's resident work force reflects the existence of a thriving high-profit economic core.

This is very much an analysis of the official data on employment and an analysis anchored in the formal labor market. The next chapter addresses the more difficult question of what the official data may not be counting or activities not encompassed by the formal labor market.

Three Cities, One Tale?

All three cities have experienced changes in their industry and occupational structure over the last two decades. Alongside the growth in the producer services and finance, discussed in Chapter Six, there were pronounced losses during the 1970s in overall job levels in New York and London and in manufacturing in all three cities. Both New York and Tokyo had severe fiscal crises in the mid-1970s, which forced their governments to take strict measures, notably cuts in government jobs and services. In London the fiscal crisis assumed the form of a more protracted shrinkage in government jobs and services. Let me illustrate with a few figures, to be developed in greater detail below.

Table 8.1 shows employment levels in New York, London, and Tokyo for 1977, 1981, and 1985; Table 8.2 shows the manufacturing and service shares for those years. The aggregate data for New York City from 1970 to 1980 show a decline in the absolute level of employment, from 3.7 million to 3 million; a 35% loss in manufacturing jobs; a 41% loss of headquarters' office jobs; a 15% overall decline in office jobs; and the depar-

TABLE 8.1

New York, London, and Tokyo: Population and Employment, 1977-1985

	1977	1981	1985
New York			
Population (N)	(5,618,000)	(5,564,000)	(5,748,000)
Employment (N)	(3,056,000)	(3,098,000)	(3,225,000)
Employment as % of population	54.4%	55.7%	56%
London			
Population (N)	(7,012,000)	(6,806,000)	(6,767,500)
Employment (N)	(3,652,600)	(3,564,800)	(3,476,000)
Employment as % of population	52.1%	52.4%	51.4%
Tokyo	*(1975)*	*(1980)*	
Population (N)	(11,663,000)	(11,655,000)	(11,828,000)
Employment (N)	(5,620,000)	(5,672,000)	(5,910,000)
Employment as % of population	48.2%	48.7%	50.0%

Sources: Employment Review, (New York State) 40, no. 5 (May 1987); *Employment Gazette,* (U.K.) 95, no. 10, historical supp. no. 2 (Oct. 1987); U.K. Central Statistical Office, *Regional Trends,* 1981 and 1987; *id., Annual Abstract of Statistics,* 1985; *Japan Statistical Yearbook* 1986.

ture of a significant number of corporate headquarters. To this should be added the decay in much of the city's infrastructure and a severe fiscal crisis in 1975–1976.

Employment in London also fell, from 4.3 million in 1961 to 3.5 million in 1985. There was a tenfold increase in unemployment from 40,000 in the mid-1960s to 400,000 in 1985, a figure that would rise if we included unregistered unemployment. Much of this unemployment was due to large cuts in public sector jobs, beginning in the late 1970s. And, as in New York City, there has been a significant decline in manufacturing jobs, from 1.4 million in 1961 to 1 million in 1971 and 572,000 in 1985, less than a fifth of all jobs.

Employment in Tokyo remained fairly constant in the decade of the 1970s and rose from 5.6 million in 1977 to 5.9 million in 1985. Though absolute losses were on a much smaller scale than in London and New York, the share of manufacturing employment also fell in Tokyo, from 30% in 1970 to 25% in 1975 and 22% in 1985. The actual components of this decline, however, are somewhat different from those in New York and London. Besides the decline of the old traditional manufacturing districts, there was a government-directed dispersal of highly polluting factories, notably chemical plants. Perhaps less known is the fact that Tokyo's deficit reached 101 billion yen in the mid-1970s, a record high for the Tokyo Metropolitan Government. In 1979, Tokyo's governor set up a committee to address and work out the financial crisis.[1]

[1] The ratio of current expenses to total revenues had been increasing for many years and

TABLE 8.2

New York, London, and Tokyo: Distribution of Employment
in Manufacturing and Service Industries, 1970s and 1980s
(percent of total employment)

New York	1977	1981	1985
Manufacturing	21.9	18.7	15.4
Tertiary industry	63.7	68.6	73.8
Wholesale/retail	19.4	20.2	20.2
FIRE	15.9	16.6	17.3
Services	28.4	31.8	36.3
London	1977	1981	1985
Manufacturing	22.0	19.2	16.0
Tertiary industry	73.0	75.2	78.5
Wholesale/retail	13.5	19.2	20.5
FIRE	9.9	15.9	18.2
Services	49.6	40.1	39.8
Tokyo	1975	1980	1985
Manufacturing	25.1	23.5	22.0
Tertiary industry	54.5	57.2	59.8
Wholesale/retail	27.5	28.5	28.4
FIRE	6.4	6.0	6.1
Services	20.6	22.7	25.3

Sources: County Business Patterns, issues for New York,
1977, 1981, and 1985; Greater London Council, Labour
Market Report, Spring 1987; id., London Labour Market
Review, 1980/1981, (1981); Tokyo Metropolitan Gov't, Plain
Talk About Tokyo, (1984); 1980 Population Census of Japan;
Japan Statistical Yearbook, 1986.
   Note: Percentages do not total 100 because the following
industries are excluded: agriculture, forestry, mining,
construction, electricity, gas, water and heat supply,
transport and communication, and government.

It is against this background of fiscal crisis and government job cuts in
all three cities in addition to absolute employment declines in New York
and London that we need to place the high growth rates in select industries discussed in the preceding chapter. An examination of the overall
economic base in these cities shows a pattern of pronounced declines and

---

had already reached deficit levels in 1975. After the severe deficit of 1978, Tokyo's government set up a commission, whose recommendations led to the implementation of a plan for
financial rehabilitation by bringing down expenses to 90% of revenues by the end of 1982.
The recommendations were as follows: (1) reductions in staffing ceilings of the Tokyo Metropolitan Government and revision of the wage scale; (2) review of projects of the Tokyo
Metropolitan Government and promotion of reasonable cost-sharing by the beneficiaries;

equally pronounced growth, especially in the case of New York and London and to a lesser extent in Tokyo.

New York

Several major facts dominate the economic history of New York City since 1960. First, there was a massive decline in manufacturing, with a loss of over half a million jobs. Second, there was a massive loss of headquarters and hence of office jobs. Third, there was a rapidly deteriorating fiscal situation, culminating in an officially declared crisis in 1975–1976. Fourth, amidst the overall decline in the period after the fiscal crisis, there was rapid growth of finance and producer services, concentrated in Manhattan, beginning in 1977, and accelerating in the early 1980s.

New York City's employment was stable at about 3.5 million in 1950 and 1960, increasing to 3.8 million in the late 1960s. After 1969, there was a relentless decline, with overall employment reaching its lowest level in 1977, after the fiscal crisis, at 3 million (including government jobs). Since then two major trends are evident. One is the continuing decline of manufacturing, notwithstanding small increases in particular branches and periods. The other is the rapid growth in the producer services, which accelerated at the turn of the decade and into the 1980s. By 1987 employment stood at 3.6 million, a significant recovery based on producer services growth. But New York's was clearly a transformed economy, with a severely reduced manufacturing sector, a thriving finance and producer services complex, and 0.2 million fewer jobs than at its peak in 1969.

Manufacturing accounted for 1 million jobs in 1950, 0.9 million in 1960, 0.8 million in 1970, half a million in 1980, and 387,000 in 1987. Between 1969 and 1987, New York City lost half of its manufacturing jobs and more than half of its office jobs in manufacturing headquarters. It

(3) reasonable sharing of administrative responsibilities and fiscal burden between the Tokyo Metropolitan Government and the wards of other municipalities; and (4) improvement of various taxation and fiscal systems through increase and expansion of taxable sources in large cities such as Tokyo, through the reform of the financial resources allocation adjustment system, and through promotion of the national government's financial assistance to maintain Tokyo's police. The Tokyo Metropolitan Government, like New York City's government, concentrated much of its effort on the first, reducing staff by 9,255 employees, in addition to a cut in services, imposition of fees on consumer services, and a reduction or abolition of subsidies. A first reduction in the deficit was reached in 1979, and a surplus by 1981, the first time in twenty years that the Tokyo Metropolitan Government did not have a deficit. Thus, Tokyo's financial rehabilitation was completed a year before the scheduled date of 1982. It went from a 101 billion-yen deficit in 1979 to a 31 billion-yen surplus in real terms in 1981.

also had severe losses in related wholesale and distribution jobs. While New York City was never as important a manufacturing center as London was in the United Kingdom, the manufacturing sector was once central to the city's economy. Thus, in their landmark study, Hoover and Vernon (1962) predicted an actual increase from 1956 to 1985 in the absolute number of manufacturing jobs. Instead of the predicted increase of 0.8 million manufacturing jobs for the region, there were losses of 0.6 million in the region and of 0.5 million in the city. New York City's was a diversified manufacturing sector, which included important concentrations of electrical engineering and machine goods manufacturing, in addition to the more traditional consumer industries of furniture and apparel. Beyond the city, the broader New York metropolitan region extending into New Jersey, contained a vast industrial complex which included chemical and instruments manufacturing and a broad range of factories producing components for military suppliers. New York's harbor and distribution facilities were an important element in the growth of this industrial complex and made it a key location for headquarters.

While it is true that average wages in production in New York City were never among the highest in the country because of the absence of such key industries as steel, auto, and aerospace, it is also true that average wages were increasing and reached their highest relative level as recently as 1970—101.2% of the national average hourly wage in production. One indicator of the extent of change in manufacturing is the decline of that wage level, which had fallen to 87.6% of the national average by 1982. (A similar relative decline can be seen in Los Angeles, whose manufacturing sector is radically different from New York City's, being dominated by aerospace and electronics; nonetheless, hourly production wages fell from 108% of the national average in 1970 to 100.7% in 1982. As in New York City, that wage level would be significantly lower if sweatshops and industrial homework were included.)

The losses in manufacturing were not simply due to closing or departing factories but also due to the departure of manufacturing headquarters, particularly those of the so-called Fortune 500 companies, the largest industrial firms in the country. In 1965 New York City had 128 of these headquarters; in 1976 there were 84, and in 1986, 53 (Drennan 1987: 25). In 1917, before there was a Fortune 500 list, data compiled from Moody's Industrials and annual reports indicate that 150 of the 500 largest industrial corporations were headquartered in New York City (Conservation of Human Resources Project 1977: 38–40). These losses represent departures to suburban locations and outside the region, acquisitions by other corporations, and corporations no longer on the list because of reclassification or changed size. The change is further underlined by the fact that there were also 28 gains: mostly companies that moved their headquarters into New York City or were added to the list because of size or reclassification (Conservation of Human Resources Project 1977: 40). It is evident that the headquarters of industrial corporations became more mobile toward the 1970s. Data for the ten largest old metropolitan areas of the Northeast and North Central states show that together they accounted for 302 of the Fortune 500 headquarters in 1957, a level they had maintained since 1917 according to the data from Moody's Industrials, when they had 316 such headquarters. But by 1974, seven of the ten metropolitan areas had losses, leaving a total of 237 headquarters (Conservation of Human Resources Project 1977: 38).

Some of the reasons that led to the decline in manufacturing in New York City are the same as in London: inadequate amount and kinds of space at a time of growing needs by industry; the development of an interstate highway system, which further contributed to the declining relative advantage of a central city location and contributed to the movement of manufacturing, wholesale trade, trucking, and warehousing outside the city; the weaknesses in certain branches, which reduced their competitiveness for land and resources with other sectors of the economy. In addition there are the general factors that affected all old industrial areas—growing international competition, inadequate investments for modernization of plants, leading to lower productivity, the development of technologies that made possible locating production and assembly facilities in low-wage countries or low-wage regions of the United States. In brief, the combination of factors that led to the large concentration of plants and headquarters in cities such as London and New York came to lose its relevance and importance in the late 1960s because of changes in international, political, economic and technical conditions.

In contrast, services, excluding FIRE, increased from half a million in 1950 to over 1 million in 1987, and FIRE went from 0.3 million to over half a million—a figure that incorporates sharp losses of insurance jobs over this period. A more refined analysis of the city's economy shows that the producer services and finance reached over 1 million jobs in 1987, in a perfect reversal of the manufacturing trajectory. None of the other major industry groups had such pronounced changes. Thus wholesale and retail trade declined from 0.7 million to 0.6 million, and transportation and utilities declined from 0.3 million to 0.2 million. After a fall to 77,000 jobs in 1980, construction, not surprisingly, regained much of its loss, almost reaching its 1950 level of 0.12 million jobs by 1987. Government jobs overall increased from 0.37 million in 1950 to 0.6 million in 1987.

In the years following the 1975–1976 fiscal crisis, when overall employment continued to decline, several industries had pronounced growth rates. The overall 17% increase in white-collar industries from 1977 to 1980 was even higher in some industries, with rates of over 50% (computer services) and others hovering around 20% to 30% (management

consulting and public relations, engineering and architecture, accounting, protective services, securities, etc.) (U.S. Department of Labor, Bureau of Labor Statistics various years). In this period employment increased by 7.7% in finance, insurance, and real estate, by 9.4% in
communications and media, and by 24.7% in business services. Also, employment expanded by 8.9% in educational services and research institutions, by 7.4% in entertainment, culture, and tourism, and by 3.9% in
social services (U.S. Department of Labor, Bureau of Labor Statistics,
various years). (See Table 8.3 for related data.)

A comparison of the industry distribution in the private sector (U.S.
Department of Commerce, Bureau of the Census, 1977–1987) for Manhattan, New York City, and the United States as a whole (see Table 8.4)
shows that the single sharpest difference is in the FIRE sector. While
23.6% of all workers in Manhattan are employed in FIRE, this share falls
to 17.4% for the city as a whole and to 7.4% for the United States as a
whole. It would be less than 7.4% if New York City were excluded, since
the city's FIRE sector accounts for 11% of the U.S. total. A second set of
differences between the occupational distribution for the city and that for
the country as a whole is in manufacturing and in retail. While 24.8% of
all workers in the United States were in manufacturing, this share fell to
16.4% for New York City and 14.6% for Manhattan, with a good number
of these in the offices of manufacturing firms. However, in an interesting
reversal also evident in other major cities, 4.4% of workers in Manhattan
were in apparel compared with 1.5% in the country as a whole. Only
9.9% of workers in Manhattan were in retail, compared with 12.5% in
New York City and 20.6% in the country as a whole. Clearly, this does
not point to inadequate retail facilities in New York City, but rather to
the marked overrepresentation of other sectors, such as FIRE. Also of

TABLE 8.3
New York: Employment Change by Industry, 1977-1985

	% Change
Legal services	62
Business services	42
Banking	23
Retail	17
Wholesale	14
Real estate	6
Transportation	-20
Manufacturing	-22
Construction	-30
Insurance	-2

Source: County Business Patterns, issues for New York,
1977 and 1985.

TABLE 8.4
United States, New York, and Manhattan: Employment
Distribution by Industry, 1984 (percent)

	United States	New York	Manhattan
Construction	5.3	3.7	2.0
Manufacturing	24.8	16.4	14.6
Apparel	1.5	4.2	4.4
Transportation, communications, and utilities	6.0	8.1	6.9
Wholesale	6.7	7.6	8.0
Retail	20.6	12.5	9.9
FIRE	7.4	17.4	23.6
Business services	4.9	8.9	11.6
Legal services	0.8	1.9	2.6
Personal services	1.3	1.0	0.7
Health services	7.9	8.1	4.9
Educational services	1.9	3.2	3.1
Other services[a]	9.2	10.3	11.0

Source: County Business Patterns, issues for the United
States and New York, 1984.
Note: Percentages do not total 100 because other categories are not listed. Such categories include agricultural
services, forestry, fisheries, mining, and nonclassifiable establishments.
[a] Other services include hotels and other lodging
services, auto repair services and garages, social services,
miscellaneous repair services, motion pictures, amusement
and recreation services, museums, botanical and zoological
gardens, and miscellaneous services.

interest to this inquiry is the fact that while less than 1% of workers in
the United States were in legal sevices, the share was more than three
times higher in Manhattan; business services showed a similar differential, accounting for 4.9% of all workers in the United States compared
with 8.9% in New York City and 11.6% in Manhattan. Most of the other
industries had similar shares of workers in all three areas under consideration.

While New York City is according to many criteria a single labor market, there are pronounced differences among the various boroughs and
especially between Manhattan and the other four boroughs. One could
argue that for certain industries we are dealing with separate markets or,
certainly, separate submarkets. The distribution of economic activity by
borough points to a number of trends. First, there is a disproportionate
concentration (60%) of all activities in Manhattan. This disproportion becomes even more accentuated when we consider certain types of activi-

ties. In 1985, over 89% of FIRE and almost 86% of business services in New York City were located in Manhattan. The extent of manufacturing concentration in Manhattan, while lower than in earlier periods, still remained high, at 59%, particularly so for apparel, with 69%. These figures also show that the concentration of apparel in Manhattan is much higher than that in other boroughs and than that of manufacturing as a whole. The distribution of economic activity within boroughs shows a few pronounced differences. Most pronounced is the greater concentration of FIRE and business services in Manhattan, totaling 35% of all the borough's workers compared with about 10% in each of the other boroughs. A second difference is the much larger share of retail activity in the four outer boroughs, where it reached about 17% of employment in 1985, while in Manhattan it was under 10%.

These growth rates together with the decline in offices and manufacturing jobs point to a recomposition in the city's economy. In 1950, manufacturing supplied almost one job in three while services supplied one in seven. By 1980, these figures were reversed. There was a parallel loss of office jobs, particularly headquarters' office jobs, which declined by 41% between 1969 (highest employment) and 1980 (Ehrenhalt 1981: 46). The producer services also had a decline in employment of 9.4% from 1970 to 1977. But over the ensuing five years, from 1977 to 1982, they grew by 19%. This sector continued to grow, but at a much slower rate, of 8% for the three-year period from 1982 to 1985 and by 2% from 1985 to 1986. By then, almost a third of New York City's employment was in these industries, while the share of manufacturing had been further reduced from 22% in 1977 to 15% in 1985.

London

Three facts dominate London's economic history since 1960: first, the loss of 800,000 manufacturing jobs in a city that was once an important center for light manufacturing; second, a rather stagnant economy for about twenty years, with steady losses in employment and population; and third, a new phase of rapid growth based on finance and producer services, beginning in 1984, with employment in these industries overtaking that in manufacturing in 1985. That was the year when net employment gains replaced net losses in London, after twenty-five years of losses. The equivalent event took place in New York City in 1984. In only fifteen years, there has been a pronounced shift from manufacturing to services. In 1971, 27% of all London jobs were in manufacturing, and 68.6% were in services. By 1986, these shares had changed to, respectively, 15% and 80%. In a period of two decades, there has been a pronounced transformation in the employment distribution of London, pointing to a restructuring of the economic base.

London's employment fell from 4.3 million in 1961 to 3.9 million in 1971 and to 3.5 million in 1981 (U.K. Office of Population and Surveys 1963, 1973, 1983).[2] It fell to its lowest level of the postwar period in 1983 at 3.4 million, and began to increase again after 1985, reaching 3.5 million by 1987 (Department of Employment estimates). As in New York City, this fall in employment was dominated by the loss of manufacturing jobs, which fell from 1.4 million in 1961 to 680,000 in 1981 and about half a million in 1985. A further loss of 100,000 jobs occurred from 1985 to 1988. This parallels trends in the rest of the country, where manufacturing has declined from 10.7 million in 1961, to 5.8 million in 1982 and 5.3 million in 1985. But it is a relatively larger loss. In the two decades after World War II, about a third of London's population was in manufacturing. In their detailed study of the London economy, Buck, Gordon, and Young (1986) established that in the postwar decades the city's manufacturing sector was, with a few exceptions, structurally sound, paying relatively good wages overall, with considerable inputs of skilled and craft work, and relatively high levels of specialization. London accounted for significant output shares in several industries.

As with any large manufacturing sector, the reasons for the decline of London's are complex. There are general reasons shared by most old industrial countries in the West: growing international competition, declining productivity as a result of insufficient investment in modernizing plants, and, in some cases and at certain times, foreign exchange rates that did not favor manufacturing exports. In addition, there are specific conditions (primarily inadequate space and high land prices) in large, older cities, such as London and New York and to some extent Tokyo, that toward the late 1960s began to exercise constraints on many industries. Fothergill and Gudgin (1982) argue that the decline of manufacturing in London was in part related to the constraints on expansion at a time of greater needs for large-scale spaces in industrial production, an argument also advanced by analysts of New York City's manufacturing decline. This would seem to explain partly the finding of Buck, Gordon, and Young (1986) that job losses in London were negatively related to national changes in manufacturing. After controlling for changes expected on the basis of the national rate of change, they found that London lost relatively more jobs in nonrecession periods and relatively fewer during national recessions. This suggests that the losses in London were in part a result of constraints on growth specific to London. It is worth not-

---

[2] The figures for 1961 are adjusted to be comparable with a Census of Employment basis. See Buck, Gordon, and Young (1986).

ing that much of London's manufacturing loss was not due to shifts of jobs out of London; it is estimated that about 200,000 job losses can be attributed to factory closures (Greater London Council 1986: 46–47) and that first-time locations outside of London, notably in the Southeast region, have also contributed to the manufacturing loss in London. In the same line of analysis, Buck, Gordon, and Young (1986) found that some of the weaker manufacturing branches in London were increasingly unable to compete under the conditions of higher prices for inputs in London, again a trend parallel to the case of several industries in New York City. London, like New York, experienced a rapid loss of low-wage manufacturing jobs in the 1960s and 1970s, especially in the apparel and furniture branches. My fieldwork in London points to a very minor expansion in some of these industries in London in the last few years, notably clothing and leather accessories. Though on a much smaller and restricted scale, it parallels New York City. In the late 1970s, New York City began to experience a renewed expansion in some of these branches, though under different conditions from the pre-1970 period.

Finally, as in New York City, London today has several fairly strong manufacturing industries notwithstanding continuing overall losses. They are high-wage, high value-added industries, such as printing (tied to London's leading industries: finance and producer services), the high-tech sector based in the M4 corridor, and the communications industries. Average wages for full-time manual workers in the larger London area are higher than the national average.

A comparison of employment changes in various industries for London and Britain shows how deep the losses were for the country as a whole since the late 1970s. From 1978 to 1985 there was an absolute decline in total employment of 5% in Britain and 4% in London. The country as a whole had a 24% decline in manufacturing jobs. London lost 10% of public service jobs compared with 3% for Britain as a whole. In addition to manufacturing and public services, other major sectors lost jobs in London during the 1970s: construction, utilities, transport and communications, and the distributive trades. From 1973 to 1983 these sectors lost 218,000 jobs. As in New York City, public sector services employment fell during the 1970s after decades of growth. Public services had continued to grow up to 1976 and since then have been cut back. Local authority and central government employment both suffered severe cuts. Construction, on the other hand, declined by 21% in London, compared with 24% for Britain.

The total of service jobs has remained more or less constant at 2.6 million jobs in London and has increased in the rest of Britain from 13.1 million to 13.6 million jobs. Behind constant levels for service jobs in London, there are declines in some industries, notably transport and communications, and increases in banking, insurance and finance jobs, which grew from 379,000 in 1971 to 633,000 in 1985. London's preeminence as a location for the latter jobs is evident from the share it holds in these jobs, which in 1985 stood at one-third of Britain's total of 1.9 million. This share increases if we exclude insurance, a sector where London lost 10% of its jobs during the 1970s. London's share of jobs is far less pronounced in other service industries—for example, 376,000 wholesale, hotel, and catering jobs out of a national total of 2.2 million, which is equivalent to its share of all workers. A high percentage of services can be expected in a large city. But London's concentration of producer services and finance is higher than the overall concentration of services.

A more detailed analysis of trends in recent years shows extremely pronounced changes in certain industries during the 1980s (see Table 8.5). From 1981 to 1987, business services increased by 30%, personal services by 20%, and banking and finance by 13%. In contrast, several key manufacturing industries had severe declines. Electrical engineering declined by 22%, footwear and clothing by 30%, and mechanical engineering and vehicles by 37%.[3]

When we compare the employment distribution by industry for the United Kingdom, London, and the City of London, the most pronounced difference is in the category of banking, insurance, and finance, with respectively, 7.8%, 15.9% and 71.7% of all workers (see Table 8.6). Correspondingly, while the United Kingdom had 27% of all its workers in manufacturing, London had 19.2%, and the City had 10.9%, with a disproportionate share of these in office jobs. Another pronounced differ-

TABLE 8.5
London: Employment Changes by Industry, 1981-1987

	% Change
Business services	30
Personal services	20
Banking and finance	13
Insurance	0
Wholesale distribution	-8
Construction	-21
Electrical engineering	-22
Footwear and clothing	-30
Mechanical engineering and vehicles	-37

Sources: Greater London Council, Labour Market Report, Spring 1987; id., London Labour Market Review 1980/81, (1981).

[3] See Massey (1984) for an examination of the complex context in which these figures need to be placed.

TABLE 8.6

United Kingdom, London, and City of London: Employment Distribution by Industry, 1981 (percent)

	United Kingdom	London	City of London
Agriculture, forestry, fishing	2.2	0.0	0.0
Energy and water supply	3.1	1.6	0.9
Manufacturing	27.0	19.2	10.9
Construction	7.0	4.5	0.8
Services	60.5	74.6	87.3
Retail and wholesale	19.2	19.2	8.4
Transport and communications	6.5	10.4	71.7[a]
Banking, insurance, and finance	7.8	15.9	
Other services	27.0	29.1	7.2

Sources: Inner London Education Authority, London Labour Market Trends, (July 1987); Census 1981, England and Wales; Census of Employment, 1981, (U.K.).
[a] Combined percentage for transport and communications and banking, insurance, and finance.

ence emerges in retail and wholesale, with about 19% of all jobs in both the United Kingdom and London but only 8.4% in the City. Finally, a very sharp differential is evident in the other services category, with over 27% of all jobs in both the United Kingdom and London, but only 7.2% in the City. In the case of retail, wholesale, and other services key factors shaping these levels are the disproportionate concentration of finance and related jobs in the City, which would contribute to bringing down the share of other sectors, and the relative absence of such services as health and education, which tend to account for significant shares of jobs nationally.

Spatial dispersion has also affected service industries, and only partly as a result of technical developments. London's share of the nation's insurance jobs went from 36% in 1971 to 30% in 1981, and its share of banking went from 39% to 36% in the same period. Except for top-level functions, which have tended to remain in London, large components of headquarter offices have relocated (U.K. Department of Employment 1986, 1987a; Greater London Council 1986), reminiscent of what happened in New York City.

There are several reasons for these changes, some specific to London and others generally found in major urban centers. Transformations in the organization of work, especially the growth of mass production and scale economies, contributed to the suburbanization of part of the production process. Some of the conditions are familiar: the search for cheaper and better housing, cheaper land for firms and fewer land use regulations, lower wages and less unionized labor. The loss of population and of jobs was a development that stretched with fluctuations over a period of time and contained a number of distinct processes. During the 1970s, the Southeast region emerged as a new area for growth and had population and job increases (excluding London) while London had losses. From 1971 to 1981, the Southeast gained 346,000 jobs and London lost 414,000 jobs. (See Table 8.7 for a breakdown of employment change percentages.) Though the Southeast lost jobs in many manufacturing branches, it gained manufacturing jobs in electrical engineering and the brick industry. This region also gained jobs in most of the other economic sectors, often at higher growth rates than in London's growth sectors (U.K. Department of Employment 1986, 1987b).

Tokyo

After the massive employment and population growth of the postwar decades, Tokyo's job levels remained rather constant from 1970 onward. Manufacturing losses were far less pronounced than in New York and London, and the FIRE sector did not quite have the sharp growth it did in those two cities. It is not easy to establish to what extent this is a function of timing and to what extent of a different economic base. The rapid growth of finance and producer services began in the late 1970s in New York and in the early 1980s in London. Perhaps in Tokyo this process only began after the mid-1980s and has several years to go before it is the overwhelming presence that it is now in London and New York.

Yet by the mid-1980s a profound transformation had taken place in Tokyo, not captured in aggregate employment figures. The dismantling and disintegration of many old industrial districts in central areas of the city has occurred along with the rapid construction of high-rise buildings in the central business district. But these two distinct processes, which in

TABLE 8.7

Great Britain: Employment Changes in London and the Southeast, 1971-1981

	% Change		
	Manufacturing	Services	Total
Inner London	-40.6	-6.1	-13.9
Outer London	-32.6	10.2	-5.8
Outer metropolitan area	-18.4	25.0	6.3
Outer Southeast	-3.5	23.9	13.6
Southeast	-23.9	10.0	-1.3
Great Britain	-24.9	14.5	-2.3
Berkshire and Buckinghamshire	-3.0	32.1	17.6
All other Southeast counties	-17.2	20.5	5.7

Source: Breheny and McQuaid 1985.

New York and London dominate economic transformation, in the case of Tokyo are embedded in a massive economic base serving a vast region with services, trade, and clerical work. Tokyo's labor force of 5.9 million is far larger than those of London and New York. And the region for which Tokyo is the central hub contains 17 million people. While this compares with the 18 million of the New York City metropolitan area or the 12 million of London's metropolitan area, the difference is the centrality of Tokyo to the whole region, evidenced by the fact that it receives 2.4 million commuters a day, most of whom are workers. The profound transformation evident in the central areas of the city is lost in the numbers describing the broader economic base.[4]

Over a period of thirty years, Tokyo's labor force more than doubled, reaching 5.6 million in 1950. It then fell to 4.5 million in 1960, rose to 5.6 million in 1970, and, after a decline in the mid-seventies, rose back to 5.6 million in 1980 and climbed to 5.9 million in 1985. There were significant transformations in the occupational and industrial distribution. Of Tokyo's 5.6 million workers in 1970, 30.2% were in manufacturing, 26.3% were in wholesale and retail industries, 5.4% were in finance, insurance, and real estate industries, and 21.3% were in service industries. By 1980 these shares had changed most markedly in manufacturing, falling to 23.5%, and in services narrowly defined, climbing to 22.7%. Most other sectors showed little growth, partly an indication of Tokyo's fiscal crisis. By 1985, with the consolidation of the finance and producer services complex, Tokyo's labor force had increased to 5.9 million, largely accounted for by an increase of 300,000 service jobs, which compensated for the 200,000 jobs lost in manufacturing (Tokyo Metropolitan Government 1987a).

Tokyo's manufacturing sector began declining in 1965, after fifteen years of growth. Manufacturing jobs grew rapidly from 834,000 in 1950 to 1.7 million in 1960, when they reached 42% of all employment. After 1960, manufacturing employment kept growing, reaching 1.88 million in 1965—but by 1970 it had declined to 1.57 million; by 1980 it had declined to 1.4 million; and by 1981 it had declined to 1.3 million. The share of manufacturing employment declined sharply from 30.2% in 1970

---

[4] Tokyo's population growth rate began to decline in the mid-1960s. By then, migration out of Tokyo had begun to surpass in-migration. Much of the population loss was due to residential suburbanization rather than actual departure from the region; consequently, the number of commuters increased. But there was also an actual decline in the number of jobs during the 1970s because of the fiscal crisis and overall economic decline in Tokyo. After 1967, when net migration began to be negative as a result of suburbanization, there was a continuing influx of people from outside the metropolitan region. Suburbanization of Tokyo's population and in-migration from outside the region have contributed to a strong increase in the metropolitan population, from a total of 7.4 million in 1955, or 8.1% of the national population, to 18 million, or 15% of the national population, in the early 1980s.

to 23.5% in 1980, in good part as a function of the massive increase in white-collar and service workers.

Behind the minor changes in aggregate figures for maufacturing lies a significant recomposition of the sector. On the one hand, there is the disintegration of the old manufacturing districts alluded to above, as well as the government-directed relocation of many of the large factories in the chemical and steel complex located on the south of Tokyo, a process that began in the 1960s. On the other hand, two types of growth trends have emerged over the last decade in manufacturing. There has been the resurgence of craft-based, small-batch factories in the old industrial districts and other parts of central Tokyo, especially in industries linked to fashion and designer markets, from apparel to furniture. The second type of growth consists of specialized, high-tech industries. Many of these firms used to be subcontractors for a particular company: they have now become more autonomous and sell in a highly specialized market where large enterprises buy components and research and development they cannot provide in house. There are also firms, mostly in electronics-related industries, that develop new products for what are basically old lines of production. The core of Tokyo's high-tech manufacturing is in the development of new products and technology for simple mass production lines. It is an important center for product development and testing. Many of these products are eventually mass produced, but increasingly Tokyo factories are also accepting contracts for small batches of highly customized production. Let me elaborate on these aspects.

The overall decline of manufacturing is in part due to the reduction in heavy industry and chemical factories. These sectors reached their highest level of growth in the 1950s. During this period, large-scale chemical factories developed along Tokyo Bay, becoming a crucial element in the economic base of the area. Since then the Tokyo government has restricted and basically made it impossible for this type of factory to be built. In the 1950s the Japanese government sought to restrict and redirect industrial development in Tokyo and Osaka through the Promotion of Replacement of Industry Act of 1952 and the Restriction of Industry and Others Act of 1959.

Before World War II the main location of factories was in the lowlands of the eastern part of Tokyo, the old shitamachi district, since its origins a working-class district. These are areas containing small factories and workshops as well as workers' residences, often combined in two- to four-story buildings. At the time, this area lay outside Tokyo's central business district and hence meant cheaper and more available land. The area was well served through rivers and canals. The southwest area had similar characteristics and offered easy access to sea transport on Tokyo Bay, close to the ports of Tokyo and Yokohama. It became the site of the massive new industrial complex that eventually made Kawasaki, an area that lies between Tokyo and Yokohama, the largest industrial complex in Japan. After World War II new factories and industrial districts were developed in the eastern and northern region of the capital region, outside Tokyo proper. Relocation of factories to the less populated areas on the west, in the mostly undeveloped Tama district, had already begun before World War II, but most of the growth is recent.[5] Some of this relocating led to the formation of new industrial suburbs.

Although manufacturing reached its peak in Tokyo in 1961 and has since declined, it is still the single largest employer in the city and Tokyo. Tokyo still ranks first in Japan in terms of numbers, with almost 100,000 factories and over 1 million employees in manufacturing. The larger Tokyo region, not unlike the Los Angeles area in the United States, contains a massive industrial complex. The whole Kanto industrial area dominated by Tokyo has well over 5 million manufacturing workers, a third of the nation's total, and 36.2% of all factories in Japan.[6] It contains advanced high-technology industries, is well connected to key areas of the country, and is expected to account for an increasing share of all industry in Japan (Murata 1988). About half of the industries in Tokyo are in metal processing and machine goods. The southern area of Tokyo and the Tama district area along the Tama river contain a large share of Japan's most important enterprises. Most factories in the southern part of Tokyo are small or medium-size because of government restrictions. Only 0.3% of the factories have more than 300 employees (Murata 1988). But most of the small and medium-sized factories use advanced technologies of production. Three types of industries are to be found among the small and medium-sized enterprises in the area: (1) specialized high-tech processing industries; (2) old-style processing industries that are not incorporating new technologies or are doing so only minimally; and (3) mostly electronics-related industries that are developing new products for older industries.[7]

According to Murata (1980, 1988), Tokyo has a distinct role as a center

[5] Among the industrial cities in the Tama district are Musashimurayama, Inagi, Akishima, Ome, and Hinto. The Tama district also contains predominantly white-collar cities, such as Tama and Kyose, and those lining what is the busiest commuter rail line in suburban Tokyo, Kunatachi, Koganei, Kokubunji, and Musachino.

[6] The Kanto area, dominated by Tokyo, contains one-third of Japan's professional and technical workers, managers and officials, and clerical workers. The corresponding figures for the Kansai area, dominated by Osaka, range from 15% to 23%. It is interesting to note that the Kanto area has a significantly larger concentration of production workers than does the Kansai area: 28%, compared to Kansai's 14.5%.

[7] Tokyo's electronics industry accounts for an overall small share of Japan's total electronics production: 30% of the country's computer manufacturing, 13% of its integrated circuits manufacturing, and 10% of its robotics industry.

for innovation and new product development. Tokyo's manufacturing industries face two problems. First, the massive concentration of economic and political functions in addition to the management of large manufacturing enterprises creates immense strains on land use and prices. Murata (1988) posits that Japan will have to strengthen an alternative center for its manufacturing industries, with Osaka, once the main manufacturing center in the country, a leading candidate for development of the support infrastructure that would be required. Second, the growing expansion of high-rise residential and office buildings in the old industrial districts of the inner city, which still house many factories, is creating growing strains between these two very different land uses and the different sectors of the population involved. High land prices and densities,[8] along with growing numbers of high bidders, have put constraints on manufacturing. The productivity of industrial land use is far lower than that of commercial uses; however, Tokyo's industrial land is twice as productive as Osaka's and seven times more productive than that of many smaller areas. Yet, as in New York City and London, manufacturing industries cannot compete with other land uses.

Against this background, it is interesting to note the recent growth of printing and publishing associated with the growth of finance and producer services and the recent growth of the apparel industry linked to fashion and associated with the existence of a critical mass of high-income, mostly rather young workers with distinct consumption patterns as well as a growing export market for Japanese designers. In the 1970s printing and publishing, textiles, and apparel declined (Ide and Takeuchi 1980). Textiles and some components of printing and publishing were moved offshore. Apparel was moved to low-wage areas in Japan and offshore. The rapid growth over the last few years in the printing and publishing industry parallels developments in New York and London. I will elaborate briefly on the apparel industry because the evidence is not generally available given the recency of this development.

Unpublished data of the Tokyo Metropolitan Government show the distribution for apparel and accessories by industry branch and describe the spatial organization of the industry. One particular area in Tokyo (Sumida) is the key location for development, design, and testing. These are mostly large and medium-sized firms and are in some ways the equivalent of the so-called "manufacturers" in New York City—large firms that "produce" label clothing but increasingly subcontract production to small firms. Harajuku and Aoyoma are the information and design centers of the industry, also locations with large concentrations of fashionable boutiques and fashion shows. This part of the industry consists of a range of firm sizes, from large to small. Wholesale activity is concentrated in Ni-

---

[8] Average density in Tokyo is 14,000 people per square kilometer, compared with 9,000 for New York City.

honbashi. These are all very central areas of the city. The large firms now have offshore production, especially in the newly industrializing countries (NICs) and in Oceania. Smaller firms tend to have production facilities in Tokyo and in the less developed areas in Japan, such as Hokaido, where apparel production has grown sharply. A broad range of fashion-linked apparel and accessories, however, are produced in Tokyo proper. Unpublished data show clearly that the largest single concentration of factories is in eastern and northern Tokyo, areas that contain many of the traditional manufacturing districts. Eastern Tokyo alone (Katsushika, Edogawa, Sumida, Kouto, Adachi) contains over 8,000 firms, comprising manufacturers of coats, knit goods, ornaments, bags and luggage, and decorative accessories and other linked industries. Farther to the north in Tokyo are another 4,000 factories in the industrial wards of Taito and Arakawa. Several wards in the west and south of Tokyo also have concentrations of firms in these industries. In brief, as in New York and London, fashion-linked apparel manufacturing has grown in the 1980s at the heart of the postindustrial core in these cities.

Overall the category of producer services increased by 71% in Tokyo from 1977 to 1985 (Japan Ministry of Labor 1986a). It reached extremely high growth rates for certain industries (see Table 8.8), notably increases of 134% in information, research and development, and advertising; 124% in real estate; 30.7% in legal services; 43.1% in accounting; over 93% in other corporate services; and over 99% in other professional services.

The extent to which Tokyo is a service center can be inferred from the

TABLE 8.8

Tokyo: Employment Changes by Industry, 1977-1985

	% Change
Information, R & D, advertising	134.0
Real estate	124.0
Legal services	30.7
Other corporate services	93.2
Accounting	43.1
Architectural services	28.6
Other professional services	99.4
Retail	10.0
Wholesale	15.0
Transportation	7.0
Construction	15.0
Insurance	1.0
Manufacturing	-12.0

Source: Japan Ministry of Labor, *White Paper on Labor, 1987* (1988).

fact that this sector accounts for 60% of all employed people in Tokyo compared with 47.6% for the country as a whole, a figure that would clearly fall if we excluded Tokyo. The percentage of workers in Tokyo in clerical, administrative, technical, retail, and services is significantly higher than in the nation as a whole, with a tendency toward further increase (Tokyo Metropolitan Government 1984b, 1987b; Japan Economic Planning Agency 1988). Over 40% of Tokyo's workers compared with 30% of workers nationwide are in clerical, technical, and administrative occupations, whereas 25% in Tokyo compared with just under 40% nationwide hold production and transport jobs. Almost 30% of Tokyo's workers compared with 20% nationwide hold sales and service jobs. The industry distribution of the national labor force (see Table 8.9) shows that of the total of 58 million workers in 1985, about one-quarter each were in manufacturing and in wholesale and retail, with only 3.8% in FIRE. The largest differences between Tokyo and the country are in agriculture, in wholesale and retail, in FIRE, and in services. These differences become more pronounced when we compare Tokyo's central business district with the country as a whole (see Table 8.10 for the 1980 comparison).

From 1950 to 1965 there were no major transformations in the occupational structure of Tokyo. The change begins to be evident after this period, when white-collar jobs grew sharply and blue-collar jobs

TABLE 8.9
Japan: Employment Distribution, 1975-1985

	1975		1980		1985	
	N ('000s)	% of Total National Employment	N ('000s)	% of Total National Employment	N ('000s)	% of Total National Employment
Agriculture and Forestry	7,354	13.9	6,110	10.9	5,418	9.3
Non-agriculture	45,619	86.1	49,639	89.1	52,695	90.7
Mining	132	0.2	108	0.2	95	0.2
Construction	4,729	8.9	5,383	9.7	5,300	9.1
Manufacturing	13,245	25.0	13,246	23.7	13,811	23.7
Energy and communication	3,686	7.0	3,853	6.9	3,870	6.6
Wholesale and retail	11,372	21.5	12,731	22.8	13,453	23.1
Finance and insurance	1,383	2.6	1,577	2.8	1,742	3.0
Real estate	372	0.7	427	0.8	485	0.8
Services	8,741	16.5	10,288	18.5	11,924	20.5
Government	1,959	3.7	2,026	3.6	2,015	3.5
All Industries	52,973	100.0	55,749	100.0	58,113	100.0

Source: Japan Statistical Yearbook, 1986.
Note: There are a few minor discrepancies among the figures in table 8.10 because they are taken from different sources. Columns do not always sum up due to rounding.

declined. In contrast to the gradually declining numbers of nonmanufacturing jobs overall, white-collar jobs increased relentlessly over the thirty-year period, from 0.7 million, or 30% of all workers, in 1950 to 1.38 million in 1960, 2 million in 1970, and 2.4 million, or 43% of all workers, in 1980. A similar rate of increase, though at a somewhat lower level, took place for sales and service workers. Their numbers grew from 0.58 million in 1950 to 1.1 million in 1960, 1.4 million in 1970, and 1.5 million in 1980. By 1980, their share was closer to that of manufacturing, having reached 27% of all workers, 17% of whom were in sales. Within services it is important to note that business services grew rapidly but personal services (laundries, barbershops, certain types of repair, movie theaters) and social services, such as education and health, are declining.

Earnings

Existing information on earnings varies considerably among the three cities under study and is rarely exhaustive. This poses problems that basically cannot be solved if the objective is a rigorous comparison of detailed characteristics of the earnings distribution in New York, London, and Tokyo. After a careful examination of the available information it became clear that for the purposes of this study greater insight could be derived from a descriptive account of earnings in each city than from standardized measures, which though facilitating comparison, would do so at the price of losing all detail and specificity. This seems particularly appropriate because the primary emphasis is on differentials within each city and country rather than among the three cities. For this same reason, I decided to keep earnings in the original currency; keep the information in the original format of each country and city; and include types of information not necessarily available for all three cities.

The aim is to understand the trajectory of wages and salaries in different industries and occupations during a period of pronounced transformation in the economic base of these cities, as described in the previous section. Central to this trajectory is the relative change in pay levels by occupation and industry. Wages and salaries are embedded in a set of broad economic and political processes that cannot be done full justice here; I will only briefly discuss this more general context in which to place the detailed information on earnings presented later.

The shift to a service economy in many of the highly developed countries has resulted in a greater share of low-wage jobs than was the case when manufacturing was the leading sector (Singelmann 1978; Stanback et al. 1981; Harrison and Bluestone 1988; Jacobson 1978; Japan Management and Coordination Agency 1988; Japan Ministry of Labor 1987; Low Pay Unit 1988a, 1988b, 1987). In addition, there has been a downgrading

TABLE 8.10

Japan, Tokyo, and Tokyo's Central Business District (CBD): Employment Distribution by Industry, 1980 (percent)

	Japan	Tokyo	CBD[a]
Agriculture and forestry	9.6	0.6	0.0
Fisheries	0.8	0.0	0.2
Mining	0.2	0.0	0.1
Construction	9.9	8.3	6.1
Manufacturing	24.7	23.5	19.1
Energy and water supply, transportation and communication	6.9	6.7	8.2
Total services	47.6	60.5	66.1
Wholesale and retail	22.5	28.5	29.6
FIRE	3.4	6.0	9.9
Services	18.1	22.7	21.8
Public services	3.6	3.3	4.8

Sources: Tokyo Metropolitan Gov't, *Plain Talk About Tokyo*, 2d ed., (1984); *id.*, *Survey of Tokyo Day-time Population*, (1983); Bank of Japan, *Economic Statistics Annual, 1987* (Mar. 1988).

[a] CBD includes Chiyoda-ku, Chuo-ku, Minato-ku, and Shinjuku-ku.

of manufacturing jobs; major new industries, notably electronics, have a high proportion of low-wage jobs in production and assembly, while several of the older industries have undergone a social reorganization of the work process resulting in a growth of nonunion plants and a rapid increase in subcontracting. Finally, sweatshops and even industrial homework have grown over the last decade, especially in large cities, such as New York and London (New York State Department of Labor 1982a, 1982b; Sassen 1988; Balmori 1983; Morales 1983; Low Pay Unit 1988a, 1988b, 1987). And in Tokyo, low-wage industries, particularly apparel, restaurants, and retail, are growing. These developments have been most thoroughly documented in the United States and the United Kingdom. The decline in the centrality of mass production in national growth in both the United States and the United Kingdom and the shift to services as the leading economic sector contributed to the demise of a broader set of arrangements. In the postwar period, the economy functioned according to a dynamic that transmitted the benefits accruing to the core manufacturing industries on to more peripheral sectors of the economy. The benefits of price and market stability and increases in productivity could be transferred to a secondary set of firms, including suppliers and subcontractors, but also to less directly related industries. Although there was still a vast array of firms and workers that did not benefit from this shadow effect, their number was probably at a minimum in the postwar period.[9] During this period unions gained legitimacy and were central to the employment relation in the leading industries. As soon as international competition and the possibility of organizing work differently emerged, concessions and cutbacks were instituted by management. By the late 1970s, the wage-setting power of leading industries and this shadow effect had eroded significantly in both the United Kingdom and the United States, and by the mid-1980s it was becoming evident in Japan.

This transformation is reflected in the evolution of wages. In the United States, inflation-adjusted average weekly wages peaked in 1973, stagnated over the next few years, and fell in the decade of the 1980s.[10] Furthermore, up to 1963 there was an increase in the degree of equality in the distribution of earnings. Since 1975, the opposite has been occurring. Harrison and Bluestone (1988), using Current Population Survey (CPS) data, have shown that the index of inequality grew 18% from 1975 to 1986. Other studies found a similar trend (Bell and Freeman 1987; OECD 1985: 90–91). The data show a clear increase in low-wage, full-time, year-round jobs and, though less pronounced, in high-income jobs since 1973. In the previous decade, from 1963 to 1973, nine out of ten new jobs were in the middle-earnings group and high-paying jobs actually lost share.[11] After 1973, only one in two new jobs was in the middle-earnings category.[12]

[9] Piore and Sabel (1984) have compiled an important set of cases showing the continuation of craft-based manufacturing throughout this period of growth in mass production.

[10] During the post-World War II period, the real, inflation-adjusted average weekly wages of workers in the United States increased, reaching almost $92 in 1965, and then declined slightly, to $89 in 1979. BLS data show that real, spendable earnings grew by 20% from 1947 to 1957; by 13% from 1957 to 1967; and by 3% from 1967 to 1977 (Blumberg 1981: 71).

[11] Research by Jacobson (1978) on what happens to workers who are displaced from basic manufacturing industries shows that a majority may face a permanent loss in earnings. Bluestone and Harrison (1982: 92) also found a loss in earnings among New England workers after displacement from traditional mill-based industries; a shift to the service sector, where job growth is occurring, entailed a decline in earnings for most of these workers. Using 1970 and 1980 Census data on earnings organized by industry-occupational cells derived from the 1976 Survey of Income and Education, I found that the two highest earnings classes increased their share of total earnings from 32% to 37%, while the two lowest ones increased their share from 32% to 38.5%; the two middle earnings classes reduced their share by 11% (Sassen 1988: 141–46).

[12] Estimates made by the Bureau of Labor Statistics in 1983 (U.S. Department of Labor, unpublished data) indicated that the highest absolute growth in jobs would be in low-paying occupations. Using unpublished data and forecasts from the Bureau of Labor Statistics, Bluestone, Harrison, and Gorham (1984) examined the 1969–1982 growth performance of 136 manufacturing and nonmanufacturing sectors monitored regularly by the Bureau and categorized them by their mean annual wage in 1980. They found that from 1969 to 1982,

In Japan, since the mid-1980s, average real earnings have been decreasing and the manufacturing sector has been losing its wage-setting influence, according to Ministry of Labor statistics. In 1985, real earnings increased by 2.9%; in 1986, they increased by 1.4%. The main components of the increase used to be bonuses and overtime, closely linked with full-time employment in manufacturing. But this category had dropped to 1% of the increase in 1985 and to a negative minus 0.5% in 1986 (Japan Economic Planning Agency 1988: 13). The annual spring negotiations for wage increases have gradually delivered lower rates of increase. Total cash compensation for full-time employees of establishments with thirty or more employees increased by 5.03% in 1985, 4.5% in 1986, and 3.2% in 1987 (Japan Economic Planning Agency, 1988). Spring wage negotiations affect mostly the very large companies—not unlike wage negotiations in the steel or auto industries in the United States. But in 1987 they were only slightly higher, at 3.56%, in the iron and shipbuilding industries, which once set the average for the country. Furthermore, unlike prior years, there were only regular wage raises and no additional increases, another indication of the declining position of the basic manufacturing industries, which have been one of the bases for rapid economic growth in the Japanese economy. The share of companies that took the iron and steel industry into account in setting wages shrank, while that of companies considering the auto, electrical machinery, and private railway industries increased. In addition, unemployment reached almost 3% in 1986, one of its highest levels since the mid-1950s.

There is considerable disagreement about the reasons for the increase in low-wage jobs. The most extensive debates have taken place in the United States, long a country where the middle class is supposed to be an expanding stratum. In the United States, several analysts maintain that the increase in inequality in the earnings distribution is a function of demographic shifts, notably the growing participation of women in the labor force and the large number of young workers as the baby boom generation has come of age. Women and youth are two types of workers who have traditionally earned less than white adult males (Lawrence 1984; Levy 1987). Harrison and Bluestone (1988: ch. 5) analyzed the data, controlling for various demographic factors as well as the shift to services; they found that these demographic variables did not explain away the increased inequality in the earnings distribution. Rather, they found that within each group (white women, young workers, white adult men, and so on) there has been an increase in earnings inequality. They

the sectors with the largest net growth in jobs were those that paid the lowest average wages in 1980. While 63% of net new jobs were found to be in industries with a 1980 average wage of less than $12,500, there was almost no net growth in industries with an average 1980 wage of $22,000 or more.

found that the sectoral shift accounted for one-fifth of the increase in inequality, but most of the rest of the growth in inequality occurred within industries so that, as with demographic groups, there has been a growth in inequality in the earnings distribution within industries (see their app. tab. A.2 for eighteen demographic, sectoral, and regional factors). They explain the increased inequality in the earnings distribution in terms of the restructuring of wages and work hours (ch. 2 and 3). Though a parallel study does not exist for either the United Kingdom or Japan, it would seem that at least some of these outcomes are also present there. There has been an increase in the labor force participation of women in the United Kingdom and in Japan. But, as in the United States, this demographic shift cannot be the only source of growth in low-wage jobs when there are declines in what were once leading industries and the major growth industries of the 1980s have above- or below-average wage levels.

A second major trend is that some of the fastest-growing service industries are characterized by larger than average concentrations of lowly and of highly paid jobs, a subject examined at length later (Stanback et al. 1981; Appelbaum 1984; Harrison and Bluestone 1988; U.K. Department of Employment 1984, 1987a, 1987b; Townsend et al. 1985). This is most clear in New York and London. It is more difficult to establish in Tokyo. The technological transformation of the work process, in part underlying the above trends, has further added to earnings polarization by either upgrading or downgrading a vast array of middle-income jobs. Mechanization and computerization have transferred skills to machines and have shifted certain operations from the shop floor to the engineering office; many middle-level management jobs have been eliminated through computerization, and many secretarial jobs have been downgraded into routinized word processing. If one were to add the increase in the numbers of workers who are not employed full time and year round, then the inequality becomes even more pronounced. This is also a subject examined at greater length in a later section.

What matters for the purposes of the analysis here is the erosion of the broader institutional framework characterized by the social compact between labor and employers in the leading industries. This compact rested on mass consumption: Workers' wages were part of the production equation because they represented a key factor in profit realization. In the case of industries geared to the export market, as are the producer services in New York City and London, such a compact is unlikely. The decline of this broader institutional framework has taken place in a context of rapid growth in several service industries. In all three countries the growth industries of the 1980s—FIRE, trade, business services— show significant shares of low-wage jobs, weak, if any, unions, and higher percentages of part-time and of female workers.

The next three sections presenting detailed information on earnings in New York, London, and Tokyo, should be read against this broader context.

New York

A number of studies and data series document various aspects of earnings distribution in the United States. The most detailed source is the decennial census. The U.S. Department of Labor has also produced extremely detailed information on earnings by occupation and industry; while geographic coverage varies, New York City is unusually well represented. At this time, the most definitive study on earnings in the 1970s and 1980s is that by Harrison and Bluestone (1988), who test the evidence against a wide range of alternative explanations—from demographic shifts to the growth of services.

An overall measure of the weight of low-wage jobs in the producer services can be found in what is at this point the most detailed analysis of 1980 census data about the impact of service growth on the creation of low-wage jobs in major metropolitan areas. Using the 1980 Census PUMS File, Sheets, Nord, and Phelps (1987) found that from 1970 to 1980 service industries had a significant effect on the growth of what they define as underemployment, that is, employment paying below poverty-level wages. They found that the growth of producer services and of retail were particularly strong contributors to low-wage jobs. The highest relative contribution resulted from what the authors call "corporate services" (FIRE, business services, legal services, membership organizations, and professional services)—a 1% increase in employment in these services was found to result in a 0.37% increase in full-time, year-round low-wage jobs. A 1% increase in distributive services was found to result in a 0.32% increase in such jobs. In contrast, a 1% increase in personal services was found to result mostly in an increase of part-time jobs and in a 0.13% increase in full-time low-wage jobs. The retail industry had the highest effect on the creation of part-time, year-round low-wage jobs: A 1% increase in retail was found to result in a 0.88% increase in such jobs.

Nelson and Lorence (1985) examined the relationship between service employment and inequality in metropolitan areas, using census data on the 125 largest such areas.[13] The question guiding their research was why male earnings are more unequal in metropolises with high levels of ser-

[13] Two clarifications on this study: (1) The 125 became 124 in 1980 with the merging of Dallas and Fort Worth. (2) The study focused only on men to facilitate comparability with previous research on individual earnings dispersion in metropolitan areas, which has been largely focused on men.

vice sector employment. The authors' interest was to establish whether
the growth of service employment also contributes to earnings inequality
through the expansion of high-income jobs, rather than, as is more commonly held, through the expansion of low-wage unskilled jobs. They
measured the ratio of median earnings over earnings at the 5th percentile
to identify the difference in earnings between the least affluent and the
median metropolitan male earners, and the ratio of median earnings over
earnings at the 95th percentile to establish the gap between median and
affluent earners. A larger ratio between the upper end and the median
in one metropolitan area than in another indicated that the more affluent
in that area had a greater economic advantage over median earners than
did high earners in the lower-ratio area; the median: lower end ratio was
similarly used as the measure of disparity between the median earners
and the lowest ones. They disaggregated service employment into four
major groups following Singelmann and Browning (1980) and included a
number of control variables (race, age, education, unemployment). Overall, they found that more inequality in the 125 areas appeared to be accounted for by earnings disparity between the highest and the median
earners than by disparity between the median and lowest earners (Nelson
and Lorence 1985: 115). Furthermore, they found that the strongest effect came from the producer services and that the next strongest was far
weaker (social services in 1970 and personal services in 1980).[14]

Using census data and the 1976 Survey on Income and Education,
Stanback et al. (1981) showed that there is a high percentage of the next-
to-lowest earnings class in all services, except distributive services and
public administration. Almost half of all workers in the producer services
are in the two highest earnings classes; but only 2.8% are in the middle
earnings class, compared with half of all construction and manufacturing
workers. Harrison and Bluestone (1988), the OECD (1985), and Bell and
Freeman (1987) found growing wage dispersion within industries and a
tendency for industries with low average wages to suffer additional declines in wages and for those with high average wages to experience additional earnings increases at the top. Finally, in a 1986 national survey
of technical and clerical pay, the Bureau of Labor Statistics examined
salary levels by occupation, controlling for industry, and found a consistent tendency for most of the jobs to pay below average in the service
industries and above average in manufacturing (U.S. Department of Labor, Bureau of Labor Statistics, 1986b).

[14] The authors regressed the various income and percentile measures on the other four
service sectors and select control variables and found that the producer services had the
most substantial relationship to overall inequality of the four service sectors and were more
highly related to inequality than most of the control variables associated with the traditional
explanations of inequality.

When we consider the evidence on different occupational and earnings distributions for various industries in combination with the locational patterns of such industries, it becomes rather clear that major cities like New York have a high proportion of industries with considerable income and occupational polarization. Two-fifths of the new jobs created in New York City from 1980 to 1985 are in the higher-pay, higher-status professional, technical, managerial, and administrative occupations (U.S. Department of Labor, Bureau of Labor Statistics, various years), and many of the remaining three-fifths are in low-paying jobs.

The statistical frequency of major service industries with growing earnings dispersion is far higher in New York than in the country as a whole. In 1985, over 26% of all employment in New York City, compared with 15% in the country as a whole, was in FIRE (SIC 60–69), the communications group (SIC 48), business services (SIC 73), and legal services (SIC 81). The frequency of these industries in New York City is also higher than in other major cities; for example, it is 17.8% in Los Angeles and 20.3% in Chicago. If we consider the producer services category as usually defined, which also includes membership organizations (SIC 86) and miscellaneous business services (SIC 89), this group of industries accounted for 35% of all employment in the city in 1985, up from 25% in 1970, for a total employment of almost 1 million workers. This group of industries accounted for 35% of the city's payroll in 1985. In Manhattan, it accounted for almost 40% of employment and 45% of payroll. It is thus a significant factor in the city's economy—and even more significant if we include its indirect impact through the housing market, commerce, and personal services.

Data for 1987 from the New York State Department of Labor show that in 1987 average unadjusted annual pay in New York City was $28,735, or an increase of 7.5% over 1986. Only two sectors had above-average increases: FIRE, up 10.3% over the preceding year, and services, up 8.4%. FIRE was the highest-paying sector, confirming national trend data, with annual average pay in New York City of $43,964 in 1987. The next-highest major industry group, transportation and public utilities, was far below this level. At the same time, unpublished data from the New York State Department of Labor based on occupational surveys in 1984, 1985, and 1986, show that 49.4% of FIRE workers are clerical workers and another 13% are service, production, and maintenance workers. Notwithstanding an average annual pay level almost twice the average for the city, only 11% are managers and in related occupations, and 14.4% are professionals and in related occupations. If we put together the information about these three different aspects it becomes evident that there is considerable earnings dispersion in this industry.

The available evidence for New York City confirms the trends toward the dispersion of earnings within industries. Data for 1981 and 1987 (see Table 8.11) show that in a range of office occupations, from secretaries, word processors, and file clerks to switchboard operators, average median weekly earnings were lower in the nonmanufacturing group of industries than in manufacturing. They were highest overall in the transport and utilities group. While the absolute levels were significantly higher, the same relative difference was found for professional and technical workers, with a few exceptions. In 1987, the overall trend in clerical occupations was toward lower salaries in nonmanufacturing industries than in manufacturing for the same occupation. Median weekly earnings of secretaries were $426 in manufacturing and $415 in nonmanufacturing; those of typists were $282 and $259; those of word processors were $395 and $348; those of switchboard operators were $353.50 and $296; and those of switchboard operator/receptionists were $307 and $290. What is important to note is that these are all numerous and growing occupations,

TABLE 8.11

New York: Median Weekly Earnings of Office Workers by Industry Group and Occupation, 1981 and 1987 (dollars).

Occupation	Manufacturing		Transportation and Utilities		Non-Manufacturing	
	1981	1987	1981	1987	1981	1987
Secretaries	288.5	426.0	303.0	480.0	279.0	415.0
Stenographers	--	--	328.5	446.0	228.5	371.5
Transcribing typists	--	--	--	--	221.0	--
Typists	193.5	282.0	232.0	315.0	182.5	259.5
Word processors	--	395.5	--	--	--	348.0
Key entry operators	205.0	301.0	282.0	446.0	222.5	305.0
Accounting clerks	230.0	346.0	333.5	443.0	224.5	322.5
Payroll clerks	242.0	356.0	304.5	363.0	226.0	365.0
File clerks	175.0	260.0	205.5	277.0	165.0	216.0
Messengers	168.0	250.0	163.0	258.0	160.0	227.0
Order clerks	227.0	344.0	--	--	209.5	279.5
Receptionists	--	284.5	--	--	--	284.0
Switchboard operators	222.0	353.5	262.5	356.5	216.5	296.0
Switchboard operator/receptionists	205.0	307.0	312.5		210.0	290.0
Computer systems analysts	541.5	786.5	641.5	825.5	531.0	785.0
Computer programmers	400.0	614.5	529.0	613.5	391.5	565.0
Computer operators	285.5	421.0	333.0	452.0	289.5	400.0
Drafters	292.0	480.0	--	--	372.5	518.0
Electronics technicians	580.0	475.5	443.5	475.5	--	--
Registered industrial nurses	392.5	590.5	395.0	--	331.5	561.5

Source: BLS, Area Wage Survey, New York, 1981 and 1987.

especially so in nonmanufacturing industries. There are some exceptions to this differential: median earnings of key entry operators were slightly above $300 in both manufacturing and nonmanufacturing, and those of payroll clerks were $356 in manufacturing industries and $365 in non-manufacturing industries.

When we compare these levels of earnings with those in 1981, we see that a few of these occupations had had lower differentials in 1981. The differential had grown, for example, for file clerks, whose median weekly earnings in 1981 were $175 in manufacturing and $165 in nonmanufac-turing but by 1987 had risen to $260 and $216, respectively; order clerks, whose median earnings were, respectively, $227 and $209 in 1981, in 1987 rose to $344 in manufacturing but only to $279 in nonmanufactur-ing; and switchboard operators rose from, respectively, $222 and $216.50 in 1981 to $353.30 in manufacturing but only to $296 in nonmanufactur-ing in 1987.

County Business Patterns data on average weekly payments by indus-try (see Table 8.12) reveal two trends. First, there is considerable varia-tion in such payments among the major industry groups. Second, Man-hattan-based jobs have higher average weekly payments in all major industry groups than do jobs in the outer boroughs of the city. These data are inadequate in that they are averages and do not indicate the distri-bution of weekly payments by occupation within industry. In 1985, weekly payment in construction ranged from a high of $689 in Manhattan to a low of $468 in Brooklyn (Kings County); in manufacturing, it ranged

TABLE 8.12

New York City: Average Weekly Earnings by Borough and Industry, 1985 (dollars)

	Bronx	Brooklyn (Kings County)	Manhattan (New York County)	Queens	Staten Island (Richmond County)
Construction	554	468	689	597	493
Manufacturing	400	342	575	405	507
Apparel	190	227	352	266	197
Transportation, utilities and communications	589	478	698	653	554
Wholesale	468	413	656	492	416
Retail	240	245	322	242	213
FIRE	344	356	732	371	369
Services	358	316	487	325	314
Business services	286	272	501	295	242
Personal services	223	244	257	210	176
Legal services	514	475	729	405	462

Source: *County Business Patterns,* issue for New York, 1985.

from $575 in Manhattan to $342 in Brooklyn; in FIRE, it ranged from $732 in Manhattan to $344 in the Bronx; in services as a whole, it ranged from $487 in Manhattan to $314 in Staten Island (Richmond County). Within the service sector, business services ranged from $501 in Manhattan to a low of $242 in Staten Island; personal services were uniformly low, ranging from $257 in Manhattan to $176 in Staten Island; and legal services ranged from $729 in Manhattan to a low of $405 in Queens.

Detailed survey data for New York from the U.S. Department of Labor by occupation, industry and sex indicate that a majority of the thirty-five clerical office occupations and of the twenty-one technical office occupations have, at least since 1960, shown a clear pattern of higher average weekly earnings in manufacturing than in nonmanufacturing industries, with the exception of public utilities (see Table 8.13 for summary data).[15]

[15] There follow some examples for four time periods. In 1960, female secretaries earned average weekly earnings of $95 in manufacturing and $89.50 in nonmanufacturing. Within the latter, they earned $89.50 in finance and $96 in public utilities. Among men, male accounting clerks (class A) had average weekly earnings of $102 in manufacturing, $93.50 in nonmanufacturing, $87 in finance and $102.50 in public utilities. Among women in these occupational groups, the earnings were, respectively, $89, $87.50, $86, and $95.50. This pattern of higher average earnings among office workers in manufacturing holds for many detailed office categories (bookkeeping, typing, stenographers, switchboard operators). It also holds for many of the blue-collar service occupations, such as custodial, maintenance, and material moving occupations (for example, elevator operators, several types of janitors, receiving clerks). In 1970 there was a tendency for these occupations to have slightly higher earnings in nonmanufacturing than in manufacturing. Dissaggregating shows that overall, however, wages remained lower in finance than in manufacturing. It is the very high earnings in wholesale and public utilities that appear to pull up average earnings for the nonmanufacturing sector. Among women accounting clerks (class A), earnings were $139.50 in manufacturing, and $140.50 in nonmanufacturing; for the latter group, they were $151 in public utilities and $145 in wholesale, but $137.50 in finance. This pattern held for the most detailed occupational categories. If there is a deviation, it is in the highest-paid categories of a given occupation; for example, the highest-paid secretaries (class A) made more in nonmanufacturing than in manufacturing, but secretaries in the remaining four categories did not. In 1980, there was a clear trend for office clerical, technical, and blue-collar service workers to have higher average earnings in manufacturing than in nonmanufacturing, with the exception of public utilities. This difference was even more pronounced in establishments employing over 500 workers. For example, secretaries in the highest-paid catergory had average weekly earnings of $335.50 in manufacturing and $326 in nonmanufacturing (but $353 in public utilities). This pattern held for three of the four other categories of secretaries. In larger establishments, the corresponding figures were $353.50, $330.50, and $353 in public utilities. We see this pattern in most of the other thirty-five office categories and in most of the twenty-one technical office occupations. Among blue-collar service workers there are some exceptions, notably for mechanics, a category with a larger share of its employment in public utilities. In 1988 there is a slightly altered version of this pattern, with overall manufacturing still paying higher average wages, but with exceptions. In the highest-paid category of secretaries, accounting for 10% of all secretaries surveyed, earnings were $621 in manufacturing and $571 in nonmanufacturing. This holds for other clerical occupations as well, notably word processing, where the highest-paid category earned $442

Disaggregating the nonmanufacturing group reveals pronounced differences, particularly the generally sharply higher earnings in all occupational categories in wholesale trade and public utilities and the often considerably lower average earnings in a majority of clerical and technical occupations in the nonmanufacturing group as a whole, with the financial industry average typically even lower than the overall nonmanufacturing one. When sex is controlled, many of these trends still hold, in good part because office jobs are quite gender typed.

In sum, detailed data on earnings by occupation, industry, and job location in the city as well as by occupation and type of institution of employment all point to significant divisions between manufacturing and nonmanufacturing, between Manhattan and the other boroughs, and between corporate services and other service industries.

London

In the United Kingdom, the evidence from the New Earnings Survey (U.K. Department of Employment 1984, 1985, 1985c) also points to greater income inequality in some of the most dynamic sectors, notably financial and professional services, than is the case in traditional manufacturing. The evidence also points to higher pay levels in these sectors in London than in Britain as a whole, and to a male-female differential. Since the concern is with differentials we have kept the following pay levels in English pounds as presented in the original data.[16]

Table 8.14 shows 1986 earnings by occupation and sex in London and Britain. Most pronounced is the significantly higher than average earn-

---

in manufacturing and $375 in nonmanufacturing. But in the lower-paid categories, earnings were higher in nonmanufacturing than in manufacturing. On the other hand, among some of the technical occupations in offices there is a variety of patterns. For example, the highest-paid category of computer systems analysts earned $891.50 in manufacturing and $912.50 in nonmanufacturing, but this was reversed among the highest-paid category of computer programmers, who earned $650 in manufacturing and $588 in nonmanufacturing. Among blue-collar service occupations in office establishments, most average earnings were higher in manufacturing (for example, guards earned hourly wages of $10.98 in manufacturing and $5.78 in nonmanufacturing), but with exceptions (for example, material-handling laborers earned $9.12 an hour in manufacturing and $11.70 an hour in nonmanufacturing). Similar trends held in large establishments with over 500 employees.

[16] The two major sources of data on the income distribution are the Family Expenditure Survey and the New Earnings Survey. The Family Expenditure Survey is the major source of information on households but covers only 1,000 households in London and underrepresents poorer households. The New Earnings Survey also tends to underrepresent low-wage earners, as it explicitly excludes people earning below the level required for National Insurance payments. This is the stratum that has increased most over the last few years and contains a large share of women.

TABLE 8.13

United States: Relative Salary Levels for Selected Occupations by Industry, 1986

Occupation	All Industries	Mining	Construction	Manu-facturing	Public Utilities[a]	Wholesale	Retail	FIRE	Services[b]
Professional and administrative									
Accountants	100	110	96	100	105	99	101	94	96
Auditors	100	117	--	105	106	93	100	93	105
Public accountants	100	--	--	--	--	--	--	--	100
Chief accountants	100	117	--	101	99	--	100	97	99
Attorneys	100	116	--	104	102	96	98	96	103
Buyers	100	119	103	99	109	100	114	100	99
Computer programmers	100	116	102	102	106	98	99	95	98
Systems analysts	100	114	--	101	106	--	102	96	98
Job analysts	100	--	--	105	114	--	93	91	98
Directors of personnel	100	113	92	99	--	--	--	96	94
Chemists	100	114	--	101	--	--	--	--	89
Engineers	100	118	101	100	103	--	--	--	94
Technical support									
Engineering technicians	100	121	--	99	114	--	--	--	95
Drafters	100	110	102	99	116	--	--	--	98
Computer operators	100	107	--	102	117	100	92	93	95
Photographers	100	--	--	101	116	96	--	91	94
Clerical									
Accounting clerks	100	112	103	101	120	97	92	90	95
File clerks	100	113	96	109	132	--	105	96	101
Key entry operators	100	114	101	103	127	97	87	92	95
Messengers	100	109	--	109	133	114	96	87	100
Personnel clerks	100	113	--	102	115	97	94	89	99
Purchasing clerks	100	--	--	99	114	--	--	--	--
Secretaries	100	109-	100	103	113	101	91	90	100
Stenographers	100	--	--	97	107	98	--	68	91
Typists	100	107	95	107	122	95	95	91	94
General clerks	100	112	90	100	123	94	95	91	96

Source: BLS, *National Survey of Professional, Administrative, Technical, and Clerical Pay*, March 1986.

Note: Dash indicates insufficient employment in one or more work levels in the occupation-industry designation to warrant separate presentation of data.

[a] Transportation (except U.S. Postal Service), communications, electric, gas, and sanitary services.

[b] Limited to engineering, architectural, and surveying services; commercially operated research, development, and testing laboratories; credit reporting and collection agencies; computer and data processing services; management, consulting, and public relations services; noncommercial educational, scientific, and research organizations; and accounting, auditing, and bookkeeping services.

TABLE 8.14

Great Britain and London: Average Weekly Earnings by Occupation and Sex, 1986 (pounds)

Occupational Group	London		Great Britain	
	Men	Women	Men	Women
Professional and related supporting management and administration	399.8	281.3	328.2	237.7
Professional and related in education, welfare, and health	293.6	204.5	261.2	183.6
Literary, artistic, and sports	357.8	243.8	283.7	213.0
Professional and related in science, engineering, technology, and similar fields	304.2	214.7	267.0	178.1
Managerial (excluding general management)	315.6	222.1	265.5	176.1
Clerical and related	209.2	168.6	181.4	137.0
Selling	229.2	145.7	200.8	114.2
Security, protective service	263.5	--	239.0	211.0
Catering, cleaning, hairdressing, and other personal service	169.0	131.9	147.6	108.2
Materials processing (excluding metals)	201.6	--	190.2	119.2
Making and repairing (excluding metals and electrical)	232.6	--	193.5	111.3
Processing, making, repairing, and related (metals and electrical)	229.6	--	539.0	130.3
Painting, repetitive assembling, inspecting, packaging, and related	200.3	127.5	179.3	122.2
All full-time workers	255.0	169.3	207.5	137.2

Source: U.K. Dep't Employment, New Earnings Survey, 1986.

ings level in the professional and related supporting management and administrative occupations in London, where men in these occupations made an average weekly salary of £292 in 1984, rising to £399.8 in 1986, compared with £255 for all full-time men in all occupations. The differential between London and Britain in this particular occupational group is higher than that for all occupations. Though at lower levels, a parallel set of differentials exists in the professional and related occupations in science, engineering, technology, and similar fields. Average weekly earnings for men in these occupations in London were £244.6 in 1984 and £304.2 in 1986, compared with £216.2 in 1984 and £267 in 1986 for Britain. An indication of the distribution of this differential by occupation is the fact that in eleven of the eighteen occupational groups, average weekly earnings for men in London were below the average for all groups in both London and Britain. Only four occupational groups in London and six in Britain accounted for all above-average earnings levels for all nonmanual occupations.

The evidence for women is far more incomplete, partly because of their small presence in several occupational groups. Though the highest average weekly earnings for women in professional and related supporting management and administration were much lower than those for their male counterparts, they showed the same sort of locational differential: £213.8 in 1984 and £281.3 in 1986 for London and £179.1 in 1984 and £237.7 in 1986 for Britain. This is a rather pronounced differential given an average for all occupations of £142.8 in 1984 and £169.3 in 1986 for London and of £117.2 in 1984 and £137.2 in 1986 for Britain. It is interesting that this differential is higher than for the men; but this group is a minority and the majority of women are heavily concentrated in lowly paid occupations. It also suggests a more skewed distribution than that of men and that female differentials between the top occupational earnings group and the next few groups are higher in London than in Britain.

When we control for manual and nonmanual occupations by industry group, very pronounced differentials in average earnings emerge in certain industry groups. Table 8.15 shows these differentials for 1986. I will first discuss men. This differential is highest in banking, finance and insurance, business services, and leasing, at £196.2 for manual workers (below the average) and £328.4 for nonmanual workers. The latter is the highest earnings level for all occupational-industrial cells in London and in Britain as a whole. Another pronounced differential is in electrical engineering (which includes some of the more dynamic industrial branches) at £194.3 for manual and £291.4 for nonmanual workers. For all manufacturing industries, average weekly earnings for men in manual occupations are £209.7 and those for men in nonmanual occupations are £307.3 in London. Among all nonmanufacturing industries, the figures are, respectively, £192.1 and £288.3. The industry group with the highest overall earnings is "manufacture of paper and paper products; printing and publishing," clearly a rather heterogeneous grouping, yet one where the differential between manual and nonmanual is relatively small. In brief, some of the most pronounced gaps in income between manual and nonmanual workers are in two of the most dynamic and technically advanced industry groups, FIRE and electrical engineering.

For Britain as a whole these differentials seem to be less pronounced. For all manufacturing industries, the average weekly earnings were £183.4 for manual and £255.7 for nonmanual men; for all nonmanufacturing industries, these levels were £167.5 and £241.2. As was the case in London, one of the highest differentials, though at lower levels, is in the banking group, at £169.6 for manual and £271.2 for nonmanual workers.

TABLE 8.15
Great Britain and London: Average Weekly Earnings by Sex, Selected Industry, and Manual/Nonmanual Occupation, 1986 (pounds)

	London				Great Britain			
	Men		Women		Men		Women	
	Manual	Non-manual	Manual	Non-manual	Manual	Non-manual	Manual	Non-manual
Electrical engineering	194.3	291.4	125.5	165.5	177.8	259.7	115.5	143.3
Food, drink and tobacco manufacturing	219.8	--	--	--	184.3	260.0	118.0	--
Construction	204.2	264.6	--	134.1	167.2	229.8	--	122.3
Wholesale, distribution, and commission agents	172.1	283.7	--	154.9	154.8	234.4	99.1	126.5
Hotel and catering	142.6	--	108.4	--	126.0	--	40.3	117.8
Retail, distribution, repair of vehicles, and consumer goods	160.8	222.0	--	140.3	141.3	187.3	100.5	109.5
Transportation and communications	211.6	285.6	165.0	174.1	190.9	256.3	143.3	149.8
Banking, finance, insurance, leasing, and business services	196.2	328.4	--	188.8	169.6	271.2	--	148.5
Professional and scientific services	168.7	272.5	120.0	181.9	147.8	242.6	98.0	165.8
Miscellaneous services	181.9	264.5	130.4	185.3	148.5	226.4	102.8	152.9
All manufacturing industries	209.7	307.3	123.8	170.0	183.4	255.7	111.6	136.7
All nonmanufacturing services	192.1	288.3	130.5	176.4	167.5	241.2	103.1	147.0
All industries	197.1	291.3	128.6	175.8	174.4	244.9	107.5	145.7

Source: *Annual Abstract of Greater London Statistics, 1986–1987, 19 (1988): tab. 37.*

The single highest occupational-industrial cell is that of nonmanual occupations in the chemical industry; other high nonmanual categories are in energy and water supply, and in manufacture of motor vehicles and parts. One significant difference between these industries and banking, etc., is the lower differential between manual and nonmanual occupations. As in London, rather high differentials between manual and nonmanual occupations can also be found in the professional and scientific service group, and the public administration, defense, and social security group.

The data on women are far less complete, especially in many of the manufacturing and extractive industries. For all manufacturing industries average weekly earnings in London for women in 1986 were £123.8 for manual and £170 for nonmanual occupations. In Britain, they were respectively, £111.6 and £136.7. For all nonmanufacturing industries, they were £130.5 for manual and £176.4 for nonmanual occupations in London and, respectively, £103.1 and £147.0 in Britain. Not only the money values but also the differentials are lower. In London one of the highest differentials is in professional and scientific services, at £120 for manual and £181.9 for nonmanual occupations. Together with the manufacture of paper, printing, and publishing group and the banking group, this is one of the highest nonmanual earnings levels for women in London. Yet these earnings levels amount to about 60 or 70% of those of men in these same industries. The most pronounced earnings differentials in Britain are, as in London, in the professional and scientific services group, at £98 for manual and £165.8 for nonmanual workers, which are, respectively, below and above average earnings for all nonmanufacturing as well as manufacturing industries. A similar, though somewhat less extreme, case is in the miscellaneous services group. Probably the lowest differential and the lowest overall levels of earnings are in retail, with £100.5 for manual and £109.5 for nonmanual occupations in Britain. See also Table 8.16, showing manual-nonmanual and male-female differentials for 1979–1985.

Besides the occupational transformation, there has been a change in pay settlements by industry and occupation. The overall effect was to favor the already better-off. On the average, from 1977 to 1984 pretax pay rose by 60% in money terms (12% in real terms)—but the increase was 98.6% for professional and managerial men and 49% for catering and cleaning women. Some workers have had cuts in real and in money terms. There have been governmental wage cutbacks in hospital work, part-time cleaning work, and other already low-paying occupations. On the average, London wage rates have kept pace with those in the rest of the country, and the margin of extra payment, given the higher cost of living, has been maintained. It has become evident that institutional bargaining mechanisms mattered; workers who lacked them have had a rel-

TABLE 8.16

London: Average Adult Full-Time Weekly Earnings, 1979-1985 (pounds)

	Manual		Nonmanual		All	
	Men	Women	Men	Women	Men	Women
1979	97.9	60.5	129.0	76.3	115.5	73.3
1982	146.4	92.1	206.8	123.9	183.0	118.9
1985	183.8	118.3	264.7	160.0	233.2	154.4

Source: Inner London Education Authority, London Labour Market Trends - Facts and Figures (July 1987).

ative loss in income (Greater London Council 1986). Groups covered by traditional London weighting allowances have been able to maintain the relative value of such allowances. On the other hand, the pay of catering, cleaning, and similarly placed workers has risen more slowly in London than elsewhere.[17]

The increase in low-paid work has particularly affected women in manual work. White-collar women have maintained their relative position with respect to men since 1980, at 62.5% of male hourly earnings. Manual women's hourly earnings as a share of men's, though higher than for white-collar women, have dropped from 75% in 1980 to 72% in 1984; and part-time women's hourly earnings as a share of men's have fallen from 68% in 1977 to 62% in 1984.

The importance of women's income is reflected in the fact that by 1984, 10% of London households with children had no adult male present, and over 30% were headed by women, two categories that have

[17] The government has weakened the labor movement as a whole, through unemployment and industrial relations legislation. The attack on wages has been strongest on lower-paid workers: Privatization has undermined the conditions of work of many low-paid workers and led to cutbacks in jobs; reform of welfare provisions has reduced eligibility among the lower-paid; and cuts in welfare expenditures have affected access to child care, health care, housing, and training of lower-income people. The government has clamped down on public sector wage increases, except for the police, and is now trying to dismantle the Wages Councils, which would entail an additional loss of protections for low-income workers. Women and minorities are disproportionately represented by the Wages Councils and will thus be particularly affected by these changes. The loss of statutory rights will further exacerbate differentials engendered by sex and race discrimination.

The share of wages in overall household income has been declining in the United Kingdom and in London, but it is still by far the largest component. It went from 73% in the United Kingdom and 75% in London in 1973 to, respectively, 64% and 66% in 1986. In contrast, income from state pensions and social security benefits showed the largest increase of all household income components (U.K. Department of Employment, various years).

been growing since. Excluding retired people, women's earnings, as opposed to welfare aid, are central to one-fifth of London households, and to 28% of the households in Inner London. In England and Wales as a whole, only half as many (nonpensioner) households are headed by women (Greater London Council 1986; Policy Studies Institute 1984).

Blacks' average income is lower than that of whites, even when controlled for qualifications and education. A survey by the Policy Studies Institute (1984) found that the average earnings of white men were about £11 higher.[18] Furthermore, black men are more likely (one-third) than white men (one-fifth) to do shift work on a regular basis.[19] The corresponding figures among women are 18% for West Indians, 14% for Asians, and 11% for whites. Only 1% of white men work only night shifts, but 4% of West Indians and 7% of Asians work the night shifts. The incidence of shift work appears related to language fluency.

When we control for location (see Table 8.17), it is quite evident that the highest absolute wage levels are in the City of London, followed by London. The Southeast as a whole has significantly lower wage levels, especially when we exclude London. Thus, for men, the average gross weekly earnings in 1986 in London were £197.1 for manual and £291.3 for nonmanual jobs; for women they were £175.8 for nonmanual jobs. When we disaggregate and consider only the City of London, earnings for men in manual jobs were £248.7, and those for men in nonmanual jobs were £340, the highest single level for all regions. For women, nonmanual jobs paid £204.6, which is somewhat higher than in London gen-

---

[18] Among those with A-level education, 84% of whites compared to 75% of Asians had nonmanual jobs. The gap is wider for those with O-level education. And among those with no qualifications, the share of whites who have nonmanual jobs is four times that of Caribbean and twice that of Asian men (Policy Studies Institute 1984).

[19] Shift work has increased very rapidly in London, faster than in the rest of the country. It is mostly related to increased capital utilization. According to the Transportation and General Workers Union (Greater London Council 1986), in 1954, one in eight factory workers was involved in shift work; by 1968, one in five; and by 1984, one in three. Official statistics on shift work are inadequate because they count only full-time workers who receive premiums for their shift work in April (the time that the New Earnings survey is taken). Using this very restricted definition, the New Earnings Survey found that the share of full-time male workers receiving shift premiums in London went from 10% in 1974 to 14% in 1984. Among full-time women workers, it went from 5% to 10%. The figures are somewhat higher for Britain. Controlling for occupation, the highest percentage is for manual work, going from 17% in 1974 to 25% in 1984 among men, and from 9% to 16% among women. This represents an overall decline of 29% among all full-time manual and nonmanual workers. In the nonmanufacturing industries, on the other hand, there was an overall increase of 35% in shift premiums, accounted for largely by nonmanual women, who also accounted for the largest single increase in actual numbers.

TABLE 8.17

Great Britain: Average Gross Weekly Earnings by Area, 1986 (pounds)

	Men		Women	
	Manual	Non-manual	Manual	Non manual
London	197.1	291.3	--	175.8
City of London	248.7	340.0	--	204.6
City of Westminster	185.8	306.4	--	185.4
Remainder of Southeast region	175.8	247.2	--	145.0
Total Southeast region	184.7	270.0	--	160.8
Total England and Wales	174.6	245.5	--	146.4
Total Great Britain	174.4	244.9	--	145.7

Source: U.K. Dep't Employment, "Part E: Analysis by Region and Age Group," *New Earnings Survey*, 1987.
Note: Dash indicates that figures not available.

TABLE 8.18

Japan and Tokyo: Average Monthly Earnings 1977-1987 (yen)

	Tokyo	Japan
1977	260,821	219,620
1978	279,816	235,378
1979	290,667	247,909
1980	310,490	263,386
1981	330,622	279,096
1982	349,819	288,737
1987	468,137	390,114

Sources: Tokyo Metropolitan Gov't, *Trends of Labor and Wages in Tokyo-to* (monthly report), Apr. 1977, Apr. 1978. Apr. 1979, Apr. 1980, Apr. 1981, Apr. 1982, and Apr. 1987; id., *Statistics Profile of Tokyo, 1984 (1985)*.
Note: Based on average earnings in establishments with thirty or more full-time workers.

erally. This clearly indicates a significant concentration of all women employed in the City in clerical rather than top professional-level jobs.

Tokyo

Average monthly earnings for full-time workers are, not surprisingly, significantly higher in Tokyo than in Japan as a whole (see Table 8.18). However, this differential has tended to increase over the last few years. Using 1980 wages as an index year, nominal earnings show that before 1980 there was a slight tendency for Tokyo to have a lower level of real wages than that for Japan as a whole. Since 1980, however, the opposite is the case. The absolute differential in average earnings for full-time workers was quite pronounced, with 288,737 yen in 1985 in Japan and 349,819 yen in Tokyo.

When we control for industry and sex some considerable differences emerge. The latest available figures are for 1988 (Tokyo Metropolitan Government 1988a) (see Table 8.19). Average monthly wages for workers in establishments with thirty or more employees stood at 311,132 yen. For men the figure was 356,686 yen, and for women, 199,183 yen. The base from which the data are drawn probably leads to an undercount of the low-income jobs likely to be found in very small establishments with fewer than thirty employees. This effect may hold for both men and women. This differential tends to hold across most industries, though it is significantly lower in several of the services, notably hotel and catering and entertainment, where average earnings are much lower for men but hold close to the overall average for women.

As was the case in London and New York, the highest absolute earning level was in finance for men. This industry also had one of the highest

TABLE 8.19
Tokyo: Average Monthly Earnings by Industry and Sex, 1988

	All Workers (¥)	Men (¥)	Women (¥)	W/M Ratio
Agriculture	318,889	355,208	167,815	0.47
Construction	323,946	347,987	173,481	0.49
Manufacturing	302,359	347,559	164,246	0.47
Energy	397,849	436,376	211,401	0.48
Transport and communication	323,546	335,569	215,859	0.64
Retail and wholesale	283,216	341,060	170,519	0.50
Finance and insurance	365,605	459,421	251,163	0.54
Real estate	358,933	406,613	216,222	0.53
Services	288,326	335,069	193,964	0.58
Hotel and catering	239,702	262,820	172,485	0.66
Entertainment	246,928	291,115	183,817	0.63
Auto services	299,230	316,665	178,838	0.56
Health services	271,308	371,456	230,570	0.62
Education	396,629	436,767	324,756	0.74
Research institutes	350,499	385,233	240,699	0.62
All industries	311,132	356,686	199,183	0.56

Source: Tokyo Metropolitan Gov't, *Trends of Labor and Wages in Tokyo-to,* (monthly report), Apr. 1988.
Note: Based on earnings in establishments with thirty or more full-time workers.

sex differentials, clearly an indication of the concentration of women in lower-paying clerical jobs in this industry group. Average monthly wages in finance were 459,421 yen for men and 251,163 yen for women, one of the highest absolute levels for women, but still only 55% of male earnings. As in London and New York, energy-related industries also had very high absolute wage levels and relatively higher levels for women than in most other industries, with 436,376 yen for men compared with 211,401 yen for women. With few exceptions, most of the service industries had significantly lower average earnings than did manufacturing and transport and communications. Hotel and catering had average monthly earnings of 239,702 yen; entertainment, of 246,928 yen; health services, of 271,308 yen; and retail and wholesale of 283,216 yen. Thus, many of the industries that are growing either pay above-average wages, as is the case with finance, insurance and real estate, or pay below-average wages as is the case with many of the other services. The same trend found in many Western cities is also evident in Tokyo: The lower the average wage level in an industry, the lower the differential between men and women is likely to be. In Tokyo, with the exception of education, which pays high average wages, the average wage of women as a share of men's is well above 60% in industries with low average wages, while it is hardly above 50% in the FIRE group, transport and communications, and other industries paying high average wages.

Data from the Ministry of Labor on earnings in establishments with thirty or more employees for full-time workers by industry show that manufacturing, utilities, transport and communications, and finance and insurance are all above the national average, while much of the service sector is not. They also show that the finance and insurance category has the highest average earnings level (Japan Ministry of Labor, 1984, 1986b, 1987, 1989). Average monthly cash earnings were 585,788 yen in finance and insurance in 1986 and 373,774 yen in manufacturing. When we control for gender, the average monthly highest earnings are still in finance and insurance for men, followed by the utilities (electricity, gas, water) at a far distance, and then the remaining major industry groups, again at a considerable distance from the utilities. For women, the highest average wages were in these same two industry groups, but in contrast to men's earnings, their level stood at 250,000 yen in both groups. This indicates that the degree of inequality between male and female earnings in finance and insurance is very pronounced, much more so than in any of the other major industry groups. The lowest average monthly earnings for women were in wholesale and retail trade and in manufacturing.

Part-Time Work

Part-time work emerged as a significant component of the labor market in advanced industrialized economies from the late 1960s onwards, as new growth sectors, notably health and education, and a tight labor market for full-time workers led employers to organize jobs in ways that permitted the use of women with children.

Data from the U.S. Bureau of Labor Statistics on part-time work show that in 1989 26.1 million U.S. workers accounting for 24% of the national labor force, were employed part time. Part-time work is defined as employment for one to thirty-four hours a week. A more detailed set of measures gives a higher figure of a third of the labor force in 1986, or 50 million workers (Newman 1988). About 80% of these 50 million part-time workers earned less than $11,000 in 1980, the level used by Harrison and Bluestone (1988) to define low-wage jobs, and only 400,000 earned at or above the high-pay level. Part-time work increased from 15% in 1955 to 22% in 1977 (Blumberg 1981: 67, 79; Deutermann and Brown 1978; Harrison and Bluestone 1988: 102). In 1988, the highest frequency of part-time work was in several major service industries: A quarter of all workers in services, excluding FIRE, were part-time workers, and so were 30% of all workers in construction, as well as 11% of workers in FIRE. In contrast, in mining and manufacturing, two sectors traditionally heavily unionized, part-time workers accounted for only around 5%. Wholesale and retail industries and service industries represented, respectively, 32.5% and 38% of all part-time workers in nonagricultural industries, or a total of almost 14 million workers out of the 19.5 million part-time workers employed in nonagricultural industries. FIRE accounted for 0.8 million part-time workers, or 4% of the total, and the self-employed accounted for almost 2 million, or 10%. Together, the service sector broadly defined accounted for over 17 million part-time workers, or 31% of all part-time workers, compared to over 35% of all full-time workers. Clearly the frequency of part-time work is significantly higher in the service sector (U.S. Department of Labor, Bureau of Labor Statistics 1990).

Corresponding data at a more dissaggregated level, such as New York City, are not available. The best approximation, and a way to examine current trends, is the information on job openings. These will tend to underestimate the incidence of part-time jobs, especially in low-wage jobs, given how these data are compiled. In 1988, the single largest concentration of openings was in service jobs, with part-time jobs accounting for 40% of openings. The next-largest concentration was in benchwork (skilled manual labour), with less than 1% of part-time openings. Professional, technical, and managerial openings were also among the larger concentrations of openings; at 56%, these occupations had the highest incidence of part-time openings of any of the major occupational groups and were sharply above the average 37.2% part-time for all openings.

Over the last few years the U.S. government has implemented a number of decisions that promote the growing use of part-time and temporary workers (U.S. Congressional Budget Office 1987). Circular A-76 by the Office of Management and Budget ordered all agencies to raise their use of private firms for service work unless the agency could demonstrate that it could do it more economically in house. The result has been a growing subcontracting out of such services as food preparation, building maintenance, warehousing, and data processing. They involve types of jobs that can be organized in terms of part-time or temporary work hours and, being labor intensive, can cut costs significantly by reducing wages. This is reminiscent of the privatization of these types of services in London, where many of these jobs went from being full-time, year-round regulated jobs with fringe benefits to being part-time or temporary jobs with no fringe benefits and lacking the regulatory protection of the state. In 1984 the government implemented a two-tiered wage system in the U.S. Postal Service, one of the largest employers among government agencies. The purpose was to create more flexible work schedules. The second tier paid wages 25% below the previous standard. In 1985 the government implemented a regulation authorizing the employment of temporary workers at all levels for up to four years and in fact urging agencies to do so "whenever possible." This represented a severe erosion of the contractual arrangement regulating the Civil Service guarantee of permanent employment after a probationary period. Finally, in 1986 the government implemented regulations that make it easier for companies to use homeworkers.

The United Kingdom has better data on this type of work than the United States or Japan. According to the 1984 New Earnings Survey in Britain, the share of women working less than sixteen hours per week increased from a quarter in 1978 to a third in 1984 (U.K. Department of Employment 1984). The data for 1984 are among the most detailed and hence will be discussed here; but the evidence for later years shows that these 1984 trends are, if anything, increasing (see, for example, Hurstfield's [1987] analysis of the 1986 Labor Force Survey). According to the 1984 survey, the trend held for both manual and nonmanual jobs. It was an underestimate because it excluded workers not covered by National Insurance categories. One estimate is that 40% of all part-time women worked less than sixteen hours per week, accounting for 20% of all women workers, both part-time and full-time. In London part-time work is less common than in the rest of the country: 36.6% of all employed women in London worked part time in 1984 compared with 46.6% of women nationwide, and 16% of the work force was made up of part-time women workers compared with 21% in Britain. This lower proportion is probably due to the large percentage of single women, minority women, and single mothers in London, who tend to be under extreme pressure to find full-time employment, a situation that parallels the conditions of similar categories of women in New York City. Furthermore, the higher cost of living in London and a long tradition of work for married women are additional inducements. The concentration of administrative and office work gives women more choices and the greater differential between full-time and part-time jobs in London compared with the rest of the country makes full-time employment relatively more attractive to women. However, as of 1984, women accounted for a larger share (85%) of all part-time jobs in London than nationwide, even though the 15% share of men did represent an increase over the previous decade. The increase in the numbers of part-time workers is evident even over a very short period of time. In 1981 there were 456,000 part-time workers; by 1984 there were 553,000, representing an increase in the share of all women workers, from 31.5% to 36.6%. For the whole of Britian, this share went from 41.9% to 46.6% (4.3 million).

Such increases in part-time work are particularly high in low-wage services. In Britain, 69% of women in the retail industry were part-time workers in 1984, up from 35% in 1961; there has also been an increase in part-time workers in the postal service. In manufacturing, the introduction of new technologies has been associated with increased part-time work. This provides a cheap way of increasing capital utilization through multiple shifts around the clock, seven days a week.

The evidence on temporary jobs is less adequate than that on part-time employment. In the United Kingdom, the Manpower Service Commission does not collect any data on them, and little information is obtained by the BLS in the United States. Furthermore, some of this employment is in violation of various regulations, either because it involves undocumented immigrants or because taxes go unreported or there is some other violation. Research on several industries by the Greater London Council (1986) indicates that both part-time and temporary jobs are increasing in London. The number of temporary agencies has also grown. Temporary work is increasing rapidly in both private and public employment, notably in the health services and in education. Workers are being hired on a daily basis, not even for the week, a development also evident in Manhattan. The privatization of public services has permitted the increasing use of temporary workers as well as subcontracting. London is experiencing the reintroduction of temporary and seasonal work in sectors where it had been eliminated (Greater London Council 1986; Hurst-field 1978).

Data from the Labor Force Survey show that by 1986 one in seven part-time workers held temporary seasonal or casual jobs. These data also show that more male (one in five) than female (one in eight) part-time workers were in temporary employment. In contrast, only one of every fifty male and one of every twenty-five female full-time workers were in temporary employment in 1986, or 3% of all full-time workers. A review of the evidence for Britain by the Low Pay Unit (Hurstfield 1987) con-cludes, "Part-time working is increasingly becoming associated with tem-porary and casual employment." The study cites an analysis of 1984 La-bor Force Survey data (Casey 1987), which found a pronounced increase of temporary employment among part-time workers. One-fifth of all workers are in part-time jobs, but the proportion is well over half for temporary workers. In industries such as retail, catering, and personal services, which have a high proportion of part-time work, over 80% of temporary workers are part time (Casey 1987).

Many of these are also industries with seasonal and day-to-day varia-tions in demand, which has increasingly led employers to hire casual workers for unspecified periods of time, some as short as one afternoon (Casey 1987). While full-time and part-time temporary workers, as well as other part-time workers, can be employed with contracts specifying length of employment, the idea behind casual workers is to eliminate even those obligations and expectations. From the standpoint of the law, such workers are frequently not defined as employees but as self-em-ployed, thereby freeing the employer from all obligation. The worker is free to accept or reject employment, and the employer is under no obli-gation to provide a minimum amount of employment (Hurstfield 1987). Casual workers are excluded from most statutory employment rights ex-cept if they can demonstrate that they are actually regular employees.

Data from the Labor Force Survey in Japan (Japan Ministry of Labor 1987, 1989) show that the share of part-time workers increased from un-der 7% of all workers in 1970 to 12% in 1987, or 5 million workers. Among women workers, this share almost doubled, from about 12% in 1970 to 22% in 1985 and over 23% in 1987, or a total of about 3.65 million women. All these figures exclude people employed in agriculture and forestry. Of 3.6 million female part-time workers, about 0.8 million were in manufacturing; 1.3 million, in wholesale and retail trade; 170,000, in FIRE; and almost 1 million, in other service industries. Thus, almost 24% of part-time women workers were in manufacturing; over 35%, in wholesale and retail trade; about 5%, in FIRE; and almost 28%, in other service industries. There are also small numbers in government, trans-port, and a few other sectors.

Part-time work in Japan is defined as a job with scheduled hours per week "substantially shorter than those of regular workers" (Japan Ministry of Labor 1984). It excludes seasonal and temporary employment and is thus an undercount of all jobs that are not full-year, full-time jobs. Part-time work is measured as regular employment of under thirty-five hours a week or those called "part-timers" or equivalent names in their places of work. "Part-timers" often work as many hours as regular full-time workers; what distinguishes them is the lack of various benefits and entitlements, or in the terms used here, a casualized employment relation. The latest available evidence shows that by 1983, 58% of all firms surveyed employed part-time workers.

The vast majority of part-time jobs are in the service sector. Wholesale, retail, and eating and drinking places have raised their relative share of part-time workers most, from 25.4% in 1970 to 35.1% in 1985 (Japan, Management and Coordination Agency 1986: 27). This represents an increase from 330,000 part-time workers in 1970 to 1.17 million in 1985 and accounts for 41% of the total increase in part-time work. The number of part-time jobs in manufacturing doubled from 400,000 in 1970 to 800,000 in 1985. Women part-time workers increased by 38.2%, or 1.5 million, from 1982 to 1987, a far larger increase than for the labor force generally. Part-time workers are paid mostly by the hour. Average hourly wages in June 1987 were 623 yen, ranging from 710 yen in services, 617 yen in wholesale, retail, and restaurants, and 584 yen in manufacturing.

Official counts of legal homeworkers in Japan show gradual decline over the last decade. In 1987 there were over 1 million such workers, almost all women (Japan Ministry of Labor 1987). The largest share of homework, 34%, is in clothing and related items, followed by 18.6% in electrical/electronic equipment (including assembly of electronic parts) and almost 16% in textiles. The remaining share includes a very broad range of activities, from making toys and lacquer ware to printing and related work. It is quite possible that the existing regulations protecting homeworkers and providing them with fringe benefits are eroding. Official figures are describing a decline in the fully entitled share of homeworkers but possibly not registering an absolute increase among homeworkers with no protection. There are some indications that the latter category may be increasing.

Conclusion

Data on earnings and employment are typically highly problematic, and they may be even more so in the case of cities since often the best data sets are at the national rather than the urban level. The object in this chapter was not a direct comparison of these three cities, a task that would be quite precarious given the differences in the types and availability of data, but rather to capture major trends in employment and earnings as well as transformations in the relative positions of industries, occupations, earnings, and sex within each city.

New York, London, and Tokyo show parallel employment and earnings trends. All three experienced losses of manufacturing jobs and above-average growth in producer services, though the timing and magnitude varied. Finance paid the highest average salaries in all three cities, but the gap between men and women is enormous. Among the fastest-growing jobs are professional and clerical occupations, the former paying some of the highest salaries and the latter paying increasingly lower salaries. Furthermore, where the evidence is available, clerical jobs in the new service industries tend to have lower salaries than do clerical jobs in manufacturing and transportation, while the reverse is the case with professional jobs. This suggests growing inequality in earnings insofar as the new service industries and professional and clerical jobs are among the fastest-growing elements in these cities. Finally, in all three cities, part-time jobs have increased and are disproportionately held by women; the available evidence shows that part-time jobs tend to be more lowly paid than full-time jobs. Perhaps the most acute case is Tokyo, where the majority of new jobs in the 1980s were part-time jobs and temporary employment agencies constituted one of the fastest growing industry branches.

Overall, the outcome of the new forms of growth and decline has been (1) an increase in the inequality between professional and clerical workers and for this inequality to be sharper in the new service industries than in older manufacturing and transportation sectors; (2) a reproduction of the earnings gap between men and women; and (3) an increase in the share of part-time jobs and in the share of women in the labor force, two trends not completely unconnected.

When we compare the leading growth sectors of the post-World War II period with today's, we can see pronounced differences in their occupational and income distributions. Today's leading sectors generate a higher share of high-income jobs and of low-wage jobs. The growth in inequality is further fed by the erosion of workers' gains in manufacturing and the high incidence of layoffs and plant closures involving unionized and well-paying jobs, especially in the United States and United Kingdom, but now also in Japan. Finally, the general shift to a service economy entails a much larger share of low-wage jobs than is the case with a strong manufacturing-based economy. The overall result is an increased income polarization.

Nine

Economic Restructuring as Class and Spatial Polarization

EMPLOYMENT AND EARNINGS statistics, such as those discussed in the previous chapter, provide only a partial description of the socioeconomic conditions in New York, London, and Tokyo under the current economic regime, one characterized by the dominance of producer services and finance. They leave out components of the economic and social order that are not captured through these kinds of figures and especially undercount, or do not count at all, employment in informal and casual labor markets as well as industrial homework. Nor do these statistics describe the specific labor markets in which employment and earnings are embedded. Finally, employment and earnings statistics do not convey the concrete conditions of life in these cities for the population at large.

I propose to address these broader questions through an examination of the specific forms assumed by socioeconomic conditions in New York, London, and Tokyo. Running through this analysis is a concern with the articulation of the leading growth sectors to other components of the economic base of these cities. The attempt is to identify key elements in the dynamics that contribute to constituting and reconstituting—whether in part or in full—the social order in these cities, beyond what is happening in the leading sectors, as discussed in the preceding chapters, but continuously raising the question of the articulation of this order.

The first section discusses the consequences of such a new economic core of advanced, high-growth industries for the organization of other economic sectors in these cities. Specifically, does the existence of a high-growth sector feed the expansion of what appear to be declining or backward economic sectors, sectors that do not conform to our image of a postindustrial economy? To what extent do the most sophisticated white-collar industries that characterize the new economic core need easy access to a broad range of industrial services, a land use that is not competitive in such cities? The second section discusses how the greater income polarization in the leading industries, as described in the preceding chapter, is constituted socially; that is to say, is it merely a change in the income distribution, or are there new social forms associated with an increase of high-income and of low-income workers? What is the social geography emerging from this transformation?

The third section examines the evidence of the growth of casual and informal labor markets. Are there conditions in the global city that stimulate the expansion of casual and informal work, or, on the contrary, do these forms of work shrink as a result of the presence of a thriving postindustrial core? Is the sphere of casual and informal work a somewhat autonomous one, not affected by conditions in the leading economic sectors, basically a remnant from an earlier economic period or, in the case of New York City and London, perhaps associated with immigration from the Third World?

The facts of immigration, ethnicity, and race need to be incorporated for an adequate understanding of labor market questions, most particularly in New York, but to some extent also in London. The fourth section discusses the available evidence on immigrant and black workers in New York and London and on the new illegal immigration in Tokyo. It examines the place of the new Third World immigration of the 1970s and 1980s in New York City, the earlier Asian and Caribbean immigration in London, and the recent illegal immigration of Asian workers into Tokyo. Is theirs a circumstantial arrival? Do they inhabit a world of work basically unconnected to the social and economic order of the global city? Or, on the contrary, are significant components of their employment articulated by economic polarization?

Overall Effects of Leading Industries

We can identify at least three major bodies of theoretical work that address the question of the articulation of leading economic sectors with the rest of the economy and, more generally, the socioeconomic conditions in cities under the current regime of advanced services. One is general economic development theory; another, the model of the economic base or export sector in urban economies and its multiplier effects; and the third, the sociological model of the postindustrial economy.

According to general economic development theory, as economic development progresses it will bring about a generalization of the market and market relations to an increasing number of institutional spheres in a society. In the case of the labor market, this entails a growing incorporation of workers, and people of working age generally, into formal work relations. This process is part of the broader expansion of the regulatory capability and intent of the state. The period of rapid growth after World War II was, indeed, characterized by the attainment of high levels of economic development in major industrialized countries and the growing incorporation of workers into the formal labor market. A series of regulatory aspects ensured that a majority of workers had full-time, year-round jobs, often with unemployment and retirement benefits. Unions were central in this expansion of formal work relations. Fordism is the most institutionalized version of this model of the labor market. This process was to continue as development proceeded to higher stages. One would, according to this thesis, expect that the leading cities in the most advanced countries would certainly be characterized by a strong expansion in the share of workers incorporated in highly developed and encompassing formal labor markets. The growth of casual work would be interpreted as a development lag or as exogenous to the advanced sectors of the economy; for example, informal labor markets could be viewed as imported through Third World immigration.

The model of basic versus nonbasic industries addresses the issue of city-building economic activities (Mayer 1969; Alexander 1954). City-building industries are those that generate more than is consumed internally and hence produce for export as well. It is this export activity that becomes a vehicle for multiplier effects in that it contributes to the expansion of the other sectors in the economy that service the basic industries. Exports provide an exogenous source of additional income for the city and induce a demand for additional support services beyond those required by the resident population. Expansion in the nonbasic sectors of the economy is basically reproductive; it cannot generate new growth. Much debate has centered on whether manufacturing, always held to be a basic sector, is indeed so in the current era. Classic arguments on services as the basic sector were developed by Blumenfeld (1955) and by Tiebout (1957); a notion of services as the basic sector seems particularly appropriate for the case of major cities that are leading centers in the production and export of producer services. This thesis would suggest that the high level of exports and the extremely high value of these exports in the three cities under consideration, should have a rather high multiplier effect and the benefits should be evident over a wide range of industries in these cities.

In its original and richest formulation, the postindustrial model posits a major transformation, one where the expansion of the highly educated work force and the centrality of knowledge industries will lead to an overall increase in the quality of life and a greater concern with social rather than narrowly economic objectives. It is impossible to recapitulate the full thesis, and unnecessary given the widespread familiarity with Bell's (1973) text. For the purposes of this discussion what matters is Bell's notion of a hierarchy in the growth of services, the first type of services developed being those linked to industry, notably transportation and distribution, and the later ones being those linked to a higher quality of life. For Bell, this latter stage in the development of services will be characterized by a more collective or communal nature, given the type of needs they respond to and the public character of provision for many of these services. Furthermore, the preeminence of theoretical and technical knowledge with a scientific base makes postindustrial society one resting on knowledge. The central problem of society is no longer that of capital or the organization of industrial work but that of the organization of scientific knowledge. This means that the class of professionals and technicians not only expands greatly but becomes the vital center of postindustrial society. This is a heterogeneous and stratified class, ranging from teachers and health workers to engineers and scientists. But at its core are the latter, engineers and scientists. It is an enlightened elite, whose politics can play a significant role in changing the social order. The transformation of work is also evident in the organization of firms and power. The preeminence of services is expected to entail a growth of smaller-sized firms, where professional knowledge is more important, contributing to making firms and the organization of work more humane and social. This represents the transition from an economic to a more sociological mode of thought in the management of firms and of society.

Several elements in this model have certainly taken place. If we consider the producer services and finance as knowledge industries, then it is evident that there has been rapid growth of such industries and that they have become the dominant sectors in advanced economies. Furthermore, as the preceding chapter indicated, there has been an expansion of highly paid professional-level jobs and a growth in the high-income stratum of workers. Finally, high-income gentrification as we see it in these three cities does in many ways represent a higher quality of life for those that benefit from it. Important questions that arise are first, whether the increase in low-wage jobs and the increase in informal and casual work are or are not articulated with these advanced, higher forms of growth. Second, does the rapid increase in the number of small firms in the advanced services alter the nature of concentration in these economies? The evidence presented in preceding chapters suggests that high levels of economic concentration continue, though often in different forms from that represented by the large manufacturing-oriented multinational corporations and the large transnational banks that dominated economic activity in the 1960s and well into the 1970s. Alongside these types of corporations, there is now a vast number of comparatively small firms, which together exercise immense control over investment and economic activity, especially in these cities. And finally, how is the vast proliferation of small firms with marginal returns and mostly low-wage jobs we see in these cities articulated with the advanced sectors of the economy?

A central question in light of the evidence presented in all the preceding chapters is to what extent these models are ultimately derived from a historical period that has come to an end, a period characterized by strong tendencies toward growth in the middle sectors of the economy. There was sharp growth in consumer and capital goods industries, construction, and other industries associated with the suburbanization of the population in the United States after World War II and in the United Kingdom beginning in the interwar period and with rapid urbanization of the population in Japan. In both the United States and the United Kingdom, growth in the economy was centered on a range of industries servicing the needs of the population. Japan's accelerated industrial growth after World War II was in basic industry and eventually consumer goods for export; however, the equally accelerated urbanization of the population—one of the fastest in the world—meant that notwithstanding a low standard of living, the construction and furnishing of housing and the provision of public services and goods were also central in Japan. What is distinct about the current period is a pronounced discontinuity in this pattern, with growth centered on finance and the production of services for firms.

Different types of economic growth promote different types of social forms. In the post-World War II era, growth was characterized by the vast expansion of a middle class and formal labor markets. This middle class was not as well off in the United Kingdom and Japan as in the United States, but it was not, ultimately, a fundamentally different process. The historical forms assumed by this expansion, notably capital intensity, standardization, and suburbanization, promoted the generalization of formal labor market relations and acted against the casualization of work. Large, vertically integrated firms in manufacturing as well as in insurance and banking, offered elaborate internal labor markets with possibilities for advancement, considerable job security, and various fringe benefits (Edwards 1979). The lifetime job security in Japan rested not only on culture, as has often been asserted, but on conditions akin to elaborate internal markets that offered possibilities for shifting workers to different jobs if necessary. The social forms accompanying this process, particularly as they shaped the structures of everyday life, reproduced and further induced a middle-class culture. A major inference that can be drawn from this is that a large middle class contributes to patterns of consumption that promote standardization in production and hence, under certain conditions, are conducive to greater levels of unionization or other forms of worker entitlement that can be derived from large plants or large offices—an entitlement which is, in turn, conducive to middle-income jobs. Many of the patterns evident today work in the opposite direction, promoting small scales, less standardization, and an increasingly casualized employment relation.

The consolidation of an economic core of top-level management and servicing activities needs to be viewed alongside the general move to a service economy and the decline of manufacturing. New economic sectors are reshaping the job supply. However, so are new ways of organizing work in both new and old sectors of the economy. Components of the work process that twenty years ago took place on the shop floor and were classified as production jobs today have been replaced by a combination of machine/service or worker/computer/engineer. Activities that were once all consolidated in a single service retail establishment have now been divided between a service delivery outlet and central headquarters. Finally, a large array of activities that were being carried out in large-scale, vertically integrated firms in the postwar decades are today increasingly characterized by small-scale, flexible specialization and subcontracting. In brief, the changes in the job supply evident in major cities are a function both of new sectors and of the reorganization of work in both new and old sectors.

These trends assume distinct forms in (1) the spatial organization of cities, (2) consumption and more generally the structures for social reproduction, and (3) the organization of the labor market. I will discuss each of these.

Social Geography

The theoretical models briefly cited above tend to correspond to prevailing notions about the spatial configuration of major cities in highly developed countries. One key element is the suburbanization of the population associated with the expansion of a middle class and understood as an increase in the quality of life associated with economic development. A second element is the continued suburbanization of jobs: in an earlier phase, suburbanization of factories as central cities became obsolete locations for large, mechanized plants, and more recently, the suburbanization of office jobs made possible by modern telecommunications. At the same time, the inner city became an increasingly powerful image in Western cities to describe central areas where low-income residents, unable to afford a house in the suburbs, were left behind. In the case of New York and London, the inner city increasingly also contained concentrations of public housing inhabited by minority residents. The continuing existence of a sizable middle class in large cities was overshadowed by the growth of suburbanization and the inner city. Generally, older cities lost population in the 1960s and 1970s. Demographic, economic, and technological factors all contributed to strengthen this image of the sociospatial configuration of major cities, one to a large extent rooted in postwar developments that continued into the 1960s.

The following discussion of sociospatial patterns in these cities aims at detecting major changes and the underpinnings of a new conception of space. An emerging body of scholarship is producing new knowledge about the social geography of advanced economies (Gregory and Urry 1985; Soja 1989; Massey 1984; Scott and Storper 1986), a subject also discussed in several preceding chapters. In addition, an important reexamination of the impact of technology on the spatial organization of the economy can be found in Castells (1989).

Have the various transformations discussed throughout this book engendered a new social geography, or have they been absorbed by the existing spatial patterning of social forms? Spatial differentiation based on social and economic characteristics is a basic trait of cities, often expressed by changes in land use. The focus here is on changes associated with the economic transformation of the last two decades, specifically the sociospatial forms through which the changes in the industrial, occupational, and earnings distribution are made concrete. These sociospatial forms are one expression of the relation between space, in this case, urban space, and the economy in major cities dominated by the new leading industries. This expression is not necessarily captured by a detailed description of the spatial distribution of various types of firms and households. The built-in rigidities of physical structures limit the spatial transformation. And the vastness of these urban economies limits the overall impact of leading industries. Thus the attempt here is to capture ruptures, instances where the leading growth trends have altered existing arrangements or where massive declines have made possible totally new land uses or sociospatial forms. Distinct sociospatial forms arising out of these processes are high-income residential and commercial gentrification, the massive construction projects described in Chapter Seven, and sharp increases in spatially concentrated poverty and physical decay. One question for us is whether we are seeing the formation of a sort of new territorial complex at the level of the spatial and institutional arrangements in cities dominated by services and finance, a complex of luxury offices and housing, massive construction projects, and appropriation of urban areas that previously had gone to middle and low-income households and to moderately profitable firms?

It has been several decades since these cities experienced such massive transformations. Notwithstanding different political systems and planning traditions, all three cities underwent large-scale, state-directed spatial reorganization in the past (Fainstein and Fainstein 1983; Savitch 1988; Ishizuka and Ishida 1988).[1] Though under different forms and with different

---

[1] Planning has an interesting history in all three cities and a vast literature, impossible to

players, New York, like London, went through a period of state-directed redevelopment (Fainstein and Fainstein 1983, 1985).[2] Under its master planner, Robert Moses, there was a rapid modernization and development of highways and bridges, there were slum clearance programs that eliminated whole neighborhoods, and there were public housing construction programs that benefited significant numbers and sectors of the working and middle classes even though they hurt and displaced others.

In London, there was massive development of the outer area in the interwar period through housing construction and location of manufacturing firms; public (authority) housing was built largely in inner London and contributed to concentrations of low-income households, as in New York City. Inner London eventually received much of the Asian and Caribbean immigration of the postwar period. This was a period when London was seen as overcongested and overpopulated; its expansion was seen as threatening the balanced development of the outer areas. One response was the Green Belt, introduced in 1934. Abercrombie's Greater London Plan of 1944 sought to strengthen the Green Belt by concentrating development in so-called New Towns within the region and controlling the development of rural land. The interwar and postwar periods were major planning eras for London and its surrounding areas, marked by the departure of people and jobs from London, the Green Belt, the New Towns, and, increasingly, the physical and economic decay of inner London.

In Tokyo, the central element in urban planning and management policy from the late 1950s had been the attempt to regulate the concentration of the commuting population and of industry in Tokyo through the development of a green belt. The decentralization of industry called for in the 1963 National Capital Region Development Plan further sought to regulate Tokyo's growth. But a much higher than expected concentration

---

list here. Among others, see Savitch (1987, 1988); Boyer (1986); and Ishizuka and Ishida (1988).

[2] Fainstein and Fainstein (1983) distinguished three types of local regimes and three stages in the postwar politics of urban development in the United States. From the mid-1940s to 1965, there was an emphasis on large-scale development projects, initially sponsored by governments. This was a period characterized by strong government participation and little popular opposition. It was followed by "concessionary regimes," a phase that lasted up to about the mid-1970s. This phase was dominated by the necessity to make concessions in addressing the urban struggles of the late 1960s and early 1970s led by minority groups and community organizations. The final period, which includes the present, is seen as dominated by business interests and characterized by a stress on fiscal stability, along with the maintenance of some of the institutions and programs stemming from the preceding concessionary regime. According to Fainstein and Fainstein (1983), New York City entered the directive period earlier than did most other cities in the United States but otherwise followed this pattern.

of population and manufacturing, forcing a vast expansion of Tokyo, led to the abolishment of the green belt concept. In the 1968 Plan, this concept was replaced by that of suburban development. The decentralization of population and manufacturing to the suburbs continued to be promoted during the 1960s and 1970s with massive construction of suburban housing and transportation systems.

In all three cities, attempts to stem population growth through decentralization were replaced by alarm at the rapid decline of central areas due to population and job losses. In all three cities, though at slightly different periods, a prevalent conception in the postwar era had been that left unattended, they would grow excessively. Planning was aimed at regulating this growth by decentralizing population and jobs. This conception prevailed even as the population in central areas was beginning to decline (see Buck, Gordon, and Young [1986: ch. 2–3] for a good account of this process in the case of London).

Important to the transformation of New York City was the massive outflow of white residents to the suburbs and a massive influx of Southern blacks and Puerto Ricans in the 1950s and 1960s; later, in the 1970s and continuing today, these flows were replaced by a large new immigration from South America, the Caribbean Basin, and Asia. The radical transformation in the city's demographic composition altered the meaning of public housing. White voters withdrew their support for what they saw as mostly housing benefiting blacks (Fainstein and Fainstein 1983). Segregation in the city increased immensely. The urban renewal programs ultimately resulted in greater segregation because they destroyed the various smaller black neighborhoods in a larger number of areas to make room for highways, large-scale public housing, or middle-class housing. Greater residential segregation also accelerated white flight to the suburbs, further increasing residential segregation. In 1940, 94% of the city's population was white. In 1985, the proportion was down to 49%.

In London, the interwar period was one of growing homeownership among workers and manufacturing expansion in the outer areas. As is the case with many old cities, inner London had long contained above-average unemployment and a considerable incidence of casual employment. Suburban growth of population and jobs at best left these conditions in inner London unchanged and at worst contributed to the decay by draining better-off people and better jobs. Furthermore, in the postwar period, the City of London was continuing to decline, a process that had begun in the interwar period. The City had increasingly become financial rather than trade oriented. The further decline of the British Empire and the collapse of the international financial system caused the City to decline. It became far less important to the London economy than it had been before the war, when international trade and banking were central to the British economy.

In Tokyo, the continuing outmigration of young people from the central wards to the suburbs led to a change in urban policy during the 1980s: The three wards that constitute the central business district—Chiyoda, Chuo and Minato—sought to encourage migration, especially of young people, into their wards through the construction of new housing at a time of extremely rapid increases in the price of land due to the large-scale construction of high-rise office buildings (Nakabayashi 1987). This points to a strong element in the government's conception of the central city: The notion that areas of the city should become completely deserted by night as a result of the lack of a critical mass of residents was strongly resisted, unlike what was the case in the United States after World War II, where the emphasis was on the suburbanization of the population and the continuing perception of central cities as undesirable places for family life. In this regard, then, Japan is closer to the European conception of the central city.

The loss of manufacturing jobs and the associated loss of people have further eroded the base of local services and commerce in central Tokyo, in turn further inducing outmigration. There is very strong concern in local ward governments with promoting a stable residential base that includes young people of working age, residential buildings, neighborhood commerce, and consumer services. There is an understanding that population loss will affect the mix of activities and lead to a quick deterioration of these areas. There is, in addition, a political loss of power associated with a declining population for the local governments of these wards.

In the 1980s, the central areas of London, New York, and Tokyo increased their specialization as high-priced locations for firms and residences on a scale and with traits that diverged markedly from earlier periods. Crucial to all three cities has been the development of large-scale, high-cost luxury office and residential complexes, as was discussed in Chapter Seven in the context of the international property market and the expansion of new growth industries. But along with these developments, there has been a continuation and consolidation of concentrated poverty and extreme physical decay in the inner cities. The appropriation of a growing area of the city for high-priced rehabilitation and redevelopment has also contributed to a sharp increase in homelessness, especially in New York, but also in London and, on a much smaller scale, in Tokyo. All three cities have long had a significant concentration of high-income residents—but not quite on this scale or quite so evident and not quite producing a complex of consumption practices and lifestyles that others could buy into, wholly or in part, depending on their incomes: the boutiques, the fine restaurants, the renovated brownstones or new condominiums in the city. And all three cities have long had a significant concentration of poor people. But the extent of the segmentation and spatial unevenness has reached dimensions not typical of earlier decades.

One process that articulates these various outcomes is gentrification. Gentrification was initially understood as rehabilitation of decaying or low-income housing by middle-class outsiders in central cities. In the late 1970s, a broader conceptualization of the process began to emerge, and by the early 1980s, new scholarship had developed a far broader meaning of gentrification, linking it with processes of spatial, economic, and social restructuring (Hamnett 1984; Holcomb and Beauregard 1981; Smith, N. 1982). Smith and Williams (1986) note that up to the late 1970s, the notion of gentrification as residential rehabilitation may have been an adequate understanding of the process, but by the early 1980s, it was becoming evident that residential rehabilitation was only one facet of a far broader process linked to the profound transformation in advanced capitalism: the shift to services and the associated transformation of the class structure and the shift toward the privatization of consumption and service provision. Gentrification emerged as a visible spatial component of this transformation. It was evident in the redevelopment of waterfronts, the rise of hotel and convention complexes in central cities, large-scale luxury office and residential developments, and fashionable, high-priced shopping districts.

When homes are also considered places of work—either unpaid housework or paid industrial homework—then the industrial geography of the city assumes new meanings. As Harris (1988) put it, there is a geography of unpaid work—and, I would add, a geography of informal work (Sassen 1988).[3] Insofar as different socioeconomic, ethnic, and racial households are embedded in different sets of relationships there may be distinct patterns by class and race. High-income households will tend to be locations for paid rather than unpaid housework, and so will the new two-career city-based households. Low-income immigrant households are often workplaces for paid industrial homework and mostly unpaid housework. Middle-class suburban and urban households may increasingly become places for a growing portion of paid housework (day nannies and cleaning women who come once a week) and for paid work (word processing, freelance professional work, etc.). This brings up a series of questions about standard descriptions and definitions of labor market areas. It suggests also that for low-income immigrants and middle-class suburban women engaged in clerical homework, the "labor market" may be a rather differ-

---

[3] Harris (1988) has pointed out that, while there are many studies about the impact of job location on place of residence and, more generally, determinants of residential change, for example, gentrification (Hoover and Vernon 1962; Ley 1986), little attention has been given to the way in which the social geography of the city affects the location of work.

ent entity than that contained in standard definitions. Increasingly seg-
regated residential areas for blacks in New York City and the small number of black suburban commuters also may be altering the geography of
the labor market.

A full account of the social geography of each city would require a
whole book in itself. The following discussion emphasizes particular processes in each of these cities. The focus will be on particular aspects. In
the case of New York, much has been written about suburban growth, so
we will limit the discussion largely to an examination of the reorganization of space in Manhattan, a key location for some of the most pronounced changes, and focus somewhat less on the rest of the city and the
suburbs. In the case of London, the key dynamic continues to be the
relationship of London to the rest of the Southeast; the concern for us
will be the extent to which the transformations in the economic base of
London and the sharp rise in the importance of finance have weakened
that relation or have created new forms of incorporation of the Southeast.
In the case of Tokyo, much has been said about its vast suburban sprawl,
its bedroom communities, and its masses of commuters to central Tokyo.
This monotony of outward suburban expansion has been sharply broken
by two developments: One is the massive construction projects discussed
in Chapter Seven and the second is the growth of an inner city. Here,
we will focus on this unexpected and little-known growth of an inner city,
reminiscent of what we see in Western cities.

New York

Manhattan's specialized role as a place for office jobs increased over the
three decades between 1950 and 1980. But it also became too expensive
for the vast majority of office workers to reside in. Using census data,
Harris (1988) found that between 1950 and 1980 the location quotient for
managerial and professional jobs in Manhattan rose from 102 to 120, and
that for clerical jobs rose from 114 to 128. The massive job losses in the
1970s become evident, however, when we compare 1970 and 1980. The
overrepresentation of clerical jobs in Manhattan declined from 141 in
1970 to 128 in 1980, a function of the departure of large offices and headquarters and the growing concentrations of clerical jobs in the suburbs.[4]
It also declined in the rest of New York City and increased in outlying
areas, especially in the inner suburban ring, where it went from 88 to 96.

---

[4] Decentralization of clerical jobs has involved moving jobs not only to suburbs, but also
a short distance to the areas surrounding the central business district or to distant locations
(Armstrong and Milder 1985; Roberts 1987).

According to some analysts (Moss and Dunau, 1986), the relative decline in Manhattan's overrepresentation of clerical jobs will probably continue. However, this can only be the case if growth of clerical jobs in the rest of the region outstrips growth in Manhattan, since the evidence for 1980–1988 indicates considerable growth in clerical jobs in Manhattan. Indeed, one could have expected that the suburbanization of the population and of many firms and the resultant need in the suburbs for various types of businesses, and for professional and clerical workers, would have led to a more pronounced reduction in the locational concentration of such jobs in Manhattan and a higher increase in the suburban quotient. But as of 1988, clerical jobs, as well as managerial and professional jobs, remained underrepresented in all areas of the region except Manhattan. Indeed, the location quotient for these jobs in the region had hardly changed over the previous decades, notwithstanding large increases in absolute numbers. In stark contrast, in 1988 Manhattan had underrepresentation of all other occupational categories (sales, crafts, operators and laborers, and service workers), while these were all overrepresented in the rest of the city and in the inner and outer suburban rings (for a more detailed account, see Harris 1988).[5]

In terms of residential patterns, Manhattan has overrepresentation of managers, professionals, and service workers. The sharpest increase has been for professionals, where the quotient rose from 148 in 1970 to 163 in 1980; that for managers rose from 112 to 127. The quotient for service workers, on the other hand, had been declining for the previous thirty years, from 190 in 1950 to 130 in 1970 and 105 in 1980. Its continuing representation as of 1980 was clearly a function of the high share of minority and immigrant workers who reside in Manhattan. From 1970 to 1980, the residential quotient for managers and professionals in the inner suburban ring actually declined, from 106 to 99 for professionals and from 120 to 109 for managers; but their absolute numbers did not decline, nor did they move out of the suburbs and into the city. Rather, the decline in the suburban quotient was a function of the sharp increase in these jobs in Manhattan and in the choice of urban residence among new job entrants. In the 1970s and 1980s, the baby boom generation came of age, and the preference for urban living among the new high-income professionals was a key element in the gentrification of large sectors of the city. The available evidence for the 1980s indicates that this trend for urban living among professionals became even stronger.

This trend is strongest among women, even though their absolute

---

[5] Retail jobs are the only major category not significantly over- or underconcentrated in Manhattan, an indication of the extent to which they follow population distribution. Harris (1988) observes that the retail industry reflects the social geography of the city, capturing the specific ethnic and class components of an area.

numbers are smaller. A far larger share of female than of male managers and professionals working in Manhattan live in Manhattan (location quotient of 168 compared with 115 for men). Women managers are more likely to be single or part of two-career households, while male managers are still more likely to have a traditional household situation, with the woman working in a nonprofessional job. Susser (1988) has shown in her work the extent to which the urban household depends on hired houseworkers.[6] In this context, it would seem, then, that women are a key factor in the process of gentrification in New York City (Rose 1984: 62; Smith, N. 1987: 158).

A more disaggregated analysis of professionals points to significant differentiation. Evidence on upper-level professionals living in New York City provides information on a central element in the restructuring of consumption and rapid gentrification in Manhattan and certain areas in Brooklyn. It should also provide information on the extent to which this sector of the population is linked to various institutional complexes. Clearly, the overall group of upper-level professionals actually working in New York City is far larger given a considerable number of commuters.

Brint (1988) classified professionals and managers into four categories based on census data: upper professionals, rank-and-file professionals, smaller employers, and marginal professionals. In Brint's analysis the first group is characterized by highly valued intellectual resources, employment in powerful organizations, and involvement with the cosmopolitan side of the economic and cultural life of the city. It includes many corporate lawyers, professionals in the leading accounting, advertising, engineering and other such firms, leading artists and designers, television executives, researchers in leading scientific and civic institutions. The other three categories do not quite fit the model of the new professional: they are teachers, social workers, engineers, government lawyers, and professionals in small, locally oriented firms. Among the small employers group, there are now significant numbers of upper professionals, but as a group, the vast majority of small employers are not upper professionals. In his examination of the upper professionals group, Brint disaggregates the census information in terms of the type of organization they are employed in.[7] Using 1980 census data, Brint (1988) found that

---

[6] There is considerable evidence on the extent to which owner-occupied houses, especially in suburban areas, contain a lot of unpaid work (Ehrenreich 1984). On the subject of unpaid work in households beyond a narrow definition of *household work*, see Gershuny and Miles's (1983) analysis of the shift of furniture, toy, and tool assembling from the factory or retailer to the household. See also Pahl (1984).

[7] Upper professionals are the central component of the new class of highly educated workers; they are the quintessential postindustrial workers. Brint argues that in order to

the highest-paid segment of professionals were those employed in the corporate headquarters and producer services and living in Manhattan.[8] They are also most likely to be white, 90% of them being non-Hispanic whites, and over half of them are under 45 years of age. The other categories of professionals living in New York City have far lower average earnings, are far more likely to live in the outer boroughs of the city, and are more likely to be black and/or women. Indeed, blacks and Asians were a presence only in the human capital services complex. Hispanic professionals in 1980 were employed only in very small numbers.

---

understand this group of workers, it is not enough to look simply at their occupation; rather, he argues, organizational attachments are crucial in defining key aspects of socioeconomic status. Organizational powers (level of resources and market scope) and organizational purposes define distinct spheres and strata in the city (Brint 1988: 4). Thus, upper professionals are those who, besides possessing highly valued intellectual resources, work for resource-rich organizations, and this distinguishes them from rank-and-file professionals. Organizational purposes are significant in understanding political and cultural divisions among professional people. Bell (1973) already pointed out the shaping influence of the organizations to which the professionals belong, beyond class commonalities. Following Hoover and Vernon (1962), Brint identifies four major institutional complexes that employ upper professionals: the corporate headquarters complex, the culture and communications complex, the civic complex, and the human capital services complex. These are the most powerful and central sectors in the city's economic and political life, and are, at least in some respects, recognized as knowledge and information based. If a "new class" of professionals exists, it is the product of forces generating the growth of these four sectors (Brint 1988: 8). Boundaries among these sectors are defined in terms of distinctiveness of resources or the resources supporting the activities of a sector.

One distinctive trait about the civic complex in New York City is its large concentration of foundations, greater than that of any other U.S. city. One-third of the largest foundations in the United States are located in Manhattan. And many of the large and small foundations in Manhattan take an active interest in civic and urban issues. In addition, vast sectors of middle-income and middle-level employees in the various organizations making up this complex have an orientation toward social justice and civic issues rather than merely economic issues. It is in this sense distinct from the other two complexes.

[8] Brint (1988) used a 5% sample from the 1980 Census data for New York. The demographic and employment information contained in this sample makes it possible to identify the differences among professionals in terms of the institutional sectors of employment. Brint (1988) defined as upper professionals all those employees who reported incomes of at least $40,000 per year for 1979 and lived in Manhattan. He included self-employed artists and writers who reported incomes of at least $40,000 because, though they lack the organizational attachments central to the upper professional, they contribute to the cosmopolitan side of the cultural life in the city. On the basis of this definition, only 1% of New York's labor force in 1980 qualified as upper professionals. Another 1% were classified as small employers; 10% as rank-and-file professionals; and 20% as marginal professionals. Small employers include owners of goods production and wholesale and retail businesses and self-employed professionals. They are oriented toward organizations and markets, are largely locally or regionally oriented, generally have lower levels of educational attainment, and are not self-consciously information and knowledge based. Even though there are a growing number of small businesses involved in specialized services, most are not.

Overall, the outer boroughs have had sharp declines in household income. In the 1950s and 1960s, they contained a vast middle class and a prosperous working class. They now have less than their share of managerial and professional households, notwithstanding gentrification in certain areas of Brooklyn, which if excluded, would bring this quotient down even further. And they have an overrepresentation of clerical and service workers, operatives, and laborers. The income distribution in the outer boroughs has a strong concentration at the lower end: In 1987 half of the households with annual incomes less than U.S. $5,000 were concentrated in the outer boroughs, compared to only 14% of those with incomes over U.S. $50,000 (Stegman 1988).

During the period 1970–1980, clerical workers, mostly women, lived in the boroughs but overwhelmingly worked in Manhattan, in contrast to professionals and managers, who worked in Manhattan and lived in either Manhattan or the suburbs. For clerical workers, the increase in their job quotient in Manhattan was not paralleled by an increase in their residential quotient, which fell from 94 in 1970 to 82 in 1980. The residences of clerical workers were overrepresented in the rest of the city, where their quotient grew from 117 in 1970 to 122 in 1980, and underrepresented in the suburbs. The available evidence suggests that few of the clerical workers who lived in the suburbs commute to Manhattan, even from Westchester County, which is quite accessible and has large numbers of high-income workers who commute to Manhattan. In 1980 only 16% of clerical workers living there commuted to Manhattan, compared with 27% of managerial and professional workers (Harris 1988: 17).

Manhattan's location quotient of blue-collar jobs (crafts, operatives, laborers) has reached an all-time low, while the location quotient of such jobs has tended to increase in the outer boroughs and neighboring New Jersey's Hudson county, places that have long had significant concentrations of blue-collar workers.[9] In 1980, the residences of these workers were severely underrepresented in Manhattan and overrepresented in the rest of the core; residences of craft workers were overrepresented in the suburbs as well. These trends have held since then. The location quotients of both the jobs and the residences of service workers have mostly decreased, except for the outer boroughs.

The expansion in the numbers of professionals, especially in the high-income segment working and living in Manhattan, has been a central fact in the gentrification of several parts of the city. It is evident in Manhattan and certain areas in Brooklyn where once poor and middle-income neigh-

[9] The location quotient for blue-collar jobs in the outer boroughs and Hudson county increased for craftsworkers from 108 in 1950 to 119 in 1980, for operatives and laborers from 107 to 132, and for service workers from 91 to 121 (Harris 1988).

borhoods now contain highly priced commercial and residential buildings: parts of Greenwich Village, the area South of Houston Street (referred to as Soho), parts of the Lower East Side (now referred to as the
East Village), large portions of the Upper West Side in Manhattan, and
the vast office and residential complex named Battery Park City at the
southern edge of Manhattan. Gentrification has also transformed Brooklyn Heights, Park Slope, and a few other neighborhoods in Brooklyn
(DeGiovanni 1984; Zukin 1982; Chall 1984).

The New York Housing and Vacancy Survey (Stegman 1985, 1988) carried out every three years provides some detailed data in this regard.
Contrary to national trends, home ownership in New York City rose from
27.4% in 1978 to 30.3% in 1987. Between 1981 and 1987, the period of
sharpest increase, the proportion of households that owned their homes
increased by 5.9% in Manhattan compared to 2.5% for the city as a
whole. Most of the increase in ownership occurred through the conversion of existing rental units into condominiums or cooperatives, both typically requiring a significant amount of money.[10] The evidence shows that
those who bought units in this period had a median income of $36,000,
compared with a median income of $16,000 among tenant households
(Stegman 1988: 100, 185). The households that bought converted units
were 77% white, and 78% had no children. Given these trends in addition to the displacement of low-income households associated with conversion, household incomes in Manhattan have risen more rapidly than
in any other borough, increasing by 18.3% from 1983 to 1986 (Stegman
1988: 100, 182, 185).

Yet Manhattan also contains areas that have experienced sharp declines
in household incomes: northern Manhattan, containing Harlem and East
Harlem, has experienced growing unemployment, sharp increases in
poverty, and sharp increases in crime and delinquency rates. There is a
ring of poverty that runs through northern Manhattan, the South Bronx,
and much of northern Brooklyn (Tobier 1985). In 1980 New York City
contained a larger number of census tracts with higher levels of poor
households than in 1970.

The low-rent housing market suffered a massive decline in the 1980s
that, along with the stagnation and decline in household incomes at the
lower end, created a situation that led to severe overcrowding and homelessness. Since 1978 there has been an absolute decline in the number of
rental units, whether occupied or vacant, of over 57,000, along with an
increase of over 101,000 in owner-occupied units. In addition to the ab-

[10] From 1981 (the first year these data became available) to 1987, over 93,000 housing
units in New York City were converted from rental to coop or condominium tenure (Stegman 1988: 175). Of these, 49% were located in Manhattan, where the ownership rate rose
by a sharp 5.9% from 1981 to 1987 alone.

solute decrease in rental units, the share of rental units lacking protection from eviction or inordinate rent increases has increased from 25% to 31% of all units, or 522,000 units. Finally, there has been a sharp decline of 26% in the share of low-cost rental units and a sharp increase of 26% in the share of high-cost rental units, with an even sharper increase of 30% for very expensive units.[11]

Several conditions produced the sharp increase of homelessness in the 1980s: the growth in low-income households, the sharp reduction in government subsidies for housing due to conversions, and high-income gentrification. While the combination of deinstitutionalization of mental patients with a shrinking in the low-priced housing supply and in subsidies may have produced much of the homelessness in the 1970s, other conditions were the major generators of homelessness in the 1980s. The sharp increase in homeless families was the clearest evidence of the transformation. By 1988, there were over 5,000 registered homeless families in city shelters, a quintupling of the estimate for 1980. And there were over 10,000 registered homeless individuals. Furthermore, for the first time, a large share of the homeless were women and children. In addition, there is an uncounted population of homeless individuals and childless families who avoid the shelters and live on the streets, in train stations, in parks, and beneath highways. There are no precise figures, but it is estimated that up to 100,000 single room occupancy units (SROs) disappeared in the 1980s as a result of conversion or demolition of these units, particularly in the more central areas of Manhattan (Tobier 1990: 311).

It is important to note that some of the conditions producing homelessness were emerging in the 1960s and 1970s, but did not produce the level and composition of the homeless evident in the 1980s. First, deinstitutionalization began in the 1950s, but the availability of single room occupancy units and, eventually, housing subsidies deterred homelessness.[12] It was only in the 1980s that the sharp increase in the demand for

[11] A category of housing units that is important for low-income people and that does not quite exist in London or Tokyo is the stock of in-rem housing held by the city's government as a result of abandonment by or tax delinquency of the owners. About half of the in-rem units are occupied by blacks and about a third by Hispanics; whites and others occupy the rest. Another important source of housing for low-income people is single room occupancy units. These are one-room rental units that lack complete plumbing and kitchen facilities for the exclusive use of the occupant(s). There were over 51,000 such units in 1987, a significant decline from earlier periods.

[12] Passage of the Community Mental Health Care Act in 1963 provided federal funds for community-based mental health facilities, setting the stage for large-scale deinstitutionalization. From 1965 to 1975, the number of patients in New York State psychiatric hospitals fell by 62%, from 85,000 to 33,000, and by the late 1980s, it was down to 19,000 (Tobier

housing made a precarious situation into a crisis. Second, the supply of low-priced housing began to shrink, mostly through urban renewal and abandonment by landlords, in the late 1960s. But again, it was only in the 1980s that the dimensions of this shrinkage reached a new scale and produced massive homelessness of families. Third, public assistance payments began to level off in the 1970s, but it was in combination with the shrinking supply of low-priced housing and massive job losses in the 1980s that the full impact of this became evident in the form of homelessness.

New York City's property tax subsidy, extended in 1976 to stimulate a languishing real estate industry, contributed to raising the profitability of rehabilitating old structures and converting low-income housing into high-priced units. In the 1960s there had been few alternative uses for many such properties. The growing demand in the 1980s for centrally located housing by high-income households contributed to the accelerated replacement of SROs by high-cost housing. In a short period of time, the profitability of the market for affordable housing had been acutely outdistanced by that of the booming market for high-priced housing. This only added to the rapid shrinkage in the supply of low-priced housing.[13]

While the luxury housing sector is a small proportion of all housing it represents much of new construction in the 1980s. This sector is also part of the international property market and can command prices that leave most of the residents in the city out of the bidding. Again, while New York, London, and Tokyo have long had a luxury housing sector, the scale of the 1980s represents a new development in that it generated a sharp expansion in the supply of such housing and hence absorbed areas of these cities that only a decade ago were considered marginal or worse. Moreover, the sharp competition and the high prices of the 1980s in central locations altered the terms defining profitability in the industry and

---

1990: 310). Single room occupancy units were cheap and abundant and disability allowances covered the cost.

[13] A fruitful area for future research would be quantification of the relationship between a concentration of high-income households and the infrastructure of service jobs associated with it. Although not directly applicable to this discussion of New York City, it is interesting to note that such an analysis of London and Britain was developed by Lee (1984) and then replicated by Thrift and Williams (1987). Using the ratio between the population of an area and service employment in that area, they obtained what could be read as a service provision ratio. This is clearly a very crude measure, and not too much can be read into it. But the findings are interesting. They found the ratio to be 3,058.95 per 10,000 population in the Southeast compared with an average for Britain as a whole of 2,466.21. Isolating specific service industries, they found this service provision ratio to be 575.96 per 10,000 population for the Southeast compared with 362 for Britain as a whole in banking, finance, insurance and business services. Wales, with 198.77, had the lowest ratio for this industry group.

induced significant increases along the price chain. While there was an increase in high-income workers and high-income households, it is also true that, with the probable exception of the top-income level, households had to allocate larger shares of income to housing than had been customary, and there were more two-earner households. Thus it would seem that the industry managed to extract a higher level of prices from households than had been the norm in preceding decades.

The distribution of household income in New York City reflects these developments. The triannual survey on housing and vacancies, the most detailed source for intercensal periods, indicates that the lowest quintile lost 15% of income between 1977 and 1986, while all other quintiles gained in income (Stegman 1988). The highest gain in real income (deflated by the Consumer Price Index) was in the top quintile, at 28%; the next to the highest gained 23.5%. The sharpest increase occurred between 1983 and 1986, with 14.2% for the top quintile and a little less than that for all other quintiles. In contrast, between both 1977 and 1980 and 1980 and 1983, there was an increase of only about 4% in each period for the top quintile, even less for following quintiles, and small negative rates for the two lowest quintiles in each of these two periods. The income distribution shows that the share of income going to the lowest quintile decreased from 4.9% in 1977 to 3.9% in 1986, equivalent to a 20% decline, while the top quintile raised its share from 45.2% to 47.3%, a small increase but still the largest gain in share of all five groups. The next two highest quintiles remained basically unchanged, and the next to lowest quintile lost about 8%, going from 9.3% to 8.6% in 1986. In sum, the concentration of household income is rather acute, not unlike the case in London.

While real incomes have risen for the upper half, and especially the upper quarter, of the city's population since 1977, they have dropped for many ethnic groups, notably Puerto Ricans (Weitzman 1989). Although a share of immigrants and blacks are in well-paid jobs, it is also clear that most are not. Poverty increased by 20% between 1980 and 1984 (Tobier 1985) and by another 15% between 1985 and 1988 (Rosenberg 1989). The poor are disproportionately black and Hispanic. They are also concentrated in female-headed households, which account for 25% of all households in New York City, compared with 15% nationwide. In 1982, about 42% of Hispanic and black children in New York City lived with their mother only, another indication of the prevalence of poverty in this group. A recent fact is that in New York City most poor are children, a situation reminiscent of Third World cities (Tobier 1985; Rosenberg 1989). The norm in highly developed countries is for most poor to be elderly.

London and the Region

Central London has long specialized in office jobs. But the number of these jobs has risen immensely. There is a strong overrepresentation of finance, banking, and insurance, with the area accounting for two-thirds of all jobs in FIRE compared with a third of all employment in London and half of all jobs in professional and business services. Manufacturing, on the other hand, is overrepresented in outer London, an area that accounts for well over three-fifths of such jobs compared with somewhat over a third of all London employment.

The most central areas of London have undergone a transformation that broadly parallels Manhattan's, though the concrete details are diverse. We see a parallel increase in the stratum of what Brint (1988) described as upper professionals, a group largely employed in the corporate services, including finance. The sharp growth in the concentration of mostly young, new high-income professionals and managers employed in central London represents a significant change from a decade ago.[14]

The internationalization of the city itself inevitably brought greater pressures toward earning levels comparable to those in other major international financial centers. It was not till the 1980s that salaries of professionals and managers in London's City began to reach such levels. Furthermore, the accelerated growth in the magnitude of operations brought about an increase in the demand for workers and a tight labor market in certain occupations, especially those involving specialized skills. The movement of foreign firms into London further accelerated these trends putting great upward pressure on salary levels. Deregulation, by opening up the market, raised the demand for certain types of specialized skills and experience and generally reduced the feasibility for many firms of simply using their old work force.

While the expansion in the number of jobs directly and indirectly associated with the growth of London as an international financial and producer services center affected a broad range of occupations, from unskilled service workers to highly specialized personnel, the upward pressure on salaries did not similarly affect all these occupations. As in New York, the overall outcome of these various trends has been the expansion of both a high-income stratum and a low-income stratum of work-

---

[14] There has been a greater demand for highly trained workers, and more university graduates are going into business occupations. In 1985 over 18% of all graduates in Britain went into finance, many of these in the City (O'Leary 1986). Alongside the increase in numbers of highly trained workers with advanced degrees, there has been a greater specialization associated with the greater complexity and multiplicity of innovations in the financial industry and in the specialized services generally.

ers. And there has been an increase in high-income residents in central areas of London, along with a growing concentration of poor in inner London (Townsend, Corrigan, and Kowarzik 1987). Using 1981 census data, Thrift and Williams (1987) found that most of the new professionals live in the affluent parts of London and in the Southeastern suburban ring.

One of the most detailed studies of the new segment of the professional and managerial stratum (Thrift and Williams 1987) shows that two categories of workers account for most of the increase in the number of high-paying jobs: a group composed of top-level managers and dealers and a group of mostly young graduates whose advancement or promotion lines lead to high-paying jobs over a fairly short period of time. This, again, parallels trends in Manhattan in the 1980s. Thrift and Williams (1987) have reported that for the first group, the whole period surrounding the 1986 deregulation saw a very large increase in the demand for their expertise. In 1985, there were only sixty-seven such employees in fourteen companies in the City who earned more than £100,000; two years later there were about 2,000 (Thrift and Williams 1987). To these earnings should be added a whole range of other types of income associated with such jobs.

Thrift and Williams (1987) note that this stratum of workers should be distinguished from the top of the corporate hierarchy, the directors and partners of the City's firms. These have received extremely high salaries for a long time, and the developments of the last few years have raised their salaries, but have lacked the dramatic impact on these salary levels and their numbers that they have had among the group of top managers and dealers described above.[15]

Among the second group, the well-paid recent graduates, Thrift and Williams (1987) found that there has been an across-the-board increase in salaries and frequently a highly accelerated rate of salary growth. This is also the group where there are at times labor shortages in certain spe-

[15] In 1985, there were 361 directors, in forty-two companies, who earned over £100,000 a year, 24 of whom earned over £250,000 a year. The continuing weight of the class system in English economic and social life is evident in the extent to which top-level executives in City firms come from upper-class backgrounds, which is not necessarily the case among the new professionals. Using various sources, Thrift and Williams (1987) estimated that about three-quarters of top executives in merchant banks, clearing banks, accountancy firms, and insurance companies; stockbrokers; and insurance brokers went to a private school. Among stockbrokers, this figure rises to 96% (cited in Thrift 1987). Furthermore, 68% of top City executives went to one of two universities: Oxford or Cambridge. To this concentration should be added that of the considerable presence of members of the aristocracy. This situation represents somewhat of a dilution compared with what it was before the 1960s, when the first conditions leading up to today's opening up of London to the international financial community were put in place.

cialties, another factor that raises salaries. A key example is that of computer experts. Young graduates make up a large share of this category. Their starting salaries have increased significantly, averaging £16,000 but often considerably above that.

As in New York City, a distinct lifestyle has emerged, and there is a sufficiently critical mass of young, high-income workers engaged in high levels of consumption that it makes itself felt in certain parts of London and its region. Much of the discretionary income is being spent "primarily on demonstrating taste" (Thrift and Williams 1987). New, elegant shops and restaurants—and sharp increases in the prices of housing— manifest the new lifestyle. There has also been high-income gentrification of several parts of London, including areas of inner London once inhabited by lower-income people, especially minorities. For example, in my 1987 fieldwork in Hackney, one of the poorest areas in London, I found a number of renovated townhouses and warehouses and factories converted to living lofts. Similarly, in the area called Little Venice, once rather grand townhouses that had decayed and been subdivided into dense tenements for immigrants in the 1950s and 1960s were being "rehabilitated" at immense speed and in large numbers in the mid-1980s. Walking through those streets in the summer of 1987 offered what is probably one of the most stunning instances of how landlords will let row after row of what had been elegant cream-colored facades fall into dark gray disrepair for decades, only to be quickly restored to their old splendor in a few months when the market calls.

The evidence shows that household income has increased faster in London and in the Southeast region as a whole than in the rest of the country (U.K. Department of Employment, 1987a, 1987b, 1987c). The Southeast has a disproportionate concentration of earnings, national income, investment income, and accumulated assets. According to one account, almost half of Britain's millionaires live there, as do 58% of those with annual earnings over £50,000, which represents a rather higher share than its 31.2% of Britain's population in 1986 (U.K. Central Statistics Office 1986; U.K. Department of Employment 1987a). This has contributed to an expansion in the consumption of goods and services and in home acquisitions. The average level of household expenditures is far higher than in other regions. The prices of houses have increased enormously and been at least 25% higher than in the rest of the country since the late 1970s. The Family Expenditure Survey (U.K. Deparment of Employment 1985) has reported that the Southeast region has higher household expenditures than does any other region of the country. These expenditures stood at £85.66 in London, £89.95 for the rest of the Southeast, and £69.4 for the United Kingdom as a whole. Though less pronounced, a parallel gap existed in household expenditures for services, which ranged from £21.81 for both London and the Southeast to £18.44 for the United Kingdom as a whole.

However, while this region contains a disproportionate concentration of high-income households, the region as a whole does not contain a disproportionate concentration of high-income jobs. This parallels the New York region, with its large numbers of high-income workers residing in the suburban ring and commuting to high-paying jobs in Manhattan. London has a disproportionate concentration of high-paying jobs. In 1986 the average weekly pay in the Southeast, excluding London, was £247.2 for nonmanual males compared with £245 for Britain as a whole (U.K. Department of Employment 1987c). Average pay levels were virtually the same among manual workers. The differences overall are not significant. The pattern changes markedly when we bring in London, and especially the City of London. The weekly average for nonmanual males in London was £365.2 in 1986. The difference becomes especially accentuated when we look at earnings in the top decile. In Britain, 10% of nonmanual males earned over £383.2 a week. The equivalent level was about the same for the Southeast, but it rises to £629 for the City of London. This pattern of differential earnings also holds for nonmanual women though their actual earnings are much lower.

The key point here is that the Southeast excluding London, while representing a large concentration of high-income households, high levels of household expenditure, and highly priced houses, is not a location with a disproportionately larger concentration of high-income jobs compared with Britain as a whole. This further suggests that the concentration of wealth and high-income households in this region is partly maintained and reproduced by the accelerated growth and high incomes generated by London's expanded role as a financial center.

Finally, the Southeast can be seen as a location for the generation of a range of jobs that service the needs of the high-income households, directly and indirectly. As in New York City, areas with large concentrations of high income households generate an infrastructure of often low-wage jobs, notably the overrepresentation of sales jobs in the suburban ring. Ethnographic materials of various kinds can be used to describe and illustrate the range of services that are purchased by high-income households, from various kinds of cleaning and maintenance work through governesses, masseuses and beauty care, to more elaborate and specialized work, such as accountants, lawyers, and trust managers. The decentralization of offices has contributed clerical jobs.

Interestingly, the Southeast is also a location for secondary servicing or production for firms in London. Some of these jobs may be high-income jobs, but a large share are likely to be low-wage, a fact perhaps partly reflected in the similarity in average earnings in the Southeast and the rest of the country, both significantly lower than those of London. Higher levels of unionization and the higher cost of living in London probably contribute to the higher earnings in London, even among manual workers and among women. But it may also reflect the different occupational composition in the Southeast, excluding London: more low-wage personal service jobs, more low-wage manufacturing jobs (for example, in electronics), fewer better-paid transportation jobs, fewer traditional manufacturing jobs. At the same time, as was discussed earlier, London's higher average earnings figures describe a shrinking segment of the city's labor force, especially if we consider that the New Earnings Survey figures do not include London's growing stratum of low-wage, part-time and casual workers.[16]

The number of clerical and blue-collar service jobs has also increased significantly in the City and in London at large. But these workers have not experienced a parallel growth in their wages and salaries. It is important to repeat that, as in New York and Tokyo, these kinds of jobs account for a large share of all workers in the new economic sectors, reaching about 50% in London's City. They constitute a significant share of the work force necessary to keep the so-called new economy going. Since as yet many of these jobs have not been relocated to lower-cost areas, these workers have to compete for housing with the expanding higher-income

[16] If we use official poverty levels, without controlling for the higher cost of living, in 1984 one in eighteen full-time male workers earned below that level; for women it was one in five, and for female part-time workers it was nearly one in two. This is a total of half a million workers in London earning under the poverty level: 100,000 full-time men, 100,000 full-time women, and 300,000 part-time women (U.K. Department of Employment 1984, 1987a; Bazen 1985).

Furthermore, this gap has widened more in London than in the rest of the country. Statistics are deficient at measuring lower-income jobs and households. One estimate is that the share of these jobs has increased: In 1977, one-fifth of all women part-time workers earned below the limit (that is, 7% of all women workers, or 3% of all workers). By 1984 this had increased to 20% of all women workers, 8% of all workers, and two-fifths of all female part-time workers. These figures represent only part-time female workers, who, while they do represent a significant share of below-poverty-level earners, are at most half of such workers. Thus the total figures are actually higher.

The evidence also points to an increase in the gap. In 1974, the poorest quarter of London households had incomes that were the equivalent of 3% of the income of the top quarter; by 1983 this had fallen to 25%. On the basis of the New Earnings Survey data, the following trends emerge. In 1974 the poorest 10% of men in full-time work earned 37% of the pay of the top 10%; in 1979 this had risen to 39%, but by 1984 it had fallen to 33%, or £102.5 per week. The decline was steeper for women, both part- and full-time ones: In 1979 the poorest 10% earned 27% of the earnings of the top 10%, or less than £70 per week for full-time work. Some of this is attributable to growth of part-time work among women, but pay differences are also increasing within full-time work. An important factor here is the shift from manufacturing to service jobs and the associated increase at both ends of the pay scale.

sectors. Not only have their incomes typically not increased; their conditions of life have often declined, given the privatization of public housing and the higher prices in gentrified commercial areas. Another trend that has accentuated this tension is the increased representation in this group of part-time and temporary workers, who are mostly women (Townsend, Corrigan, and Kowarzik 1987). This is undermining those full-time jobs in this group that have above-average salaries compared with national standards. Furthermore, much clerical work is becoming deskilled and routinized, which is gradually leading to lower average salaries at the same time that most higher-level occupations are becoming more specialized and leading to higher average salaries.

A third major component of the social geography of London is the consolidation of areas of concentrated poverty and other multiple disadvantages. Violent confrontations in 1976 in Notting Hill and in 1977 in East London's Lewisham brought out in full force the facts of severe decay, high unemployment, and poverty in many places in Britain's major cities, and especially London.[17] These areas became known as "the inner city." Blacks and Asians were disproportionately concentrated in the inner city, especially in London, which had the largest share of this population. The 1974–1975 recession and the continuing loss of manufacturing and low-level warehousing and distribution jobs in combination with discrimination in employment and in housing against Asians and blacks all contributed to their high unemployment. Unemployment also rose sharply among whites, especially among working-class youths, low-wage workers, the unemployed, and the elderly (Friend and Metcalf 1982). The sharp rise of unemployment in the 1980s and the continuing loss of manufacturing jobs extended these problems to areas beyond the inner city as understood in the 1970s.

Between 1971 and 1981, over 20% of whites left London for the suburbs or elsewhere compared with 10% of minorities; among Afro-Caribbeans four out of five stayed in the inner city between 1971 and 1981, while half of inner city Indians moved out, mostly to the suburbs. The Bengali population, however, was still highly concentrated in East London and heavily involved in the garment industry, thus resembling the

[17] The great worry for the government was that urban uprisings on the scale of those in the United States in the 1960s were going to take place in London and other British cities (Friend and Metcalf 1982). There were many violent clashes; the National Front grew and became very violent in its racism, and the police made hundreds of arrests. In September 1976, the Secretary of State for the Environment announced that the government was beginning a major review to address urban decay. Development resources were switched from outer areas and New Towns to inner city areas; the special urban aid program, started in the 1960s, was expanded; and special efforts to help small businesses in the cities were implemented.

first generation of many immigrant groups in the United States and the United Kingdom. In the late 1980s many of these differences remained among blacks and Asians.

It is increasingly evident that there are two major areas of minority concentration in London: the inner city boroughs of Hackney, Haringey, Lambeth, Lewisham, and Wandsworth and the outer city boroughs of Brent, Ealing, Hounslow, and Waltham Forest. These two areas of concentration are increasingly diverse in terms of the predominant population, with the former mostly Afro-Caribbean and the latter mostly Asian. The exceptions are Tower Hamlets and Brent, which have fairly mixed populations and are among the poorest (Townsend, Corrigan, and Kowarzik 1987).

Using a deprivation index for 1984, Townsend, Corrigan, and Kowarzik (1987) found that in the most deprived boroughs, a majority of households had incomes under £6000 per year.[18] The five most deprived boroughs reported in the 1984 data were Hackney, Tower Hamlets, Islington, Lambeth, and Newham. Their deprivation indices ranged from 9.21 in Hackney, the highest, to 6.75 in Newham. Only 3% of households in Hackney and Tower Hamlets had annual incomes of over £15,000. The highest shares of households with incomes over £15,000 in the most deprived boroughs were 9% and 10% in, respectively, Islington and Lambeth. The least deprived boroughs were Havering, Bromley, Berkley, Sutton, and Harrow; between 10% and 16% of households in these boroughs had incomes of over £15,000. It is astounding to see, however, that significant shares of households in these boroughs had incomes under £6,000: about 44% in Havering and 37% in Bromley.

Townsend, Corrigan, and Kowarzik (1987), working from government statistics, have estimated that in 1985–1986 there were 1.8 million people in London living in poverty or on the margins of poverty.[19] This represents a doubling of the 1960 figure. A large part of the increase occurred from 1979 to 1983. Though the government has not published later figures, other kinds of evidence point to additional growth in poverty: Increases in dependency, in early retirement, and in the number of people over seventy-five years old all feed the expansion of a low-income population. Compared to Townsend's (1979) earlier study, Townsend, Corrigan, and Kowarzik's (1987) found more poverty and far more severe pov-

[18] The deprivation index is a standardized measure based on the share of a borough's population constituted by residents who are unemployed, are overcrowded, lack basic amenities, or are single parents, one-person pensionner households, black immigrants, or unskilled working class.

[19] This study was a representative sample survey of the population of Greater London in 1985–1986 and was based on available evidence on deprivation and mortality in the 755 wards of the city.

erty, with people living far below the poverty threshold, and in the most extreme cases becoming homeless. The number of homeless people is rapidly growing in London, where it is now estimated at 75,000.

The distribution of income clearly reflects these conditions. The New Earnings Survey for various years shows that relative to the median income top earnings increased in the early and mid-1980s and bottom earnings decreased. When we add to this the increase in resources at the top and the reduction in various types of benefits at the bottom, then the gap is even larger than the earnings figures indicate. Tax changes have favored those with higher incomes. Thus if we were to measure the gap in posttax income, it would be even wider. The average company director's income has increased by 43%; the average income for households with an unemployed head of household fell by 12%. There has been a growth in unearned income, a growth in the earnings gap, and a growth in households headed by single persons, the aged, and the unemployed.

In constant 1985 prices, gross household income per week in London declined by about 4% from 1981 to 1986 for the lowest decile and by 6% for the lowest quartile. In contrast, it increased by 17% for the top quartile and by 25% for the top decile, again indicating that a growing share of income was going to a fairly small share of households at the top (U.K. Department of Employment 1985, 1986). These same trends hold for the United Kingdom as a whole, only with greater declines at the lower end and smaller increases at the top.[20] Data from the Family Expenditure Survey (cited in Logan and Taylor-Gooby n.d.) show that the ratio of the top to the lowest quintile of the household income distribution in London has been increasing. It was 2.93 in 1979–1980, 3.15 in 1982–1983, and 3.54 in 1985–1986. The income distribution in London in actual 1985 pounds shows a far larger differential than in Britain as a whole: In London, households in the lowest decile had an average weekly income of £47 and those in the highest decile had an average weekly income of £473 (Townsend, Corrigan, and Kowarzik 1987: 46).

Average income in London is higher than in the rest of the country. The Family Expenditure Survey of 1985 reported that average household

[20] The income distribution in the United Kingdom has grown more unequal (U.K. Central Statistics Office, various years). In 1976, the bottom 20% received 0.8% of household income, while 44.4% went to the top 20%. By 1986 these shares were, respectively, 0.3% and 50.7%. After taxes and various government transfers, disposable income still showed an increase in inequality, with the bottom fifth accounting for 7% of all household income in 1976 and 5.9% in 1986 and the top fifth accounting for 38.1% in 1976 and 42.2% in 1986. Disposable income among the second- and the third-lowest fifths also declined, from, respectively, 12.6% to 11% and from 18.2% to 16.9%. Only the two top fifths raised their share, with most of it concentrated in the top fifth.

income in London was 34% above the national average.[21] But the distribution of these higher average earnings across income classes shows that
the lower-income groups have a very small differential with national averages, while the higher-income groups have a rather high differential
(see Townsend, Corrigan, and Kowarzik 1987). In other words, there is
an unequal distribution of the income differential across income classes.
Thus, the income gap or the spread of inequality is much higher in London than in the rest of the country.

Tokyo

The social geography of Tokyo exhibits far less differentiation than that of
London and New York. This is in good part because Tokyo's expansion
took place in such a brief period and was influenced by a different cultural and political conception guiding the allocation of resources, one which
gave strong priority to the development of industry rather than to increasing the standard of living. The vast size of Tokyo's population and
the rapidity of urbanization have produced a landscape dominated by the
modest dwellings of the enormous numbers of middle- and lower-income
workers who commute to central Tokyo every day. There are in central
Tokyo areas, such as Minato and generally the hilly western side called
the Yamanote, that have long contained the residences of the wealthy and
now are also inhabited by many of the new top corporate officials, including foreigners. The central business district has, like central areas in
Manhattan and in London, evolved into a highly specialized place for
offices, while Shinjuku has become a second major commercial center.
High-income gentrification in several older areas of central Tokyo and
new luxury developments have grown rapidly in the 1980s. The elements
of an expensive lifestyle centered around fashion, designer stores, and
elegant restaurants are also becoming evident, for example, in the Rop-

[21] Gross normal average weekly household income in 1985 was £216.23 in the United
Kingdom and £248.60 in London (U.K. Department of Employment 1986: 91). And 11.5%
of London households, compared with 6.6% of United Kingdom households, had gross normal weekly incomes of £450 or more in 1985 (U.K. Department of Employment 1986: 76).
Earnings from employment were 20% above the national level for men and 22% above it
for women. This disparity between income and earnings points to the concentration of
wealth in London. The Greater London Council (1986) has argued that the lower but still
higher differential in earnings was due to (1) the lower percentage of persons exclusively
dependent on social security benefits; (2) a greater concentration of highly paid professional
and administrative jobs; and (3) a concentration of better-organized and -paid manufacturing
activities, except for clothing. At the same time the cost of living in London was 15% higher
than in the nation as a whole.

pongi area of Minato. Indeed, there has been a sharp increase in imports of luxury goods, including German cars and Italian designer clothes.[22]

As in New York and London, the growth in corporate and financial services has raised the demand for professional workers. This has particularly been the case in finance, information research and development, advertising, accounting, architecture, and engineering services. Between 1975 and 1985, the number of professional workers in Tokyo rose by 200,000 in service industries; these workers were mostly between twenty-four and thirty-four years of age (Japan Management and Coordination Agency 1988). This figure excludes a growing category of highly trained professional women workers who are being hired as part-time workers in these occupations (Japan Ministry of Labor 1989). The growing need for professional workers and their strategic location in leading industries have put strong upward pressure on salaries. This has fed, along with the rapid increase in domestic and foreign corporate staff generally, the expansion of the high-priced housing market in central Tokyo. The growth of the luxury housing market and the demand for office space have further induced sharp rises in the cost of housing. There is now a

---

[22] An interesting question concerns the impact on consumption of the revaluation of the yen after 1985, which the Japanese refer to as "endaka." Using the OECD model for calculating multilateral purchasing power parities, Japan's Economic Planning Agency found that Japan's parity had increased during the strong increase in the value of the yen from October 1985 to March 1987 compared with other currencies. Purchasing power parities are comparative figures for each country's own currency with which the same amount of a particular consumer good or service can be bought in each country. This is clearly complicated by differences in lifestyle and consumption patterns, the lack of comparability on many consumer items, and great variations in standards and quality. During that eighteen-month period the yen/dollar rate was changing more rapidly than were the purchasing power parities. This was partly because the purchasing power of the yen includes land and services, which are not traded and hence do not reflect changes in currency value. It also takes longer for changes in currency values and prices of imported goods to be reflected in the purchasing power parities. Therefore, the Japanese did not feel that the purchasing power inside Japan had increased much, notwithstanding huge increases in the value of the yen (Japan Economic Planning Agency 1988). The increase in the yen in 1985 had an effect on luxury imports (Japan Economic Planning Agency 1988: 38). Imports from France and Italy, which are mostly expensive or luxury clothing items, also increased. Automobile imports increased by 98.5% over 1985; imports of arts and antiques, by 68.4%. Imports from South Korea, China, and Taiwan had been growing throughout the 1980s; but in 1986 they grew by 40%, to 50% over the 1985 level. Imports from South Korea and Taiwan of toys and play equipment, which formerly had been exports from Japan, increased by 79.6% in 1986. According to the Japan External Trade Organization (JETRO), in 1986 about forty import consumer items grew by more than 50% over 1985. JETRO found a new trend toward imports of certain expensive consumer goods, especially luxury cars, paintings, calligraphic works, other art objects, antiques, and tropical fruits, all items not formerly imported. A survey of consumers (Japan Economic Planning Agency 1988: 43) found that 66.8% did not care whether an item was imported or domestic as long as the quality and price were satisfactory; only 21.3% reported that they tended to choose domestic products.

large number of young Japanese professionals and employees of foreign firms who are likely to reside in central Tokyo and have the consumption and lifestyle patterns evident among such workers in London and Tokyo. Areas such as Roppongi, Aoyama, and Akasaka resemble equivalent areas in New York and London. Tokyo has long had elegant restaurants and shopping districts for wealthy Japanese and foreigners and corporate elites. Now there is an expansion of a less exclusive version of such districts, where a fashion-oriented lifestyle, or fragments of it, can be bought. There also has been a growth in new luxury residential and office complexes, such as Ark Hill, which, like Trump Tower in New York City, are sites for the new corporate elite.

The city also contains a growing number of jobs in new and old industries that pay rather low wages. For these workers, access to housing in Tokyo is increasingly difficult. There has been a vast growth in personal services, with many new types of services being sold. Jobs in these industries are mostly low-wage and held by women. Many of the professional jobs in high demand are being filled by part-time workers, many of whom are women. Another growth occupation, clerical work, is employing an increasing number of part-time workers. Seventy percent of women part-time workers are in clerical jobs. Furthermore, the gap between full-time and part-time women has increased: In 1977 part-time workers' earnings stood at 80% of those of full-time workers; by 1987 they stood at 65%. Thus, the gap between Tokyo's female part-time clerical workers and male full-time professional workers, two growing categories, is increasing.

For the mass of workers in Tokyo, affordable housing increasingly entails a two-hour trip to work. The rate of homeownership declined in the 1980s, and the average size of new apartments in Tokyo fell, after increasing in the 1970s. The average floor space of newly built apartments fell to under 49 square meters in 1983 and 46 square meters in 1987, from 57 square meters in 1980 (*Economist*, August 31, 1987). Homeownership in Tokyo stood at 54% in 1987 compared with 64% in Japan (Japan Economic Planning Agency 1989). Tokyo residents paid about 20% of their salary in rent compared with 15% for the nation as a whole (Tokyo Metropolitan Government 1988a, b); but for central locations this ratio clearly has very different absolute values. Commuting distances have kept growing, and prices of housing even in distant locations have made ownership increasingly impossible, to the point that ninety-nine-year mortgages are now available.

These two divergent trends parallel conditions in New York and London, and, as in these cities, assume concrete forms in the spatial organization of the city. Gentrification articulates both the expansion of a housing supply for high-income households (either through renovation of old structures or their demolition and construction of new ones) and the displacement of low-income households (either through direct physical displacement or through their elimination from the bidding and from effective demand). The familiar outcomes are increasingly evident in Tokyo as well: the emergence of fashionable residential and commercial districts along with growing poverty, including homelessness, particularly among older residents displaced by gentrification.

But perhaps the most important process of change in the social geography of Tokyo is, at this point, the emergence of an inner city. It deserves some detailed discussion.

TOKYO'S INNER CITY

There has been some discussion as to whether the decline of manufacturing in central Tokyo and the outmigration of working-age residents from these areas may have contributed to the development of what in the West is often referred to as an inner city problem (Okimura 1980; Kimijima 1980; Narita 1980; Sakiyama 1981; Komori 1983; KUPI 1981). The very rapid growth of the economy in Tokyo, extensive construction of public and private sector projects, the decline in the young population in central Tokyo, and the loss of many traditional manufacturing firms could conceivably contribute to a decline in the employment base and in the physical conditions of older areas in central Tokyo that have not been incorporated into the new types of growth evident in the city, especially in the 1980s.

The most detailed empirical study of this issue is by the geographer Nakabayashi (1987), who addressed this question through an examination of government data on thirty-two variables for each of Tokyo's twenty-three wards in 1986. These range from basic demographic variables to employment, land prices, environmental conditions, and the presence of minority populations. Data on these variables were organized into four indices of socioeconomic conditions. The degree to which these conditions were present and their degree of geographic concentration allowed the author to establish the extent to which there are in Tokyo social, economic, and physical conditions resembling the inner-city problem in cities such as New York and London, and the extent to which such conditions, if present, are concentrated in Tokyo's inner areas. The four indices are neighborhood social decline; local economic decline; physical and housing decline; and presence of disadvantaged minorities, including immigrants. Nakabayashi's findings are as follows (for the sake of clarity and because there is much reason to believe the trends still hold, I have set these forth in the present tense).

In terms of the first index, there is a rather clear pattern of social decline in old downtown areas of wards characterized by mixed commercial, residential, and traditional manufacturing uses. These, especially Taito and Sumida Wards, are the most problematic, having clearly suffered from a severe loss of jobs and young people. A second tier of problematic areas are to be found in both the traditional manufacturing districts, such as Arakawa and in the central business district wards of Chiyoda and Chuo. All of these areas are characterized by extreme declines in the resident population and a sharp relative increase in the share of old people in the resident population. A good share of those who have outmigrated are people who lived and worked in these areas for at least twenty years; thus the outmigration has not been confined to the young. In the evaluation of the author, these communities "are dying as social units" (Nakabayashi 1987: 122).

In terms of economic decline, the most affected areas are those where manufacturing was once a thriving economic base supporting a whole array of other commercial and service activities as well as a significant residential and commuting work force. Most severely affected are the wards of Arakawa, Sumida, Kita, Koto, and Ota. These areas thus offer a sharp contrast to others in Tokyo where there has been a massive increase in the level of economic activity and in the numbers of commuting workers. But clearly this growth involves very different economic sectors.

In terms of decline in physical and housing conditions, the most severe cases are Toshima and Kita wards, which have a high density of both poor housing and poor people. These areas have a high proportion of tenement housing with no private bathrooms or kitchens. It is worth noting that poor housing conditions and blight were also found in two of the wards in the central business district, Chuo and Minato, where land fetches the highest prices and the most elegant homes, hotels, office towers and shops are located. This is not unlike Manhattan, which contains both some of the poorest and some of the most expensive housing. Other areas with poor housing and blight are located in the wards immediately surrounding the central business district; they are areas characterized by significant concentrations of small houses for rent, factories, shops, and offices, with continuing high population density notwithstanding a gradual decline in absolute numbers. In the central business district wards there is simultaneously a very high density of buildings, contributing to the deterioration of living conditions, and a growing number of unoccupied rental housing (one of the results of the increase in residential land prices). The dominant fact in these three wards is the rapid expansion of the highly dynamic business center and the rapid decline of the residential population.

In terms of the fourth element, the association between social disadvantage and minority residents, the types of data available make it difficult to establish such an association. However, there is little doubt that the presence of minority residents has not been a significant factor in the development of an inner-city area of economic and social decline. Furthermore, this factor plays itself out quite differently in Tokyo than in New York or London, where the evidence clearly indicates the higher prevalence of poverty, unemployment, poor housing conditions, and residence in blighted areas among immigrants and blacks than among native-born whites.

Given common conceptions of a totally homogenous society held both by many Japanese and by many commentators abroad, it is important to point out that there is a growing Southeast Asian immigrant population (discussed in greater detail later in this chapter). Nakabayashi (1987) expanded the research on the spatial distribution of socially disadvantaged and ethnic minorities, including foreign residents. The most disadvantaged locations were found in the Taito and Arakawa wards and, to a lesser extent in the Sumida, Kita, Toshima, Shinjuku, and Shibuya wards. These are all areas that are part of inner Tokyo, immediately surrounding the three central business district wards. The wards of Shinjuku, Shibuya, and Toshima comprise the major subcenter of Tokyo, and Shinjuku, of course, is the new seat of the Tokyo Metropolitan Government and a major area for new business development. Shinjuku and Shibuya contain a significant Korean community and most of the foreign Asian women recruited as "entertainers," who live there, as do many of the new illegal male immigrants from South and Southeast Asia. These are wards where I found extremely dense concentrations of very poor housing and small restaurants catering to these legal and illegal immigrants who are clearly in a condition of severe social, economic, and political disadvantage.

When all four of Nakabayashi's sets of characteristics are considered, the areas with the strongest incidence of these various conditions are the Arakawa, Taito, and Sumida wards, all immediately adjacent to the central business district. The loss of traditional manufacturing lies at the heart of the social, economic, and physical decline of Arakawa and Sumida. Taito has long had high concentrations of poor and low-income households. It now also has a high incidence of crime. Taito ward contains the largest concentration of daily laborers; it is one of the four major hiring camps for such workers in Japan, heavily controlled by gangsters. Arakawa and Taito now also have socially disadvantaged minority and immigrant populations.

In brief, the greatest social, economic, and physical decline is not in the central business district but in the areas immediately surrounding it, which were once centers for manufacturing and trading. While they are losing population they continue to have very high residential density and deteriorating housing conditions. There is a high incidence of poverty, illness, and crime in the worst areas, such as Taito, but also in Toshima and Kita. According to Nakabayashi (1987), the key factor in the social, economic and physical decline of inner areas in Tokyo has been the decline of traditional manufacturing and trading, which in turn affects the viability of a whole range of secondary local activities. Nakabayashi also sees this decline as linked to some of the factors associated with the rapid growth evident in central Tokyo, notably the high price of land.

Consumption

Economic inequality in major cities has assumed distinct forms in the consumption structure, which in turn has a feedback effect on the organization of work and the types of jobs being created. There is an indirect creation of low-wage jobs induced by the presence of a highly dynamic sector with a polarized income distribution. It takes place in the sphere of consumption (or social reproduction). The expansion of the high-income work force, in conjunction with the emergence of new cultural forms in everyday living, has led to a process of high-income gentrification, which rests, in the last analysis, on the availability of a vast supply of low-wage workers. As I have argued at greater length elsewhere (Sassen 1988), high-income gentrification is labor intensive, in contrast to the typical middle-class suburb, which represents a capital-intensive process—tract housing, road and highway construction, dependence on private automobile or commuter trains, heavy reliance on appliances and household equipment of all sorts, and, in the United States, large shopping malls with self-service operations. High-income gentrification in a city, on the other hand, is labor intensive: Renovation of townhouses and storefronts and designer furniture and woodwork all require workers, directly and indirectly. Behind the gourmet food stores and specialty boutiques lies an organization of the work process that differs from that of the self-service supermarket and department store. High-income urban residences in luxury apartment buildings depend to a much larger extent on hired maintenance staff than do the less urban homes of middle-level-income workers, epitomized by the middle-class suburban home in the United States, with its heavy input of family labor and of machinery from household appliances to lawn mowers.

The differences in the organization of the work process are evident in both the retail and the production phase (Sassen 1988). High-income gentrification generates a demand for goods and services that are typically not mass produced or sold through mass outlets. Customized production and limited runs of production will tend to be associated with

labor-intensive methods of production and sold through small, full service outlets. Subcontracting part of this production to low-cost operations, including sweatshops and households, is not uncommon. The overall outcome is an increase in low-wage jobs and in small firms for
production and retailing. The large department stores and supermarkets,
on the other hand, need large quantities and standardized products; they
will tend to buy from mass producers, often located in other regions and
involving large-scale transportation and distribution. Mass production,
standardization, and mass distribution facilitate unionization. Customized production, limited runs, and small retail outlets can promote the
informalization and casualization of work.

Professionals and managers have long been important occupational
groups in large cities such as New York, London, and Tokyo. But two
traits distinguish the current period from earlier times. One is the extent
to which these occupational groups have grown. For instance, census
data show salaried professionals and managers represented under 5% of
New York City residents in the nineteenth century and early twentieth
century; today they constitute 30%. The second is the extent to which
they, along with other high-income workers, have become a very visible
part of city life through distinct consumption patterns, lifestyles, and
high-income gentrification.

It is the magnitude in the expansion of high-income workers, their concentration in cities, and their high levels of spending that contribute to
this outcome. New York, London, and Tokyo, like all major cities, have
long had a core of wealthy residents and commuters. And while this core
has probably been expanded by a large influx of wealthy foreigners, especially in New York and London, and now increasingly in Tokyo, by
itself it could not have created the large-scale residential and commercial
gentrification recently evident in these cities, discussed in the preceding
section. As a stratum, the new high-income workers are to be distinguished from this core of wealth, or upper class. Their disposable income
is usually not enough to make them into important investors. Furthermore, their level of disposable income is also a function of lifestyle—
spending rather than saving—and demographic patterns, such as post-
poning having children and setting up two-career households. The critical point here is that this disposable income reached a level sufficient for
a significant expansion in the demand for highly priced goods and services—that is to say, sufficient to ensure the economic viability of the
producers and providers of such goods and services. The extent to which
this dynamic operates is reflected in the losses registered by restaurants,
designer shops, and certain kinds of service providers in New York City
beginning in 1988, when the financial industry began to lay off significant
numbers of employees. By late 1989 similar effects were becoming evi-

dent in London. This indicates that this relatively very small segment of consumption of highly priced goods and services is intimately connected to the new economic core in these cities and is distinct from older forms of elite consumption.

Thus, the existence of major growth sectors, notably the producer services, generates low-wage jobs directly, through the structure of the work process, and indirectly, through the structure of the high-income lifestyles of those therein employed and through the consumption needs of the low-wage work force. Even a technically advanced service industry, such as finance, generates a significant share of low-wage jobs with few educational requirements. High-income residential and commercial gentrification is labor intensive and raises the demand for maintenance, cleaning, delivery, and other types of low-wage workers. And the massive array of low-cost service and goods-producing firms selling to the expanded low-wage work force further contributes to the growth of low-wage jobs.

Beyond this impact of the new economic core, there have been broader transformations in the forms of organizing production, with a growing presence of small-batch production, small scales, high product differentiation, and rapid changes in output. These have promoted subcontracting and the use of flexible ways of organizing production. Today many industrial branches need to accommodate rapid changes in output levels and in product characteristics. There has been an overall decline in the production of basic goods and consumer durables, the leading growth industries in manufacturing in the postwar period. The most rapidly growing sectors within manufacturing in the 1980s were the high-technology complex and craft-based production, which also grew in traditional branches, such as furniture, footwear, and apparel. Flexible forms of production can range from highly sophisticated to very primitive and can be found in advanced or in backward industries.

Such ways of organizing production assume distinct forms in the labor market, in the components of labor demand, and in the conditions under which labor is employed. Indications of these changes are the decline of unions in manufacturing, the loss of various contractual protections, and the increase of part-time and temporary work or other forms of contingent labor. An extreme indication of this downgrading is the growth of sweatshops and industrial homework. The expansion of a downgraded manufacturing sector partly involves the same industries that used to have largely organized plants and reasonably well-paid jobs but replaces these with different forms of production and organization of the work process, such as piecework and industrial homework. But it also involves new kinds of activity associated with the new major growth trends. The possibility for manufacturers to develop alternatives to the organized factory becomes particularly significant in growth sectors. The consolidation of a downgraded manufacturing sector, whether through social or through technical transformation, can be seen as a politicoeconomic response to a need for expanded production in a situation of growing average wages and militancy, as was the case in the 1960s and early 1970s, and intense competition for land and markets, as was the case in the late 1970s and 1980s.

The expansion in the low-wage work force has also contributed to the proliferation of small operations and the move away from large-scale standardized factories and stores. The decline in wages has reached the point where sweatshop production in New York or London has become price competitive with cheap imports from Asia. The consumption needs of this work force are met in good part by production and retail establishments that are small, often fail to meet safety and health standards, and frequently rely on family labor—that is, work situations that further expand the low-wage work force. The growth of sweatshop production of garments in New York and London, for example, has meant that some of it can replace cheap Asian imports in meeting the demand for low-cost products.

It is my hypothesis that this form of economic polarization brought about by growth trends contains conditions that promote the informalization and casualization of work in a wide range of activities (Sassen-Koob 1984). Linking the informalization and casualization of work to growth trends takes the analysis beyond the notion that the emergence of informal "sectors" in such cities as New York and London is due to the large presence of immigrants and their supposed propensity to replicate survival strategies typical of Third World countries. It suggests, rather, that basic traits of advanced capitalism may promote conditions for informalization. The presence of large immigrant communities then can be seen as mediating in the process of informalization rather than directly generating it: The demand side of the process of informalization is therewith brought to the fore. The same argument holds for women and the growth of part-time jobs: The fact of inadequate child care support may make them more likely to seek part-time work, but the growth of part-time jobs is rooted in economic conditions. These are subjects I examine in the next section.

All these trends are operating in major cities, in many cases with greater intensity than national average data describe. This greater intensity is rooted in at least three conditions. First, there is locational concentration of major growth sectors with highly polarized income distributions in major cities. The evidence on different occupational and earnings distributions for various industries in combination with the locational patterns of such industries indicates that major cities, and especially New York and London, have a high proportion of industries with considerable income and occupational polarization. Second, there is a proliferation of small, low-cost service operations, made possible by the massive concentration of people in such cities, in addition to a large daily inflow of nonresident workers and tourists. The ratio between the number of these service operations and resident population is most probably significantly higher than in an average city or town. Furthermore, the large concentration of people in major cities will tend to create intense inducements to open up such operations, as well as intense competition and very marginal returns. Under such conditions, the cost of labor is crucial—hence the likelihood of a high concentration of low-wage jobs. Third, for these same reasons, together with other components of demand, the number of small, labor-intensive, low-wage manufacturing firms would tend to be larger in London, New York, or Tokyo than in average-sized cities. Indeed, in many cities such a downgraded manufacturing sector is not a significant factor if present at all.

Casual and Informal Labor Markets

There has been a pronounced increase in casual employment and in the informalization of work in both New York City and London. This trend is also emerging, under different form, in Tokyo where the increase in the number of casual workers, particularly "daily laborers" and part-time workers has led the government to express alarm publicly. The increase in various types of casual work is often thought of as a function of the increased participation of women in the labor force. Indeed, part-time, temporary, and seasonal jobs are more common among women than among men in all three cities. However, all the evidence points to significant increases of such jobs among men over the last decade. More generally, the industry/occupational mix prevalent among such jobs indicates that they account for a significant share of new jobs created in these economies. In addition, jobs that were once full-time ones are now being made into part-time or temporary jobs, pointing to a transformation in the employment relation. While so-called flexible work arrangements may be a development of advanced economies associated with a higher quality of life, the vast majority of casual jobs hardly fits this category. A majority are low-wage jobs, with no fringe benefits and no returns to seniority—a way of organizing work that reduces costs for employers. However there is a new trend that I consider significant in this study: High-income professional and managerial employees in many of the new specialized service and financial firms are more vulnerable to dismissal and have fewer claims on their employers than was the case with their equivalents in the large commercial banks and insurance houses. This greater "flexibility" in the employment relation is another way of saying that these jobs have become casualized as well. I will return to this subject, which has received no attention in the pertinent literature.

The growth of service jobs is crucial to the expansion of part-time jobs. The pressures to reduce labor costs in industries with limited profit margins, such as catering, retail, and cleaning, assumes added weight when these account for a growing share of jobs. In addition, many service industries require work at night, on weekends, and on holidays, which would entail costly overtime payments for full-time workers. And since many of these jobs do not require many skills or training, they can be downgraded into part-time, more lowly paid jobs. As these service industries have grown, the gap between the work week in such industries as retail, reaching seventy hours a week, and the forty-hour full-time work week has grown in weight. Part-time jobs can recruit women more easily, create greater flexibility in filling various shifts, and reduce labor costs by avoiding various benefits and overtime payments required by full-time workers. In its review of part-time employment trends in advanced industrialized countries, the OECD (1983) found that the shift to services was a major factor. In its analysis of the retailing industry, the National Economic Development Office (NEDO 1985) in Britain found a substitution of full-time jobs for part-time ones and that much of the employment growth in the industry was actually a function of this substitution and of the hiring of part-time workers to meet cyclical and seasonal demand rather than of the generation of full-time permanent jobs (NEDO 1985).

There is also evidence pointing to an expansion of the underground economy. Of interest to the analysis here is one particular component of the underground economy, informal work.[23] This encompasses work that is basically licit but takes place outside the regulatory apparatus covering zoning, taxes, health and safety, minimum wage laws, and other types of standards.[24] In other words, this is work that could be done in the formal

[23] We can distinguish at least three very different components of the underground economy: (1) criminal activities, which by their very nature could not be carried out aboveground; (2) tax evasion on licit forms of income (all governments confront this and have implemented mechanisms to detect and control tax evasion); and (3) the informal economy.

[24] The concept of an informal economy describes a process of income-generating activity characterized by lack of regulation in a context where similar activities are regulated (Castells and Portes 1989). The term *regulation* here refers to the institutionalized intervention of the state in the process of income-generating activity. Thus, while particular instances of informal work in highly developed countries may resemble those of an earlier period, they are actually a new development in the organization of work, given decades of institutionalized regulation that have led to a pronounced reduction and in many sectors virtual elimination of unregulated income-generating activity. Because the particular characteristics of

economy, unlike the criminal activities that are also part of the underground economy. Government regulations play a particularly important role in the rise of informal production because of the costs that they impose on formal businesses through their various licensing fees, taxes, and restrictions. Labor costs also have an effect on the formation and expansion of the informal economy: directly, in terms of the wage paid, and indirectly, in terms of various contributions demanded by law. One question is whether the importance of these inducements to informalization varies by industry and location.

The specification of this particular component, the informal economy, has implications for theories on the nature of advanced capitalism and the postindustrial society. While criminal activities and underreporting of income are recognized to be present in advanced industrialized economies, informal sectors are not. The literature on the informal sector has mostly focused on Third World countries and has, wittingly or not, assumed that as a social type such sectors are not to be expected in advanced industrialized countries. And the literature on industrialization has assumed that as development progresses, so will the standardization of production and generalization of the "formal" organization of work. Since much of the expansion of the informal economy in developed countries has been located in immigrant communities, this has led to an explanation of its expansion as being due to the large influx of Third World immigrants and their assumed propensities to replicate survival strategies typical of their home countries. Related to this view is the notion that backward sectors of the economy are kept backward, or even kept alive, because of the availability of a large supply of cheap immigrant workers. Both of these views posit or imply that if there is an informal sector in advanced industrialized countries, the sources are to be found in Third World immigration and in the backward sectors of the economy—a Third World import or a remnant from an earlier phase of industrialization.

A central question for theory and policy is whether the formation and expansion of informal and casual labor markets in advanced industrialized countries is the result of conditions created by advanced capitalism. Rather than assume that Third World immigration is causing informalization and the entry of mothers into the labor force is causing the casualization of work, what we need is a critical examination of the conditions that may be inducing these processes. Immigrants, insofar as they tend to form communities, may be in a favorable position to seize the opportunities represented by informalization. And women, insofar as they have children and inadequate access to child care may be interested in part-

informal work are derived from the existence of a context where such work is regulated, the informal economy can be understood only in its relation to the formal economy.

time or temporary job opportunities. But the opportunities are not necessarily created by immigrants and women. They may well be a structured outcome of current trends in the advanced industrialized economies. Similarly, what are perceived as backward sectors of the economy may or may not be remnants from an earlier phase of industrialization; they may well represent a downgrading of work connected to the dynamics of growth in leading sectors of the economy.

There is a strong tendency for the service sector overall to produce or make possible more part-time jobs than does manufacturing. This tendency is clearly embedded in a number of basic institutional arrangements and in specific historical conditions. The institutionalization of the family wage was closely interlinked with the rise of powerful manufacturing-based unions and a male-dominated "labor aristocracy." The family wage is—or, rather, was—the institutionalized principle that a man's wage should be high enough to support his family. Thus, it contributed to establishing the gender-based occupational work structure characteristic of industrialized economies (Hartmann 1981). "The perpetuation of the family wage system has depended on two things, one a fact, the other an assumption. The fact is that men, on the average, earn more than women. The assumption is that men use their higher wages to support women, and hence that most women are at least partly supported by men" (Ehrenreich 1984: 8).

The shift in the economy toward a prevalence of service industries contains what one could think of as a structurally induced erosion of the—albeit limited—institutional bases for the family wage. The growth of part-time work, the growth in the numbers of female-headed households, the decline of manufacturing-based unions, and the large-scale displacement of male workers—all these conditions have contributed to an erosion of the institution of the family wage, limited as its implementation was, especially in the United States, and to an erosion of the ideology of the family wage. One important question is whether the current conditions—a sort of disarray compared with the ideal type presupposed in the family wage—represent a transition to less gender-based structures of work or are yet another step in the formation of a supply of cheap and powerless workers.

The overall effect is the casualization and informalization of the employment relation. The differences among these three cities stem partly from the distinct institutional arrangements through which work is organized. In the United Kingdom, the government has until recently played a rather fundamental role as supplier of a vast range of services and goods, from housing to health services, which in the United States are largely delivered through the private market. The net effect was to incorporate a vast number of workers who were employed by the government or public authorities. This carried with it a considerable degree of government regulation over large sectors of the labor market. The recently implemented withdrawal of the government from these various markets through the privatization of services and goods has created a situation that has facilitated the transformation of many of these jobs from regular full-time, year-round jobs with the requisite fringe benefits into various kinds of part-time temporary jobs, as well as the subcontracting of work. The historical obligation assumed by a government to enforce its own regulations covers a shrinking share of the work force and an increasingly restricted set of labor markets. The recency of this transformation in the government's role in the economy and the rapidity of the process of privatization has provided the conditions for a pronounced spread of part-time and temporary work, while the growth of service industries further facilitates the expansion of part-time work.

In the United States, the government's role in the economy, while strong, has not been centered on the labor market or oriented toward the provision of housing and health services on a national scale. The mere absence of a national health system entails a much less encompassing role for government in shaping the characteristics of jobs. Economic conditions in the postwar era—the dominance of consumer-oriented industry, large unions, the expansion of a middle class, the growth of standardized production—all promoted the expansion of a large number of jobs that respected the regulatory framework. Thus, the outcome was similar to that in Britain in the postwar era, but was effected through different channels. The key vehicle in the expansion of part-time work over the last decade was the combination of a shift to services and the dismantling of the manufacturing-based unions, which had the power to impose wage standards on broad sectors of the economy.

Beyond the trend toward an increase in part-time work arising from these various conditions, we see the expansion of informal work arrangements, at times resembling an informal sector with a fairly elaborate set of relations of production, distribution, and markets for labor and inputs—that is to say, informal arrangements that do not simply consist of a few individuals working off the books. In the case of the United States there has not been such rapid wide-scale privatization of the production and delivery of various public goods and services as in Britain, but there has been a somewhat similar development in terms of the shift of a growing number of jobs from highly regulated formal labor markets to semiregulated, unregulated, or casual labor markets. Much work in the informal economy is not casual strictly speaking in that it is part of a well-organized chain of production and involves full-time, year-round work. But much of it is casual, this flexibility being precisely the key advantage of informal work for employers or contractors.

In Japan, rapid industrialization, immensely rapid urbanization, and culture have created very specific conditions. The securing of a reliable industrial work force under conditions of extremely rapid growth and different cultural preferences and expectations from those in the West has contributed to the development of the so-called lifelong job security system. This system now accounts for only a fifth of all workers, having also suffered from the shift to and rapid growth of service industries. The growing participation of women in the labor force has assumed the form of a rapid growth in part-time and temporary jobs. However, the growth of the category of daily laborers and the rapid erosion of the institutional arrangements that are supposed to cover daily laborers, are reminiscent of the casualization and informalization of work evident in Britain and the United States.

While present in all three cities under study, these developments assume rather specific forms and operate through distinct social arrangements. The available evidence suggests that the most pronounced form over the last decade in London was the growth of part-time work; in Tokyo it was the expansion of daily labor; in New York, the growth of informal work. The following sections discuss each of these instances of the casualization of the employment relation.

Informalization in New York City

A small but growing body of evidence points to the expansion of informal work in major cities of the United States over the last decade (Fernandez-Kelly and Garcia 1989; Stepick 1989; Sassen-Koob 1984, 1989). These studies are based mostly on ethnographic research. They are to be distinguished from studies that aim at overall estimates of the underground economy based on aggregate figures for the supply and circulation of money (Gutman 1979; Spitznas 1981; Tanzi 1982). As categories for analysis, the underground economy and the informal economy overlap only partly. Studies on the underground economy have sought to measure all income not registered in official figures, including income derived from illicit activities, such as drug dealing. Studies on the informal economy focus on the production and sale of goods and services that are licit but produced and/or sold outside the regulatory apparatus covering zoning, taxes, health and safety, minimum wage laws, and other types of standards.

The difference in focus has major consequences for the kind of information produced and issues raised. General measures of unregistered income make the underground economy into a homogeneous category; the distinction between underground income derived from criminal activities (for example, drug sales) and underground income derived from such activities as an unregistered, non-taxpaying shop cannot be applied to these aggregate monetary measures. Studies on the informal economy based on fieldwork document the existence of a diverse group of activities in need of diverse policy responses.

Grover and I investigated these activities from 1986 to 1989 (Sassen-Koob and Grover 1986; Columbia University 1987; Sassen-Koob 1989). The concern was to specify a relationship between the growth of informal activities in New York City and overall conditions in the economy and the existing regulatory environment. In this context, one can think of informalization as an emergent, or developing, "opportunity" structure that avoids or compensates for various types of constraints, from regulations to market prices for inputs. This type of inquiry requires an analytical differentiation of immigration, informalization, and the characteristics of the current phase of advanced industrialized economies in order to establish the differential impact of (1) immigration and (2) conditions in the economy at large on the formation and expansion of the informal economy. The theoretical and policy implications associated with the primacy of one or the other will vary. For theory, the primacy of economic structure would point to the need for further theoretical elaboration on the current understanding of the nature of advanced capitalism. For policy, the primacy of immigration would suggest, at its crudest, that controlling immigrant activity in the informal economy would eradicate the latter; it would, then, also reinforce standard theories on advanced industrialization or the postindustrial society, which allow no room for such developments as an informal economy.

The industries covered were construction; garments; footwear; furniture; retail activity; and electronics. We did field visits in all the boroughs of New York City (for a detailed account see Sassen-Koob 1989). On the basis of our fieldwork, interviews, and secondary data analysis, we found the following profile of the informal economy in the New York City area: (1) A rather wide range of industrial sectors use informal work—apparel, general construction contractors, special trade contractors, footwear, toys and sporting goods, electronic components, and accessories. (2) Informal work is also present in lesser measure in particular kinds of activities, such as packaging notions, making lampshades, making artificial flowers, jewelry making, distribution activities, photoengraving, manufacturing of explosives, etc. (3) There is a strong tendency for informal work to be located in densely populated areas with very high shares of immigrants. (4) There is an emergent tendency for "traditional" sweatshop activity (notably in garments) to be displaced from areas undergoing partial residential and commercial gentrification; such areas engender new forms of unregistered work, catering to the new clientele.

There are several patterns in the organization of the informal economy in New York City that are of interest to an examination of its articulation with leading growth trends. One pattern is the concentration of informal activities in immigrant communities, where some activities meet a demand from the communities and others meet a demand that comes from the larger economy. A second pattern is the concentration of informal activities in areas undergoing rapid socioeconomic change, notably gentrification. A third is the concentration of informal activities in areas that emerge as a type of manufacturing and industrial servicing area in a context where both regulations and market forces do not support such activities; while these are frequently located in immigrant communities, they cater to the larger economy. There follows a more detailed description of each.

The first pattern contains what are possibly two very different components of the informal economy. One is the use of immigrant workers and communities to lower the costs of production and raise the organizational flexibility of formal sector industries. The garment industry is the clearest example. Certain components of the construction industry, footwear industry, and industrial services also illustrate this pattern. Immigrant communities can be seen as collections of resources that facilitate informal production or distribution of certain activities (Sassen-Koob 1989). These resources consist of cheap, willing, and flexible labor supplies; entrepreneurial resources in the form of individuals willing to engage in the long hours and often low returns involved and the availability of family labor; various informal credit arrangements that make possible small-scale capital formation; and a supply of low-cost space available for a multiplicity of uses, some of them in violation of regulated uses. The issue of space may be far more important for firms using informal operations than is usually recognized. The sharp competition for land by high bidders, regulations that do not support manufacturing or industrial services, and the need for such activities to be easily accessible may make the availability of informal workspaces, whether sweatshops, basements, or homes, as important as the low cost of labor.

The other component of the informal sector in immigrant communities represents a type of neighborhood subeconomy. It consists of a variety of activities that meet the demand for goods and services inside the community, including immigrants residing in other neighborhoods that may lack commercial facilities. These goods and services may be of a kind not provided by the larger economy, or provided at too high a price, or provided in locations that entail a long or cumbersome trip. Certain aspects of the informal transportation system are illustrative, notably "gypsy" cabs servicing low-income or immigrant areas not serviced by the regular cabs. Also illustrative are certain aspects of the construction industry, especially renovations and small-store alteration or construction. A wide array of personal services are informally provided, frequently in the home of the buyer or provider. Certain types of manufacturing, including production of garments and footwear, and, at least in a few cases, furniture, are carried out in the community and meet local demand. Such a local economic base may well represent a mechanism for maximizing the returns on whatever resources are available in the communities involved. In this regard, these activities may help stabilize low-income areas by providing jobs, entrepreneurship opportunities, and enough diversification to maximize the recirculation of money spent on wages, goods, or services inside the community where the jobs are located and the goods and services produced.

A second pattern is characterized by the concentration of informal activities in areas undergoing high-income residential and commercial gentrification. The leading industrial sectors involved are construction and various forms of woodwork, including furniture making. Also involved in this process are various industries supplying the goods and services sold by the new commercial facilities associated with high-income gentrification—clothing boutiques, gourmet food shops selling prepared dishes, shops selling customized household items. But unlike construction and customized woodwork, many of the latter activities are not necessarily located in the area undergoing gentrification. While immigrant workers often were found to provide the requisite labor, including highly skilled craftswork, the demand for the goods and services clearly stems from the larger economy.

The third pattern we can discern is the concentration of manufacturing and industrial services in certain areas, which emerge as a type of manufacturing district or service market. For example, in one particular location in the New York City borough of Queens we found shops doing glasswork for buildings and vehicles; shops doing refinishing of restaurant equipment; auto repair shops; garment shops; carpentry shops that make frames for furniture and then send them to other locations for finishing; cabinetmakers. All these shops are operating in violation of various codes, and they are located in an area not zoned for manufacturing. This area has emerged as an informal manufacturing district. The city government is well aware of its existence but has, it seems, opted for disregarding the violations, probably because of the scarce supply of manufacturing space in Manhattan and the city's interest in retaining small businesses. The concentration of manufacturing shops in this area of Queens has brought about a whole array of related service shops as well as contributing to the development of a zone where new industrial uses are occurring. One implication in this case is that what may initially be a small cluster of manufacturing shops operating informally may, under certain conditions, develop into an industrial district with agglomeration economies that will draw an increasing number of industrial users. This becomes a de facto manufacturing zone. We found significant clusters of auto repair shops in several areas of the city. The number of shops and cars involved was large enough to point to a service being sold beyond the neighborhood. It is a development that goes against prevailing notions of the economic base in "post-industrial" cities, and points to an ongoing need for manufacturing firms and industrial services.

In sum, we can identify different types of locations in the spatial organization of the informal economy. Immigrant communities are a key location for informal activities meeting both internal and external demand for goods and services. Gentrifying areas are a second important location; these areas contain a large array of informal activities in renovation, alteration, small-scale new construction, woodwork, and installations. A third location can be characterized as informal manufacturing and industrial service areas serving a citywide market.

An examination of what engenders the demand for informal production and distribution indicates several sources: (1) One of these is competitive pressures in certain industries, notably apparel, to reduce labor costs to meet massive competition from low-wage Third World countries (Safa 1981). Informal work in this instance represents an acute example of exploitation. (2) Another source is a rapid increase in the volume of renovations, alterations, and small-scale new construction associated with the transformation of many areas of the city from low-income, often dilapidated neighborhoods into higher-income commercial and residential areas. What in many other cities in the United States would have involved a massive program of new construction was mostly a process of rehabilitation of old structures in the case of New York City. The volume of work, its small scale, its labor-intensiveness and high skill content, and the short-term nature of each project all were conducive to a heavy proportion of informal work. (3) A third source is inadequate provision of services and goods by the formal sector. This inadequacy may consist of excessively high prices, inaccessible or difficult-to-reach location of formal provision, or actual lack of provision. It would seem that this inadequacy of formal provision involves mostly low-income individuals or areas. (4) The existence of a cluster of informal shops can eventually generate agglomeration economies that induce additional entrepreneurs to move in. (5) The existence of a rather diversified informal economy making use of a variety of labor supplies may lower entry costs for entrepreneurs and hence function as a factor inducing the expansion of the informal economy. This can be construed as a type of supply-side factor.

We can distinguish different types of firms in the informal economy, particularly in terms of the locational constraints to which firms are sub-

ject. For some firms, access to cheap labor is the determining inducement for a New York City location. While access to the city's final or
intermediate markets (or the city's sheer size, which facilitates informalization) may also be significant, it is ultimately access to cheap labor, specifically low-wage immigrant workers, that determines location, because
it allows these firms to compete with Third World factories. Many of
these shops could be located in a diversity of areas with cheap labor.
Certain segments of the garment industry are illustrative.[25] In contrast,
many of the shops engaged in customized production or operating on
subcontracts evince a whole host of locational dependencies on New York
City. These firms are bound to the city (or to any large city they might
be located in that is undergoing the kinds of socioeconomic transformations we identified for New York City) for some or all of the following
reasons: (1) localized demand, typically involving specific clients or customers; (2) proximity to design and specialized services; (3) brief turnover
time between completion of design and production; (4) demand predicated on the existence of a highly dynamic overall economic situation that
generates a critical volume of demand and spending capability on the
part of buyers; and/or (5) the existence of immigrant communities, which
have some of the traits associated with enclave economies.

Finally, we can distinguish differences in the types of jobs we found in
the informal economy. Many of the jobs are unskilled, with no training
opportunities, involving repetitive tasks. Another type of job demands
high skills or acquisition of a skill. The growth of informalization in the
construction and furniture industries can be seen as bringing about a certain reskilling of the labor force. In the case of highly skilled work for
which there is a considerable demand, for example, stonecutters and

[25] Interviews with homeworkers confirmed what is generally accepted, that hourly or
piece rate wages are extremely low. However, we also found a new trend toward an up-
graded version of homework. One pattern we found was for designers (typically free-lance
or independent designers) to have immigrant workers come into their homes (typically large
converted lofts in lower Manhattan) and work off the books. The other pattern was for
middle-class women to take in very expensive cloth and clothes to do finishing work at
home or do highly specialized knitting on special machines purchased by the workers themselves; the cases we studied all involved Chinese or Korean households in middle-class
residential neighborhoods in the city. The overall evidence from our ongoing research
points to the existence of a very dynamic and growing high-price market where production
has been organized so as to incorporate sweatshops and homes (of poor and middle-class
immigrants and of designers) as key workplaces. Finally, a distinct pattern of ethnic ownership characterizes the informal sector in this industry. The new Hispanic immigrants,
especially Dominicans and Colombians, have replaced Puerto Ricans as the leading group
of owners in the Latino population; the Chinese have increased their number of shops
immensely over the last ten years; and the Koreans are emerging as the fastest-growing
new ethnic group setting up sweatshops and homework arrangements.

woodworkers for architect-designed buildings, informalization served as the vehicle for making use of undocumented immigrants with such skills.

It would seem from our study that important sources of the informalization of various activities are to be found in characteristics of the larger economy of the city. Among these are the demand for products and services that lend themselves to small scales of production, or are associated with rapid transformations brought about by commercial and residential gentrification, or are not satisfactorily provided by the formal sector. This would suggest that a good share of the informal economy is not the result of immigrant survival strategies, but rather an outcome of structural patterns or transformations in the larger economy of a city such as New York. Workers and firms respond to the opportunities contained in these patterns and transformations. However, in order to respond, workers and firms need to be positioned in distinct ways. Immigrant communities represent what could be described as a "favored" structural location to seize the opportunities for entrepreneurship as well as the more and less desirable jobs being generated by informalization.

The Casualization of Work in London

There has been a great increase in part-time, casual, and sweated labor in construction, clothing, catering, retailing, tourism, cleaning, and even printing in London and in the United Kingdom generally. The growth of unorganized and low-paid labor can drag down the pay and working conditions of the better-paid, organized workers. This is contributing to a further erosion of the socioeconomic conditions of low-income workers. While the vast majority of part-time workers in the United Kingdom, as well as in most developed countries, are women, the share of men has grown over the last decade. In the early 1970s, men accounted for a small share of part-time workers. By 1981, 19% of all part-time workers in the United Kingdom were men. Not only is part-time work increasing, part-time contracts are becoming shorter (see Chapter Eight).

Studies by the Greater London Council and the Low Pay Unit estimate that over 20% of workers in the hotel and catering sectors are on temporary contracts. There is a job center for casual employment, with lines forming every morning at six and waiting until the center opens at eight. The regular use of casual labor has also increased in this industry, not simply as a response to seasonal demand in hotel and catering, but largely as a way to cut costs and avoid addressing poor working conditions and low pay. There has also been an increase of these practices in the construction industry. Every morning there is a hiring hall in certain areas and a scramble for jobs. These jobs carry no benefits, and workers are often classified as self-employed in order to exempt the employer from taxes and other responsibilities. Again we see here parallels with what is occurring in New York City.

These practices, however, are not confined to the more traditional industries. In such specialized service industries as architectural and engineering services and banking there has also been an increase of workers paid by the hour and a reduction in part-time workers with the same rights as full-time workers. These workers, mostly women, have no sick pay, no overtime pay, no holiday pay, and no job security. Yet they work as much as a regular worker. As in the garment or construction industries, these workers are also classified as self-employed by their employers. These practices contribute to the income polarization evident in the advanced services sector.

The growth of part-time jobs is not only a function of the increase in service jobs or a tight labor market and hence the need to accommodate married women with child care responsibilities. Part-time jobs allow for wage cuts, greater flexibility in work force size and in a firm's response to fluctuations in demand, use of workers on night and weekend shifts or overtime without added cost, the replacement of men by women, no unions, no overhead. Employers are exempt from paying various taxes and fringe benefits.

Homework and sweated work have also increased. The clearest case is apparel. To be able to use the cheapest workers, ethnic minorities and women, smaller textile and clothing firms now tend to be concentrated in London and other cities. The London clothing industry consists of about 3,000 firms, a few of which employ over 100 workers. London has lost all its large factories, as many of the large manufacturers no longer do production: They subcontract to overseas or domestic producers. And in the 1960s the big retailers began subcontracting as well, initially to Hong Kong and Taiwan and now also to domestic firms. As a result, the number of firms and workers has increased, especially "fly-by-night" factories. The majority of the workers are from ethnic minorities and up to a third are homeworkers. Many are part-time or temporary workers, employed in the busy season. The vast majority of homeworkers and part-time workers in clothing are women. It has been estimated that the number of homeworkers and other unregistered workers in women's light wear increased by 17,000 between 1978 and 1982 (Mitter 1986). As in New York and Tokyo, the whole new emphasis on fashion and luxury—or simulated luxury—has also led to a new need for quick turnover from design to finished product and hence for producers close by. The estimate is that 30% to 50% of all East End and northeast London garment production is through homework and that at least half of these homeworkers are Bangladeshi or Pakistani women; of the rest, a large number of women in garment work are from Cyprus. And in fieldwork in 1989, I found a significant presence of recently arrived Turkish entrepreneurs and workers. Homework is taking place not only in clothing but also in other lines of production, including the making of lampshades, electrical goods, painted toys, and zippers.

The levels of unemployment and its duration changed markedly over the two decades between 1965 and 1985 (Greater London Council. Intelligence Unit 1988). Total unemployment levels went from about 25,000 for men and almost 6,000 for women in the late 1960s to 277,524 and 124,722, respectively, in 1985, or a total of 400,000 unemployed in a work force of 3.4 million. Furthermore, registered unemployment figures are known to be underestimates in periods of high unemployment, because they exclude workers who have used up their allowance and discouraged workers, including those who decided not to enter the labor force.

Yet another strong trend emerges when we control for duration of unemployment. The number of unemployed men with two weeks or less of registered unemployment went from 7,000 in 1965 to 17,375 in 1985; those with two but no more than eight weeks went from 6,800 to 32,500; and those with eight weeks or more went to 227,672. For women, the total levels were much smaller in each of the categories, but the trends were similar. Thus a vast majority of the increase in unemployment was among those unemployed for eight weeks or more, a group that was in 1985 twenty-one times larger than in 1965 for men and sixty times larger for women. Among those with two to eight weeks' unemployment, the increase was far less pronounced: a fivefold increase for men and a ninefold one for women. In the under-two-weeks category it was 2.5 times larger for men and 5.2 times larger for women in 1985 than in 1965.

Reviewing the evidence for Britain, Hurstfield (1987) found that by far the greatest savings to employers derived from using part-time employees seem to be on National Insurance contributions, by keeping part-time workers' earnings below the threshold (Hart 1986). This was further suggested by another study, which found that in Britain the threshold was twice as high as in Germany, thus facilitating the creation of part-time jobs with wages below the National Insurance threshold, especially in industries with low average pay (Schoer 1987).

As in the United States, the government has passed legislation that further weakens the position of part-time workers, creates additional incentives for employers to use part-time workers, and legitimizes the use of part-time workers. Compared with other European countries, Britain has lost significant ground in terms of the protection of workers, though it is probably still more generous than the United States. At present, part-time workers employed at least sixteen hours a week in continuous employment are entitled to various rights. Below this threshold, the employer has few if any obligations to the workers. In a recent White Paper entitled "Building Businesses . . . Not Barriers," there are proposals for raising this threshold to twenty hours. About 95% of the workers affected by these changes would be women.

Tokyo's Daily Laborers

Daily laborers, especially in construction, construction-related industries, and longshoring—all major industries in Japan—are supposedly registered and entitled to unemployment compensation and other benefits according to their work records. They have work carnets in which are registered the days worked every week and month—necessary to establish the amount of unemployment compensation a worker is entitled to. There are specific locations where jobs are listed and allocated by government employees, who staff the various desks or counters, give workers their job slips, and write the information in the workers' carnets. These workers supposedly also can write themselves into a waiting list for housing and have accesss to other services. There was a time when their numbers were smaller, fairly well-paying jobs in longshoring were their main occupation, and daily laborers generally were better incorporated in mainstream society.

The recent massive expansion of this category of workers has meant that a minority of them are actually covered by these regulations. Daily labor has increasingly become a residual category, formed by those who were fired from other jobs, including white-collar workers, elderly men who no longer can work in the jobs they once held, and young men unable to get any other job. In my fieldwork in Yokohama's daily laborers' camp, I found university graduates, including one who had been a political militant at the University of Tokyo and had subsequently been blacklisted. Daily labor has also become a key employment form for new illegal immigrants from several Asian countries. In my fieldwork I found that a number of these immigrants had actually attended university in their home countries.

There are four major hiring halls for daily laborers in the country, two in the Tokyo-Yokohama area and one each in Nagoya and Osaka. The largest of these hiring halls is in the Taito ward in Tokyo. It has a reputation for being a rather dangerous place. While the Japanese version of Western-style gangsters or Mafia, the "yakusa," are known to control all four of the large hiring halls in the country, Taito's is supposed to be the worst. As I discussed above in describing Tokyo's inner city, Taito is one of the most deprived wards in the city, with growing rates of criminality, poverty, and unemployment. There is clearly a massive breakdown of the system that was supposed to protect daily laborers and low-income residents generally. The hiring halls are also frequently places for homeless men.

On my first visit to one of these halls, Kotobuki-cho in Yokohama, we walked over at five in the morning. It was still dark. There was a gray concrete structure, the equivalent of four stories, with wide-open platforms at street level and one at the equivalent of two stories up, covered by a flat, slablike roof. It was a square structure with about 50 meters per side. Both on the street level and on the second-story platform on one of the enclosed sides were what looked like train station ticket counters, with long lines of men at each one. Through the ticket window I could see lists of jobs, with wages listed. At the other end of the platform were large groups of men, lying on the ground or just rising, clearly homeless, covered with tattered clothes, lying on dirty blankets, unshaven, unhealthy. An image of absolute misery. There were also young, neat men, among them many immigrants, and many older men standing in line. Amongst this vast and varied sea of men walked about twenty flashy, flamboyant men, arrogant and aggressive looking, with dark sunglasses notwithstanding the predawn darkness. They were the yakusas. They acted in rather threatening ways toward me, circling me. But I knew I was safe for a complicated set of reasons, not the least being that murder is still extremely rare even in the absolute bottom of the Japanese social structure. At about 8 a.m., the contractors have left with their hired laborers, and the large numbers that stay behind have nothing much to look forward to. They sit at the edges of the streets and talk, play various games. There is no place beneath this place.

I visited some of the living quarters of those who had been left behind. You enter an old, minute version of a New York City tenement: a long, very dark and narrow hallway, with an extremely low ceiling. There is an endless row of roughly made wooden doors. Behind each door is a cubicle the size of a narrow double bed and, at least in the ones I saw, a small window. Some of the quarters I visited were extremely neat, the occupant clearly intent on salvaging as much as he could of his dignity. Some of the daily laborers are extremely clean and neat in appearance; they make use of the public showers, for which they are willing to pay. They have not been morally broken. At least not yet; they may still have the hope of a better job.

The meager evidence we have and the fate of the older, less employable daily laborers suggest that increasing hardship and demoralization lie ahead for the mass of daily laborers. One can still see amidst the misery and the darkness and the dankness the behavior of individuals who consider themselves integrated in a wider society; there is in fact no exit for most of them. The distance between the world of the daily laborer and the rest of society, the world of regular, full-time jobs, has grown immensely in only a few years. So has the distance between the world of the daily laborer and the society of men and women and families and children. This is a world exclusively of men. I had been warned that many of the older men had probably not seen women, live and up close, for many years, that they would come up to me and stare and try to touch me, innocently, with no mean intent. They did. This is a world far removed from the Japan we think of in the West. It is neither the old, foreign culture nor the new, modern Japan. It is a place of no name, with no image to call it forth.

A group of daily laborers have sought to organize the union of daily laborers. This would represent a threat to the place and source of money of the yakusa. The top leader of the newly born "Union of Daily Workers" was murdered, an event which received considerable attention because it was viewed as truly unusual and stepping beyond all boundaries. The second in command is now supposed to be on the death list and is keeping a low profile. My reading is that it is a quid pro quo: you keep a low profile and we stay away from you. I was at a large meeting of daily laborers where this organizer attended briefly, gave a speech, and left. It was being described as an act of extreme courage, but I do believe that the key context is one that is quite different from, for example, the drug business in the United States in that murder is not as common an occurrence yet among the Japanese. Most of the labor-related murders have thus far been of illegal immigrants, including women in the sex industry.

Daily labor in Japan is, perhaps, the sharpest instance of casualization in the employment relation. Along with female part-time work, it represents a growing stratum of the labor force.

Race and Nationality in the Labor Market

It is impossible to disregard the facts of race and nationality in an examination of social and economic processes in New York. To a lesser extent this is also the case with London. Tokyo, on the other hand, is rather different, since Japan has lacked a history of immigration. The very recent new illegal immigration of the last few years does raise a number of questions about the future. Thus, while Tokyo is indeed to be distinguished from New York and London, it would seem important to present the available information on the new immigration insofar as it may signal the beginning of a new process of labor force formation in the context of the internationalization of the Japanese economy.

While there are complex reasons that explain the patterning and the directionality of international migration flows (Sassen 1988) this still leaves unanswered a number of questions about the place of Third World immigrants in the leading economic centers of the world. The argument that New York keeps receiving immigrants because it has always been a city of immigrants emerges as clearly inadequate given the formation of a completely new illegal immigration into Japan and Tokyo in the last three years. In London, we see the continuation over two generations of Asian and Afro-Caribbean populations highly concentrated in London and with employment patterns quite distinct from those of the majority population. It raises questions about (a) the conditions in these cities that bring about the highest number of immigrant entries ever in the history of New York; (b) a continuing differentiation of Asians and Afro-Caribbeans in London, as well as a new illegal immigration into that city after a long period of little or no immigration; and (c) a first-time immigration into Tokyo, a city in a country that has never before had a major immigration and has firmly resisted the notion.

If immigrant and native minority workers had the same earnings and occupational distributions as native workers and similar residential patterns, then there would be less purpose in examining these populations here. But they do not. Notwithstanding great differences in the three cities and among the multiplicity of nationalities involved, they are still, in the end, disproportionately concentrated in large, central cities and in low-wage jobs and casual labor markets. The following sections emphasize the specificity of each of these processes and the concrete details characterizing each city.

New York City's Minority and Immigrant Work Force

Alongside the increase in high-income jobs, there has been a second, perhaps less noted growth trend in New York City's labor force since 1980. Blacks and Hispanics increased their share of all jobs, while whites lost share. Half of all resident workers in New York City are now minority. The evidence also shows that blacks and Hispanics are far less likely than whites to hold the new high-income jobs and far more likely than whites to hold the new low-wage jobs. Thus, one can infer a trend toward replacement of whites in existing lower-income jobs by blacks and Hispanics as well as these minorities' entry into new lower-income jobs. A third trend that is expected to become more pronounced over the next few years is the growing share of jobs held by women from all groups. The share of women in New York City's resident work force increased from 39% in 1970 to 45% in 1986. Several projections show that by 1990 more resident workers will be women than men.

Of the 3.2 million resident labor force, 1.6 million are non-Hispanic whites, 663,000, or 20.5%, are Hispanic (both native and foreign born), and 928,000, or 28.8%, are black and other non-Hispanic workers. Most of the growth in New York City's labor force since 1977, when the new economic phase began, was accounted for by minority workers and women. The resident labor force grew by 169,000. Minority workers increased by 237,000, or 30%, compared with a loss of 68,000 whites. The Hispanic work force is estimated to have increased by 20%. Labor force participation rates were 52.5% for blacks, 47% for Hispanics, and 54.7% for whites. While minority workers now represent almost half of the resident work force, they account for only 10% of the 700,000 workers who commute to the city daily.

In terms of numbers, the critical components of the labor force in New York City are native-born whites and blacks and native- and foreign-born Hispanics. The largest industry gains among native-born blacks were in public sector employment, professional services, business services, and FIRE. The largest gains for foreign-born Hispanics were in manufacturing, retail, FIRE, business services, and the public sector.

Occupational gains show rather diverse patterns. For the city as a whole, the largest increase for the 2.8 million workers registered in the 1980 census were in white-collar occupations, notwithstanding a loss of 68,000 such jobs over the 1970 level. This change was not evenly distributed, with losses concentrated among native-born whites and foreign-born Hispanics. The largest single concentrations of white-collar jobs among foreign-born Hispanics are in clerical and managerial jobs, the latter largely accounted for by self-employment and family business. In other words, a large share of the white-collar jobs held by Hispanics are rather low-paying jobs.

Minority workers continue to be underrepresented in higher-level jobs (U.S. Department of Labor, Bureau of Labor Statistics 1988). In 1986, still the phase of high growth, 16% of all Hispanics and 21% of all employed blacks and other races held managerial, professional, and technical support jobs as compared to 36% of whites. These occupational groups represent the major sector of employment growth for New York City. From 1983 to 1986, a period of sharp job growth, 213,000 resident workers, or three-fourths of net employment growth, were in these occupational groups. Hispanics and blacks in these occupations tend to be concentrated in social and health services. The figures for whites are underestimates in that they exclude commuters, 90% of whom are white and many of whom have higher-level jobs. Among Hispanics there continues to be overrepresentation in manufacturing compared with their share in the labor force. As of 1986, 23% of Hispanics, compared to 12% of non-Hispanics, were semiskilled and unskilled machine operators, assemblers, and inspectors. But clearly, in absolute numbers, the vast majority of Hispanics in the labor force are not in manufacturing but in services. Compared with the nonimmigrant population in New York, most immigrants are disproportionately concentrated in blue-collar and service jobs. Those groups that are better educated on the average, such as Koreans, Japanese, Filippinos, and South Asians, tend to be self-employed or to hold jobs in government and the health services.

Another indication of a disadvantaged labor market situation can be inferred from educational data. According to the 1980 census, 42% of the city's blacks aged twenty-five and over and 60% of Hispanics had no high school diploma. About 80% of the 50,000 youths aged sixteen to nineteen who dropped out of school were minority. The available evidence indicates that dropouts tend to be unemployed or concentrated in low-income jobs. More than one in four immigrants residing in New York do not speak English well or at all: half of all Dominicans, 27% of all Latinos, 37% of all Chinese, 29% of all Koreans. Half of all such immigrants had eight years or less of education, including school attendance both in New York City and abroad. In New York City, 49% of the population have high school degrees, but only 23% of Dominicans, 26% of Puerto Ricans, and 41% of South Americans.

An important question, particularly from the perspective of major cities with large concentrations of immigrant workers, is whether the expansion of low-wage jobs is a function of the large new Third World immigrant influx. DeFreitas (1986) analyzed the sector and skill distribution of workers in the United States by country of birth and found a rather similar concentration of native-born Anglos and foreign-born Hispanics in his grouping of "immigrant intensive industries" (industries where at least one-fifth of the work force are immigrants). This would suggest that it is the economy rather than the immigrants which is producing low-wage jobs. Race and nationality segment the labor force and contribute to a supply of low-wage workers.

London's Black and Asian Work Force

During the period of high immigration in the 1950s, almost half of the Afro-Caribbean and Asian entrants settled in London, and most of the rest settled in other large cities. They doubled their share in Britain's labor force from 1971 to 1981, accounting for 5% and 1.1 million of all British workers in 1981. By 1981, they numbered 945,000, or 14.6% of London's total population and 19.4% of inner London's population. This share rose to about a third of the population in three inner London boroughs (Hackney, Haringey, and Brent) and about a fourth in several other London boroughs (Lambeth, Newham, Ealing). The average concentration was below 5% in the rest of London. The largest groups were and remain Asians, followed by Afro-Caribbeans (West Indians and Guyanese), also referred to as blacks. The strong concentration in major cities and particularly London has continued, though with increasingly divergent patterns (Stuart 1989). While those of Caribbean origin remain overwhelmingly concentrated in inner London, a good number of Asians have moved to the suburbs. The evidence shows that Afro-Caribbeans are less likely to move out of the inner city than Asians and the general population.

Originally, Commonwealth citizens had been encouraged to come to Britain to meet shortages of unskilled labor in several industries. But by 1962 the first of a series of immigration laws restricting their entry was implemented.[26] Furthermore, in 1979 temporary work permits were eliminated. The tourist and catering industry had used temporary work permits to recruit workers mostly from non-Commonwealth countries: Turkey, Spain, Greece, the Philippines, and Colombia.[27] Now work permits can be issued on a temporary basis to employers who apply for them; but they have increasingly been issued to white professionals. For example, in 1984, of all the permits issued, 5,480 went to North Americans and 30 to Bangladeshi.

There is also an increasing number of "illegal" migrant workers in low-wage service jobs. For temporary workers, dismissal is equivalent to deportation, so they are forced to keep the jobs they have and to accept low wages, a condition that parallels that of undocumented migrant workers in the United States today after passage of a new law in 1986. Most migrants with temporary work permits come from outside the New Commonwealth. A very high proportion of these temporary workers are women. Although work permits for unskilled and semiskilled workers were abolished in 1970, in fact many of these workers continue to be employed illegally, because they have overstayed their visas, because their pre-1980 permits have run out, or because they are women who

[26] An even stricter law was introduced in 1968. By the early 1970s, no new workers were being allowed to enter for permanent settlement; only close relatives of those already in Britain were allowed to enter on a permanent basis, but even this was not easy, and many applications were rejected. Finally, the Nationality Act of 1981 redefined the status of certain British passport holders so that they no longer had automatic rights of entry or citizenship. One result was an increase in deportations.

[27] From the late 1960s until 1979, when temporary work permits no longer were issued, there was an inflow of workers from Turkey, Greece, Spain, the Philippines, Malaysia, Latin America (especially Colombia), and elsewhere, whose status was highly vulnerable and who lacked the right to settle. These migrant workers were used by the London tourist industry, among others, and were subjected to frequent raids by the police and immigration authorities (Greater London Council 1986).

have married and separated without obtaining U.K. citizenship (Greater London Council 1986). They work in tourism, catering, domestic service, and the public health service and as homeworkers. Migrant workers are generally the most vulnerable and desperate of all minority workers in Britain.

Controlling for industry, the 1981 Labor Force Survey found that black workers were much more concentrated in manufacturing than white workers. Manufacturing accounted for 25% of Asian workers and 27% of black ones, compared with 12% of white male workers. Black workers have strong concentrations in industries such as engineering and vehicles, food, and textiles. They are absent from industries that tend to involve more skilled work or have strong unions, such as gas, water, electricity, printing, dock work, and property development industries. Most blacks work in production-related activities, such as packing, and, to a lesser extent, in service and maintenance activities in manufacturing. Asians and blacks are overrepresented in industries that have been most affected by decline. Pakistanis and Bangladeshis are particularly concentrated in clothing, textiles, and leather, especially in East London, and also in the furniture trades. There are few Asians in the construction industry. Other ethnic groups, such as Greeks, Cypriots, and Italians, are also found in textiles and clothing.

From 1971 to 1981, the sharpest growth rates (though not necessarily the greatest absolute numbers) among all men were in professional business services and the public sector; for women, they were in the public sector and in professional services. For all minority men, the highest rates were in construction; for black men, they were in construction and business services. For minority women, the highest rates of growth were in miscellaneous services and in retail; there was also growth, though minimal, in business services and, for Indian women, in transport and utilities. All other sectors accounted for declining shares among minority workers. In terms of occupation, white men raised their shares of professional, managerial, crafts, transport, and service jobs; white women raised their shares of managerial and other service occupations. Minority workers raised their shares of clerical jobs and, with some exceptions, service jobs. Indian men and women also raised their shares of managerial jobs, as did Pakistani and Bangladeshi men, partly a function of self-employment. The largest single increases were in clerical jobs among black and Indian women, followed by service jobs among Afro-Caribbean men and women.

While whites and West Indians have similar percentages in services, the industry distribution differs strongly. Fewer blacks are in public administration, and they have not entered the expanding professional, banking, and financial industries in London. Neither have Asians. Afro-

Caribbean men are overrepresented in transport and communications, and Caribbean women are overrepresented in the health services. This concentration in the health services explains why in Britain as a whole 40% of black women are in the professional and scientific category compared with 25% of white women and 16% of Asian women. There are interesting parallels with the United States, where Caribbean women are also highly represented in the health services, particularly nursing and various forms of home care delivery. Among Asian women, 14% work in the distributive trades, compared with 8% of Caribbean women. This is partly explained by the high number of Asian shopowners. But these figures are still much lower than the 27% for white women. Black men and women have considerable concentrations in public service and vehicle maintenance. As a result they have been severely affected by government cutbacks and by privatization.

The 1981 Labor Force Survey found that 20% of Asian men were self-employed, a share considerably higher than the 7% of Caribbean men and the 12% of all other men. Furthermore, for both Asians and Caribbeans, this represents an increase over the 1979 figures of, respectively, 15% and 1%, compared with no change for other men. The 1981 figures for women also show a higher share for Asians: 12% compared with 1% for Caribbeans and 7% for others. These figures represent an increase of 2% for Asian women and no change for Caribbeans and others. Self-employment among Asians is concentrated in clothing, textiles, food stores, and catering; among Caribbeans, in hair salons, retail stores for records and household goods, and, to a lesser extent, food and catering (Aldrich et al. 1981; Wilson and Stanworth 1985; Jones 1982; Greater London Council 1985; Lee 1981; Shah 1975). Long work hours, use of family labor, and undercapitalization are key characteristics in these firms.

There is a 10% concentration in the professional and the employers and managers categories among Indian, Pakistani, and Bangladeshi men, compared with 3% among black men. And the 50% concentration of the former group in the skilled and semiskilled manual occupations is smaller than the three-quarters concentration of black men in these occupations. But clearly, manual work accounts for the majority of all black workers. Among the Asians, the highest concentration of manual jobs is among the Bangladeshis, of whom nearly 70% are semiskilled or unskilled, compared with 40% of Indians and 25% of African Asians. The largest single concentration among black women is to be found in nonmanual occupations, mostly clerical, and the teaching and health professions. Over half of all jobs held by black women are in these two occupational groups. The women have a far more pronounced occupational concentration than the men, a pattern that holds for all women in London. The occupational concentration of black men is far more pronounced than that of all men, while that of black women is somewhat less pronounced than that of all women. Black workers in London, and in Britain overall, are generally in worse jobs than are whites. Thus, a larger number of Asians who are employers are actually owners of small shops and engage in long work hours and use family labor. Half the Asian managers in London are self-employed.

The growth in contracting out and in the casualization of labor has particularly involved black workers and other ethnic minorities. These practices are spreading rapidly and are affecting a growing number of jobs not only in catering and cleaning, health, education, and local services but also in postal service and in food manufacturing at such places as Heathrow airport. These practices are also spreading in the tourism industry. Many of the workers in tourism are migrants with a legal status even less secure than that of resident immigrants from former British colonies.

The 1981 Labor Force Survey found higher unemployment rates among blacks than among whites. Unemployment rates for all those of working age stood at 16% for West Indians and 12% for Guyanese, compared with 8% for the work force as a whole. These rates were much higher among youth: 37% among West Indians and 23% among Asians aged sixteen to nineteen, and somewhat lower among those aged twenty to twenty-four. While black workers have generally lower educational levels than whites, when we control for education it becomes evident that black workers are at a disadvantage even when they have the same educational level as whites (Policy Studies Institute, 1984). By the early 1980s, increasing numbers of young black men and women were leaving full-time education to get jobs, and unemployment rates among young blacks were becoming extremely high, particularly in certain boroughs, for example, 60% in Lambeth in 1982 (Policy Studies Institute 1984). Almost 82% of blacks who lived in London's inner city in 1971 still lived there in 1981 compared with 53% of Indians and 63% of Pakistanis and Bangladeshis. Departures were mostly to outer London.

Many of these trends have held over the ensuing years, particularly the overrepresentation in declining industries and in low-wage service industries. Labor Force Survey data for 1985–1987 show a further shift into low-wage service industries and a shift out of metal manufacture and into other forms of manufacture. By 1986, 21% of minority men were in services, and so were 47% of minority women (U.K. Department of Employment 1988). While Asian women are still overrepresented in non-metal manufacturing, they are increasingly moving into service jobs. In 1986, a fourth of black and white men were in manufacturing compared to 36% of Asian men; almost 16% of black men compared to 22% of Asian men and 13% of white men were in distribution and catering; and 30% of black men compared to 10% of Asian men and 24% of white men were in other services. Among women, the largest single concentration for black women was in other services; this also held for white women. But among Asian women, the largest single concentration, at 43%, was in manufacturing, with another 32% in other services.While both Asian and black men clearly have disadvantaged labor market positions compared with that of whites, the Asians do better than do the Afro-Caribbeans. But Afro-Caribbean women have a better earnings distribution than that of Asian women, probably a consequence of low levels of activity and overconcentration in apparel among certain Asian groups, particularly Bangladeshi women. Policy Studies Institute survey data for 1982 (Brown 1984) show somewhat less distance in earnings between white women and minority women than is the case for men. The evidence also indicates that there is considerable differentiation among Asian men. Townsend, Corrigan, and Kowarzik (1987) found that minorities earn about four-fifths as much as whites do, with black men showing the greatest disadvantage. The concentration of blacks in areas with declining industries and low-wage jobs may also affect their occupational and earnings distribution. Labor Force survey data for London show that minority workers as a group are more disadvantaged than whites. The highest unemployment rates in 1986 and 1987 were 30% among Pakistani and Bangladeshi men, followed by 25% among black men; among white men, unemployment stood at 11%. Among white women it was 11%, but it was twice that level among minority women.

There is growing evidence that inner London minority workers are disproportionately affected by the loss of jobs in manufacturing and the declining conditions in many service jobs that were once part of the public sector. And there is some evidence that would lend support to spatial explanations of unemployment (Cross 1988), given the high concentration of minority workers in inner cities and the high unemployment and decline in these areas. Cross (1988) finds that an explanation in terms of skills mismatch is perhaps especially inadequate, since Labor Force survey data show that the gap between white and black unemployment rates is at least as wide at higher skill levels as at lower skill levels. The ratio between white and black unemployment for men aged sixteen to sixty-four was 1:1.8 overall, but for those with higher levels of qualifications it was 1:3 (U.K. Department of Employment 1988: 642). Thus, it could be that spatial concentration is feeding this differential; but racism may also be at work.

The New Illegal Immigration in Japan

In Japan massive rural migrations to a few major urban areas provided the needed labor supply during the 1950s and 1960s, a period of accelerated industrialization in a country closed to foreign immigration but

with massive labor reserves in the countryside. It was also a period of
large-scale construction of public and private infrastructure in order to
accommodate the industrialization of the economy and the urbanization
of the people. In brief, the demand for labor was immense. It was the
kind of period in which countries such as the United States or those of
Western Europe have relied on foreign workers. In Japan, rural migration to the cities took the place of immigration. The scale and the speed
of rural outmigration reached historic dimensions. Whole villages were
reported to have voted to abandon their settlements together, rather
than leave a few members behind (Douglass 1987: 11). From 1955 to
1965, the height of this migration, more than half of the nation's forty-six
provinces experienced an absolute decline in population, and fourteen
others had annual growth rates of less than 1%. Tokyo, Osaka, and Nagoya, the three largest metropolitan areas, were the main destinations of
this massive migration. From 1960 to 1970, these three areas raised their
populations by 10 million and came to account for 40% of the national
population. The Greater Tokyo Metropolitan Area increased by 10 million between 1950 and 1970, reaching 17.7 million people. In 1950, almost 50% of Japan's labor force was in agriculture; by 1970 this figure
was down to 19%.

Elsewhere (Sassen 1988) I have posited that one of the properties of an
immigrant work force is its condition as a mobilized work force. Once
uprooted, such workers will accept options that settled members of a
community would not. They will take jobs, accept hours and wages, and
travel distances to their workplaces that "native" workers would not. Japan's vast work force, formed through massive rural outmigration, is such
a mobilized work force. This condition may have contributed, along with
culture, to the well-established qualities of Japanese workers in this period: hard work, willingness to travel long distances to jobs, endurance
of extremely uncomfortable and harsh living conditions.

The current immmigration of Asian workers is occurring in a completely different phase of the Japanese economy. The second, urban-born
generation is fully grown and in the labor force; there is a large demand
for workers at all occupational levels; and it has become increasingly clear
that there are labor shortages in very arduous jobs (for example, ocean
fishing), and in a growing percentage of low-wage jobs. Though fragmen-
tary, the evidence clearly points to a rapid increase over the last few
years in the number of foreigners who are working illegally in Japan,
mostly in the Tokyo metropolitan area, Nagoya, and Osaka. Typically,
they have entered the country with tourist visas and overstayed their
officially permitted time. The estimate is that by mid-1988 there were
200,000 illegal male workers in Japan in manual work, from construction
to restaurant kitchens. Almost all of these were from Asia. The estimate

is that the largest single groups were from Taiwan, South Korea, Bangladesh, the Philippines, and Pakistan.

Classifying entries into Japan by nationality clearly indicates that Taiwan and South Korea account for the largest contingent, with respectively 300,272 and 299,602 entries in 1986, increasing to over 360,000 entries from each in 1987. (See Tables 9.1 and 9.2 for related data.) Over the last five years, entries from these countries have hovered about these levels, though 1988 shows a distinct increase, especially for Koreans. The third largest group over this period has been from the Philippines. Its levels have almost doubled, from about 48,000 entries in 1983 to 85,300 in 1988. If what we have seen in the United States is also occurring in Japan, then it is quite possible that a growing number of these entrants are actually coming not to visit but to work. Government figures registered increases in apprehensions of illegal residents, from 51,368 in 1982 to 77,437 in 1987. There also has been an increase recently in the numbers of forced deportations, from 5,399 in 1987 to 13,771 in 1988.

The total legal alien population stood at 2.1 million in 1987. About 1

TABLE 9.1

Japan: Entries of Asians by Country of Origin, 1983-1987

| | % of Total Entries | | | | | % Change, |
	1983	1984	1985	1986	1987	1983-1987
Taiwan	17.4	17.2	15.8	14.9	16.7	-0.7
Republic of Korea	14.9	14.9	13.1	14.8	16.7	1.8
Philippines	2.5	2.4	2.9	4.0	3.9	1.4
China	1.4	2.5	4.5	3.7	3.4	2.0
Malaysia	2.8	3.2	3.1	3.2	1.9	-0.9
Singapore	2.2	2.2	1.9	1.7	1.7	-0.5
Thailand	2.3	2.3	2.0	1.5	1.6	-0.7
Hong Kong	3.4	2.6	2.2	1.6	1.4	-2.0
Indonesia	1.7	1.9	2.1	1.6	1.1	-0.6
India	1.0	1.0	1.1	1.0	1.0	0.0
Iran	0.2	0.5	1.1	0.8	0.9	0.7
Others	1.9	1.8	2.0	2.4	2.4	0.5
Stateless	0.2	0.2	0.2	0.2	0.1	-0.1
Total Asia	51.7	52.0	51.7	50.2	52.6	0.9
Total (N)	(1,900,597)	(2,036,488)	(2,259,894)	(2,021,450)	(2,161,275)	13.7
Asia total(N)	(982,688)	(1,057,926)	(1,168,254)	(1,014,787)	(1,136,710)	16.7

Source: Japan Immigration Office, Statistics on Foreigners and Japanese Arriving and Leaving Japan in 1987 — Summary Report (1987).
Note: Discrepancies in Asia total N, and Percentage change are the result of rounding.

TABLE 9.2

Japan: Entries of Foreigners by Continent of Origin, 1986

	N	%
Asia	1,014,787	50.2
Europe	358,365	17.6
Africa	10,771	0.5
North America	550,200	27.4
South America	26,488	1.3
Oceania	56,784	2.8
Stateless	4,055	0.2
Total	2,021,450	100.0

Source: Same as in Table 9.1.

TABLE 9.3

Japan: Selected Entries of Foreigners by Type of Visa, 1987

Purpose	Visa Type	N	Asian Share (%)
Student	4-1-6	5,182	67.1
Trainee	4-1-6-2	17,081	78.7
Teacher	4-1-7	350	14.3
Cultural activities	4-1-8	1,739	53.6
Entertainer	4-1-9	59,693	69.1
Religious missionary	4-1-10	1,934	2.6
Correspondent	4-1-11	410	4.6
Technical personnel	4-1-12	24	8.3
Skilled worker	4-1-13	465	82.0
Dependent of all above	4-1-15	6,559	41.1
Spouse and children of Japanese	4-1-16-1	3,442	72.2
All entries	All visas	2,161,275	52.6

Source: Same as in Table 9.1.

million were foreign personnel; most of the remaining million were from other Asian countries. The vast majority of Asians, over 800,000, were first-time entrants. Almost all, or 727,000, of these entered on temporary ninety-day visas, and half of these gave sightseeing as the reason for their visits. A more detailed analysis of those entering on work and other types of visas (see Table 9.3) shows that the largest single category is that of entertainer, which accounted for 59,693 entrants. Of these, over 41,000 were Asians, with 36,000 from the Philippines, 2,500 from Taiwan, and over 800 from Korea, in addition to small numbers from many other countries.

Given prevalent perceptions about Japan's work force it is probably worth noting that among those entering on work visas, 465 entered as skilled laborers, the vast majority of whom were from Asia. It should also be pointed out that of the total of 13,900 officially entering to study at Japanese-language schools, over 12,000 were from Asia. Several investigations by Japanese authorities found that this form of entry is being used for purposes of work. As in the United States, a number of these language academies are fronts for facilitating the entry of people in search of work.

Juxtaposing entries and departures suggests that in recent years there were significantly more entries than departures, compared with earlier years. This can clearly be a function of a number of reasons, from planned multiple-year stays to administrative miscount. But for certain nationality groups, it will tend to support other types of evidence we have, such as information obtained from deportees, that show a growing number of entrants with short-term visas are coming to work illegally. Among the nationality groups, there were over 360,000 entries in 1987 from Taiwan and 314,000 departures. Similarly, over 360,000 Koreans entered in 1987, and 149,300 departed. There were 85,300 entries from the Philippines and 57,600 departures. It is important not to read too much into these figures, especially because entries may have been registered in one year and departures in another. However these figures do support deportation data and my own interviews with illegal immigrants indicating a growing illegal migration through overstaying of tourist visas.

There is considerable debate within the Japanese government about what to do regarding the new illegal immigration. The centrality that this issue has assumed for the Japanese government is evident from the fact that all the major ministries have set up working parties to study and consult on the issue, and most have come up with position papers. Among these are the Ministry of International and Foreign Affairs, the Ministry of Justice, the Ministry of International Trade and Industry, the Ministry of Labor, and, not unexpectedly, the Ministries of Construction, Fisheries, and Transportation, three industries that are hiring foreign workers. A review of the main positions asserted by each of the ministries points to the complexity the issue has already assumed and also to the fact that the growing employment of illegal foreign workers is generally recognized as a given and a growing development.[28]

[28] A survey of 266 small to medium-size manufacturing firms in Tokyo in 1989 carried out by Iyotani (1989) found that three out of every five firms interviewed could not find enough employees, particularly young male workers, to fill the available positions. The reasons given were as follows: Many respondents said that young Japanese tend to want better, higher-paying jobs; almost 60% said that young men did not want to work in skilled manual labor; and 20% said they lacked training in manual skilled work. In order to cope with this labor shortage, firms are considering improvements in automation; almost 15% are considering employing foreign workers; 14% are considering bringing in rural young men and

The Ministry of Labor had initially proposed formation of a guest-worker program, giving foreign workers short-term contracts for specific jobs. It proposed opening the Japanese job market to foreigners by implementing a law that would require them to obtain a full-time employment status permit from the ministry. But the Ministry of Justice held that such a law would further complicate an already complicated immigration process and that it would create a competitive disadvantage for Japanese workers. The added opposition of several sectors of the economy to the employment permit proposal led the Ministry of Labor to postpone its proposal.

The Ministry of Justice has proposed its own immigration law, which contains provisions on permanent residency, sanctions against employers who hire illegal workers, and a number of other issues concerning foreign workers. Key aspects of the proposed law are (1) expansion of the eighteen categories of professional workers whom the Japanese government already allows prolonged stays for work to include other categories, notably technicians, software engineers, teachers, professors, employees of

---

women; and some are considering several other types of adjustments. Over 11% of the firms interviewed said that they were employing foreign workers, and almost 13% said that they had hired foreign workers even if currently they had none on the payroll. Thus, about a quarter of all the firms interviewed had at one point or another hired foreign workers. The largest single concentration, 26.8%, of foreign workers in the survey was in metal-related factories; another 21% were in printing and publishing, and about 16% were in electric and electronic goods. Over 15% of the firms asserted that they would not hire foreign workers. In terms of the treatment of foreign workers, 3% of firms believed that foreign workers should be treated exactly like Japanese workers. Over 34% believed that foreign students should be allowed to work without restrictions. And well over a quarter believed that professional foreign personnel should be increased. Well over half of all the firms interviewed asserted that they had no objections to the hiring of foreign workers, while a third said that they would rather not do so in order to avoid problems with foreigners who do not speak Japanese and do not understand the culture.

A 1988 survey by the Agency of Management and Coordination found that 45% of the 10,000 respondents believed in accepting unskilled foreign workers, but with certain conditions. Asked what they thought about foreign workers doing a job that Japanese did not want to take, almost 35% responded that it was all right if the foreign worker did not object. But over one-third said that it was indecent to offer foreign workers jobs that Japanese would not accept. A fourth said that it was not a good idea, but that if that was the only option for the foreign workers and they were willing to take these jobs, then that was all right.

The law preceding the recent changes in the immigration law already forbade the entry of unskilled foreign workers for employment. But the younger age groups among respondents showed far more flexibility toward accepting unskilled foreign workers. And only one-fourth of all respondents said that unskilled foreign workers should not be allowed to enter and work in Japan. But well over half said that skilled and highly educated workers should be allowed to enter. Almost half said that they could understand why foreign workers came to Japan and worked illegally; and over 60% said that it was understandable because they had to support their families back in their home countries.

foreign firms, lawyers, public health professionals, doctors, students, and refugees; (2) a permit entitling the holder to accept employment with a Japanese firm if the foreign worker is the most suitable person for the job; and (3) heavy penalties for employers who knowingly hire illegal foreign workers. The Ministry of Justice is intent on protecting Japanese workers, and it maintains that supply and demand in the labor market should be examined carefully from the perspective of firms. In this context, the Ministry of Labor is assuming a rather different stance, maintaining that in the long run what will be needed is a system of support for what is de facto a foreign work force and one that is expanding rapidly. Furthermore, the Ministry of Labor maintains that its own proposals for facilitating employment and legalization of foreign workers will be insufficient to control the problem of foreign workers, given the rapid growth in their numbers.

The position taken by the Ministry of Foreign Affairs is that it is important for Japan to accept its new place in the world and that the government should handle the foreign labor question from the perspective of Japan's new power. The Ministry of Foreign Affairs maintains that the government should control the numbers of foreign workers in order to protect the Japanese labor market, but recognizing that Japan's protectionist era is over and the country must assume its role as one of the economic leaders in a "global economy." Finally, it has urged the Ministry of Justice to reconsider its position on foreign workers and stressed that the key to the issue is to support economic development in countries with high emigration to Japan.

A rather different set of positions has emerged from ministries that are clearly representing sectors of the economy that need a supply of workers willing to take very low-paying or dangerous jobs. Thus, the Ministry of Fisheries, in conjunction with private sector organizations, produced a report asserting its need and willingness to hire foreign unskilled laborers, especially for ships operating in international waters and on long-distance expeditions. This is extremely hard and dangerous work, and Japanese fishermen are, according to this report, hesitant to take these jobs. The position of the fishing industry is that Taiwan and South Korea have a growing advantage because their workers are far cheaper than Japanese fishermen. In sum, the Ministry of Fisheries would like to see the Japanese labor market opened to foreign workers, even if on a limited scale. Another type of situation is exemplified by the Ministry of Transportation. The transportation industry hires large numbers of foreign sailors even though there is no shortage of Japanese sailors. The hiring of foreign sailors cuts the cost of wages sharply for the large companies who own the international shipping industry. Limited hiring of foreign transportation workers is already permitted, but the ministry has asserted that the market should be further opened to foreign workers and has denied that foreign workers are taking jobs away from Japanese ones or reducing wages. The Ministry of Construction, representing an industry that is probably a large employer of illegal foreign workers, has maintained strong opposition to the entry of unskilled laborers. It asserts that the presence of foreign unskilled illegal workers is bringing down wage levels and hence creating increasingly unattractive conditions for native Japanese youth; health insurance is minimal among foreign workers and is further being eroded by their presence, as are the general conditions of work.

The Japanese Parliament eventually approved several amendments to the immigration law that seek to control immigration. On the one hand, the amendments expand the number of job categories for which the country will accept foreign workers to twenty-eight. These are mostly for professional workers, ranging from lawyers, investment bankers, and accountants with international expertise to medical personnel. On the other hand, the amendments restrict and control the inflow of unskilled and semiskilled workers. Moreover, for the first time, the amendments provide sanctions against employers employing illegal workers. Employers can be fined up to $14,000 for such practices and can be imprisoned for up to three years if they continue to employ illegal workers after the first violation. Japan is, then, in many ways replicating the efforts of the United States to control who can come into the country. It will be interesting to observe whether it succeeds in view of the growing internationalization of its economy (Sassen 1988). Perhaps a concerted effort at this early a stage of the immigration process can stem the flows that are in place now.

I spent many hours speaking with illegal immigrants in Tokyo and in Yokohama in an attempt to learn how and why they decided to migrate to Japan, given its reputation as a closed society. It is impossible to do full justice to their answers here, but the main points were as follows: First, they were individuals who had, in one way or another, become mobilized into migrant labor; second, Japan's growing presence in their countries, together with the consequent availability of information about Japan, had created linkages and made Japan emerge in their minds as an option for emigration. One interesting question here is, To what extent are we witnessing the emergence of alternative "lands of opportunity" to the United States? The new law will undoubtedly deter some employers; but cases as diverse as the United States, Western Europe, and the Middle Eastern oil-exporting countries have all sought to control immigration and not quite succeeded in the intended way.

My hypothesis is that the segmentation and casualization of the labor market now increasingly evident in Japan have facilitated the labor market incorporation of the new illegal immigration. Casualization opens up the hiring process, reduces the regulatory constraints on employers, and lowers the indirect and typically also direct costs of labor. The relative decline of manufacturing and the growth of services have contributed to a critical mass of small, freestanding firms not incorporated in the large economic groupings into which much of the Japanese economy is still organized—yet another form of casualization. The overall effect may well be to undermine the efficacy of regulatory enforcement, including the new immigration regulations.

Immigration in Economic Restructuring and Social Geography

What is the place of immigration in the economic recomposition process in such cities as New York and London? A common view in the literature is that the bulk of the immigrants provide low-wage labor to declining, backward sectors of capital. This is correct in part, but incomplete. I see two additional roles for immigration, both pertaining to the recompositon process.

First, immigration can be seen as providing labor for the low-wage service and manufacturing jobs that service both the expanding, highly specialized service sector and the high-income lifestyles of those employed in the specialized, expanding service sector (Sassen-Koob, 1982). Some of these jobs held by immigrants may routinely be classified as belonging to declining sectors of the economy. But in fact, insofar as they service the most dynamic sector of the city's economy, we need to make a distinction between "backward jobs"—which they often are—and declining sectors of the economy, which they are not necessarily.

Second, immigration is a factor in the occupation of areas both in New York in the 1970s and in London in the 1960s that would otherwise have had a high proportion of abandoned housing and closed stores. Through the immigrant community, immigrants become agents actively engaged in rehabilitating both spatial and economic sectors of the city. The immigrant community can be seen as representing a small-scale investment of direct labor (through neighborhood upgrading) and of capital (through neighborhood commerce) in a city's economy. Another way of putting it is that the immigrant community is a structure or vehicle that maximizes the benefits of individual investments of direct labor and money for the community, by concentrating such investments spatially, a concentration effected by residential segregation. Thus, home repairs by multiple households become neighborhood upgrading; differences of language and food preferences create a captive market for ethnic shopkeepers.

Elsewhere (Sassen 1988), I have argued at length that the large influx of immigrants into the United States from low-wage countries over the last fifteen years, which reached massive levels in the 1980s, cannot be understood separately from this restructuring. The expansion in the supply of low-wage jobs generated by major growth sectors is one of the key factors in the continuation of ever-higher levels of the current immigration. The magnitude, timing, and destination of the current migration to the United States becomes more understandable when juxtaposed with these developments. While changes in United States immigration legislation in 1965 and the existence of prior immigrant communities are important factors explaining immigration over the subsequent decade and a half, they are not sufficient to explain the continuation of this flow at ever-higher levels, even in the late 1970s and early 1980s, a time of growing unemployment in the United States and rather high employment growth in the immigrants' countries of origin (see Sassen 1988). Nor are they sufficient to explain the disproportionate concentration of immigrants in major cities. New York and Los Angeles have the largest Hispanic populations of all U.S. cities, respectively, 2 million and 1.5 million, sizes significantly larger than in Chicago and Miami, each with about 580,000 Hispanics. New York City and Los Angeles also contain, together with San Francisco, the largest concentration of Asians. Finally, New York City is the major recipient of West Indians.

New York accounts for 12% of all foreign-born U.S. residents, compared with 3% of the total U.S. population. And since 1980, the city has accepted an even larger share, 15% of all new arrivals. On the basis of the 1980 Census count of foreign-born residents, the INS count of new arrivals since 1980, and a low estimate for the undocumented population, Armstrong (1988) estimated that by 1987 New York City had 2.6 million foreign-born residents, accounting for 35% of the city's total population. While this is not the highest percentage of foreign-born residents in the history of New York City, it is the highest absolute number. In 1935, the prior high, the city's foreign-born numbered 2.3 million; the highest percentage was in the early 1900s, when the foreign-born accounted for 40% of the city's population. The estimate for the year 2000 is that the immigrant population (foreign born and second generation) will account for over 50% of the city's population. While New York has long been the major port of entry for immigrants, it is more difficult to explain this concentration today than in the past, when the city accounted for a far larger share of all jobs in the United States and transportation was far less developed.

The expansion in the supply of low-wage jobs, particularly pronounced in major cities, can thus be seen as creating objective employment opportunities for immigrants even as middle-income blue- and white-collar native workers are experiencing high unemployment because their jobs are being either downgraded or expelled from the production process.

Conclusion

The central question in this chapter was whether the increase in various types of inequality has brought about new social forms. There is now greater inequality in earnings distribution and in household income, a greater prevalence of poverty, and a massive increase in foreign and domestic investment in luxury commercial and residential construction. Do these merely represent changes in magnitude along an upward or downward gradient, or are they ruptures and discontinuities in the social fabric of these cities?

Gentrification is not a new process. But what is different from earlier episodes is the scale on which it has taken place in all three cities and the extent to which it has created a commercial infrastructure that anyone can buy into, fully or in part. It has engendered an ideology of consumption that is different from that of the mass consumption of the middle classes in the postwar period, which was centered around the construction and furnishing of new suburban housing and the associated infrastructure. Style, high prices, and an ultraurban context characterize the new ideology and practice of consumption, rather than functionality, low prices, and suburban settings. This is not merely an extension of elite consumption, which has always existed and continues to exist in large cities. It is quite different in that it is a sort of new mass consumption of style, more restricted than mass consumption per se because of its cost and its emphasis on design and fashion. There are distinct areas in all three cities where this new commercial culture is dominant and where one finds not only high-income professionals for whom it is a full-time world, but also "transients," from students to low-income secretaries, who may participate in it for as little as one hour. Poverty is not new either. What is new is its severity, leading in the extreme to homelessness on a scale not seen in a long time in highly developed countries.

Similarly, these cities have long been key centers for international business and finance. But the enormity of major central city projects in all three cities, discussed in Chapter Seven, constitutes yet another instance of a transformation of urban areas that is not simply a continuation of old trends but, rather, represents a massive appropriation of public resources and urban space.

The second major subject of concern in this chapter was the transformation of the employment relation. Transient and casual employment is likely to be part of any large city, but developments over the last decade in New York, London, and Tokyo point to the institutionalization of casual labor markets. These have become a growing and central part of the employment relation in these service-dominated economies. The increase in various types of part-time work is the most general and largest trend. But the dynamics of casualization assume specific forms in each of these cities, and it is important to capture this distinctiveness.

I decided to focus on forms of casual employment somewhat distinct to each city. In New York, one of the more unexpected and dynamic forms of the growth of casual labor markets has been the emergence of an informal economy. This informal economy has had the overall effect not only of cheapening production costs for firms in both growth industries and declining ones, but also of increasing flexibility in the organization of production. Such flexibility is particularly important in a city where leading sectors can easily outbid all other sectors for space, but at the same time need to have access to these other industries. The informal economy can thus be seen as providing a flexible arrangement to accommodate firms that are necessary for the operation of leading sectors but could not compete in the open market. Similarly, it reduces the costs of reproduction for low-wage workers, who are in demand in the new economy but would find it difficult to compete for all goods, services, and housing in the open market. In London, perhaps the most dramatic form of the casualization of employment has resulted from the privatization of many of the services once provided by the state. Jobs that used to be full-time and carry a full array of fringe benefits, have now been thrown into the open market, where they have been transformed into part-time, subcontracted jobs at even lower wages. The key here is that even though many of these jobs have long been rather low-paid ones, now they have become part of a growing casual labor market, institutionally a far more vulnerable employment condition. Finally, in Japan what used to be a flexible but protected labor force, "daily laborers," is now a rapidly growing and increasingly heterogeneous stratum of workers, with a sharp erosion in regulatory protection and wage levels.

A third issue discussed in this chapter is that of race and nationality in the economy of these cities. If blacks, Asians, and other immigrants had employment and earnings distributions basically similar to those of whites and/or natives, then this would not be an issue. But they do not. Blacks and Third World immigrants in New York City are disproportionately concentrated in lower-paying, more traditional service industries, notably health and social services and in the low-paying jobs of the producer services. In London, notwithstanding the closing of immigration, there has been a continuing influx of illegal or semilegal immigrants, who tend to hold low-wage jobs. And there is now a second and a third generation, descendants of Caribbean and Asian immigrants, who continue to have distinct labor market positions, with high rates of unemployment and, especially among blacks, a disproportionate concentration in public housing and inner city areas in severe economic and physical decay. As in New York City, blacks and Asians in professional occupations tend to hold the lower-paying jobs in both growth and declining industries and to be disproportionately concentrated in the central city. And in both we also see the emergence of persistent and concentrated poverty among these populations and a growing share of young adults who have never held a regular job. We see a dual tendency toward the growing isolation and economic irrelevance of a growing share of these workers and households on the one hand, and on the other hand, the full incorporation of others in the form of a casual, highly flexible, low-cost labor force. Even in Tokyo, a new illegal immigrant work force similarly occupies low-wage jobs in manufacturing and services, while a growing number of legal immigrants provide necessary technical and professional skills.

The new illegal immigration to Tokyo raises a number of important questions, especially in view of Japan's strong anti-immigration stance and historical absence of immigration. I posit that this new immigration is one outcome of the intersection of two basic processes in these advanced countries: first, the rapid internationalization of the economy, notably the growth in direct foreign investment, foreign aid, and offshore manufacturing facilities in those countries that have been the main sources of the new illegal immigration; and second, the growing presence of casual labor markets and generally a growing casualization of the employment relation, which has facilitated the absorption of the new illegal immigrants.

This suggests that a similar dynamic may be partly underlying some of the new immigration to New York and the United States generally. The notion that New York City keeps receiving immigrants because it has always been a city of immigrants is simply insufficient. Migrations are produced, and this requires specific conditions (Sassen 1988). Along with the continuation of older immigrations, we may be seeing a set of new conditions producing the increased immigration to the United States and to New York, which received a quarter of all the immigrants in the 1980s. The case of Japan suggests the formation of a new social process, rather than merely the continuation of an old pattern. It would seem that two of the basic processes identified in this book—the internationalization of the economies of these countries, particularly centered in their premier cities, and the casualization of the employment relation—contribute to producing new migrations and facilitating their absorption.

IN CONCLUSION

Ten

A New Urban Regime?

Do the changes described in this book amount to a significant transformation in the place of New York, London, and Tokyo in their respective nation-states and in the world economy, and, secondly, have those changes brought about a significant realignment in the social and economic structure of these cities? Are we seeing a new type of city, the global city? And if so, how does this affect the urban hierarchy? Is there a new type of urban hierarchy, a new urban system, as a consequence of the global role of major cities, or is this transformation just affecting these cities themselves? Finally, what happens to city politics when the leading economic forces are oriented to the world market?

A central proposition organizing the inquiry was that in order to understand the pronounced social and economic changes in major cities today, we need to examine fundamental aspects of the new world economy. Such changes cannot be adequately explained merely in terms of the shift from manufacturing to services in developed economies. The first part of the book analyzed and documented key trends in the world economy: the growth of the international financial market, the expansion of the international trade in services, and the repatterning of direct foreign investment. Next, it examined the form of this internationalization, one characterized by an increasingly global network of factories, service outlets, and financial markets, along with continued economic concentration. A limited number of countries account for most of the flows and international transactions; very large firms dominate some of the flows; a few cities emerge as leading centers for international transactions.

The most pronounced development is the massive increase in the volume of transactions of the financial industry, by far the most significant international industry. While in the 1950s and 1960s direct foreign investment in primary activities was the main type of international flow, by the late 1970s and especially in the 1980s financial transactions dwarfed the former. In direct foreign investment, a new pattern has emerged, with most of the flows directed to two major areas, the United States and Southeast Asia. In contrast, Latin America and Europe, which were among major recipients in the 1950s and 1960s, became less significant recipients in the 1980s. By far the largest importer of capital in the 1980s was the United States; and Japan has become the leading net exporter of capital. Most direct foreign investment is now in services.

Having confirmed the growth of international transactions in the economy and the central place of a limited number of countries, notably the United States, the United Kingdom, and Japan, in these transactions, the question then was how cities fit into this globalization of economic activity—particularly the major cities for international business and finance, New York, London, and Tokyo. A central thesis organizing this discussion is that increased globalization along with continued concentration in economic control has given major cities a key role in the management and control of such a global network.

Many of these patterns in the development of a global economy express themselves in terms of territory. Within this context, the territory of major cities as a site for world economic activity was explored. We were concerned with understanding why the extremely rapid growth of finance and business services took place and why their location patterns were characterized by such high concentration in major cities. There are two hypotheses that we explored. One is that the spatial dispersion of production and the reorganization of the financial industry over the last decade have created new forms of centralization in order to manage and regulate the global network of production sites and financial markets. The second is that these new forms of centralization entail a shift in the locus of control and management: In addition to the large corporation and the large commercial bank there is now also a marketplace with a multiplicity of advanced corporate service firms and nonbank financial institutions. Correspondingly, we see the increased importance of such cities as New York, London, and Tokyo as *centers* of finance and as *centers* for global servicing and management.

The spatial dispersion of production, including its internationalization, has contributed to the growth of centralized service nodes for the management and regulation of the new space economy. Major cities, such as New York, London, and Tokyo, have greatly expanded their role as key locations for top-level management and coordination. And the reorganization of the financial industry has led to rapid increases in the already significant concentration of financial activities in major cities. The pronounced expansion in the volume of financial transactions has magnified the impact of these trends. Finally, the reconcentration of a considerable component of foreign investment activity and the formation of an international property market in these major cities has further fed this economic core of high-level control and servicing functions. In brief, alongside well-known decentralization tendencies, there are less known centralization tendencies.

Different locations manifest different aspects of these developments.

To a considerable extent, the weight of economic activity over the last fifteen years has shifted from production places, such as Detroit and Manchester, to centers of finance and highly specialized services. While the dispersion of plants speeds the decline in old manufacturing centers, the associated need for centralized management and control feeds growth in servicing centers. Similarly, the ascendance of the advanced services in economic activity generally has shifted tasks out of the shop floor and into the design room and has changed management from what was once an activity focused on production to one that is finance focused today.

Key questions for investigation concerned the actual work involved in such management and control and what exactly is the work that takes place in major cities. This examination was the subject of Part Two of the book. The organizing concept is that of the *practice* of global control— the activities involved in producing and reproducing the organization and management of the global production system and the global labor force. The argument organizing the discussion was that the maintenance of centralized control and management over a geographically dispersed array of plants, offices and service outlets cannot be taken for granted or seen as an inevitable outcome of a "world system." The possibility of such centralized control needs to be produced. Central to its development is the production of a vast range of highly specialized services and of top-level management and control functions.

The focus on production serves several purposes. First, it provides an empirical referent for identifying specific modes of integration of global cities in the world economy. Besides being nodal points in a vast communications and market system, these cities are also sites for the production of global control capability. Second, a focus on production introduces the categories of labor and work process into the analysis. If we look only at power issues, the tendency is to think of, for example, financial factors in terms of highly specialized financial outputs rather than the wide range of jobs, not all of which have to do with highly specialized financial know-how, involved in *producing* such outputs. Third, a focus on production does not have as its unit of analysis the powerful actors, be they multinational corporations or governments, but the site of production—in this case, major cities. Thus, even though global control capability is a basic mechanism that allows large corporations to operate a widely dispersed domestic and global production system, this should not necessarily be taken to mean that the production of this capability can be contained within the corporation. If we look at the production of this capability, we can incorporate in the analysis a rapidly expanding market of freestanding specialized service firms. Such firms, an important growth sector in New York, London, and Tokyo, would be left out if the focus were on the power of large firms. Fourth, a focus on production and production sites brings to the fore the role of a few key cities in the current phase of the world economy as well as the differences among major cities in the highly industrialized countries.

This second part of the book established that the whole array of activities that make up or facilitate the various internationalization processes discussed in Part One has indeed grown over the last fifteen years, is heavily concentrated in major cities, particularly New York, London, and Tokyo, and is a significant factor in the economies of these cities. There is a complex of industries, such as advertising, accounting, legal services, business services, certain types of banking, engineering and architectural services, etc., which assist, facilitate, complement, and in many cases make possible, the work of large and small firms and of governments. A central and growing component of this complex of industries is linked to the servicing of firms engaged in international transactions and with a far-flung domestic and/or international network of service outlets, factories, and markets. In the case of finance, part of the industry fulfills this servicing function. But in the 1980s, a growing sector of the industry, the book argues, became akin to a commodity sector, where the buying and selling of instruments has its own sphere of circulation and does not function as a service industry in the narrow sense of the word. New York, London, and Tokyo are the leading marketplaces for this sector of the industry, as well as functioning as a single, transterritorial marketplace.

This part of the book also examined other major cities in these countries to specify what, if anything, is distinct about New York City, London, and Tokyo. The salient difference is the extent of concentration of the producer services and finance. But many cities have growing producer services sectors, as do these countries as a whole. Part of this growth is clearly related to the overall transformation in the composition and organization of the economy, beyond the mere growth in services. There is a greater proportion of services in many industries and more service inputs in many kinds of work. Furthermore, the development of regional and national markets and networks of service outlets and factories also has created the same pressures toward expanded central functions for regional or national-level firms. And we see, indeed, that trends similar to those evident in New York, London, and Tokyo are also emerging in other major cities, though on a lower order of magnitude and based on regional- rather than global-level processes. The proliferation of producer services firms has itself created a demand for more service inputs bought on the market rather than produced in house. And the growing complexity faced by governments has also created a demand for more specialized services bought in the market. There is, then, a fundamental relationship between the growth of these kinds of service industries catering to the needs of complex organizations and various aspects of economic restructuring in the last two decades. I argue that it is these transformations that constitute the shift to a service-dominated economy, rather than the mere fact of a shift in employment from manufacturing to services, a process usually centered on the growth of consumer services. On the contrary, I posit that the period of massive growth of consumer services is associated with the expansion of mass production in manufacturing.

A third issue addressed in this part of the book is the question of urban hierarchies: How has the globalization of economic activity affected the whole notion of urban hierarchies, or urban systems, which the specialized literature typically sees as nationally based? Are New York, London, and Tokyo actually part of two distinct hierarchies, one nation-based and the other involving a global network of cities? Each of these three cities is the preeminent urban center in its country, though none quite to the extreme that London is in the United Kingdom. And unlike London and Tokyo, New York City is part of a tier of major cities that includes Los Angeles, Chicago, Boston, San Francisco, and, because it is the national capital, Washington, D.C. Yet the evidence made it clear that New York City emerged over the last decade as the leading international financial and business center in the United States, with Los Angeles a far second.

Through finance more than through other international flows, a global hierarchy of cities has emerged, with New York, London, and Tokyo not only the leading cities, but also the ones fulfilling coordinating roles and functioning as international marketplaces for the buying and selling of capital and expertise. Stock markets from a large number of countries are now linked with one another through New York, London, and Tokyo. In the era of global telecommunications, we have what is reminiscent of the role of an old-fashioned marketplace, which serves as a connecting and contact point for a wide diversity of often distant companies, brokers, and individuals.

Furthermore, the book sought to show that in many regards New York, London, and Tokyo function as one transterritorial marketplace. These three cities do not simply compete with each other for the same business. They also fulfill distinct roles and function as a triad. Briefly, in the 1980s Tokyo emerged as the main center for the export of capital; London as the main center for the processing of capital, largely through its vast international banking network linking London to most countries in the world and through the Euromarkets; and New York City as the main receiver of capital, the center for investment decisions and for the production of innovations that can maximize profitability. Beyond the often-mentioned need to cover the time zones, there is an operational aspect that suggests a distinct transterritorial economy for a specific set of functions.

The management and servicing of a global network of factories, service outlets, and financial markets imposes specific forms on the spatial organization in these cities. The vastness of the operation and the complexity of the transactions, which require a vast array of specialized services, lead to extremely high densities and, at least for a period, extremely high agglomeration economies, as suggested by the rapid building of one high-rise office complex after another in all three cities, extremely high land prices, and sharp competition for land. This process of rapid and acute agglomeration represents a specific phase in the formation and expansion of an industrial complex dominated by command functions and finance.

There are two questions at this point. One concerns the durability of an economic system dominated by such management, servicing, and financial activities; the second one concerns the durability of the spatial form associated with the formation and expansion of this industrial complex in the 1980s.

Regarding the first, there is considerable debate as to whether a service-dominated economy can grow, or keep on growing, without a strong manufacturing sector. This point can be argued from different perspectives. Simplifying, some argue that manufacturing is actually a key factor in service growth. For example, Cohen and Zysman (1987) found that a third of producer service sector output in the United States is linked to manufacturing and that it is precisely the most important and dynamic service industries that have this characteristic. Others argue, more specifically for the United States, that the only way to overcome a severe budget deficit—and by implication this would hold for any major country with a budget deficit—is to develop a strong manufacturing sector and engage in exports. Such a manufacturing sector, in this view, should be one with good, well-paying jobs, to avoid becoming an economy with a high percentage of low-wage jobs and a low standard of living (Thurow 1989). These are analyses that are oriented toward nations.

What comes out of this book is that the globalization of manufacturing activity and of key service industries has been a crucial factor in the growth of the new industrial complex dominated by finance and producer services. Yes, manufacturing matters, but from the perspective of finance and producer services, it does not have to be national. This is precisely, as this book sought to show, one of the discontinuities (between major cities and nations) in the operation of the economy today compared with two decades ago, the period when mass production of consumer goods was the leading growth engine. One of the key points developed in this book is that much of the new growth rests on the decline of what were once significant sectors of the national economy, notably key branches of manufacturing that were the leading force in the national economy and promoted the formation and expansion of a strong middle class.

Furthermore, the new industrial complex has contributed to a transformation in the social structure of major cities where it is concentrated. This transformation assumes the form of increased social and economic polarization. While some of this may not affect the functioning and expansion of the new industrial complex, some of it does. The growing inequality in the bidding power of firms has meant that a whole array of firms that produce goods and services that indirectly or directly service the firms in the new industrial core have growing difficulty surviving in these cities. They must either resort to various mechanisms for reducing costs of production—notably subcontracting, employing undocumented immigrants at below-average wage levels and in below-standard work conditions—or have to raise their prices to the point where it begins to affect the costs of operation of the core sector and eventually makes these cities less attractive locations, with a changing trade-off between agglomeration economies and location costs. Finally, the growing inequality in the bidding power for space, housing, and consumption services means that the expanding low-wage work force that is employed directly and indirectly by the core sector has increasing difficulty living in these cities. This may reduce the *effective* supply of such workers and lead to a deeper impoverishment of significant sectors of the population, something that has indeed happened over the last decade in all three cities. At what point do these tensions become unbearable? At what point is the fact of homelessness a cost also for the leading growth sectors: How many times do high-income executives have to step over the bodies of homeless people till this becomes an unacceptable fact or discomfort? At what point does the increasing poverty of large numbers of workers begin to interfere with the performance of the core industries either directly or indirectly? It is perhaps the social involution that this mode of growth brings about in significant sectors of a national economy that may be more devastating than the decline of manufacturing at the national level, since there is significant manufacturing growth globally, and in that sense there is grist for the mill of the producer services complex.

Another major tension derives from the fact that much of the new growth rests on a weakening of the national state. For instance, the national budget deficits in the United States and in Japan were a crucial source of growth for the financial industry and specialized service industries. Much recent policy has favored internationalization and finance, with the corresponding decline of significant manufacturing sectors in the United States and in the United Kingdom (and now increasingly in Japan) contributing to large trade deficits. How will this tension between the conditions for growth of leading industries in major cities and the decline of significant national economic sectors be managed? Will there be a point when national decline will exercise downward pressure on the economy of these cities?

Regarding the durability of the spatial form associated with this mode of economic growth, a critical question concerns the development of telecommunications technologies for centralizing functions. Up till now the major outcome of the development of telecommunications capability has been to expand the spatial dispersion of the economy. But this dispersion has required the expansion of central functions. At what point will telecommunications be applied to centralizing functions and the complex of professional, managerial, and executive functions at the top? The urban form that has developed in the last two decades associated with this spatial reorganization of economic activity has clearly been one of growing densities and extreme locational concentration of central functions and of the production of innovations. Are we reaching the limit of this urban form, notwithstanding the massive high-rise office complexes still under construction in London and Tokyo, with a few more planned for New York? Clearly the case of New York suggests that we may have reached the limits in the centralizing of functions, partly because of an increasingly disadvantageous trade-off between the benefits and costs of this agglomeration.

An important factor that needs to be considered is the massive infrastructural investments required by a telecommunications system. This effectively creates barriers to entry. While in principle any city could consider developing telecommunications capability of the first order and hence compete for a number of functions now concentrated in major cities, in practice entry costs are so high, in addition to the costs of continuous incorporation of the newest technology, that for the foreseeable future, major cities, such as New York, London, and Tokyo have an almost absolute advantage. Arguably, a new phase of innovation in telecommunications technology might make the current infrastructure obsolete and lead to the equivalent of the earlier "suburbanization" of large-scale manufacturing that resulted from the obsolescence of the physical structures that housed manufacturing in the large cities. At that point we could, conceivably, enter a whole new phase in the development of urban economic systems.

In this context, the Japanese case is of interest. In many regards the Japanese have built the most advanced form of office complexes and telecommunications infrastructure—the so-called "intelligent buildings" housing only computers, the teleport city being built on land extracted from Tokyo Bay, and especially the proposals to rearrange the capital city and its crucial functions in more "rational" ways. One of these proposals would link Tokyo, Osaka, and Nagoya by means of a high-speed train of the most advanced type and through telecommunications. The effect would be that of the structure of a single agglomeration in the form of a line—not what is conventionally represented as an agglomeration. A rational allocation of functions along this line would make maximum use of the comparative advantages of each point along this line. This is a very different conception of urban form from that of the concentric or axial pattern characterizing the market-led, often haphazard development of major cities today. It would link everything to a single axis, a fact that would matter for the movement of certain elements in the economy—notably workers, goods, and certain type of services—but not for those aspects subject to telecommunication. It would, arguably, be a design that would recognize that we are not a purely informational economy, that a lot of components still have very much a physical dimension, and that the juxtaposition of an ideology of telecommunications and a reality that is only partly subject to the latter or reducible to information results in massive tensions and congestions embedded in the spatial structure of large cities today. What the arrangement of crucial functions along a line would mean for politics and society is a different type of question.

The third part of the book addresses the impact of this new industrial complex on the economic and social structure of the city. We know that manufacturing, as epitomized by the two decades after World War II in the United States, had a strong multiplier effect and contributed to the expansion of a strong middle class. In the period when manufacturing based on mass consumption and large scales of production was the leading economic sector, there was a pronounced orientation in the general economy toward the production of housing, roads, shopping centers, new schools, and all the other components of the suburbanization process that dominated economy and society. The decline of Fordism entailed a change in the economic and political place of unions and mass production as well as the demise of a broader institutional framework sustained by that model of production, one with significant shadow effects for larger sectors of the economy.

The historical forms assumed by economic growth in the post-World War II era—notably capital intensity, standardization of production, and suburbanization-led growth—contributed to the vast expansion of a middle class. And so did the cultural forms accompanying these processes, particularly as they shaped the structures of everyday life insofar as a large middle class contributes to mass consumption and thus to standardization. At the same time, suburbanization also left behind a mass of poor and disadvantaged people in the older central areas in all three cities, which eventually became a factor in the formation of so-called inner cities. Nevertheless, overall, these various trends were conducive to greater levels of unionization or other forms of workers' empowerment that can be derived from large scales in production and the centrality of mass production and mass consumption in national economic growth and profits. In the case of Britain, there was, in addition, a massive expansion in public services, which entailed a corresponding growth in full-time, year-round jobs with the requisite fringe benefits, the state being the employer. It is in that postwar period extending into the late 1960s and early 1970s when the incorporation of workers into formal labor market relations reached its highest level in all three countries.

This combination of processes was important for the expansion of a middle class and generally rising wages. In the post-World War II period and into the early 1970s, a growing proportion of firms in all three countries organized their labor force in terms of full-time jobs and internal labor markets with training and career opportunities. During this period, unions in the United States and the United Kingdom gained legitimacy and were central to the employment relation in the leading industries. Economic growth in this period was based largely on providing a critical mass of people with houses, roads, cars, furniture, appliances. This was particularly strong in the United States. In the case of the United Kingdom, there was less of a process of suburbanization than in the United States and more of a process of social provisioning along with the infrastructure and organizations required for this; most notable was the development of a national public health system and of public housing. In Japan, the choice was toward massive reinvestment to expand the infrastructure for production rather than that for social reproduction, as in the United States. The delay in investment in infrastructure to house and service the population led to a significantly lower standard of living in Japan. Considerable suburbanization occurred as a sheer consequence of the need to house a vastly expanded urban population, swollen by extremely rapid and large-scale rural-to-urban migrations in the 1950s and into the 1960s. However, by far the leading growth factor in the economy was the expansion of the production apparatus, Japan in that period being, after all, far behind the United States and United Kingdom as an industrial power. One common thread was the formation and expansion of a vast middle class, though a much poorer one in Japan than in the United States. The decline of the centrality of production for mass consumption in national growth and the shift to services as the leading economic sector contributed to the demise of this broader set of arrangements. This has been the case especially in the United States and the United Kingdom, but is now also becoming evident in Japan.

As discussed in the third part of the book, today growth is based on an industrial complex that leads not to the expansion of a middle class but to increasing dispersion in the income structure and in the bidding power of firms and households. There is social and economic polarization, particularly strong in major cities which concentrate a large proportion of the new growth industries and create a vast direct and indirect demand for low-profit services and low-wage jobs.

Furthermore, growth in the new industrial complex is based less on the expansion of final consumption by a growing middle class than on exports to the international market and on intermediate consumption by other firms and governments or, more generally, consumption by organizations rather than individuals. The key, though not necessarily the largest, markets are not the consumer markets but the global markets for capital and services. These are the markets that shape society and economy.

Does this make a difference? The evidence presented in this book suggests that it makes a large difference. The book argues that there has been a pronounced transformation, characterized by major class realignments and major changes in the institutional framework within which the employment relation takes place. There has been a generalized dismantling of a system that provided a measure of job security, health benefits, and other components of a social wage to a critical mass of workers. This compact rested ultimately on an economic necessity: the fact that the consumption capacity of a critical mass of workers was of central importance to profit realization for the leading industries in the economy. But out of this economic necessity grew a series of social and political arrangements that went beyond the specific economic relation. These arrangements were supported by a series of other processes. While much has been said about the household becoming a secondary and unimportant arena in society in this period compared with the farm household, a genuinely productive unit, it is also true that the household is the key unit of consumption, and in an economy based on final consumption, this mattered immensely. Confinement of women to housework created full-time workers for the organization and management of the consumption of goods and services by the household. The notion of a family wage and the responsibility of the whole economic and political system toward maintaining and supporting the institution of the family (understood as the nuclear family) was probably nowhere as developed as in the United States. This is not surprising given that it was also here that mass production reached its highest level of development, and that suburbanization—the key mechanism to stimulate massive consumption—was nowhere as developed. Today the institution of the family wage and the social compact between labor and employers has been severely eroded in the United States and the United Kingdom and is beginning to erode in Japan. There now are more part-time workers, temporary workers, and workers without pension and health benefits, fewer workers with seniority rights, and, in the case of Japan, a pronounced shrinking in the category of workers with "life-long job security," along with an increase in "daily" workers. There are also many more women in the labor force, and, in the case of the United States, many more minority and immigrant workers.

This development raises a number of questions about the intersection of economics and politics and about the "natural" tendencies of capitalist economies. Was the social compact of the postwar period the result of the weight of local politics in a phase of economic development that gave local claims unusual powers? And is what we are seeing today—increased economic and social polarization—the "natural" outcome of the operation of the economic system when political claims carry little weight? A central question for politics is what happens to accountability when the leading economic sectors are oriented to a world market and to firms rather than to individuals. The uncomfortable question is whether the sudden growth in homelessness, especially in New York and in London but now also beginning in Tokyo, the growth of poverty generally, the growth of low-wage employment without any fringe benefits, and the growth of sweatshops and industrial homework are all linked to the growth of an industrial complex oriented to the world market and significantly less dependent on local factors than, for example, household durables manufacturers in the 1950s. To this should be added the growth of what amounts to an ideology of globalism, whereby localities are seen as powerless in an era of global economic forces.

There is clearly one class of workers who benefited from this new industrial complex. They are the new professionals, managers, brokers of all types, whose numbers increased dramatically in these three cities, and to some extent in all cities. How do they fit into the economic and political system of the city? The evidence in this book suggests that it is important to distinguish this new class of high-income workers from the wealthy, also a significant presence in leading cities. This is definitely a class of high-income workers, who, unlike top-level executives and managers, have no significant control or ownership in the large corporations and investment banks for which they work. They are not really part of C. Wright Mills's "power elite." They are ultimately a stratum of extremely hard-working people whose alliance to the system leads them to produce far more profit than they get back in their admittedly very high salaries and bonuses. In some ways it could be argued that they engage in self-exploitation insofar as they work extremely hard, put in very long hours and ultimately make significantly less money than the stratum of top-level managers and executives, who earn ten to twenty times as much. The recent crisis in the stock market, which eventually led to the dismissal of significant numbers of these workers, especially in New York, has laid bare the extent to which they have no claim on the system or their employers, unlike top-level managers who, when displaced by mergers, can claim large sums of compensation or "golden parachutes." This book also suggests that high-income gentrification and the type of conspicuous consumption associated with it serves a strong ideological function of securing the alliance of these workers to a system for which they produce immense profits in exchange for relatively low returns and few claims.

The new high-income workers are the carriers of a consumption capacity and consumption choices that distinguish them from the traditional middle class of the 1950s and 1960s. While their earned income is too little to be investment capital, it is too much for the basically thrifty, savings-oriented middle class. These new high-income earners emerge as primary candidates for new types of intermediate investments: arts, antiques, and luxury consumption. The conjunction of excess earnings and the new cosmopolitan work culture creates a compelling space for new lifestyles and new kinds of economic activities. It is against this background that we need to examine the expansion of the art market and of luxury consumption on a scale that has made them qualitatively different from what they were even fifteen years ago—a privilege of elites. The growth of a stratum of very high income workers has produced not only a physical upgrading of expanding portions of global cities, but also a reorganization of the consumption structure.

The high income of the new workers is not sufficient to explain the transformation. Less tangible factors are considerable. The new work culture is a cosmopolitan one, for the objective conditions of work are world oriented, being embedded in a context of growing internationalization in the economies of these cities. The growing number of young professional women has further contributed to an urbanization of the professional class rather than the suburbanization typical of an earlier period. Concomitantly, we see what amounts to a new social aesthetic in everyday living, where previously the functional criteria of the middle class ruled. An examination of this transformation reveals a dynamic whereby an economic potential—the consumption capacity represented by high disposable income—is realized through the emergence of a new vision of the good life. Hence the importance not just of food but of *cuisine*, not just of clothes but of designer labels, not just of decoration but of authentic objets d'art. This transformation is captured in the rise of the ever more abundant boutique and art gallery. Similarly, the ideal residence is no longer a "home" in suburbia, but a converted former warehouse in ultraurban downtown. Consequent to this new social aesthetic is, of course, a whole line of profitmaking possibilities, from "nouveaux" restaurants to a thriving art market. What is notable is the extent to which a numerically small class of workers imposed such a visible transformation—of the nature of commerce and consumption—on strategic areas of these extremely large cities. This is, I argue, connected to questions of the social reproduction of a strategic but powerless class of workers.

Immigrants in New York and London, in turn, have produced a low-cost equivalent of gentrification. Areas of New York once filled with shut-up storefronts and abandoned buildings are now thriving commercial and residential neighborhoods. On a smaller scale, the same process has occurred in London. The growing size and complexity of immigrant communities has generated a demand and supply for a wide range of goods, services, and workers. In both cities, the residential and social separateness of the immigrant community becomes a vehicle to maximize the potential it contains. Small investments of money and direct labor in homes and shops by individuals become neighborhood upgrading because of the residential concentration of immigrants. This upgrading does not fit the conventional notions of upgrading, notions rooted in the middle-class experience. Its shapes, colors, and sounds are novel. They, like the cosmopolitan work culture of the new professionals, are yet another form of the internationalization of global cities.

The changes in the economic base and the new income structure in global cities cannot explain this configuration fully. For a number of reasons we have seen the ascendancy of the arts as an arena containing elements central to the quotidian, that is, the structures of everyday life. One reason for this ascendancy can be found in the practices of artists that became prevalent in the 1960s. These practices in turn were generated by economic and other constraints on artists. For example, artists moved into what were at the time undesirable areas of large cities, such as the warehouse district in New York, in part because it was impossible to afford studio space in better areas. Once this move happened, however, it generated its own possibilities for new types of artistic practices and strategies for economic survival of artists. Eventually, artists came to imbue the environment in old warehouse districts with "value," notably aesthetic value. That these elements soon were translated into an arrangement highly desirable for nonartists, does not, however, necessarily flow from the fact that the artists imbued their "neighborhood" with aesthetic and existential value. But the vision, the capacity, the talent, the faith, the obsession that these residents could muster—often unwittingly—to give it that value acquire weight given other conditions.

These other conditions bring us back to the sphere of the economy, particularly the new consumption capacity represented by the large increase in high-income earners. For example, real estate developers picked up on the "value-giving power" of artists and made it into a profitmaking tactic. In the early 1980s, one firm bought a set of buildings on the Lower East Side of New York, at a time when it was not yet fashionable but merely a very run-down section of Manhattan, and turned them into artists' residences and studios for rent. The rationale, as the real estate developer put it, was as follows: If artists move in, we accomplish two things with one stroke; we can charge higher rents than those of the present residents, and we upgrade the area and make it desirable for much higher income people. This model-setting power attributed to artists as a group is, clearly, not inherent to the condition of being an artist. We know from past epochs that artists were mostly regarded as fundamentally undesirable types by the bourgeoisie and certainly by the new rich. In the current economic situation, this model-setting power becomes a vehicle for crystallizing new profitmaking opportunities, ranging from real estate development to luxury consumption.

There are political implications in this implementation of a new vision of the good life for those with the money to buy it. The workers holding the good jobs translate their incomes into lifestyles that clash with traditional middle-class values. There is, then, not only an economic schism, in that the elimination of middle-income jobs from the production process is one of the conditions for the new high-income jobs; there is also a cultural-ideological distancing that captures this schism on another level. Is politics far behind?

In brief, the third part of the book examined the local consequences of the globalization of economic activity, and asked whether the transformations evident in the social and economic structure of each city amount to a new urban regime. By focusing on production processes in the new industrial complex, the analysis makes it possible to see in relation to one another the full range of jobs, firms, and households involved in each city, from the top to the bottom, from those that are quintessentially postindustrial to those that look as though they belong to an earlier industrial era but are necessary to the operations of the new industrial complex. In this perspective, such developments as the growth of an informal economy and the casualization of the labor market—evident in all three cities—emerge not as anomalous or exogenous to these advanced urban economies, but as in fact part of them. A new class alignment is being shaped, and global cities have emerged as one of the main arenas for this development: They contain both the most vigorous economic sectors and the sharpest income polarization. The concrete expression of this new class alignment in the structures of everyday life is well captured in the massive expansion of a new high-income stratum alongside growing urban poverty.

This book has examined the consequences for cities of a global economy. Beyond their sometimes long history as centers for world trade and finance, some cities now function as command points in the organization of the world economy, as sites for the production of innovations in finance and advanced services for firms, and as key marketplaces for capital. In the literature of both urbanism and political economy, there are important gaps in our knowledge of the regulation, management, and servicing of spatially dispersed but globally integrated economic activities. This book sought to fill these gaps in current knowledge by showing how certain cities function in concert to fulfill such tasks.

These cities play, then, a strategic role in the new form of accumulation based on finance and on the globalization of manufacturing. The clearest representation, if one were to abstract a simplifying image from the complexity of this reality, is that the global city replaced the industrial/regional complex centered on the auto industry as the key engine for economic growth and social patterning. This is not to say that finance was unimportant then and manufacturing is unimportant today. Nor is it simply that the financial industry has replaced the auto industry as the leading economic force. It is to emphasize that a whole new arrangement has emerged for accumulation around the centrality of finance in economic growth. The sociopolitical forms through which this new economic regime is implemented and constituted amount to a new class alignment, a new norm of consumption where the provision of public goods and the welfare state are no longer as central as they were in the period dominated by mass manufacturing. A focus on the actual work processes involved in these various activities reveals that it has contributed to pronounced transformations in the social structure, directly through the work process in these industries—finance, producer services, and the range of industrial services they require—and indirectly through the sphere of social reproduction, the maintenance of the high-income and low-income workers it employs. It is this combination of a new industrial complex that dominates economic growth and the sociopolitical forms through which it is constituted and reproduced that is centered in major cities and contains the elements of a new type of city, the global city.

APPENDICES

A

Classification of Producer Services by U.S., Japanese, and British SIC

United States		Japan		United Kingdom	
60	Banking	J	Financial and Insurance Services	814	Banking
61	Credit			815	Other Financial Institutions
62	Commodity Brokers				
63	Insurance Carriers	67	Insurance	82	Insurance
64	Insurance Agents				
65	Real Estate	K	Real Estate	834	House and Estate Agents
66	Combined Real Estate and Insurance				
67	Holding, Investment Office				
73	Business Services	84	Information Services, Research, and Advertisement	839	Business Services
81	Legal Services	85	Other Services for Business	81	Legal Services
		861	Legal and Patent Offices		
		862	Notary Publics, Judicial Scriveners		
86	Membership Organization	83	Cooperative Unions	9631	Trade Unions, Business and Professional Associates
		90	Religion		
		94	Political, Economic and Cultural Organizations		
89	Miscellaneous Business Services	95	Other Services	831/2	Auxilliary Services to Bank/Insurance
				837/8	Professional Technical Services and Advertising
				841-3	Hiring Out Machinery and Equipment

B

Definitions of Urban Units: Tokyo, London, New York

WHEN THE TERM *Tokyo* is used, it refers to the Tokyo Metropolis consisting of twenty-three central wards, the Tama district, and the Islands. The heart of Tokyo's economy, Tokyo's business district, consists of about one-tenth of the central ward area. Probably a better unit to use is central Tokyo, consisting of the twenty-three central wards and in some ways akin to the region represented by Manhattan and the four outer boroughs. For example, if one were to go from one of the three central business district wards to Setagaya, one of the outer ring wards, often referred to as bedroom communities because the inhabitants mostly commute to Tokyo, one would first have to take the subway to one of the train stations and then spend about thirty minutes on a train, for a total commute that could take anywhere from forty minutes to one hour. This is not unlike what it would take to get from midtown Manhattan to some of the more distant areas in the other boroughs of New York City.

The twenty-three central wards have 8.35 million people, or 71% of Tokyo's population, and they cover a total of 598 square kilometers. Population density is 14,000 per square kilometer, compared with New York City's density of 9,000 per square kilometer. The Tama area is inhabited by 3.4 million people, and covers 1,160 square kilometers. The Islands cover 400 square kilometers and have 30,000 people. It should be noted that some of the Islands are located 1,000 or more kilometers from the mainland. These are clearly part of an administrative rather than a labor market area. Overall Tokyo covers an area of 2,162 square kilometers, or 0.6% of Japan's area. Overall density is 5,471 per square kilometer. This area contains 11.93 million people, or 9.8% of Japan's total population.

Tokyo's central twenty-three wards, often referred to as central Tokyo, contain considerable diversity. They are not a central business district, but rather more the equivalent of New York City's five boroughs. The equivalent of Manhattan's midtown and Wall Street areas or central London and the City is to be found in a core of what until recently comprised three wards; two or three more wards are rapidly being added to this core. The Tokyo Metropolitan Government has designated an official central business district consisting of the three wards of Chiyoda, Chuo, and Minato. These are, indeed, locations in which governmental offices, corporate headquarters, banks, and now a growing number of foreign firms, are centralized. The area contains the government district, the financial district, and the corporate district for firms with national and international markets. It contains elegant shopping and residential districts, foreign embassies, restaurants, and nightclubs. The rapid growth of Tokyo has, however, incorporated other wards into an expanding central business district. Most notable is Shinjuku, whose growing importance as a location for business has been anchored by the decision of the Tokyo Metropolitan Government to move all of its offices to a massive new complex in that ward, expected to be completed in March 1991.[1]

A considerable share of central Tokyo consists mostly of residential areas, not unlike many parts of New York City or London. There is an extreme concentration of workplaces in four or five of these wards and much commuting by workers from a very broad geographic area. This is not very different from New York City. Except for the growing density in its City and the immediately adjacent areas, London has a somewhat more dispersed set of workplace locations.

Much of what is called the Tokyo Metropolis consists of areas, including a number of islands, that are not viable as residential areas for people working in Tokyo; thus, they constitute separate geographic labor market areas. Many of these are very sparsely inhabited, even though the outer ring of the commuting belt has been pushed further and further out. The Tokyo Metropolitan Government is planning to develop a good share of the western part of the Tokyo Metropolis in the so-called Tama district as a group of economic subcenters in an attempt to stem growing agglomeration of economic activities in Tokyo. The Tama district accounts for one-third of Tokyo's land area but a fourth of its population.

The Tokyo Metropolitan Region, distinct from the Tokyo Metropolis, includes, besides the latter, the three prefectures ("*ken*") of Chiba, Saitama, and Kanagawa. There are areas in these three prefectures that are closer to Tokyo's central business district than are the more outlying western areas of the central twenty-three wards. In many ways, these three prefectures are more articulated with the central Tokyo economic

[1] The six city subcenters that are being developed or already have been developed are Shinjuku, Shibuya, Ikebukuro, Ueno and Asakusa, Kinshicho and Kameido, and Osaka. The Tokyo Metropolitan Government wants to add a reclamation site to the Tokyo Bay reclamation project to make it into a sophisticated central telecommunications center linking the city's business operations with the rest of the world, and including an "intelligent building," which would operate twenty-four hours a day. Since it would be expected that many foreign businesses would move in, the Tokyo Metropolitan Government would also provide touring, recreation, etc. There would be joint private and public development projects, such as those for the Takeshiba dock area of Tokyo and expected for the Shibaura and Hinode districts on Tokyo Bay.

base than are many areas of the Tokyo Metropolis. The Tokyo Metropolitan Region contains 25% of the nation's population.

Finally a third entity is the National Capital Region. This, the largest of the three units, is so spread out that it hardly functions as an economic unit. This is truly an administrative region, clearly dominated by Tokyo but containing many minor economic subcenters.

In many ways, London is an aggregation of communities governed by local councils. It lacks a unifying organ such as New York City's powerful Office of the Mayor. London consists of 32 boroughs divided into 755 wards. These form the Greater London Conurbation, which in this book is simply referred to as London. The Metropolitan Green Belt surrounds the conurbation, and beyond it lies the Outer Metropolitan Area, a widespread region with freestanding villages and towns. It consists of Bedfordshire, Hertfordshire, Essex, Kent, Surrey, West Sussex, Hampshire, Berkshire, and Buckinghamshire. As in the case of New York's outer metropolitan region, this is the area where most of the growth took place in the postwar period until the massive central city construction projects of the 1980s. London has a population of 6.7 million, and including the Outer Metropolitan Area, the London region has a population of 12.1 million.

The creation of the Greater London Council (GLC) in 1965 gave London an overall planning authority. As in New York, the relation of the region to the city was not clearly resolved at the political and regulatory level (Herbert 1960). It is far clearer in Tokyo, where there is a Tokyo Metropolitan Government with a Governor.

In 1985 the Thatcher government abolished the GLC, which had become a vehicle for interests antithetical to those of the national government, and transferred greater power to local development corporations, which are far more responsive to business interests. Probably the most notorious of these is the Docklands Development Corporation, which launched the largest construction project of any European city. Local borough councils have also lost power and resources. The central political forces in London in the late 1980s were the development corporations and the national government.

New York City consists of five boroughs: Manhattan, Brooklyn, Queens, the Bronx, and Staten Island (respectively, New York, King's, Queens, Bronx, and Richmond Counties). This is the unit we will refer to simply as New York in the book. The city is divided into areas under the jurisdiction of community planning boards. Its metropolitan region includes twelve counties in addition to the five listed above: Westchester, Rockland, Suffolk, Nassau, Bergen, Passaic, Morris, Essex, Hudson, Union,

APPENDIX B 345

Somerset, and Middlesex. The population of the city reached about 8 million during much of the 1980s, and that of the metropolitan region reached about 18 million during the same period. New York City has a municipal government headed by a mayor who is by far the most powerful officer in the city's government. Each of the boroughs has a borough president. A major revision of the city charter implemented in 1989–1990 has the potential of altering the distribution of power somewhat, giving the city council, community planning boards, and the City Planning Commission more power. In addition, an institution that was a key venue for borough presidents, the Board of Estimates, was declared illegal by the U.S. Supreme Court and eliminated, thus potentially enhancing the power of the mayor and the other bodies listed above.

C

Population of Selected Prefectures and Major Prefectural Cities

Prefecture	Total Population	Major City Population	Major City Population as % of Prefecture Population
Tokyo	11,618,281	Tokyo 8,351,983	72
Aichi	6,221,638	Nagoya 2,087,902	34
Osaka	8,473,446	Osaka 2,648,180	31

Number of Cities, Towns and Villages in Selected Prefectures by Size

Prefecture	Total	Total Cities[a]	Number with Population ('000s) of: Over 500	300-500	200-300	100-200	50-100	Under 50
Tokyo	42	27	1	1	1	10	11	18
Aichi	96	30	1	1	4	5	23	62
Osaka	44	31	3	4	3	9	12	13

Source: Japan Statistical Yearbook, 1982.

Notes: From these 1982 data, one can infer that for the 1970-1987 period under study the city of Tokyo is reasonably represented by Tokyo Prefecture, as in 1982 it was the only major city exceeding 500,000 people in the prefecture and it had 72% of the total prefecture population. Nagoya was also the only major city in Aichi Prefecture, but its share of the prefecture's population was only 34%. Osaka had the lowest prefecture population share of these three major cities. Osaka Prefecture has three cities with more than 500,000 people, making the city of Osaka less dominant than Tokyo or Nagoya within their respective prefectures.

[a] Settlements with populations less than 50,000 are not "cities."

D

Tokyo's Land Market

THE RAPID economic transformation in Tokyo has probably expressed itself most clearly in the land market. From 1986 to 1987, prices for residential land increased by 95% and those for commercial land increased by 79%. The most pronounced relative increases have occurred in areas as yet quite undeveloped but primed for development. Thus, the Tama district, where the Tokyo Metropolitan Government's ambitious master plan calls for massive investment and development by the government, has experienced some of the highest increases. If we compare the actual price levels of land per square meter in the Tama district with those in more central locations, it becomes evident that the actual sale prices are quite low and that the high rates of increase are in good part a function of very low past price levels. Yet one can also see in the extremely high increases a dynamic at play that goes beyond what one would expect as average price increases. Indeed, the figures for earlier years show mostly mild increases of a few percentage points, compared to the 8% in the Tama district in 1987. What we are seeing, even in this very distant area, is an extension of the highly speculative and immensely profitable land market of Tokyo. This is a situation where high liquidity makes investment in land a most desirable form of investment and thereby brings about extremely high increases in prices of land.

A brief review of actual transactions in central locations shows that the price per square meter in central Tokyo is far above that in other major cities, notably New York City and London. In the central business district, the average price of a square meter in Chiyoda went from $33,480 in 1986 to $46,256 in 1987. (These values are based on the 1987 rate for the dollar.)

Another extremely high average price of $43,040 per square meter was paid in 1987 for land in Minato, in the Akasaka area, one in high demand. In the commercial market, the prices are double and triple those in the residential market. It is worth noting that land prices in Shinjuku were among the highest. Shinjuku is not one of the three central business district wards, but it is where the Tokyo Metropolitan Government is developing its massive new headquarters and where a vast number of luxury high-rise office buildings have been built over the last five years.

In 1987, a square meter of developed space fetched an average of

$136,564 in Shinjuku and $140,969 in Chuo. The difference is that while Chuo has long been one of the three wards forming the central business district, Shinjuku was until recently largely a working-class district. One still sees block after block of working-class houses and shops there. Out of this vast low-rise sea of small, low-income houses and shops rises a complex of tall luxury office buildings, several over 100 stories high, with vast designer plazas, a homogeneous space that one could find in any major city in the West. In their shadow, if one happens to take a wrong turn, one can find short, narrow, almost invisible streets lined with small, very old houses with flowerpots in front and vegetable patches. Clearly, with the activity in the land market and the proposed government complex, these will not last for long.

Average residential land values for Tokyo's twenty-three central wards had an overall increase of 30.5% from 1985 to 1986 and of almost 95% from 1986 to 1987. The overall increases for commercial land were 40.5% from 1985 to 1986 and 70.3% from 1986 to 1987. There was a huge increase in the price of industrial land from one period to the next, even though manufacturing was declining in Tokyo. These acquisitions of industrial land may have been aimed at commercial development, or they may have been linked with the high-tech sector, for which Tokyo is the key location. From 1985 to 1986, overall average land prices went up by 11.5%, and from 1986 to 1987 they went up by 78%. In both periods, activity was concentrated in only five of the twenty-three central wards. One of these was the downtown ward on the bay, which has long been an industrial area. It is also worth noting that this ward, Koto, borders on one of the three wards making up the central business district. The other acquisitions occurred in wards at the outer edge of the central Tokyo area. In Tokyo's Tama area, the average prices for residential land increased by 8.1% from 1985 to 1986 and by 95.4% from 1986 to 1987, and those for commercial land increased by 18.5% from 1985 to 1986 and by 125.4% from 1986 to 1987. Industrial land also showed marked increases: 3.1% from 1985 to 1986 and 21.2% from 1986 to 1987. Finally, in the Islands, there was hardly any real estate activity and none with price increases above 1%.

For the entire Tokyo Metropolis, the average increases in land prices for the two periods 1985 to 1986 and 1986 to 1987 were, respectively, 18.8% and 93% for residential land; 34.4% and 79% for commercial land; 16% and 80.7% for mixed-use land; and 10.7% and 71.6% for industrial land. There were thus across-the-board increases. Furthermore, there were significant increases, though at much lower prices, in the more peripheral regions that are undergoing massive development, initially by the government and now by the private sector as well (see Table D.1 for a breakdown of residential land prices by district). Except for the Islands, no area in Tokyo seems to be escaping the dynamics of a real estate market that is generating immense profits through vast increases in the price of land.

Tokyo's expanded and new functions as an international financial center have put immense pressure on the prices of land. The 1987 Fourth Comprehensive National Development Plan contained proposals for the dispersion of central government offices to reduce the concentration of administrative functions in Tokyo, a proposal to impose a new tax system that discourages businesses from maintaining their offices in Tokyo, and other such proposals aimed at dispersal in order to reduce the pressure on the price of land and the congestion in central Tokyo. The overall recommendation of the plan was to implement a multipolar urban system, with several subcenters and core cities. Land and taxation were crucial priorities for the government. One example was the Tokyo Metropolitan Government's enforcement of a regulation requiring reports of land transactions in areas designated by the Governor; another was the July 1987 instruction by the Ministry of Finance requesting financial institutes to curb loans for land transactions.

When studies for the Fourth Plan began in September 1984, it was decided for the first time ever that the plan should include land-related

TABLE D.1
Tokyo: Residential Land Price by District, 1986-1987 (dollars)

	Average Residential Land Price per Square Meter	
District	1986	1987
Central	10,359.03	21,745.81
Surburban	3,342.73	6,944.93
Surrounding	1,833.48	3,711.01
Central, suburban and surrounding	2,851.54	5,877.53
North Tama	1,173.13	2,646.26
South Tama	789.87	1,438.77
West Tama	544.05	722.03
Tama	981.50	2,049.34
Island	41.41	41.85
Total area	1,897.36	3,922.03

Source: Tokyo Metropolitan Gov't, "Land Value Shift December 1986 - December 1987" (in Japanese) (unpublished report, 1988).

measures. The National Land Agency's interim report of the Fourth Comprehensive National Development Plan, issued in December 1986, was intended to guide land use up to the year 2000. It envisioned even greater concentration of facilities and functions in Tokyo and surrounding prefectures and recommended further development of Tokyo as an international financial and information center. Immense protests against this plan led to its revision. The draft of the Fourth Plan, presented on May 28, 1987, deemphasized Tokyo's role and called for a multipolar, dispersed pattern of national land development. Much of the plan focused on the development of large-scale projects, such as road construction, building up of industries and information services in each region, and urban redevelopment, which local governments had been requesting. It is doubtful, according to some experts, that the measures contained in the plan will alleviate the excessive concentration in Tokyo.[1]

In central Tokyo, land prices have reached 30 million yen per square meter and more. The government faces immense costs if it wants to build infrastructure, from housing to roads. A much cited case is a 1.3-kilometer section of a road in central Tokyo that cost 500 billion yen, with construction per se amounting to only about 2 or 3 billion yen and the rest going for land. As land prices rise, the effectiveness of funds allocated for social capital declines, and selling land to real estate developers becomes the most profitable through tax revenues. Furthermore, it leads to distortions in the development of social infrastructure when so much of the economy is concentrated in one region. For example, the construction of new subways can contribute to rather than alleviate congestion, since new housing will be developed around the new lines and stations and bring in more people to the city; the same is true of the proposed bridge over Tokyo Bay, which will open new areas for urban development, and the 10,000 hectares of land to be reclaimed from Tokyo Bay.[2]

According to some, the only solution to the accelerating rise in prices is to reduce land demand in Tokyo and the only way of doing this is to reverse the concentration of facilities and functions in Tokyo. There have been proposals for a corridor or megalopolis linking Tokyo and Osaka. A magnetically levitated train (Maglev) capable of 500 kilometers per hour, would take one hour between Osaka and Tokyo, making it one "city."

[1] Note that estimates of latent demand for buildings in central Tokyo range from ninety to a hundred buildings the size of the Kasumigaseki Building, the first skyscraper completed in Japan, in 1968, which has thirty-six floors aboveground and is 147 meters high. If one assumes 10,000 square meters of land per building, this is a total land requirement of up to 2 million square feet, or a minimum of 900,000 square meters of land. The Tokyo Bay area that is being redeveloped is about 3,000 hectares, and only four kilometers from the center of Tokyo.

[2] With current technologies, land can be reclaimed at a rate of 500 hectares a year at most.

Intelligent buildings (fully computerized facilities) would be built along-side train stations in Nagoya and Kofu. Together with the Kasumigaseki-Marunouchi district in Tokyo, these three special sectors, each 100 to 300 hectares in area and wired to permit application of the latest telecommunication and data processing technology, would become the nerve centers of a megalopolis that would serve as Japan's new economic capital. The central government's twelve ministries and eight agencies headed by state ministers, currently concentrated in Tokyo's Kasumigaseki district, would be dispersed across the 500-kilometer corridor, with three or four of them relocated in each of the three new districts.

The question of land-related constraints on economic development had already surfaced at the end of the high growth period. In 1972 there was a strong increase in the price of land, linked to Prime Minister Tanaka's plan to remodel or modernize the whole Japanese archipelago. The major difference between the 1972 increase in prices and the current one is that the 1972 increase affected the whole country while the current one is limited largely to Tokyo's commercial districts and adjacent residential areas. At that time, the boom caused by the so-called remodeling dramatically pushed up all prices, not only those of land. Eventually land prices stabilized as a result of the tight credit policy, and land-related constraints began receiving less attention. In the 1980s, excess liquidity stemming from various conditions, including a series of cuts in interest rates as the yen rose, again induced land prices to rise rapidly. While land prices in several areas of Japan rose relative to Tokyo's prices (see Table D.2), they declined in overall relative terms. (See also Table D.3 for related data.) It was, in the words of Tatsuo Izumi, "an era of bipolar land prices" (in his book Chika o Yomu [Reading the Land Prices]). Others saw it as a transition period, after which land prices would rise sharply throughout the country. It is quite possible that land prices will rise all over Japan if easy credit prevails for long. It is unlikely, however, that the money supply will be allowed to grow at an annual rate of more than 20%, as it did before the massive inflation rise in the early 1970s. Given the pressures on land in central Tokyo, overall measures designed to increase the general supply of land through conversion of rural areas in the urban metropolitan area to commercial uses would not affect land prices in central Tokyo, though they would stabilize land prices in Japan as a whole.[3] A tight credit policy helped stabilize land prices in the 1970s, when the price of everything else rose. But this would be less effective with polarized land prices.

[3] In Tokyo, farmland helps compensate for the absence of green zones. Currently, Tokyo's green zone ratio is two square meters per person, which is one-tenth that of New York City and one-fifteenth that of London.

TABLE D.2

Japanese Prefectural Cities: Average Residential Land
Prices Relative to Tokyo, 1985-1986

	1985 Index (Tokyo = 100)	1986 Index (Tokyo = 100)	Change 1985-1986[a]
Tokyo	100.0	100.0	0.0
Sapporo	15.6	12.5	-3.1
Aomori	16.1	12.8	-3.3
Morioka	18.8	15.1	-3.6
Sendai	19.5	15.8	-3.7
Akita	14.2	11.3	-2.9
Yamagata	17.5	13.7	-3.8
Fukushima	15.6	12.4	-3.2
Mito	16.4	13.1	-3.3
Utsunomiya	16.0	13.1	-2.9
Maebashi	19.2	15.2	-4.0
Urawa	50.4	39.9	-10.5
Chiba	33.3	26.5	-6.7
Yokohama	47.2	38.3	-9.0
Niigata	21.0	16.4	-4.6
Toyama	18.7	15.0	-3.6
Kanazawa	24.8	19.7	-5.2
Fukui	24.0	19.2	-4.8
Kobe	20.3	16.6	-3.7
Nagano	20.4	16.5	-3.9
Gifu	24.6	20.4	-4.2
Shizuoka	34.1	27.5	-6.6
Nagoya	36.9	29.7	-7.2
Tsu	13.5	11.5	-1.9
Ohtsu	26.6	21.7	-4.9
Kyoto	56.8	46.5	-10.2
Osaka	61.6	51.0	-10.6
Kobe	46.1	36.3	-9.8
Nara	31.8	25.4	-6.4
Wakayama	28.2	22.5	-5.7
Tottori	19.6	15.1	-4.4
Matsue	16.8	13.5	-3.4
Okayama	16.1	13.0	-3.1
Hiroshima	33.1	26.3	-6.8
Yamaguchi	11.5	9.3	-2.1
Tokushima	26.3	20.9	-5.5
Takamatsu	25.8	22.0	-3.7
Matsuyama	22.7	18.0	-4.6
Ko Chi	29.8	23.6	-6.2
Fukuoka	25.0	20.0	-5.0
Saga	14.7	11.7	-3.0
Nagasaki	21.5	10.8	-10.7
Kagoshima	25.0	19.6	-5.4
Naha	33.0	27.5	-5.5

Source: Same as in Table D.1

[a] Indicates change in price relative to Tokyo's change in price.

TABLE D.3

Japan: Land Prices in Major Cities, 1985 (yen per square meter)

	Residential	Proposed Residential	Residential Land in UCAs	Commercial	Industrial
Tokyo	196,500	48,700	36,200	1,299,400	92,500
Osaka	168,900	47,300	45,400	822,200	124,900
Nagoya	97,100	30,100	38,300	332,700	58,500
Cities with over 500,000 pop.	74,200	26,900	23,400	394,800	51,900
Cities with over 300,000 pop.	71,600	29,800	25,900	344,300	40,000
Others	54,000	24,200	19,900	213,000	30,700

Source: OECD, Urban Policies in Japan (1986).
Note: UCA (undeveloped central areas).

The bipolarization in land prices suggests that attention should be paid to how land is used rather than the mere availability of land. It is not just a matter of the land supply. In the competition for creating an international center for finance and business, the infrastructure and the availability of excellent locations is more important than the extent of available land. Agglomeration economies are high for these kinds of economic activities.

Japan's national government is addressing the land price issue by selling off national land to the highest bidder. The Tokyo Metropolitan Government does not seem to agree with this policy.[4] In the case of national land in Tokyo, this only intensifies the pressure on prices. National land sold to private developers is exempt from the restrictions placed on the sale of privately held land. One site in Chiyoda Ward was auctioned off for 8.5 million yen per square meter in 1986. The Ministry of Transpor-

[4] In September 1986 the Tokyo Metropolitan Government passed an ordinance empowering the Governor to require prior notification of transactions involving 500 square meters or more in designated districts. The National Land Use Planning Act, older than the Tokyo ordinance, is designed to keep land prices in check by requiring that the prefectural governments (including the Tokyo Metropolitan government) be notified in advance of any real estate transaction involving 2,000 square meters or more. If the asking price is significantly higher than the value at which the National Land Agency has appraised it, the Governor can formally recommend that the price be renegotiated. There are penalties for failure to notify, but the Governor's recommendations have no binding force. It is expected that the fact that the price will become public knowledge should have some deterrent effect. Tokyo passed the subsequent ordinance because most transactions involve less than 2,000 square meters, and there was no way to control such deals. The National Land Use Planning Act was amended on June 2, 1987, to incorporate most of the restrictions of real estate transactions included in the 1986 ordinance. When the new law took effect in August 1987, Tokyo eliminated its ordinance.

tation's intended sale of 163 hectares of Japanese National Railways lands in Tokyo by competitive bidding led to immense increases in prices of adjacent land, even before the site was bought. (Japanese National Railways has land slated for sale throughout Japan.)[5] The Tokyo Metropolitan Government has asked Japanese National Railways to sell its Tokyo land to Tokyo, as it is setting up a land trust; the purpose of this trust is to avoid selling land at high profits but still obtain a return so as to avoid feeding the price spiral.[6]

[5] One concern is that one key Japanese National Railways land piece in Minato ward (Shidome, in the Shimbashi area), if sold to the private sector, will be used for a large concentration of high-rises, becoming, in Governor Suzuki's words, "a disorderly thicket of skyscrapers like Manhattan's urban jungle" (Reference Reading Series 19, Foreign Press Center, Land price program: 16). In the case of the Shidome plot, Governor Suzuki proposed that the Tokyo Metropolitan Government acquire the land, put in roads and the other infrastructure, and then sell off some plots and put others in land trust. This is what the Tokyo Metropolitan Government did in the Shinjuku subcenter, built on the site of a water purification plant. It set aside 45% of the area for parks and roads, "something that would never have happened if the land had simply been sold to the highest bidder" (ibid.).

[6] Cf. the Singapore model: a freeze on land prices and governmental planning; most housing is government owned and so is most land.

Bibliography

Abu-Lughod, Janet L. 1980. *Rabat: Urban Apartheid in Morocco*. Princeton, N.J.: Princeton University Press.

Aglietta, Michael. 1979. *A Theory of Capitalist Regulation: The U.S. Experience*. Norfolk, Great Britain: Lowe and Brybone Printers.

Aldrich, A. et al. 1981. "Business Development and Self-segregation: Asian Enterprise in Three British Cities." In C. Peach, V. Robinson, and S. Smith, eds., *Ethnic Segregation in Cities*. London: Croom Helm.

Alexander, I. 1979. *Office Location and Public Policy*. London: Longmans.

Alexander, J. 1954. "The Basic-Nonbasic Concept of Urban Economic Functions." *Economic Geography* 30(3): 246–61.

Allinson, Gary D. 1979. *Suburban Tokyo: A Comparative Study in Politics and Social Change*. Berkeley: University of California Press.

Altschul, James S. 1984. "Japan's Elite Law Firms." *International Financial Law Review* 3(6): 6–12.

American Banker. 1982. "500 Largest Banks in the World." *American Banker*, July 28, 145–47.

——. 1986. "The Top 300 Commercial Banks in the United States." *American Banker*, March 18, 57–58.

AMPO. 1986. *The Challenge Facing Japanese Women*. Special issue of *Japan-Asia Quarterly Review* 18 (2, 3).

——. 1987. *Japanese Industry Moves Out: Expansion Abroad, Depression at Home*. Special issue of *Japan-Asia Quarterly Review* 19(1).

——. 1988. *Japan's Human Imports: As Capital Flows Out, Foreign Labor Flows In*. Special issue of *Japan-Asia Quarterly Review* 19(4).

Appelbaum, Eileen. 1984. *Technology and the Redesign of Work in the Insurance Industry*. Project report, Stanford University, Institute of Research on Educational Finance and Governance.

Armstrong, Regina. 1972. *The Office Industry*. New York: Regional Plan Association.

——. 1988. *New York and the Forces of Immigration*. New York: Citizens Budget Commission.

Armstrong, Regina, and D. Milder. 1985. "Employment in the Manhattan CBD and Back-Office Location Decisions." *City Almanac* 18:1–2, 4–18.

Aronson, Jonathan David, and Peter F. Cowhey. 1984. *Trade in Services: A Case for Open Markets*. Washington and London: American Enterprise Institute.

Asian Development Bank. Various years. *Yearbook of National Accounts*. New York: United Nations.

Asian Women's Association. 1988. *Women from Across the Seas: Migrant Workers in Japan*. Tokyo: Asian Women's Association.

Attali, Jacques. 1981. *Les Trois Mondes*. Paris: Fayard.

Bach, C. L. 1987. "U.S. International Transactions, Fourth Quarter and Year 1986." *Survey of Current Business* 67(3): 32–64.

Bacon, Robert, and Walter Eltis. 1978. *Britain's Economic Problems: Too Few Producers.* London: Macmillan.

Baker, James C. 1978. *International Bank Regulation.* New York: Praeger.

Baker, James C., and M. Gerald Bradford. 1974. *American Banks Abroad: Edge Act Companies and Multinational Banking.* New York: Praeger.

Balmori, Diana. 1983. "Hispanic Immigrants in the Construction Industry: New York City, 1962–1982." Occasional Papers, no. 38, Center for Latin American and Caribbean Studies, New York University.

Bankers Monthly. 1981. "21st Annual Financial Industry Survey." *Bankers Monthly*, May 15, 14–21.

Bank of England. Various years. *Quarterly Bulletin.* London: Bank of England.

Bank for International Settlements. 1986. *Recent Innovations in International Banking.* Basel: BIS, Monetary and Economic Department.

———. 1987. *International Banking Developments.* Basel: BIS Monetary and Economic Department.

Bank of Japan. 1986. *Kokusai hikaku tokei* (Comparative International Statistics). Tokyo: Bank of Japan.

———. 1988. *Economic Statistics Annual 1987.* Tokyo: Bank of Japan, Research and Statistics Department.

Baran, Barbara, and Suzanne Teegarden. 1983. "Women's Labor in the Office of the Future." Paper presented at Berkeley Roundtable on the International Economy, University of California, Berkeley.

Basche, James R. 1986. *Eliminating Barriers to International Trade and Investment in Services.* Economic and Policy Analysis Program, Research Bulletin no. 200. New York: The Conference Board.

Bavishi, V., and H. E. Wyman. 1983. *Who Audits the World: Trends in the Worldwide Accounting Profession.* Storrs, Conn.: University of Connecticut, Center for Transnational Accounting and Financial Research.

Bell, Daniel. 1973. *The Coming of Post-Industrial Society: A Venture in Social Forecasting.* New York: Basic Books.

Bell, Linda, and Richard B. Freeman. 1987. "The Facts about Rising Industrial Wage Dispersion in the U.S." *Proceedings*, Industrial Relations Research Association, May.

Beneria, Lourdes. 1989. "Subcontracting and Employment Dynamics in Mexico City." In A. Portes et al., eds., *The Informal Economy: Studies in Advanced and Less Developed Countries.* Baltimore: Johns Hopkins University Press.

Benston, George J. 1983. "Federal Regulation of Banking: Analysis and Policy Recommendations." *Journal of Bank Research* (Winter): 216–44.

———. 1984. "Financial Disclosure and Bank Failure." *Economic Review* (March). Atlanta: Federal Reserve Bank of Atlanta.

Berger, Suzanne, Michael L. Dertouzos, Richard K. Lester, Robert M. Solow, and Lester C. Thurow. 1989. "Toward a New Industrial America." *Scientific America* 260(6): 39–47.

Bergsten, C. Fred. 1987. "The U.S.–Japan Economic Problem: Next Steps." In

H. Patrick and R. Tachi, eds., *Japan and the United States Today: Exchange Rates, Macroeconomic Policies, and Financial Market Innovations*. New York: Columbia University Press.

Berry, Brian J. L. 1961. "City Size Distributions and Economic Development." *Economic Development and Cultural Change* 9(4): 573–88.

————. 1971. "City Size and Economic Development." In L. Jakobson and V. Prakash, eds., *Urbanization and National Development*. Newburg Park, Calif.: Sage.

Bestor, Theodore. 1989. *Neighborhood Tokyo*. Stanford, Calif.: Stanford University Press.

Bhagwati, J. N. 1984. "Splintering and Disembodiment of Services and Developing Nations." *World Economy* 7(2): 133–43.

Bleeke, Joel, and James Goodrich. 1981. *Capitalizing on Opportunities Created by Deregulation of the Banking Industry*. Chicago: McKinsey and Co.

BLS. See U.S. Department of Labor, Bureau of Labor Statistics.

Bluestone, Barry, and Bennett Harrison. 1982. *The Deindustrialization of America*. New York: Basic Books.

Bluestone, Barry, Bennett Harrison, and Lucy Gorham. 1984. *Storm Clouds on the Horizon: Labor Market Crisis and Industrial Policy*. Boston: Economic Education Project.

Blumberg, P. 1981. *Inequality in an Age of Decline*. New York: Oxford University Press.

Blumenfeld, H. 1955. "The Economic Base of the Metropolis." *Journal of the American Institute of Planners* 21 (Fall): 114–32.

Blunden, George. 1975. "The Supervision of the U.K. Banking System." *Bank of England Quarterly Bulletin*, June: 188–89.

Boulding, Kenneth. 1978. "The City as an Element in the International System." In L. S. Bourne and J. W. Simmons, eds., *Systems of Cities*. New York: Oxford University Press.

Boyer, Christine. 1983. Dreaming the Rational City, Cambridge, Mass.: MIT Press.

Boyer, Robert, ed. 1986. *La flexibilité du travail en Europe*. Paris: La Decouverte.

Breheny, Michael J., and Ronald W. McQuaid. 1985. "The M4 Corridor: Patterns and Causes of Growth in High Technology Industries." In *Geographical Papers*, University of Reading, Department of Geography.

Brett, E. A. 1983. *International Money and Capitalistic Crisis: The Anatomy of Global Disintegration*. London: Heinemann.

Brint, Steven. 1988. "The Upper Professionals of the 'Dual City': A High Command of Commerce, Culture, and Civic Regulation." Paper prepared for a meeting of the Dual City Working Group held in New York City, November 11–12. New York: Committee on New York City, Social Science Research Council.

Briston, R. J. 1979. "The U.K. Accountancy Profession: The Move Towards Monopoly Power." *Accountants' Magazine*, November, 458–60.

Brosnan, P., and F. Wilkinson. 1987. *Cheap Labour: Britain's False Economy.* London: Low Pay Unit.

Brown, C. 1984. *Black and White Britain.* London: Heinemann.

Browne, L. E. 1983. "High Technology and Business Services." *New England Economic Review,* July–August: 5–16.

Browning, H. L., and J. Singelmann. 1978. "The transformation of the U.S. Labor Force: The Interaction of Industry and Occupation." *Politics and Society* 8 (3 and 4): 481–509.

Buck, N., I. Gordon, and K. Young. 1986. *The London Employment Problem.* Oxford: Clarendon Press.

Buckley, John W., and Peter R. O'Sullivan. 1981. "International Economics and Multinational Accounting Firms." In John C. Burton, ed., *The International World of Accounting: Challenges and Opportunities.* Proceedings of the Arthur Young Professors' Roundtable held at Reston, Va., 1980.

Bundesbank. Various years. *Monatsbericht der Deutsche Bundesbank.* Berlin: West Germany.

Bungei Shunju. 1986. "Kokutetsu vochi kyoso nyusatsu ni igi ari" (Opposition to competition in bidding for Government railroad land). *Bungei Shunju,* December: 176–82.

Bureau of National Affairs. 1982. *Layoffs, Plant Closures, and Concession Bargaining.* Washington, D.C.: Bureau of National Affairs.

Burton, John C., ed. 1981. *The International World of Accounting: Challenges and Opportunities.* Proceedings of the Arthur Young Professors' Roundtable held at Reston, Va., 1980.

Business Week. 1977. "Annual Survey of Bank Performance." *Business Week,* April 18.

———. 1986. "Annual Survey of Bank Performance." *Business Week,* April 6.

Candilis, Wray O., ed. 1988. *United States Service Industries Handbook.* New York and London: Praeger.

Cargill, Thomas F. 1981. "The Impact of Deregulation on the Financial System." *Issues in Bank Regulation,* Winter:10–14.

———. 1986. *Money, the Financial System, and Monetary Policy.* Englewood Cliffs, N.J.: Prentice Hall.

Cargill, Thomas F., and Gillian G. Garcia. 1985. *Financial Reform in the 1980s.* Stanford, Calif.: Hoover Institution Press.

Casey, B. 1987. "The Extent and Nature of Temporary Employment in Great Britain." *Policy Studies* 8(1): 64–75.

Castells, Manuel. 1977. *The Urban Question: A Marxist Approach.* Cambridge, Mass.: MIT Press.

———. 1989. *The Informational City: Information Technology, Economic Restructuring, and the Urban-Regional Process.* London: Blackwell.

Castells, Manuel, and Alejandro Portes. 1989. "World Underneath: The Origins, Dynamics, and Effects of the Informal Economy." In A. Portes, et al., eds., *The Informal Economy: Studies in Advanced and Less Developed Countries.* Baltimore: Johns Hopkins University Press.

Caves, R. E. 1976. "International Corporations: The Industrial Economics of Foreign Investment." *Economica*, new ser., 38(149): 1–27.

———. 1980. "Industrial Organization, Corporate Strategy and Structure." *Journal of Economic Literature* 28(1): 64–92.

Chall, Daniel. 1984. "Neighborhood Changes in New York City during the 1970s. Are the Gentry Returning?" *Federal Reserve Bank of New York Quarterly Bulletin*, Winter 1983–1984: 38–48.

Chandler, Alfred. 1977. *The Visible Hand: The Manager in American Business.* Cambridge, Mass.: Harvard University Press.

Chaney, Elsa, and Constance Sutton, eds. 1979. "Caribbean Migration to New York." Special issue of *International Migration Review* 13 (Summer).

Chase-Dunn, C. 1984. "Urbanization in the World System: New Directions for Research." In M. P. Smith, ed., *Cities in Transformation*. Beverly Hills, Calif.: Sage.

———. 1985. "The System of World Cities, A.D. 800–1975." In M. Timberlake, ed., *Urbanization in the World-Economy*. New York: Academic Press.

Christaller, Walter. 1966. *Central Places in Southern Germany*. Englewood Cliffs, N.J.: Prentice Hall.

City of Nagoya. 1988. *Statistical Sketch of Nagoya 1987*. Nagoya, Japan.

City of New York. 1985. *Atlas of the Census*. New York: Department of City Planning.

Clairmonte, Frederick F., and John H. Cavanagh. 1984. "Transnational Corporations and Services: The Final Frontier." *Trade and Development: An UNCTAD Review* 5:215–73.

Clark, Colin. 1940. *The Conditions of Economic Progress*. London: Macmillan.

Clark, Gordon L. 1981. "The Employment Relation and Spatial Division of Labor: A Hypothesis." *Annals of the American Association of Geographers*: 412–24.

———. 1983. *Interregional Migration, National Policy, and Social Justice*. Totowa, N.J.: Rowman and Allenheld.

Cohen, R. 1987. *The New Helots: Migrants in the International Division of Labour*. London: Avebury.

Cohen, Robert. 1981. "The New International Division of Labor, Multinational Corporations and Urban Hierarchy." In Michael Dear and Allen Scott, eds., *Urbanization and Urban Planning in Capitalist Society*. New York: Methuen.

Cohen, Stephen S., and John Zysman. 1987. *Manufacturing Matters—The Myth of the Post-Industrial Economy*. New York: Basic Books.

Columbia University. 1987. "The Informal Economy in Low-Income Communities in New York City." New York: Columbia University, Program in Urban Planning.

Conference Board. 1983. "International Trade in Services: A Growing Force in the World Economy." *World Business Perspectives*, no. 75 (October). New York: Conference Board.

Congdon, T. 1988. *The Debt Threat: The Dangers of High Real Interest Rates for the World Economy*. Oxford: Basil Blackwell.

Conservation of Human Resources Project. 1977. *The Corporate Headquarters Complex in New York City.* New York: Columbia University. Conservation of Human Resources Project.

Coombes, M. G., J. S. Dixon, J. B. Goddard, S. Openshaw, and P. J. Taylor. 1982. "Functional Regions for the Population Centres of Great Britain." In D. T. Herbert and R. J. Johnston, eds., *Geography and the Urban Environment.* Vol. 5. Chichester: John Wiley.

Cooper, Kery, and Donald R. Fraser. 1984. *Banking Deregulation and the New Competition in Financial Services.* Cambridge, Mass.: Ballinger.

Corden, W. Maxwell. 1985. *Inflation, Exchange Rates, and the World Economy.* Oxford: Oxford University Press.

County Business Patterns. *See* U.S. Department of Commerce, Bureau of the Census, 1977–1987.

Cox, Gabrielle. 1988. *The Pay Divide.* Low Pay Briefing Papers, no. 10. Manchester, England: Greater Manchester Low Pay Unit.

Crabb, Kelly C. 1983. "Providing Legal Services in Foreign Countries: Making Room for the American Attorney." *Columbia Law Review* 83(7): 1767–1823.

Cross, M. 1988. "Ethnic Minority Youth in a Collapsing Labour Market: The U.K. Experience." In C. Wulpert, ed., *Entering the Working World.* London: Grower.

Crouch, Colin, ed. 1979. *State and Economy in Contemporary Capitalism.* London: Croom Helm.

Crozier, Michel. 1963. *Le Phénomène bureaucratique.* Paris: Le Seuil.

Daly, Maurice. 1987. "Rationalization of International Banking and the Implications for the Pacific Rim." In J. Friedman, ed., *International Capital and Urbanization of the Pacific Rim.* Proceedings of conference held at the Center for Pacific Rim Studies, UCLA, March 26–28.

Daniels, Peter W. 1975. *Office Location.* London: Bell.

——. 1985. *Service Industries: A Geographical Appraisal.* London and New York: Methuen.

Daniels, Peter, Andrew Leyhson, and Nigel Thrift. 1986. "U.K. Producer Services: The International Dimension." Working Paper, St. David's University College, Lampter and University of Liverpool, August.

Davis, Mike. 1985. "Urban Renaissance and the Spirit of Postmodernism." *New Left Review* 151:113.

DeFreitas, Gregory. 1986. "The Impact of Immigration on Low-wage Workers." Unpublished manuscript. Department of Economics, Barnard College, New York City.

DeGiovanni, F. 1984. "Neighborhood Revitalization in Fort Greene and Clinton Hill." *New York Affairs* 8(2): 86–104 (1984).

Delaunay, Jean Claude, and Jean Gadrey. 1987. *Les Enjeux de la Société de Service.* Paris: Presses de la Fondation des Sciences Politiques.

Denison, Edward. 1979. *Accounting for Slower Economic Growth: The U.S. in the 1970s.* Washington, D.C.: Brookings Institution.

Deutermann, Jr., W. V., and S. C. Brown. 1978. "Voluntary Part-Time Workers: A Growing Part of the Labor Force." *Monthly Labor Review,* June: 101.

deVries, Rimmer. 1987. "International Imbalances and the Search for Exchange-Rate Stability." In H. Patrick and R. Tachi, eds., *Japan and the United States Today: Exchange Rates, Macroeconomic Policies, and Financial Market Innovations*. New York: Columbia University Press.

DiLullo, Anthony J. 1981. "Service Transactions in the U.S. International Accounts, 1970–1980." *Survey of Current Business* (November): 29–46.

Dore, Ronald P. 1958. *City Life in Japan: A Study of a Tokyo Ward*. Berkeley: University of California Press.

Douglass, Mike. 1987. "Transnational Capital and Urbanization in Japan." In J. Friedman, ed., *International Capital and Urbanization of the Pacific Rim*. Proceedings of conference held at the Center for Pacific Rim Studies, UCLA, March 26–28.

Drennan, Matthew. 1983. "Local Economy and Local Revenues." In R. Horton and C. Brecher, eds., *Setting Municipal Priorities 1984*. New York and London: New York University Press.

———. 1987. "Local Economy and Local Revenues." In Charles Brecher and Raymond D. Horton, eds., *Setting Municipal Priorities 1988*. New York and London: New York University Press.

Dunford, Mick. 1989. "Industrial Paradigms and Social Structures in Areas of New Industrial Growth." Typescript. School of European Studies, University of Sussex.

Dunning, J. H., and G. Norman. 1987. "The Location Choice of Offices of International Companies." *Environment and Planning A* 19:613–31.

Echeverri-Carroll, Elsie. 1988. *Economic Impacts and Foreign Investment Opportunities: Japanese Maquilas—A Special Case*. Austin, Texas: University of Texas, Graduate School of Business, Bureau of Business Research.

Economic Consulting Services. 1981. *The International Operations of U.S. Service Industries: Current Data Collection and Analysis*. Washington D.C.: Economic Consulting Services, Inc.

Economic Intelligence Unit. 1984. *Multinational Business Quarterly*, no. 1. London: Economic Intelligence Unit.

Economic Planning Agency, Japan. 1980. *Standard Revised National Economic Accounting*. Tokyo: Japan Government.

———. 1983. *National Economic Accounting*.

———. 1985. *White Paper on the Global Economy, 1985*.

———. 1986. *Outline of the Economy, 1985*.

———. 1987. *Economic Survey of Japan, 1986–1987*.

———. Various years a. *Indices of External Economic Trends*.

———. Various years b. *Report on Revised National Accounts*.

Economist, The. 1986a. "Investment Management Survey." *Economist*, November 8.

———. 1986b. "Global Investment Management." *Economist*, November 8.

Edel, Matthew. 1981. "Capitalism, Accumulation and the Explanation of Urban Phenomena." In Michael Dear and Allen Scott, eds., *Urbanization and Urban Planning in Capitalist Society*. New York: Methuen.

Edwards, Franklin R. 1987. "The Dark Side of Financial Innovation." In H. Patrick and R. Tachi, eds., *Japan and the United States Today: Exchange Rates, Macroeconomic Policies, and Financial Market Innovations.* New York: Columbia University Press.

Edwards, L. E. 1982. "Intra-Urban Office Location: A Decision-Making Approach." Ph.D. diss., University of Liverpool.

Edwards, Richard. 1979. *Contested Terrain: The Transformation of the Workplace in the Twentieth Century.* New York: Basic Books.

Ehrenhalt, Samuel M. 1981. "Some Perspectives on the Outlook for the New York City Labor Market." In *Challenges of the Changing Economy of New York City.* New York: The New York City Council on Economic Education.

——. 1988. "New York City in the New Economic Environment: New Risks and a Changing Outlook." New York: U.S. Bureau of Labor Statistics, Mid-Atlantic Regional Office.

Ehrenreich, Barbara. 1984. *The Hearts of Men: American Dreams and the Flight from Commitment.* Garden City, N.Y.: Anchor Books.

Eisenbeis, Robert A. 1981. "Regulation and Deregulation of Banking." *Banking Magazine,* March–April: 25–33.

Ellis, Richard. 1985. *World Rental Levels.* London: Richard Ellis.

El-Shakhs, Salah. 1972. "Development, Primacy and Systems of Cities." *Journal of Developing Areas* 7 (October): 11–36.

Ernst, Dieter. 1986. "U.S.–Japanese Competition and the Worldwide Restructuring of the Electronics Industry—a European View." Paper prepared for the Pacific-Atlantic Interrelations Conference held at the Institute of International Relations, University of California, Berkeley, April 24.

Euromoney. 1983. "Foreign Banks in America." *Euromoney,* August, supplement no. 6.

——. 1987. "The Euromoney/InterSec 250: The Largest Investors outside the U.S.; the 75 Largest U.S. Investors." *Euromoney,* September: 365–80.

European Economic Community. 1984. *Study on International Trade in Services.* Document I/420/84-EN. Brussels.

Fainstein, N. I. 1987. "The Underclass/Mismatch Hypothesis as an Explanation for Black Economic Deprivation." *Politics and Society* 15(4): 403–51.

Fainstein, Susan S., and Norman I. Fainstein. 1983. "Regime Strategies, Communal Resistance, and Economic Forces." In Susan S. Fainstein et al., eds., *Restructuring the City.* New York: Longmans.

——. 1985. "Citizen Participation in Local Government." In D. R. Judd, ed., *Public Policy across States and Communities.* Greenwich, Conn.: JAI Press.

Fainstein, S., N. Fainstein, R. C. Hill, D. R. Judd, and M. P. Smith. 1983. *Restructuring the City.* New York: Longman.

Fainstein, S., I. Gordon, and M. Harloe. n.d. *Divided Cities: Economic Restructuring and Social Change in London and New York.* London: Basil Blackwell. Forthcoming.

Feagin, J. R. 1987. "The Secondary Circuit of Capital." *International Journal of Urban and Regional Research* 11:171–92.

————. 1988. *Houston Boomtown*. New Brunswick, N.J.: Rutgers University Press.

Feagin, J. R., and Michael P. Smith. 1987. "Cities and the New International Division of Labor: An Overview." In M. P. Smith and J. R. Feagin, eds., *The Capitalist City: Global Restructuring and Community Politics*. Oxford: Basil Blackwell.

Federal Reserve Bank of Atlanta. 1983. "Signals from the Future: The Emerging Financial Services Industry." *Economic Review*, September: 20–32.

Feige, E. L. 1979. "How Big Is the Irregular Economy?" *Challenge*, November–December: 14–17.

Fernandez-Kelly, M. P., and A. M. Garcia. 1989. "Informalization at the Core: Hispanic Women, Homework, and the Advanced Capitalist State." In A. Portes et al., eds., *The Informal Economy: Studies in Advanced and Less Developed Countries*. Baltimore: Johns Hopkins University Press.

Filed, Peter. 1981a. "M & A: The Transatlantic Battle." *Euromoney* (January): 82–97.

————. 1981b. "Regulation and Financial Innovation: Implications for Financial Structure and Competition among Depository and Nondepository Institutions." *Issues in Bank Regulation*, Winter: 15–23.

Ford, William F. 1982. "Banking's New Competition: Myths and Realities." *Economic Review*, January: 3–11. Published by Federal Reserve Bank of Atlanta.

Foreign Press Center. 1987. *Facts and Figures of Japan*. Tokyo: Foreign Press Center of Japan.

Fothergill, S., and G. Gudgin. 1982. *Unequal Growth: Urban and Regional Employment Change in the UK*. London: Heinemann.

Freeman, Richard. 1984. *Aspects of Recent Japanese Financial Markets Liberalization*. Washington, D.C.: Board of Governors of the Federal Reserve System.

Frenkel, Jeffrey A. 1984. "The Yen-Dollar Agreement: Liberalizing Japanese Capital Markets." In *Policy Analysis in International Economics*, publication no. 9. Washington, D.C.: Institute for International Economics.

Friedman, David. 1988. *The Misunderstood Miracle: Industrial Development and Political Change in Japan*. Ithaca, N.Y.: Cornell University Press.

Friedmann, John. 1964. "Cities in Social Transformation." In J. Friedmann and W. Alonso, eds., *Regional Development and Planning*. Cambridge, Mass.: MIT Press.

————. 1986. "The World City Hypothesis." *Development and Change* 17: 69–84.

Friedmann, John, and Goetz Wolff. 1982. "World City Formation: An Agenda for Research and Action." *International Journal of Urban and Regional Research* 6(3): 309–44.

Friend, A., and A. Metcalf. 1982. *Slump City: The Politics of Mass Unemployment*. London: Pluto Press.

Fröbel, Folker, Jurgen Heinrichs, and Otto Kreye. 1980. *The New International Division of Labor*. London: Cambridge University Press.

Fuchs, Victor. 1968. *The Service Economy*. New York: National Bureau of Economic Research and Columbia University Press.

Fujita, Kuniko. 1988. "The Technopolis: High Technology and Regional Development in Japan." *International Journal of Urban and Regional Research* 2(4): 566–94.

Fujita, K., and Richard Child Hill. 1987. *Toyota's City: Corporation and Community in Japan*. Sociology Working Paper no. 5, Department of Sociology, Michigan State University.

Fukuhara, Masahiro. 1981. *Keizai seicho to ginko tempo* (Economic growth and banking outlets). Tokyo: Kokon Sho-in.

Gad, G. 1975. *Central Toronto Offices: Observations on Location Patterns and Linkages*. Toronto: City of Toronto Planning Board.

———. 1979. "Face-to-Face Linkages and Office Decentralization Potentials: A Study of Toronto." In P. W. Daniels, ed., *Spatial Patterns of Office Growth and Location*. London: Wiley.

Galbraith, J. K. 1969. *The New Industrial State*. London: Hamish Hamilton.

Gans, Herbert. 1984. "American Urban Theory and Urban Areas." In Ivan Szelenyi, ed., *Cities in Recession*. Beverly Hills, Calif.: Sage.

GATT (General Agreement on Tariffs and Trade). Various years. *International Trade*. Geneva: GATT.

Gelb, Joyce. 1991. "Japanese Women: The Search for Equal Opportunity." *Kaleidoscope*. Forthcoming.

Gershuny, Jonathan. 1978. *After Industrial Society?: The Emerging Self-Service Economy*. London: Macmillan.

Gershuny, Jonathan, and Ian Miles. 1983. *The New Service Economy: The Transformation of Employment in Industrial Societies*. New York: Praeger.

Giarini, Orio, ed. 1987. *The Emerging Service Economy*. Oxford and New York: Pergamon Press.

Gillespie, A. E., and A. E. Green. 1987. "The Changing Geography of Producer Services Employment in Britain." *Regional Studies* 21(5): 397–412.

Ginzberg, Eli, and George J. Vojta. 1981. "The Service Sector of the U.S. Economy." *Scientific American* 244 (March): 48–55.

Glickman, N.J. 1979. *The Growth and Management of the Japanese Urban System*. New York: Academic Press.

Goddard, J. B. 1973. "Office Linkages and Location: A Study of Communications and Spatial Patterns in Central London." *Progress in Planning* 1:109–232.

———. 1975. *Office Location in Urban and Regional Development*. Oxford: Oxford University Press.

Goddard, J. B., and R. Pye. 1977. "Telecommunications and Office Location." *Regional Studies* 11: 19–30.

Gottdiener, M. 1985. *The Social Production of Urban Space*. Austin, Tex.: University of Texas Press.

Greater London Council. 1986. *The London Labour Plan*. London: Greater London Council.

———. Industry and Employment Branch. 1985. *Ethnic Minority Retailing*.

———. Industry and Employment Branch. 1986. *Textiles and Clothing: Sunset Industries*.

———. London Manpower Committees. 1981. *London Labor Market Review 1980/1981*.

———. London Regional Manpower Intelligence Unit. Various years. *Labor Market Report*.

———. Intelligence Unit. 1988. *Annual Abstract of Greater London Statistics, 1986–1987*. Vol. 19.

Greenbaum, Stuart I., and Charles F. Haywood. 1981. "Secular Change in the Financial Services Industry." *Journal of Money, Credit and Banking*, May: 571–89.

Greenfield, H. I. 1966. *Manpower and the Growth of Producer Services*. New York: Columbia University Press.

Greenwood, M. 1980. "Metropolitan Growth and the Intra-Metropolitan Location of Employment, Housing and the Labor Force." *Review of Economics and Statistics* 62:491–501.

Gregory, Derek, and John Urry, eds. 1985. *Social Relations and Spatial Structures*. London: Macmillan.

Gurr, T., and D. S. King. 1987. *The State and the City*. Chicago: University of Chicago Press.

Guth, Wilfried. 1986. "Bank Strategy in an Age of Rapid Change." *Banker* 136 (722): 36–45.

Gutmann, P. M. 1979. "Statistical Illusions, Mistaken Policies." In *Challenge*, November–December, 14–17.

Gyooten, Toyoo. 1987. "Internationalization of the Yen: Its Implications for the U.S.-Japan Relationship." In H. Patrick and R. Tachi, eds., *Japan and the United States Today: Exchange Rates, Macroeconomic Policies, and Financial Market Innovations*. New York: Columbia University Press.

Haig, R. M. 1972. *Major Economic Factors in Metropolitan Growth and Arrangement*. New York: Committee on Regional Plan for New York and Its Environs.

Hall, Peter. 1963. *London 2000*. London: Faber and Faber.

———. 1964. "Industrial London: A General View." In J. Coppock and H. Prince, eds., *Greater London*. London: Faber and Faber.

———. 1966. *The World Cities*. New York: McGraw-Hill.

Hall, Peter, M. Breheny, R. McQuaid, and D. Hart. 1987. *Western Sunrise*. London: Allen and Unwin.

Halliday, J. 1975. *A Political History of Japanese Capitalism*. New York: Pantheon Books.

Hamnett, C. 1984. "Gentrification and Residential Location Theory: A Review and Assessment." In D. Herbert and R. Johnston, eds., *Geography and the Urban Environment, Progress in Research and Application*. Chichester: Wiley.

Hamnett, C., L. McDowell, and P. Sarre. 1989. *The Changing Social Structure*. London: Sage.

Hamnett, C., and Bill Randolph. 1986. "Tenurial Transformation and the Flat Break-Up Market in London: The British Condo Experience." In Neil Smith and Peter Williams, eds., *Gentrification of the City.* London, Sydney, and Boston: Allen Unwin.

Haringey Women's Unemployment Project. 1984. *Survey of Women's Unemployment in Haringey.* London: Haringey Women's Unemployment Project.

Harris, Richard. 1988. "Home and Work in New York since 1950." Paper prepared for a meeting of the Dual City Working Group held in New York City, February 26–27. New York: Committee on New York City, Social Science Research Council.

Harrison, Bennett, and Barry Bluestone. 1988. *The Great U-Turn.* New York: Basic Books.

Hart, P. E., ed. 1986. *Unemployment and Labour Market Policies.* London: Gower.

Hartman, Chester. 1984. *The Transformation of San Francisco.* Totowa, N.J.: Rowman and Allanheld.

Hartmann, Heidi. 1981. "The Unhappy Marriage of Marxism and Feminism: Towards a More Progressive Union." In Lydia Sargent, ed., *Women and Revolution.* Boston: South End Press.

Harvey, David. 1973. *Social Justice and the City.* Baltimore, Md.: Johns Hopkins University Press.

———. 1985. *The Urbanization of Capital.* Oxford: Basil Blackwell.

Hattori, Kenjiro, Nobuji Sugimura, and Setsuo Higuchi. 1980. "Urbanization and Commercial Zones." In Association of Japanese Geographers, eds., *Geography of Japan.* Tokyo: Teikoku-Shoin, United Nations University.

Haussermann, Hartmut, and Walter Siebel. 1987. *Neue Urbanität.* Frankfurt: Suhrkamp Verlag.

Heller, Robert H. 1987. "Future Directions in the Financial Services Industry: International Markets." *World of Banking* 6(3): 18–21.

Henderson, Jeff. 1986. "The New International Division of Labour and American Semiconductor Production in South-East Asia." In D. Watts, C. Dixon, and D. Drakakis-Smith, eds., *Multinational Companies and the Third World.* London: Croom Helm.

Henderson, Jeff, and Manuel Castells, eds. 1987. *Global Restructuring and Territorial Development.* London: Sage.

Herbert, Sir E. 1960. *Report for the Royal Commission on Local Government in Greater London 1957–1960.* Cmnd. 1164 (HMSO).

Herman, Edward. 1982. *Corporate Control, Corporate Power.* New York: Cambridge University Press.

Hicks, D. A. 1983. "Urban and Economic Adjustment to the Postindustrial Era." In D. A. Hicks and N. J. Glickman, eds., *Transition to the 21st Century: Prospects and Policies for Economic and Urban-Regional Transformation.* Greenwich, Conn.: JAI Press.

Hill, Richard Child. 1987. "Global Factory and Company Town: The Changing Division of Labour in the International Automobile Industry." In J. Henderson and M. Castells, eds., *Global Restructuring and Territorial Development*. London: Sage.

Hill, T. P. 1977. "On Goods and Services." *Review of Income and Wealth* 23(4): 315–38.

Hino, Masateru. 1984. "The Location of Head and Branch Offices of Large Enterprises in Japan." *Science Reports of Tohoku University (Sendai, Japan), Geography Series* 34(2).

Hinojosa, R. A., and R. Morales. 1986. "International Restructuring and Labor Market Interdependence: The Automobile Industry in Mexico and the United States." Paper presented at the Conference on Labor Market Interdependence held at El Colegio de Méjico; Mexico, September 25–27.

Hirasawa, Sadaaki. 1988. "Role of Japanese Banks in the Internationalization Process." *Business Japan* 33(1): 37–39.

Hiroshi, Tanaka. 1987. "Foreign Workers and Their Rights." In *The Problem of Foreign Workers*. Report of Japan Ministry of Justice.

Hoffman, Dieter H. 1971. "German Banks as Financial Department Stores." *Federal Reserve Bank of St. Louis Review*. November: 8–13.

Holcomb, H. B., and R. A. Beauregard. 1981. *Revitalizing Cities*. Washington, D.C.: Association of American Geographers.

Holleman, Leon. 1982. "Japan's New Banking Laws." *Banker*, January, 37–39.

Hoover, Edgar M., and Raymond Vernon. 1962. *Anatomy of a Metropolis*. New York: Anchor.

Hoppe, John C., and Zachary Snow. 1974. "International Legal Practice—Restrictions on the Migrant Attorney." *Harvard International Law Journal* 15(2): 298–332.

Horvitz, Paul M. 1983. "Reorganization of the Federal Regulatory Agencies." *Journal of Bank Research* (Winter): 245–63.

Hoselitz, Bert. 1955. "Generative and Parasitic Cities." *Economic Development and Cultural Change* 3 (April): 278–94.

Howells, J., and A. E. Green. 1986. "Location, Technology and Industrial Organization in U.K. Services." *Progress in Planning* 26 (pt. 2): 85–185.

Hurstfield, Jennifer. 1978. *The Part-Time Trap*. Low Pay Pamphlet, no. 9. London: Low Pay Unit.

———. 1987. *Part-timers: Under Pressure*. London: Low Pay Unit.

Hymer, Stephen. 1971. "The Multinational Corporation and the Law of Uneven Development." In J. W. Bhagwati, ed., *Economics and World Order*. New York: Macmillan.

Ide, Sakuo, and Akio Takeuchi. 1980. "Jiba Sangyo: Localized Industry." In Association of Japanese Geographers, eds., *Geography of Japan*. Tokyo: Teikoku-Shoin, United Nations University.

IMF, *see* International Monetary Fund.

Inner London Education Authority. 1987a. *London Labour Market Trends—Facts and Figures*. London: Inner London Education Authority.

———. 1987b. *The London Labour Market: Facts and Figures*. London: Inner London Education Authority.

International Labor Office (ILO). 1981. *Employment of Multinational Enterprises in Developing Countries.* Geneva: ILO.

―――. 1985. *Women Workers in Multinational Enterprises in Developing Countries.*

International Monetary Fund (IMF). 1977. *Balance of Payments Manual.* 4th ed. Washington, D.C.: IMF.

―――. 1982. *Balance of Payments Statistics Yearbook.* Vol. 33, pt. 2.

―――. 1987a. *Direction of Trade Statistics, October 1987.*

―――. 1987b. *Balance of Payments Statistics Yearbook.* Vol. 38, pts. 1 and 2.

―――. 1988a. *World Economic Outlook,* April.

―――. 1988b. *International Financial Statistics* 41(8).

―――. 1988c. *Balance of Payments Statistics Yearbook.* Vol. 39, pt. 2.

―――. 1988d. *Balance of Payments Statistics Supplement.* Vol. 39, supplement.

―――. 1988e. *Direction of Trade Statistics Yearbook.*

―――. 1989. *Balance of Payments Statistics Yearbook.* Vol. 40, pts. 1 and 2.

―――. 1990. *International Financial Statistics* 43(2).

InterSec Research Corp. 1988. *Foreign Investment of Private Sector Pension Funds 1980–1990.* Stamford, Conn.: InterSec Research Corp.

Isard, Walter. 1956. *Location and Space-Economy: A General Theory Relating to Industrial Location, Market Areas, Land Use, Trade, and Urban Structure.* New York: Wiley.

Ishizuka, Hiromichi. 1980. "Methodological Introduction to the History of the City of Tokyo." Project on Technology Transfer, Transformation and Development: The Japanese Experience. HSDRJE-2/UNUP-85. Tokyo: Teikoku-Shoin, United Nations University.

Ishizuka, Hiromichi, and Yorifusa Ishida. 1988. *Tokyo: Urban Growth and Planning: 1968–1988.* Center for Urban Studies, Tokyo Metropolitan University.

Ito, Tatsuo, and Masafumi Tanifuji. 1982. "The Role of Small and Intermediate Cities in National Development in Japan." In O. P. Mathur, ed., *Small Cities and National Development.* Nagoya: UNCRD.

Iyotani, Toshio. 1989. "The New Immigrant Workers in Tokyo." Typescript. Tokyo University of Foreign Studies.

Jacobson, Louis S. 1978. "Earning Losses of Workers Displaced from Manufacturing Industries." In W. G. DeWald, ed., *The Impact of International Trade and Investment on Unemployment.* Washington, D.C.: GPO.

Japan Daily Labor Union Meeting Report. 1988. *The Solutions to Foreign Labor Problem.* May 30. Tokyo: Japan Daily Labor Union.

Japan Development Bank. 1988. *Growing Foreign Investors' Activities and the Future of Internationalization.* Tokyo: The Japan Development Bank.

Japan Economic Planning Agency. 1987. *Economic Survey of Japan, 1986–1987.* Tokyo: Economic Planning Agency. *See* Economic Planning Agency, Government of Japan.

―――. 1988. *Annual Report on the National Life for Fiscal 1987.*

―――. 1989. *Annual Report on the National Life for Fiscal 1988.*

Japan External Trade Organization (JETRO), *see* JETRO.

Japan Management and Coordination Agency. 1982. *1980 Population Census of Japan*. Tokyo: Management and Coordination Agency Statistics Bureau.

———. 1986. *Japan Statistical Yearbook*. Tokyo: Management and Coordination Agency Statistics Bureau.

———. 1987a. *Labor Force Survey*. Tokyo: Management and Coordination Agency Statistics Bureau.

———. 1987b. "Japanese Statistics, 1986." In *Facts and Figures of Japan*. Japan: Foreign Press Center. P. 12.

———. 1988. *Japan Statistical Yearbook*. Tokyo: Management and Coordination Agency Statistics Bureau.

Japan Ministry of Construction. 1987. *1987 Tokyo's Average Land Price Listings*, September 30: 1–6. Tokyo: Ministry of Construction.

———. 1988a. *1987: Direct Investments to Foreign Markets and Domestic Market*, May 31.

———. 1988b. *The Situation of Increasing Unskilled, Illegal Aliens*.

———. 1988c. *White Paper on Construction*.

———. 1988d. *A Report to Prevent Illegal Aliens Getting a Job in Construction Firms*. Report, November 10. Tokyo: Ministry of Construction.

Japan Ministry of Foreign Affairs. 1986. *Kaigai zairyu hojinsu chosa tokei* (Survey of Japanese living overseas). Tokyo: Ministry of Foreign Affairs.

———. 1987. *Statistical Survey of Japan's Economy*.

———. 1988. *Statistics on Japan*.

———. Various years. *Foreign Trade Statistics*.

Japan Ministry of Justice. Immigration Office. 1985. *Annual Report on Entries and Departures*. Tokyo: Ministry of Justice.

Japan Ministry of Labor. 1984. *Monthly Labour Statistics and Research Bulletin*. Tokyo: Ministry of Labor.

———. 1986a. *Rodo hakusho* (White Paper on Labor). Tokyo: Ministry of Labor.

———. 1986b. *Rodo tokei yoran* (Labor statistics manual).

———. 1987. *Monthly Labour Statistics and Research Bulletin*.

———. 1988. *Rodo hakusho* (White Paper on Labor).

———. 1989. *Labor Conditions of Women 1988*.

Japan National Land Agency. 1985. Capital Restructuring Plan. Tokyo: National Land Agency.

———. 1986. *"Price Index Report": Average Price Index of Residential Land Prices In Prefectural Cities*.

Japan Office of the Prime Minister. 1987. *New National Plan of Action Towards the Year 2000*. Tokyo: Headquarters for the Planning and Promoting of Policies Relating to Women, May.

Japan Statistical Yearbook. *See* Japan Management and Coordination Agency.

Japan Tariff Association. Various years. *Summary Report, Trade of Japan*. Tokyo: Japan Tariff Association.

Jessen, Johann et al. 1987. "The Informal Work of Industrial Workers." Paper presented at the 6th Urban Change and Conflict Conference held at University of Kent at Canterbury, United Kingdom, September 20–23.

JETRO (Japan External Trade Organization). 1981. *Japan Manufacturing Operations in the United States.* Tokyo: JETRO.

―――. 1987a. *The World and Japanese Direct Foreign Investment 1986.* Tokyo: JETRO.

―――. 1987b. *Japan's Overseas Investment Entering a New Phase with the Yen's Appreciation.* White Paper on World and Japanese Overseas Direct Investment.

―――. 1989. *New Phase in Foreign Direct Investments and Strategic Alliances.* White Paper on World Direct Investments.

Johnson, Chalmers. 1982. *MITI and the Japanese Miracle: The Growth of Industrial Policy, 1925–1975.* Stanford, Calif.: Stanford University Press.

Johnson, Manuel H. 1987. "The Yen-Dollar Relationship: A Recent Historical Perspective." In H. Patrick and R. Tachi, eds., *Japan and the United States Today: Exchange Rates, Macroeconomic Policies, and Financial Market Innovations.* New York: Columbia University Press.

Jones, E. 1981. *Accountancy and the British Economy 1840–1980: The Evolution of Ernst and Whitney.* London: Batsford.

Jones, Randall S. 1985. *Japan's High Savings Rate: An Overview.* Report no. 46A. Washington, D.C.: Japan Economic Institute.

Jones, T. 1982. "Small Business Development and the Asian Community in Britain." *New Community* 9(3): 467–77.

Judd, D. R., and M. Parkinson. 1989. "Urban Revitalization in America and the U.K.: The Politics of Uneven Development." In M. Parkinson, Foley, and D. R. Judd, eds., *Regenerating the Cities: The U.K. Crisis and the U.S. Experience.* Glenview, Ill.: Scott, Foresman.

Kakabadse, Mario A. 1987. "International Trade in Services: Prospects for Liberalization in the 1990s." In *Atlantic Paper*, no. 64. The Atlantic Institute for International Affairs. London, New York, and Sydney: Croom Helm.

Kakumoto, Ryohei. 1978. "Metropolis and Megalopolis—A General Survey of the Tokaido Region from the Standpoint of Transportation." *Waiseda Business and Economic Studies* 14:65–98.

Kaldor, Nicholas. 1966. *Causes of the Slow Rate of Economic Growth of the United Kingdom.* Cambridge: Cambridge University Press.

Kane, Edward J. 1987. "Competitive Financial Regulation: An International Perspective." In R. Portes and A. Swoboda, eds., *Threats to International Financial Stability.* Cambridge: Cambridge University Press.

Kantor, P., and D. Stephen. 1988. *The Dependent City: The Changing Political Economy of Urban America.* Chicago: Scott Foresman.

Kasarda, J. D. 1985. "Urban Change and Minority Opportunities." In P. Peterson, ed., *The New Urban Reality.* Washington D.C.: Brookings Institution.

―――. 1988. "Economic Restructuring and America's Urban Dilemma." In *The Metropolitan Era*, vol. 1, *A World of Giant Cities*, M. Dogan and J. D. Kasarda, eds., Newbury Park, Calif.: Sage.

Katouzian, Homa. 1970. "The Development of the Service Sector: A New Approach." *Oxford Economic Papers* 22:362–82.

Keeble, D. E., P. L. Owens, and C. Thompson. 1982. *Centrality, Peripherality and EEC Regional Development*. London: HMSO.

Kennedy, H. Patrick. 1982. "The Role of Foreign Banks in a Changing U.S. Banking System." *Banker* (February): 101–03.

Kenney, Martin, and Richard Florida. 1988. "Beyond Mass Production: Production and Labor Process in Japan." *Politics and Society* 16(1): 121–58.

Khoury, Srakis J. 1980. *Dynamics of International Banking*. New York: Praeger.

Kimijima, T. 1980. "Inner-City Problems of Kawasaki City." *Jutaku: A Monthly of Housing* 29(7): 55–61. Tokyo: Japan Housing Association.

Kindleberger, C. P. 1974. "The Formation of Financial Centers: A Study in Comparative Economic History." In *Princeton Studies in International Finance*, no. 36.

King, A. 1986. "Margins, Peripheries and Divisions of Labor: U.K. Urbanism and the World Economy." In Dennis Hardy, ed., *On the Margins: Marginal Space and Marginal Economies*. Middlesex Polytechnic Geography and Planning Paper no. 17.

Kobayashi, Noritake. 1981. "The Present and Future of Japanese Multi-National Enterprises: A Comparative Analysis of the Japanese and U.S.–European Multi-National Management." *Wheel Extended* 9(3): 10–18.

Komori, S. 1983. "Inner City in Japanese Context." *City Planning Review* 125:11–17.

Krieger, Joel. 1986. *Reagan, Thatcher and the Politics of Decline*. New York: Oxford University Press.

Krueger, R. C. 1988. "U.S. International Transactions, First Quarter 1988." *Survey of Current Business* 68(6): 28–69.

Krugman, Paul. 1986. "Is the Strong Dollar Sustainable?." Working Paper no. 1644. Washington, D.C.: National Bureau of Economic Research.

KUPI. 1981. *Policy for Revitalization of Inner City*. Kobe: Kobe Urban Problems Institute.

Lash, Scott, and John Urry. 1987. *The End of Organized Capitalism*. Cambridge: Polity Press.

Law, C. M. 1988. *The Uncertain Future of the Urban Core*. London: Routledge.

Lawrence, Robert Z. 1984. "Sectoral Shifts and the Size of the Middle Class." *Brookings Review* 3(1): 3–11.

Leborgne, D., and A. Lipietz. 1988. "L'après-fordisme et son espace." *Les Temps Modernes* 43(601): 75–114.

Lee, C. H. 1984. "The Service Sector, Regional Specialization, and Economic Growth in the Victorian Economy." *Journal of Historical Geography* 10:139–56.

Lee, Chung H., and Seiji Naya, eds. 1988. *Trade and Investment in Services in the Asia-Pacific Region*. Center for International Studies, Inha University, Korea.

Lee, F. 1981. "Ethnic Minority and Small Firms: Problems Faced by Black Firms—Lambeth Case Study." In *Planning Studies*, no. 14. London: Polytechnic of Central London.

Leipert, Christian. 1985. "Social Costs of Economic Growth as a Growth Stimu-
    lus." Paper presented at the Conference for a New Economics, The Other Eco-
    nomic Summit, held at Bedford College, London, April 16–19.
Leontieff, W., and F. Duchin. 1985. *The Future Impact of Automation on Work-
    ers*. New York: Oxford University Press.
Leopold, Ellen. 1987. *Inequality at Work in London's Small Firms*. London:
    London Strategic Policy Unit.
Levich, M. 1988. "Financial Innovations in International Financial Markets." In
    M. Feldstein, ed., *United States in the World Economy*. Chicago: University
    of Chicago Press.
Levitt, Theodore. 1976. "The Industrialization of Services." *Harvard Business
    Review* 54:63–74.
Levy, Frank. 1987. *Dollars and Dreams: The Changing American Income Distri-
    bution*. New York: Russell Sage Foundation.
Ley, D. 1986. "Alternative Explanations for Inner-City Gentrification. A Cana-
    dian Assessment." *Annals of the Association of American Geographers* 76(4):
    521–35.
Leyson, Andrew, Peter Daniels, and Nigel Thrift. 1987. "Large Accountancy
    Firms in the U.K.: Spatial Development." Working Paper, St. David's Univer-
    sity College, Lampter, U.K., and University of Liverpool.
Light, Ivan. 1972. *Ethnic Enterprises in America*. Berkeley: University of Cali-
    fornia Press.
———. 1979. "Disadvantaged Minorities in Self-Employment." *International
    Journal of Comparative Sociology* 20:31–45.
———. 1983. *Cities in World Perspective*. New York: Macmillan.
Light, Ivan, and Edna Bonacich. 1988. *Immigrant Entrepreneurs: Koreans in Los
    Angeles 1965–1982*. Berkeley: University of California Press.
Lipietz, Alain. 1986. "New Tendencies in the International Division of Labor:
    Regimes of Accumulation and Modes of Regulation." In Allen Scott and Mi-
    chael Storper, eds., *Production, Work, Territory*. Boston: Allen and Unwin.
———. 1987. *Mirages and Miracles: The Crises of Global Fordism*. London:
    Verso.
Logan, John. 1978. "Growth, Politics, and the Stratification of Places." *American
    Journal of Sociology* 84(2): 404–15.
Logan, J. R., and M. Molotch. 1987. *Urban Fortunes: Making Place in the City*,
    Berkeley: University of California Press.
Logan, J. R., and P. Taylor-Gooby. n.d. "New Patterns of Inequality in London
    and New York." In S. Fainstein, I. Gordon, and M. Harloe, eds., *Divided Cit-
    ies: Economic Restructuring and Social Change in London and New York*. Lon-
    don: Basil Blackwell. Forthcoming.
Lomnitz, Larissa. 1978. "Mechanisms of Articulation between Shantytown Set-
    tlers and the Urban System." *Urban Anthropology* 7:185–205.
London Research Centre. 1988. *Annual Abstract of Greater London Statistics,
    1986–1987*. Vol. 19. London: London Research Centre.
London Strategic Policy Unit. 1986. *Black Workers*. The London Labour Plan.
Losch, August. 1965. "The Nature of Economic Regions." In J. Friedmann and

W. Alonso, eds., *Regional Development and Planning*. Cambridge, Mass.: MIT Press.

Low Pay Unit. 1987. *Cheap Labour: Britain's False Economy*. Prepared by Peter Brosnan and Frank Wilkinson. London: Low Pay Unit.

———. 1988a. "Poverty: Is the Government Being 'Statistical with the Truth'?" *Low Pay Review* 34 (Summer): 8–13.

———. 1988b. *The Great Pay Robbery*. Prepared by Chris Pond. London: Low Pay Unit.

Machlup, F. 1962. *The Production and Distribution of Knowledge in the United States*. Princeton, N.J.: Princeton University Press.

Marcuse, Peter. 1986. "Abandonment, Gentrification, and Displacement: The Linkages in New York City." In Neil Smith and Peter Williams, eds., *Gentrification of the City*. Boston: Allen and Unwin.

Markusen, A. 1981. "City Spatial Structure, Women's Household Work, and National Urban Policy." In C. Stimpson, E. Dexler, M. J. Nelson, and K. B. Yatrakis, eds., *Women and the American City*. Chicago: University of Chicago Press.

———. 1985. *Profit Cycles, Oligopoly, and Regional Development*. Cambridge, Mass.: MIT Press.

Marquand, J. 1979. *The Service Sector and Regional Policy in the United Kingdom*. Research Series no. 29. London: Centre for Environmental Studies.

Marshall, J. N. 1979. "Corporate Organisation and Regional Office Employment." *Environment and Planning A* 11:553–64.

———. 1982. "Linkages between Manufacturing and Business Services." *Environment and Planning A*. 14:1523–40.

———. 1983. "Business Service Activities in British Provincial Conurbations." *Environment and Planning* 15:1343–59.

Marshall, J. N. et al. 1986. *Uneven Development in the Service Economy: Understanding the Location and Role of Producer Services*. Report of the Producer Services Working Party, Institute of British Geographers and the ESRC, August.

Martin, J. E. 1966. *Greater London: An Industrial Geography*. London: G. Bell and Sons.

Martin, R. 1988. "Industrial Capitalism in Transition: The Contemporary Reorganization of the British Space Economy." In D. Massey and J. Allen, eds., *Uneven Re-Development: Cities and Regions in Transition*. London: Hodder and Stoughton.

Massey, Doreen. 1984. *Spatial Divisions of Labour: Social Structures and the Geography of Production*. London: Macmillan.

Mastropasqua, Salvatore. 1978. *The Banking System in the Countries of the EEC: Institutional and Structural Aspects*. Germantown, Md.: Sijthoff and Noordhoff.

Mayer, H. 1969. "Making a Living in Cities: The Urban Economic Base." *Journal of Geography* 18(2): 70–87.

Michigan State, City of Detroit. 1983. *Annual Overall Economic Development Program Report and Program Projection*. Detroit: Planning Department.

Miles, I. 1985. *The Service Economy and Socioeconomic Development.* Paper prepared for UNCTAD Science Policy Research Unit, University of Sussex.

Mineo, Imai. 1988. "Foreign Employment I: Special Report, No More 'Pure-Blood Principle,' the Age of Internal Internationalism." *Toyo Keizai Weekly Magazine*, March 12, 5–10.

MITI (Japan Ministry of International Trade and Industry). 1974. *Foreign Trade of Japan, 1974.* Tokyo: MITI.

———. 1985a. *Statistics on Japanese Industries, 1985.*

———. 1985b. *White Paper on Economic Cooperation, 1985.*

———. 1985c. *White Paper on International Trade, 1985.*

———. 1986. *White Paper on International Trade, 1986.*

———. 1987. *White Paper on Small and Medium Enterprises in Japan, 1987.*

Mitter, S. 1986. "Industrial Restructuring and Manufacturing Homework: Immigrant Women in the U.K. Clothing Industry." *Capital and Class*, no. 27: 37–80.

Miyakawa, Yasuo. 1983. "Metamorphosis of the Capital and Evolution of the Urban System in Japan." *Ekistics* 50:110–22.

Miyamoto, Ken'ichi, Yokota Shigeru, Nakamure Kojiro, 1990. *The Regional Economy.* Tokyo: Yichikaku.

Miyazaki, Isamu et al. 1987. *Opinions on Japan's Economic Restructuring.* Reference Reading Series 18. Tokyo: Foreign Press Center.

Mollenkopf, John. 1984. *The Corporate Legal Services Industry.* A Report to New York City's Office of Economic Development.

Mollenkopf, John, and Manuel Castells, eds. n.d. *Dual City: The Restructuring of New York.* New York: Russell Sage Foundation. Forthcoming.

Moody's Investors Service. 1984. *Moody's Bank and Finance Manual.* New York: Moody's Investors Service.

Morales, Rebecca. 1983. "Immigrant Workers in the Auto Industry." Typescript. School of Architecture and Urban Planning, University of California, Los Angeles.

Morgan Guarantee Trust. Various years. *World Financial Markets*, various issues. New York: Morgan Guarantee Trust.

Morgan Stanley. 1987. *Morgan Stanley Capital International Perspectives*, October. New York: Morgan Stanley.

———. 1988a. *Morgan Stanley Capital International Perspectives*, January.

———. 1988b. *Morgan Stanley Capital International Perspectives*, October.

———. 1990. *Morgan Stanley Capital International Perspectives*, January.

Moss, Mitchell L. 1986. "Telecommunications and the Future of Cities." *Land Development Studies* 3:33–34.

———. 1988. "Telecommunications and International Financial Centers." *Information and Behavior* 3:239–52.

Moss, Mitchell L., and A. Dunau. 1986. "Office, Information Technology, and Locational Trends." In R. Lipper, A. Sugarman, and R. Cushman, eds., *Teleports and the Intelligent City.* New York: Dow-Jones-Irwin.

Multinational Monitor. 1983. *Focus: Women and Multinationals.* Special issue of *Multinational Monitor* 4(8) (August 1983).

Murakami, Yasuske, and Yukata Kosai, eds. 1986. *Japan in the Global Community: Its Role and Contribution on the Eve of the 21st Century*. Tokyo: University of Tokyo Press.

Murata, Kiyoji. 1980. *An Industrial Geography of Japan*. New York: St. Martin's Press.

————. 1988. *Tokyo no Sangyokozo no Henbo* (Industry Restructuring in Tokyo). Typescript, Chuo University.

Nakabayashi, Itsuki. 1987. "Social-Economic and Living Conditions of Tokyo's Inner City." Reprinted from *Geographical Reports of Tokyo Metropolitan University*, no. 22.

Nakamura, Hachiro. 1985. *Development of Chonaikai in Prewar Days of Tokyo*. Special issue of *Tsukuba Journal of Sociology* 9 (1 and 2). English reprint available from University of Tsukuba, Tsukuba, Japan.

————. 1986. *Tokyo in the Last Few Decades*, Special issue of *Tsukuba Journal of Sociology* 10. English reprint available from University of Tsukuba, Tsukuba, Japan.

————. 1988. *Urban Growth in Prewar Days of Modern Japan*. Special issue of *Tsukuba Journal of Sociology* 13. English reprint available from University of Tsukuba, Tsukuba, Japan.

Nariai, Osamu. 1988. *Progress of Japan's Economic Restructuring and Future Taxes*. Reference Reading Series no. 20. Tokyo: Foreign Press Center, Japan.

Narita, K. 1980. "Inner-City Problems in European and American Cities." *Jutaku: A Monthly of Housing* 29(7): 21–27. Tokyo: Japan Housing Association.

Nash, June, and M. P. Fernandez-Kelly, eds. 1983. *Women, Men and the International Division of Labor*. New York: State University of New York Press.

National Economic Development Office, *see* NEDO.

Nederlandse Bank. 1988. *Survey of Current Business*. Quarterly statistics. Amsterdam: Nederland.

NEDO (National Economic Development Office). 1985. *Employment Perspectives and the Distributive Trades*. London: NEDO.

Nelson, Daniel. 1975. *Managers and Workers: Origins of the New Factory System in the United States, 1880–1920*. Madison: University of Wisconsin Press.

Nelson, Joel I., and Jon Lorence. 1985. "Employment in Service Activities and Inequality in Metropolitan Areas." *Urban Affairs Quarterly* 21(11): 106–25.

Nelson, Kristin. 1984. *Back Office and Female Labor Markets: Office Suburbanization in the San Francisco Bay Area*. Ph.D. diss., University of California, Berkeley.

Netzer, Dick. 1974. "The Cloudy Prospects for the City's Economy." *New York Affairs* 1(4): 22–35.

Newman, K. 1988. *Falling from Grace*. Glencoe, Ill.: Free Press.

Newsam, P. 1986. *Annual Report of the Commission for Racial Equality, 1985*. London: Commission for Racial Equality.

New York State Department of Labor. 1982a. *Report to the Governor and the Legislature on the Garment Manufacturing Industry and Industrial Homework*. Albany.

————. 1982b. *Study of State-Federal Employment Standards for Industrial Homework in New York City.*

————. 1986. *Occupational Employment in Finance, Insurance and Real Estate, New York State.*

————. 1989. *Occupational Needs, 1988–1990, New York City.* New York: Division of Research and Statistics.

————. Various years. *Employment Review.*

New York State Department of Taxation and Finance. 1986. *The Task Force on the Underground Economy: Preliminary Report.* Albany.

New York State Office of Management and Budget and Office of Economic Development. 1982. *Report on Economic Conditions in New York City: July–December 1981.* Albany: Office of Management and Budget and Office of Economic Development.

————. 1986. *Report on Economic Conditions in New York City: January–April 1986.*

————. 1989. *Report on Economic Conditions in New York City: July–December 1988.*

Nomura Sogo Kenkyujo. 1982. *Bunsankei kezai shakai o mezashita kotsu. Tsushintai ni kansuru chosa II—kokusai kotsu yuso kiban no seiritsu joken kiso chosa.* (Investigation of the Transport and Communication Structure with the Emphasis on a Dispersion Model of Economic Society—Fundamental Research into the Conditions for Establishing an International Base in Transport and Communications). Tokyo: Nomura Sogo Kenkyujo.

Noyelle, Thierry. 1984. *The Coming of Age of Management Consulting: Implications for New York City.* Report to New York City's Office of Economic Development.

————. 1986. *New York City and the Emergence of Global Financial Markets.* Report to the Regional Plan Association, New York, November.

Noyelle, Thierry, and A. B. Dutka. 1988. *International Trade in Business Services: Accounting, Advertising, Law and Management Consulting.* Cambridge, Mass.: Ballinger Publishing.

Noyelle, Thierry, and T. M. Stanback. 1985. *The Economic Transformation of American Cities.* Totowa, N.J.: Rowman and Allanheld.

Nusbaumer, Jacques, ed. 1987. *Services in the Global Market.* Boston, Dordrecht, and Lancaster: Kluwer Academic Publishers.

O'Connor, David C. 1983. "Changing Patterns of International Production in the Semiconductor Industry: The Role of Transnational Corporations." Mimeo.

Odaka, Konosuke. 1985. "Is the Division of Labor Limited by the Extent of the Market? A Study of Automobile Parts Production in East and Southeast Asia." In K. Ohkawa and G. Ranis, eds., *Japan and the Developing Countries: A Comparative Analysis.* London: Basil Blackwell.

OECD, *see* Organization for Economic Cooperation and Development.

Office of the U.S. Trade Representative. *See* United States Department of Commerce, Office of the U.S. Trade Representative.

Ogilvie, Nigel. 1980. "Foreign Banks in the U.S. and Geographic Restrictions on Banking." *Journal of Bank Research*, Summer: 72–79.

Okimura, T. 1980. "Inner Area Problems and Housing." *Jutaku: A Monthly of Housing* 29(7): 13–20. Tokyo: Japan Housing Association.

Olson, Margrethe H. 1983. *Overview of Work-at-Home Trends in the United States*. New York: New York University Graduate School of Business Administration.

Organization for Economic Cooperation and Development (OECD). 1978. *Investing in Developing Countries*. Paris: OECD.

———. 1981. *International Investment and Multinational Enterprises: Recent International Direct Investment Trends*.

———. 1983. *OECD Employment Outlook*.

———. 1985. *OECD Employment Outlook*.

———. 1986a. *Main Economic Indicators, September 1986*. Department of Economics and Statistics.

———. 1986b. *Urban Policies in Japan*.

———. 1988a. *Financial Market Trends*, no. 40 (May).

———. 1988b. *Financial Statistics Monthly: International Markets*, April.

———. 1989a. *Financial Market Trends*, no. 43 (May).

———. 1989b. *Financial Statistics Monthly: International Markets*, June.

———. Various years a. *Economic Outlook*, various issues.

———. Various years b. *Monthly Statistics of Foreign Trade*, various issues.

———. Various years c. *Recent International Direct Investment Trends*, various issues.

———. Various years d. *Statistics on Foreign Trade*.

Oriental Economist. 1983. *Japan Economic Yearbook, 1981–1982*.

Osaka Municipal Government. 1987. *Brief Sketch of Osaka*. Osaka, Japan.

———. 1988. *Economic Profile of Osaka City*.

Pahl, R. 1984. *Divisions of Labor*. London: Oxford University Press.

———. 1988. "Some Remarks on Informal Work, Social Polarization and the Social Structure." *International Journal of Urban and Regional Research* 12(2): 247–67.

Parker, A. J. 1975. "Hypermarkets: The Changing Pattern of Retailing." *Geography* 60:120–24.

Patrick, Hugh T., and Ryuichiro Tachi, eds. 1987. *Japan and the United States Today: Exchange Rates, Macroeconomic Policies, and Financial Market Innovations*. New York: Columbia University Press.

Pigott, Charles. 1983. "Financial Report on Japan." *Economic Review* (Federal Reserve Bank of San Francisco), Winter: 25–45.

Piore, M., and C. F. Sabel. 1984. *The Second Industrial Divide: Possibilities for Prosperity*. New York: Basic Books.

Policy Studies Institute. 1984. *Black and White Britain*. London: Policy Studies Institute.

Pollert, Anna. 1988. "The 'Flexible Firm': Fixation or Fact?" *Work, Employment and Society* 2(3): 281–316.

Pond, Chris. 1988. *The Great Pay Robbery*. London: Low Pay Unit.

Porat, Marc U. 1976. *The Information Economy*. Ph.D. diss., Stanford University. 2 vol.

Porter, Richard D., Thomas D. Simpson, and Eileen Mauskopf. 1979. "Financial Innovation and the Monetary Aggregates." In *Brooking Papers on Economic Activity*, 213–29.

Portes, Alejandro. 1983."The Informal Sector: Definition, Controversy, and Relation to National Development." *Review* 7 (Summer): 151–74.

Portes, Alejandro, Manual Castells, and Lauren Benton, eds. 1989. *The Informal Economy: Studies in Advanced and Less Developed Countries*. Baltimore: Johns Hopkins University Press.

Portes, Alejandro, and John Walton. 1981. *Labor, Class and the International System*. New York: Academic Press.

Porzecanski, Arturo C. 1981. "The International Financial Role of U.S. Commercial Banks: Past and Future." *Journal of Banking and Finance* 5 (December): 5–16.

Pred, A. R. 1976. "The Interurban Transmission of Growth in Advanced Economies: Empirical Findings versus Regional Planning Assumptions." *Regional Studies* 10:151–71.

———. 1977. *City Systems in Advanced Economies*. London: Hutchinson.

Pred, A. R., and P. J. Coppock. 1978. *The United Kingdom Economy*. London: Weidenfeld and Nicholson.

Preteceille, E. 1986. "Collective Consumption, Urban Segregation, and Social Classes." *Environment and Planning D: Society and Space* 4:145–54.

Quinn, James Brian. 1987. "The Impacts of Technology in the Service Sector." In B. R. Guile and Harvey Brooks, eds., *Technology and Global Industry: Companies and Nations in the Third World Economy*. Washington D.C.: National Academy Press.

Regional Plan Association of New York. 1987. *New York in the Global Economy: Studying the Facts and the Issues*. Research Document. New York: Regional Plan Association.

Renooy, P. H. 1984. *Twilight Economy: A Survey of the Informal Economy in the Netherlands*. Research Report, Faculty of Economic Sciences, University of Amsterdam.

Revell, Jack. 1973. *The British Financial System*. London: Macmillan.

Riddle, Dorothy L. 1985. "Stimulating Economic Development via the Service Sector." Paper prepared for meeting on Services and Development held at UNCTAD, Geneva, December 2–4.

Rimmer, P. J. 1986. "Japan's World Cities: Tokyo, Osaka, Nagoya or Tokaido Megalopolis?" *Development and Change* 17(1): 121–58.

———. 1988. "Japanese Construction Contractors and the Australian States: Another Round of Interstate Rivalry." *International Journal of Urban and Regional Research* 12(3): 404–24.

Rimmer, P. J., and J. A. Black. 1982. "Land Use–Transport Changes and Global Restructuring in Sydney since the 1970s: The Container Issue." In R. V. Cardew, J. V. Langdale, and D. C. Rich, eds., *Why Cities Change: Urban Development and Economic Change in Sydney*. Sydney: Allen and Unwin.

Roberts, Bryan, Ruth Finnegan, and Duncan Gallie, eds. 1985. *New Approaches to Economic Life/Economic Restructuring: Unemployment and the Social Division of Labor*. Manchester: Manchester University Press.

Roberts, Sam. 1987. "If Companies Move to Suburbs, It Still Hurts." *New York Times*, May 28, B1.

Rodriguez, Nestor P., and J. R. Feagin. 1986. "Urban Specialization in the World System." *Urban Affairs Quarterly* 22(2): 187–220.

Rose, D. 1984. "Rethinking Gentrification: Beyond the Uneven Development of Marxist Theory." *Environment and Planning D: Society and Space* 2(1): 47–74.

Rosenberg, Terry J. 1989. "Poverty in New York City, 1985–1988: The Crisis Continues." Working Paper prepared by the Community Service Society of New York.

Rossi, Frank A. 1986. "Government Impediments to Trade in Accounting Services." *University of Chicago Legal Forum* 1(1): 135–68.

Ryu, Ohtomo. 1988. "Foreign Employment III: 'Modern Paradise': Japan for the Third World Countries; Report on Illegal Aliens." *Toyo Keizai Weekly Magazine*, March 12, 15–17.

Safa, Helen I. 1981. "Runaway Shops and Female Employment: The Search for Cheap Labor." *Signs* 7 (Winter): 418–33.

Sakiyama, K. 1981. "Urbanization and Urban Problems: On the Decline of Metropolis." In K. Sakiyama and K. Yoshioka, eds., *Decline and Redevelopment of Metropolis*. Tokyo: Tokyo University Press.

Salomon Brothers, Inc. Various years. *Prospects for Financial Markets*. U.S. ed. Bond market research.

Sapir, Andre, and Ernst Lutz. 1981. "Trade in Services: Economic Determinants and Development Related Issues." World Bank Staff Working Paper, no. 480.

Sassen, Saskia. 1988. *The Mobility of Labor and Capital: A Study in International Investment and Labor Flow*. London: Cambridge University Press.

———. 1990. "The Interdependence of Cities." In *The Committee on Urban Studies Report for 1989*. Report prepared for the UNESCO Committee on Urban Studies. Submitted to UNESCO, Paris.

Sassen-Koob, Saskia. 1980. "Immigrants and Minority Workers in the Organization of the Labor Process." *Journal of Ethnic Studies* 8 (Spring): 1–34.

———. 1982. "Recomposition and Peripheralization at the Core." In M. Dixon, S. Jonas, and D. McCaughey, eds., *The New Nomads: Immigration and the New International Division of Labor*. San Francisco: Synthesis Publications.

———. 1984. "The New Labor Demand in Global Cities." In M. P. Smith, ed., *Cities in Transformation*, 139–71. Beverly Hills, Calif.: Sage.

———. 1986. "New York City: Economic Restructuring and Immigration." *Development and Change* 17:85–119.

———. 1989. "New York City's Informal Economy." In A. Portes et al., eds., *The Informal Economy: Studies in Advanced and Less Developed Countries*. Baltimore: Johns Hopkins University Press.

Sassen-Koob, Saskia, and Catherine Benamou. 1985. "Hispanic Women in the Garment and Electronics Industries in the New York Metropolitan Area." Research progress report prepared for the Revson Foundation, New York.

Sassen-Koob, Saskia, and W. Grover. 1986. "Unregistered Work in the New York Metropolitan Area." Working Paper, Columbia University, Program in Urban Planning.

Sauvant, Karl. 1986. *International Trade in Services: The Politics of Transborder Data Flows.* Boulder, Colo., and London: Westview Press.

Sauvant, Karl, and Zbigniew Zimny. 1985. "FDI and TNCs in Services." *CTC Reporter*, no. 2: 24–28.

Savage, Mike, Peter Dinkins, and Tony Fielding. 1988. "Some Social and Political Implications of the Contemporary Fragmentation of the 'Service Class' in Britain." *International Journal of Urban and Regional Research* 12(3): 455–76.

Savitch, H. 1987. "Post-Industrial Planning in New York, Paris, London." *Journal of the American Planning Association* 53(1): 80–144.

———. 1988. *Post-Industrial Cities.* Princeton, N.J.: Princeton University Press.

Sazanami, Yoko. 1988. "Japan's Trade and Investment in Finance, Information, Communications, and Business Services." In C. H. Lee and S. Naya, eds., *Trade and Investment in Services in the Asia-Pacific Region.* Center for International Studies, Inha University, South Korea.

Scherer, F. M. 1980. *Industrial Market Structure and Economic Performance.* Chicago: Rand MacNally.

Schoenberger, Erica. 1985. "Foreign Manufacturing Investment in the United States: Competitive Strategies and International Location." *Economic Geography* 61(3): 241–59.

Schoer, K. 1987. "Part-Time Employment: Britain and West Germany." *Cambridge Journal of Economics* 11(1): 83–94.

Schwartz, Robert 1988. *Equity Markets.* New York: Harper and Row.

Scott, Allen J. 1986. "Industrialization and Urbanization: A Geographical Agenda." *Annual of the Association of American Geographers* 76:25–37.

———. 1988. *Metropolis. From the Division of Labor to Urban Form.* Berkeley: University of California Press.

Scott, Allen J., and Michael Storper, eds. 1986. *Production, Work, Territory.* Boston: Allen and Unwin.

Sekio, Sugioka. 1987. *Internationalization and Regional Structure.* Chiba, Japan: Chiba University.

Shah, S. 1975. *Immigrants and Employment in the Clothing Industry—the Rag Trade In London's East End.* London: Runnymede Trust.

Shaiken, Harley. 1985. *Work Transformed: Automation and Labor in the Computer Age.* New York: Holt, Rinehart and Winston.

Shapira, Philip. 1984. "The Crumbling of Smokestack California: A Case Study in Industrial Restructuring and the Reorganization of Work." Institute of Urban and Regional Development Working Paper, no. 437. Berkeley, Calif.

Shapira, Philip, and Plant Closure Project. 1983. *Shutdowns and Job Losses in California: The Need for New National Priorities.* Testimony prepared for the Subcommittee on Labor Management Relations, Subcommittee on Employment Opportunities, U.S. House of Representatives, Hearing on H.R. 2847, Los Angeles, Calif., July 8.

Sheard, P. 1982. "Auto-Production Systems in Japan: Some Organisational and Locational Features." *Australian Geographical Studies* 21:49–68.

Sheets, R. G., S. Nord, and J. J. Phelps. 1987. *The Impact of Service Industries on Underemployment in Metropolitan Economies*. Lexington, Mass.: D. C. Heath and Company.

Shelp, Ronald Kent. 1981. *Beyond Industrialization: Ascendancy of the Global Service Economy*. New York: Praeger.

Shibata, Tokue. 1988. "The Post-War Japanese Economy and Its Infrastructure." Typescript. Tokyo Keizai University.

Silber, William. 1983. "The Process of Financial Innovation." *American Economic Review* 73(2): 89–95.

Singelmann, J. 1974. "The Sectoral Transformation of the Labor Force in Seven Industrialized Countries, 1920–1960." Ph.D. diss., University of Texas.

———. 1978. *From Agriculture to Services: The Transformation of Industrial Employment*. Beverly Hills and London: Sage.

Singelmann, J., and H. L. Browning. 1980. "Industrial Transformation and Occupational Change in the U.S., 1960–70." *Social Forces* 59: 246–64.

Sinkey, Joseph F. 1979. *Problem and Failed Institutions in the Commercial Bank Industry*. Vol. 4 of *Contemporary Studies in Economic and Financial Analysis*. Greenwich, Conn.: Jai Press.

Sklair, Leslie. 1985. "Shenzhen: A Chinese 'Development Zone' in Global Perspective." *Development and Change* 16:571–602.

Skocpol, Theda. 1985. "Bringing the State Back In: Strategies of Analysis in Current Research." In Peter Evans, Dietrich Rueschemeyer, and Theda Skocpol, eds., *Bringing the State Back In*. New York: Cambridge University Press.

Smith, Beverly. 1986. "Democracy Derailed: Citizens' Movements in Historical Perspective." In Gavan McCormack and Yoshio Sugimoto, eds., *Democracy in Contemporary Japan*. New York: M. E. Sharpe.

Smith, Carol A. 1985. "Theories and Measures of Urban Primacy: A Critique." In M. Timberlake, ed., *Urbanization in the World-Economy*. New York: Academic Press.

Smith, M. P. 1987. "Global Capital Restructuring and Local Political Crises in U.S. Cities." In J. Henderson and M. Castells, eds., *Global Restructuring and Territorial Development*. London: Sage.

———. 1988. *City, State and Market: The Political Economy of Urban Society*. New York: Basil Blackwell.

Smith, M. P., and J. R. Feagin. 1987. *The Capitalist City: Global Restructuring and Community Politics*. Oxford: Basil Blackwell.

Smith, N. 1982. "Gentrification and Uneven Development." *Economic Geography* 58(2): 24–35.

———. 1984. *Uneven Development: Nature, Capital and the Production of Space*. New York: Basil Blackwell.

———. 1987. "Of Yuppies and Housing: Gentrification, Social Restructuring, and the Urban Dream." *Environment and Planning D: Society and Space* 5:151–72.

Smith, N., and P. Williams. 1986. *Gentrification of the City*. Boston: Allen and Unwin.

Smith, Paul F. 1982. "Structural Disequilibrium and the Banking Act of 1980." *Journal of Finance* (May):385–98.

Soja, Edward W. 1989. *Postmodern Geographies: The Reassertion of Space in Critical Social Theory*. London: Verso.

Soja, Edward, R. Morales, and G. Wolff. 1983. "Urban Restructuring: An Analysis of Social and Spatial Change in Los Angeles." *Economic Geography* 59(2): 195–230.

Spitznas, Thomas. 1981. "Estimating the Size of the Underground Economy in New York City." *The Regional Economic Digest* (semiannual publication of the New York Regional Economists' Society) 1(1): 1–3.

Stanback, Thomas M., Jr., 1979. *Understanding the Service Economy*. Baltimore: Johns Hopkins University Press.

Stanback, Thomas M., Jr., Peter J. Bearse, Thierry J. Noyelle, and Robert Karasek. 1981. *Services: The New Economy*. Totowa, N.J.: Allanheld, Osmun.

Stanback, Thomas M., Jr., and Thierry J. Noyelle. 1982. *Cities in Transition: Changing Job Structures in Atlanta, Denver, Buffalo, Phoenix, Columbus (Ohio), Nashville, Charlotte*. Totowa, N.J.: Allanheld, Osmun.

Standing, Guy. 1989. "The 'British Experiment': Structural Adjustment or Accelerated Decline?" In A. Portes et al., eds., *The Informal Economy: Studies in Advanced and Less Developed Countries*. Baltimore: Johns Hopkins University Press.

Stegman, M. 1985. *Housing in New York: Study of a City, 1984*. New York: Department of Housing Preservation and Development, New York City.

———. 1988. *Housing and Vacancy Report, New York City, 1987*. New York: Department of Housing Preservation and Development, New York City.

Stephens, J. D., and B. P. Holly. 1981. "City System Behaviour and Corporate Influence: The Headquarters Locations of U.S. Industrial Firms, 1955–75." *Urban Studies* 18:285–300.

Stepick, Alex. 1989. "Miami's Two Informal Sectors." In A. Portes et al., eds., *The Informal Economy: Studies in Advanced and Less Developed Countries*. Baltimore: Johns Hopkins University Press.

Steven, Rob. 1983. *Classes in Contemporary Japan*. Cambridge: Cambridge University Press.

Stigler, George. 1951. "The Division of Labor Is Limited by the Extent of the Market." *Journal of Political Economy* 59(3): 185–93.

Stoffaës, C. 1981. "L'emploi et la révolution informationnelle." *Informatisation et Emploi, Menace ou Mutation?* Paris: La Documentation Française.

Stone, Charles F., and Isabel V. Sawhill. 1986. *Labor Market Implications of the Growing Internationalization of the U.S. Economy*. National Commission for Employment Policy Research Report, no. RR8620. Washington, D.C.

Storper, Michael, and David Walker. 1983. "The Labor Theory of Location." *International Journal of Urban and Regional Research* 7(1): 1–41.

Strober, Myra H., and Carolyn L. Arnold. 1987. "Integrated Circuits/Segregated Labor: Women in Computer-Related Occupations and High-Tech Industries."

In Heidi I. Hartmann, ed., *Computer Chips and Paper Clips*. Washington, D.C.: National Academy Press.

Stuart, A. 1989. *The Social and Geographical Mobility of South Asians and Caribbeans in Middle-Age and Later Working Life*. LS Working Paper, no. 61, City University, London.

Survey of Current Business, International Investment Division. 1981a. "U.S. Business Enterprises Acquired or Established by Foreign Direct Investors in 1979." *Survey of Current Business* 61(1): 28–39.

———. 1981b. "1977 Benchmark Survey of U.S. Direct Investment Abroad." *Survey of Current Business* 61(4): 29–37.

———. 1984. "Plant and Equipment Expenditures, First and Second Quarters and Second Half of 1984." *Survey of Current Business* 64(3): 26–31.

———. 1985a. "Foreign Direct Investment in the United States: Country and Industry Detail for Position and Balance of Payments Flows, 1984." *Survey of Current Business* 65(8): 47–66.

———. 1985b. "U.S. Direct Investment Abroad: Country and Industry Detail for Position and Balance of Payments Flows, 1984." *Survey of Current Business* 65(8): 30–46.

———. 1986a. "U.S. Direct Investment Abroad: Detail for Position and Balance of Payments Flows, 1985." *Survey of Current Business* 66(8): 40–73.

———. 1986b. "Foreign Direct Investment in the U.S.: Detail for Position and Balance of Payments Flows, 1985." *Survey of Current Business* 66(8): 74–88.

———. 1987. "U.S. Sales of Services to Foreigners." *Survey of Current Business* 67(1): 22–39.

———. 1988a. "Foreign Direct Investment in the United States: Detail for Position and Balance of Payments Flows, 1987." *Survey of Current Business* 68(8): 69–83.

———. 1988b. "International Services: New Information on U.S. Transactions with Unaffiliated Foreigners." *Survey of Current Business* 68(10): 27–34.

———. 1988c. "U.S. Direct Investment Abroad: Detail for Position and Balance of Payments Flows, 1987." *Survey of Current Business* 68(8): 42–68.

———. 1989a. "The International Investment Position of the U.S. in 1988." *Survey of Current Business* 69(6): 41–49.

———. 1989b. "U.S. Direct Investment Abroad: Detail for Position and Balance of Payments Flows, 1988." *Survey of Current Business* 69(8): 47–61.

———. 1989c. "Foreign Direct Investment in the U.S.: Detail for Position and Balance of Payments Flows, 1988." *Survey of Current Business* 69(8): 62–88.

Susser, I. 1982. *Norman Street, Poverty and Politics in an Urban Neighborhood*. New York: Oxford University Press.

———. 1988. "Households, Social Reproduction and the Changing Economy of New York City." Paper prepared for a meeting of the Dual City Working Group held in New York City, November 11–12. New York: Committee on New York City, Social Science Research Council.

Suzuki, Y. 1987. "Comparative Studies of Financial Innovation, Deregulation, and Reform in Japan and the United States." In H. Patrick and R. Tachi, eds.,

Japan and the United States Today: Exchange Rates, Macroeconomic Policies, and Financial Market Innovations. New York: Columbia University Press.

Suzuki, Y., and H. Yomo, eds. 1986. *Financial Innovation and Monetary Policy: Asia and the West.* Proceedings of the Second International Conference. Tokyo: University of Tokyo Press.

Takashi, Machimura. 1988. "Mechanism of the World Urbanization—New International Distribution and a System of Urbanization Movement." Paper presented at the Japan Urban Sociology Conference held at Tsukuba University, Tsukuba, August.

Tanzi, Vito. 1982. *The Underground Economy in the United States and Abroad.* Lexington, Mass.: D. C. Heath.

Tauchen, H., and A. D. Witte. 1983. "An Equilibrium Model of Office Location Contact Patterns." *Environment and Planning A* 15:1311–26.

Taylor-Gooby, P. 1989. *Polarization, Privatization and Attitudes to Poverty.* Mimeo. University of Kent at Canterbury, Social Policy Department.

Terasaka, Akinobu et al. 1988. "The Transformation of Regional Systems in an Information-Oriented Society." *Geographical Review of Japan* 61(1): 159–73.

Tetsu, Naito. 1988. "Foreign Employment II: Demand-Supply Theory No Longer Applies; Receiving of Unskilled Laborforce." *Toyo Keizai Weekly Magazine* 12:12–14.

Thomas, Margaret. 1983. "The Leading Euromarket Law Firms in Hong Kong and Singapore." *International Financial Law Review* (June): 4–8.

Thrift, N. 1987. "The Fixers: The Urban Geography of International Commercial Capital." In J. Henderson and M. Castells, eds., *Global Restructuring and Territorial Development.* London: Sage.

Thrift, N., and P. Williams, eds. 1987. *Class and Space.* London: Macmillan.

Thurow, Lester C. 1980. *The Zero-Sum Society.* New York: Basic Books.

———. 1989. "Regional Transformation and the Service Activities." In Lloyd Rodwin and Hidehiko Sazanami, eds., *Deindustrialization and Regional Economic Transformation.* Boston: Unwin Hyman.

Tiebout, C. 1957. "Location Theory, Empirical Evidence, and Economic Evolution." *Papers and Proceedings of the Regional Science Association* 3:74–86.

Tienda, Marta, Leif Jensen, and Robert L. Bach. 1984. "Immigration, Gender and the Process of Occupational Change in the U.S., 1970–1980." *International Migration Review* 17(4): 1021–24.

Timberlake, Michael, ed. 1985. *Urbanization in the World-Economy.* Orlando, Fla.: Academic Press.

Tobier, Emanuel. 1985. *The Changing Face of Poverty: Trends in New York City's Population in Poverty, 1960–1990.* New York: Community Service Society of New York.

———. 1990. "The Homeless." In C. Brecher and R. Horton, eds., *Setting Municipal Priorities 1991.* New York: New York University Press.

Tokyo Department of City Planning. 1988. *Report 1: The Problem of Foreign Labor—Opinions of Ministries.* Tokyo: Department of City Planning.

Tokyo Metropolitan Government. 1983. *Survey of Tokyo Daytime Population.* Tokyo: TMG.

————. 1984a. *Long-Term Plan for Tokyo Metropolis.*

————. 1984b. *Plain Talk about Tokyo, 1984.* TMG Municipal Library publication.

————. 1985. *Report on Land-Related Data, 1984.*

————. 1986. "Distribution of Tokyo's Fashion Industries." Unpublished report.

————. 1987a. *Tokyo Statistical Yearbook 1985.*

————. 1987b. *Plain Talk about Tokyo, 1987.*

————. 1987c. *Tokyo Emergency Land Use Report,* 1–5. October 15.

————. 1988a. *Statistical Annual Report on Metropolitan Citizens' Incomes.*

————. 1988b. *Trends of Labor and Wages in Tokyo-to, Monthly Report.* April.

————. 1988c. "Land Value Shift December 1986–December 1987." Unpublished report.

————. Various years. *Monthly Labor Survey.*

Tokyo Stock Exchange. 1988. *Tokyo Stock Exchange 1988 Fact Book.* Tokyo: Tokyo Stock Exchange.

Touraine, Alain. 1969. *La Société post-industrielle.* Paris: Denoel.

Townsend, P. 1979. *Poverty in the United Kingdom.* Harmondsworth, Middlesex: Penguin Books.

————. 1985. "A Sociological Approach to the Measurement of Poverty—A Rejoinder to Professor Amartya Sen." *Oxford Economic Papers* 37(4): 659–68.

Townsend, P., with P. Corrigan, and U. Kowarzik. 1987. *Poverty and Labour in London—Interim Report of a Centenary Survey.* London: Low Pay Unit.

Toyoshima, Toshihiro. 1988. *Growing Foreign Investors' Activities and the Future of Internationalization.* Report no. 12. Tokyo: Japan Development Bank.

Trachte, K., and R. Ross. 1985. "The Crisis of Detroit and the Emergence of Global Capitalism." *International Journal of Urban and Regional Research* 9:216–17.

Tucker, K. A., and Mark Sundberg. 1988. *International Trade in Services.* London and New York: Routledge.

Tucker, K. A., M. Sundberg, and G. Seow. 1983. "Services in ASEAN-Australian Trade." In *ASEAN-Australian Economic Papers,* no. 2. Kuala Lumpur and Canberra.

United Kingdom Central Statistical Office. 1986. *Regional Trends.* London: HMSO.

————. Various years. *Annual Abstract of Statistics.*

United Kingdom Department of Employment. 1982. *Census of Employment, 1981.* London: HMSO.

————. 1984. *New Earnings Survey.* London: HMSO.

————. 1985. *Annual Family Expenditure Survey, 1985.* London: HMSO.

————. 1986. *Employment Gazette, 1986.*

————. 1987a. "Census of Employment, 1984." *Employment Gazette,* January.

————. 1987b. *Employment Gazette.* Historical Supplement no. 2, October.

————. 1987c. *New Earnings Survey.* London: HMSO.

————. 1988. "Ethnic Origins in the Labour Market." *Employment Gazette,* March: 164–77.

————. Various years. *Annual Family Expenditure Survey.* London: HMSO.

United Kingdom Inner London Education Authority. 1987. *The London Labor Market—Facts and Figures*. May.

United Kingdom Office of Population and Surveys. 1963. *Census 1961, England and Wales*. London: HMSO.

———. 1973. *Census 1971, England and Wales*.

———. 1983. *Census 1981, England and Wales*.

United Nations Centre on Transnational Corporations. 1979. *Transnational Corporations in World Development: A Re-Examination*. New York: UN Centre on Transnational Corporations.

———. 1981. *Transnational Banks: Operations, Strategies, and Their Effects in Developing Countries*.

———. 1985. *Trends and Issues in Foreign Direct Investment and Related Flows*.

———. 1989a. *Transnational Service Corporations and Developing Countries: Impact and Policy Issues*.

———. 1989b. *Transnational Corporations and International Economic Relations: Recent Developments and Selected Issues*.

———. 1989c. *Transnational Corporations and the Growth of Services: Some Conceptual and Theoretical Issues*.

———. 1989d. *Foreign Direct Investment and Transnational Corporations in Services*.

United States Congress. 1978. Senate Committee on Banking, Housing and Urban Affairs. *International Banking Act of 1978*. Washington, D.C.: GPO.

———. 1981. House Committee on Banking, Finance and Urban Affairs. *Financial Institutions in a Revolutionary Era*. 97th Cong., 1st sess. Committee Print 97-98. Washington, D.C.: GPO.

———. 1982. Senate Committee on Banking, Housing and Urban Affairs. *Foreign Barriers to U.S. Trade: Service Exports*. Washington, D.C.: GPO.

———. 1985. Office of Technology Assessment (OTA). *Automation of America's Offices*. OTA-CIT-287.

———. 1986. Office of Technology Assessment. *Trade in Service Export and Foreign Revenues, Special Report*. OTA-ITE-316, September. Washington, D.C.: GPO.

United States Congressional Budget Office. 1987. *Contract Out: Potential for Reducing Federal Costs*. Washington, D.C.: GPO, June.

United States Department of Commerce, Bureau of the Census. 1977–1987. *County Business Patterns*, issues for the United States, California, Illinois, Michigan, Massachusetts, New York, and Texas for 1977, 1980, 1981, 1982, 1984, 1985, 1986, and 1987.

———. 1981. *1980 Census of Population, Supplementary Report*.

———. 1982a. *1980 Census of Population and Housing Supplementary Report: Provisional Estimates of Social, Economic, and Housing Characteristics*.

———. 1982b. *Annual Housing Survey, 1976 (United States): SMSA Files*. Ann Arbor: Inter-university Consortium for Political and Social Research.

———. 1983. *Statistical Abstracts of the United States, 1983*.

————. 1984. *Annual Housing Survey, 1983 (United States): SMSA Files.* Ann Arbor: Inter-university Consortium for Political and Social Research.

————. 1984. *Place of Work.*

————. Various years a. *Statistical Abstracts of the United States,* various issues.

————. Various years b. *Microdata from the Survey of Income and Education.* Data Access Description no. 42.

United States Department of Commerce, International Trade Administration. 1970. *Economic Factors Affecting the Use of Items 807.00 and 806.30 of the Tariff Schedules of the United States.* Washington, D.C.: International Trade Administration. *See* United States International Trade Administration.

————. 1980a. *Current Developments in the U.S. International Service Industries.*

————. 1980b. *Import Trends in TSUS Items 806.30 and 807.00.*

————. 1980c. *Selected Data on U.S. Investment Abroad, 1966–1978.*

————. 1982. *Foreign Economic Trends and Their Implications,* various issues.

————. 1984. *International Direct Investment: Global Trends and the U.S. Role.*

————. 1988. *U.S. Industrial Outlook: Commercial Banking.* (Cited as U.S. Industrial Outlook)

United States Department of Commerce, Office of the U.S. Trade Representative. 1983. *U.S. National Study on Trade in Services.* Washington, D.C.: GPO.

United States Department of Labor, Bureau of Labor Statistics. 1979. *Employment and Earnings, for States and Areas, 1939–1978.*

————. 1982a. *Area Wage Survey, New York, 1981.*

————. 1982b. *Geographic Profiles of Employment and Unemployment, 1981.*

————. 1984. *Occupational Employment in Selected Services.*

————. 1985. *Geographic Profiles of Employment and Unemployment, 1984.*

————. 1986a. *Geographic Profiles of Employment and Unemployment, 1985.*

————. 1986b. *National Survey of Professional, Administrative, Technical, and Clerical Pay, March 1986.*

————. 1988. *Area Wage Survey, New York, 1987.*

————. 1989. *The 1989 Mid-Year Report.* New York: BLS, Middle Atlantic Region.

————. 1990. *Employment and Earnings for States and Areas.* Bulletin 1370-24.

————. Various years. *News.* Middle Atlantic Region.

United States Immigration and Naturalization Service. 1972. *Annual Report.* Washington, D.C.: GPO.

————. 1981. *Annual Report.*

————. 1985. *Annual Report.*

United States International Trade Administration. 1980. *Market Share Reports.* Document Service. United States Department of Commerce, International Trade Administration.

United States Office of Management and Budget. 1972. *Standard Industrial Classification Manual,* 278–90.

United States Office of Trade Representative. *See* United States Department of Commerce, Office of the U.S. Trade Representative.

United States President's Commission for a National Agenda for the Eighties. 1980. *Urban America in the Eighties*. Washington, D.C.: GPO.

Vernon, Raymond. 1966. "International Investment and International Trade in the Product Cycle." *Quarterly Journal of Economics* 80:190–207.

———. 1979. "The Product Cycle Hypothesis in a New International Environment." *Oxford Bulletin of Economics and Statistics* 41(4): 255–67.

Waite, Donald. 1982. "Deregulation and the Banking Industry." *Bankers Magazine*, January–February: 26–35.

Wall Street Journal. 1986. "Global Finance and Investment." Annual special report. *Wall Street Journal*, September 29.

———. 1987. "Global Finance and Investment." Annual special report. *Wall Street Journal*, September 18.

———. 1988. "Global Finance and Investment." Annual special report. *Wall Street Journal*, September 23.

———. 1989. "World Business." *Wall Street Journal*, September 22.

Walter, Ingo. 1985. *Barriers to Trade in Banking and Financial Services*. London: Policy Research Center.

———. 1988. *Global Competition In Financial Services*. Cambridge, Mass.: Ballinger-Harper and Row.

Walters, Pamela Barnhouse. 1985. "Systems of Cities and Urban Primacy: Problems of Definition and Measurement." In M. Timberlake, ed., *Urbanization in the World-Economy*. New York: Academic Press.

Ward, Kathryn B. 1985. "Women and Urbanization in the World-System." In M. Timberlake, ed., *Urbanization in the World-Economy*. New York: Academic Press.

Weber, A. 1909. *Theory of the Location of Industries*. Chicago: University of Chicago Press.

Weitzman, Phillip. 1989. "Worlds Apart: Housing, Race/Ethnicity and Income in New York City, 1978–1987." Working Paper prepared by the Community Service Society of New York.

Whichard, Obie G. 1981. "Trends in the U.S. Direct Investment Position Abroad, 1950–1979." *Survey of Current Business* 61(2): 39–56.

White, James Wilson. 1976. "Social Change and Community Involvement in Metropolitan Japan." In J. W. White and F. Munger, eds., *Social Change and Community Politics in Urban Japan*. Chapel Hill: University of North Carolina, Institute for Research in Social Sciences.

———, ed. 1979. *The Urban Impact of Internal Migration*. Chapel Hill: University of North Carolina, Institute for Research in Social Sciences.

Whittemore, F. 1987. "Internationalization of Investment Banking." In H. Patrick and R. Tachi, eds., *Japan and the United States Today: Exchange Rates, Macroeconomic Policies, and Financial Market Innovations*. New York: Columbia University Press.

Williamson, B. 1980. *The Banking and Insurance Industries in London*. Greater London Council Central Policy Unit.

Williamson, Oliver. 1978. *Markets and Hierarchies: Analysis and Antitrust Implications*. West Drayton, Middlesex: Collier Macmillan.

————. 1980. "Transaction Costs Economics: The Governance of Contractual Relations." *Journal of Law and Economics* 22(2): 233–61.

Wilson, P.E.B., and J. Stanworth. 1985. *Black Business in Brent.* London: Small Business Research Trust.

Wilson, W. J. 1987. *The Truly Disadvantaged: The Inner City, the Underclass and Public Policy.* Chicago: University of Chicago Press.

Winder, Robert. 1986. "France: Le Big Bang." *Euromoney*, January supplement, *Euromarkets 1986: Rough Ride Ahead,* 44–58.

Wood, P. A. 1984. "The Regional Significance of Manufacturing-Service Sector Links: Some Thoughts on the Revival of London's Docklands." In B. M. Barr and N. M. Waters, eds., *Regional Diversification and Structural Change.* BC Geographical Series. Vancouver: Tantalus Research.

————. 1987. "Producer Services and Economic Change: U.K. Reflections on Canadian Evidence." In K. Chapman and G. Humphry, eds., *Technological Change and Industrial Policy.* London: Blackwell.

World Bank. 1980. *World Tables, 1980.* Baltimore: John Hopkins University Press.

————. 1988. *World Development Report, 1988.* Washington, D.C.: World Bank.

Yamaguchi, Takashi. 1979. "Japan's Urban System—An Overview." *Proceedings, Department of Humanities, University of Tokyo* 69:1–15.

Yamaguchi Fighting Group and Supporting Group. 1988. "Show The Anger!" July 10. Pamphlet. Japan.

Yoshihara, Kunio. 1982. *Shogo Shosha: The Vanguard of the Japanese Economy.* New York: Oxford University Press.

Zukin, S. 1982. *Loft Living, Culture and Capital in Urban Change.* Baltimore: Johns Hopkins University Press.

Index